Juno Beach

———

JUNO

MARK ZUEHLKE

BEACH

CANADA'S D-DAY VICTORY:

JUNE 6, 1944

Douglas & McIntyre
Vancouver/Toronto/Berkeley

Douglas & McIntyre
2323 Quebec Street, Suite 201
Vancouver, British Columbia
Canada v5t 4s7
www.douglas-mcintyre.com

National Library of Canada Cataloguing in Publication Data
Zuehlke, Mark
Juno Beach: Canada's D-Day victory, June 6, 1944 / Mark Zuehlke.

Includes bibliographical references and index.
ISBN 1-55365-050-6

1. World War, 1939–1945—Campaigns—France—Normandy.
2. Canada. Canadian Army—History—World War, 1939–1945. I. Title.

D756.5.N6z83 2004   940.54'21422   C2004-901051-4

Library of Congress information is available upon request

Editing by Elizabeth McLean
Jacket and text design by Peter Cocking
Jacket photograph Gilbert Alexander Milne, NAC PA–137013
Typesetting by Rhonda Ganz
Printed and bound in Canada by Friesens
Printed on acid-free paper
Distributed in the U.S. by Publishers Group West

We gratefully acknowledge the financial support of the
Canada Council for the Arts, the British Columbia Arts Council,
and the Government of Canada through the Book Publishing Industry
Development Program (BPIDP) for our publishing activities.

Everything in war is simple, but the simplest thing is difficult.
CARL VON CLAUSEWITZ

What is War? A barbaric profession,
of which the only art is to be stronger
at a given place.
NAPOLEON, SEPTEMBER 6, 1812
ON THE EVE OF BORODINO

We came in at the beach, but 'twas hard to reach,
And many lost their lives.
We won our goal, but the terrible toll
Caused grief to far off wives.
BOMBARDIER R.A. EGO,
3RD CANADIAN INFANTRY DIVISION

Dip gently your scythe good reaper now
O'er the fields of the hallowed dead
For young men fought and young men died
Near the sea, where the earth is red.
CAPTAIN STANLEY E. HIGGS,
3RD CANADIAN INFANTRY DIVISION

[CONTENTS]

I N 2003, with the publication of *The Gothic Line*, I completed a
three-volume history of the major battles fought by Canadians during World War II's Italian campaign and was left to ponder the question, "What next?" My interest in Canada's experiences in World War
II was undiminished and I suspected many a story still remained to
be told. With the Italian campaign books, I had forayed onto a field of
combat that had been little regarded by Canadian writers—academic
or popular. So there had been a satisfaction in pulling back the mist
that had begun to cloak that major historical period and shining a
light upon it. Consequently, my first instinct was to look for other
forgotten campaigns that had slipped for whatever reason from the
national consciousness. Casting about through Canadian official
accounts, the popular histories, and the academic treatises regarding
various battles, I was surprised to find that areas once thought well
mined appeared less so. My searches brought me to the Normandy
invasion and more specifically June 6, 1944—D-Day.

In my imagining, the Canadian experience of this seminal his-
toric day had to have been well trodden by past writers, but on closer
inspection I discovered the truth to be entirely different. In fact,
Canada's D-Day was something treated only in passing by most
writers looking at the Normandy invasion and subsequent campaign
of almost three-month duration. Those books that were primarily

dedicated to June 6 were slight, little more than leaflets. On the opposite side of the balance were a number of monolithic renderings relying on virtually untouched veteran accounts that were generally
published by the associations of the regiments present on June 6.
Although these latter works contained vast amounts of rich reminiscences, they were organized rather randomly so that readers were left
with no context in which to align the described experiences.

A gap in the telling of Canada's D-Day story became evident. So
into this gap I ventured and this book is the outcome.

In the Italian trilogy, I drew heavily on veteran accounts and approached many old soldiers who had never before been asked what
happened to them on those fields of battle. By sifting their personal
stories in with the historical records generated by the army at the
time, it was possible to develop a dramatic narrative that depicted the
course of the battle in detail but also enabled the reader to experience
combat at a soldier's eye level. I have followed the same method here.

There are those, particularly academic historians, who consider
veteran accounts suspect and so rely almost entirely on the official
record. In my own experience, I have found that the veteran memory
is trustworthy and, where the record is contradicted, tend to accept
the account as rendered by the soldiers who lived it. Normally, it is
possible to compare the versions of an event as recalled by several veterans and find sufficient common ground to develop a clear sense of
what happened at a particular place and time. It is in this manner that
events hinted at in the historical record but not explained are also revealed. Take, for example, a singular mention in the Sherbrooke
Fusiliers Regiment war diary of its tanks carrying North Nova Scotia
Highlanders off the beach aboard "porpoises." What was this? Interviews with Fusiliers unearth the fact that ammunition bins were
slung under their tanks for the landing. These were alternatively
nicknamed porpoises or alligators. Then a North Nova veteran re-
counts how he and the other men in his section jumped onto an ammunition "catamaran" that was hooked to the back of the tank and
were dragged like kids on a horse-drawn sleigh over snow off to their
war in Normandy's interior. A little mystery solved.

Veteran memory, of course, is dimming with the passage of time. These days, the researcher is generally left with fragments of events rather than a complete narrative retelling. But the fragment from one veteran, stitched onto the sliver of memory offered by another and informed by the official records and accounts makes it possible to develop a credible narrative. More so, I think, than if only veteran memory or official account is trusted. Inevitably, there are points where the collective veteran memory and that of the official record stand in stark disagreement, with no reconciliation possible. At those times, I have tended to trust my gut instinct and must confess that most of the time it is the veteran version that is accepted.

Ultimately, it is the veterans of D-Day who lived through one of the most intensely horrific long days in history, buried friends who did not, and carried the memory of June 6 for the rest of their lives. This is their story.

ACKNOWLEDGEMENTS

A SPECIAL DEBT OF THANKS is owed to the many veterans whose stories appear in this book. Without them, *Juno Beach* would not exist. It is impossible to mention all of the veterans here, but they are all listed in the bibliography. I would like to single out, though, Stan Richardson, who trusted his time-worn diary tracing his service as a telegraphist on the minesweeper HMCS *Bayfield* to Canada Post so I might study it. My trepidation remained high as I undertook copying the diary and accompanying photos and then waited anxiously until it returned safely to Stan's home in Powell River.

This time out, I was assisted immensely in gathering veteran interviews by John Gregory Thompson of Ingersoll, Ontario. John tirelessly and enthusiastically visited veterans scattered throughout southern Ontario, spending many hours conducting taped interviews on my behalf. It is to his credit that so many veterans are included here. Ken MacLeod of Langley, B.C., shared the interviews he has gathered over the years in both video and audio form of veterans in the Vancouver area. Major Michael Boire, associate professor at Royal Military College, generously interviewed lieutenant colonels Don Mingay and Ernest Côté—key officers in 3rd Canadian Infantry Division's headquarters—on my behalf.

In Normandy, Isabelle Bodin-Benjamin went out of her way to gather a group of elderly gentlemen who lived through the invasion and tried to translate the resulting happily chaotic interview at the PMU Bar in Courseulles-sur-Mer. At home, the tape of this interview ended up in the capable hands of Ottawa translator and good friend Alex MacQuarrie. He and colleague Claude Bolduc somehow managed to sort out the wheat from the chaff of people placing bets in the background and everyone in the bar tossing in their two Euros' worth to make sense of the interview. Also in Normandy, Jean-Pierre Benamou, a local historian, allowed me to tag along for part of a briefing on the invasion that he was giving a fresh batch of interpreters at the Juno Beach Centre.

The Royal Winnipeg Rifles Association (British Columbia Association) kindly donated a copy of their compiled collection of veteran accounts entitled *Perspectives*.

At the Canadian War Museum, Roger Sarty very helpfully directed me to the best source documents that could be found at the Department of National Defence's Directorate of Heritage and History Archives with reference to the Royal Canadian Navy's role in the invasion. That led to Major Michel Litalien tracking them down for me and then Stephanie Burton undertaking the colossal photocopying task. Steve Harris at the directorate was also, as always, a great help. Back at the Canadian War Museum archives, Carol Reid was a delight to spend an afternoon burrowing through documents with, and in the library there Liliane Reid Lafleur was of great assistance. Thanks also to staff at the National Archives of Canada and the University of Victoria Special Collections.

I am indebted to Professor Jack Granatstein for granting permission to consult his files on Major General Rod Keller at York University.

Thanks, too, to Rosalie A. Hartigan for permission to quote passages from the late Dan Hartigan's book, *A Rising of Courage*. Also used with permission from his *Battle Diary: From D-Day and Normandy to the Zuider Zee*, by Charles Martin (Toronto: Dundurn, 1994), are several passages written by the eminently respected Company Sergeant Major of the Queen's Own Rifles of Canada.

A major chunk of the work on *Juno Beach* was carried out while writer-in-residence at the Berton House in Dawson, Yukon. My thanks to the Berton House Writers Society for giving me this opportunity for a three-month stay there and to Pierre Berton for donating the home for this use in the first place. Thanks also to the BC Arts Council, whose financial assistance helped make researching and writing this book possible.

My new publisher, Scott McIntyre, at Douglas & McIntyre deserves much praise for having rescued the Italian trilogy from disappearing into the realm of out-of-print books after the collapse of Stoddart Publishing in 2002. His enthusiasm for *Juno Beach* and commitment to future works on Canada's World War II experience is heartening to see. Scott sets a tone at D&M that obviously works because everyone there is a pleasure to work with, whether editors, publicists, or designers.

Speaking of editing, immense thanks to Elizabeth McLean for agreeing to step once more into the breach of working on a book about battle. C. Stuart Daniel also stepped up to the plate again to provide the maps. My agent Carolyn Swayze continues to ensure this writer's career prospers sufficiently to keep writing such research-intensive books possible.

Another person who came forward to help was Colonel Tony Poulin, a veteran of the Royal 22nd Regiment who some readers will remember from *The Gothic Line*. Tony had become a good friend over the years and kindly consented to translate Le Régiment de la Chaudière war diary entries and relevant parts of the text of their regimental history into English for me. Soon after he completed this task, Tony suffered a fatal injury during a tragic fall at his home in St. Bruno, Quebec. He is dearly missed.

Finally, I remain blessed to have the continued support of Frances Backhouse, a true partner in this writing life who's always game to trudge a battlefield come rain or shine.

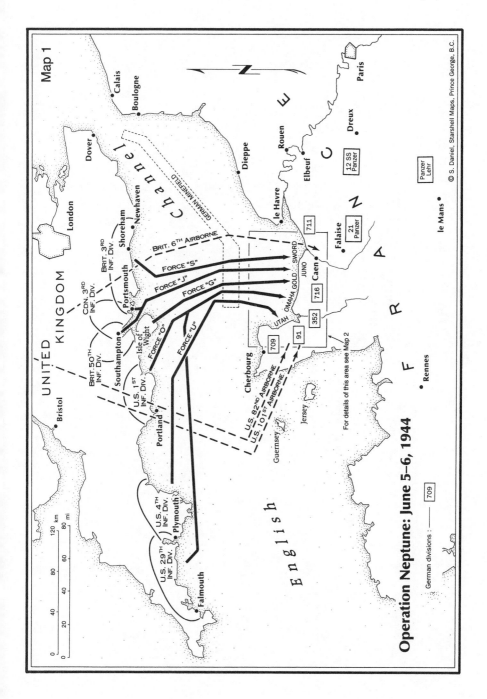

Map 1

© S. Daniel, Starshell Maps, Prince George, B.C.

Operation Neptune: June 5–6, 1944

German divisions : ——— 709

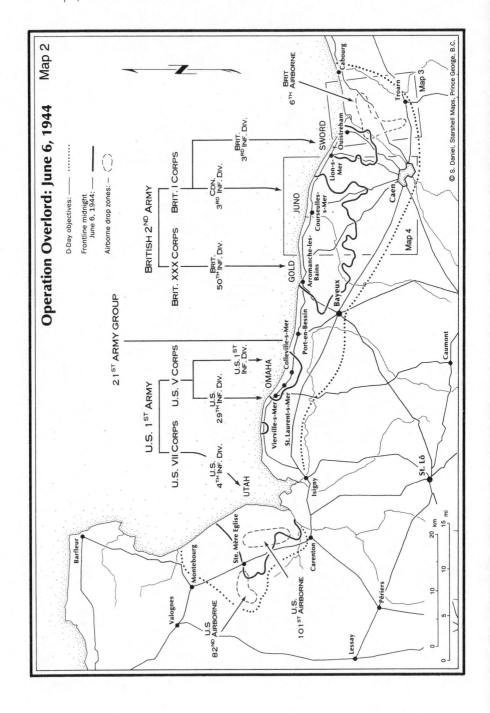

Operation Overlord: June 6, 1944   Map 2

D-Day objectives: ——·····
Frontline midnight June 6, 1944: ——
Airborne drop zones: — ◠

21ST ARMY GROUP

BRITISH 2ND ARMY

BRIT. XXX CORPS   BRIT. I CORPS

BRIT. 50TH INF. DIV.
CDN. 3RD INF. DIV.
BRIT. 3RD INF. DIV.

U.S. 1ST ARMY

U.S. VII CORPS   U.S. V CORPS

U.S. 4TH INF. DIV.
U.S. 29TH INF. DIV.
U.S. 1ST INF. DIV.

GOLD   JUNO   SWORD
OMAHA
UTAH

BRIT. 6TH AIRBORNE
U.S. 82ND AIRBORNE
U.S. 101ST AIRBORNE

Cabourg
Troarn
Map 3
Ouistreham
Lion-s-Mer
Courseulles-s-Mer
Caen
Map 4
Arromanche-les-Bains
Bayeux
Port-en-Bessin
Colleville-s-Mer
Vierville-s-Mer
St. Laurent-s-Mer
Caumont
St. Lô
Isigny
Carentan
Périers
Lessay
Ste. Mère Eglise
Montebourg
Valognes
Barfleur

0   5   10   20 km
0   5   10   15 mi

© S. Daniel, Starshell Maps, Prince George, B.C.

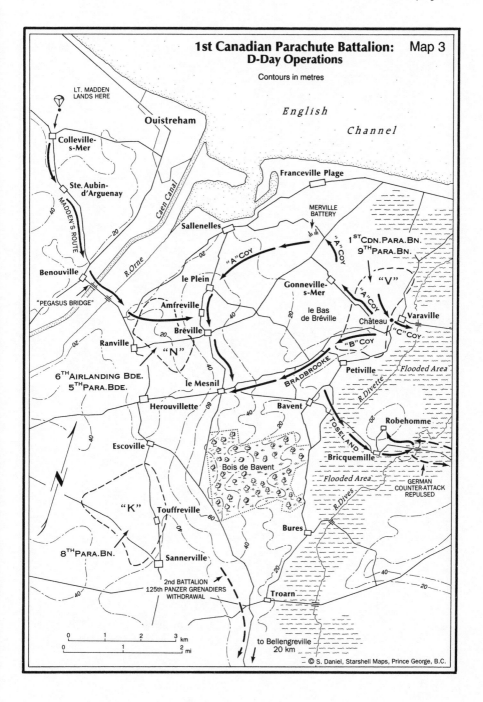

1st Canadian Parachute Battalion: Map 3
D-Day Operations

Contours in metres

English Channel

LT. MADDEN LANDS HERE

Ouistreham

Colleville-s-Mer

Ste. Aubin-d'Arguenay

MADDEN'S ROUTE

Francevelle Plage

Caen Canal

R. Orne

Sallenelles

MERVILLE BATTERY

le Plein

"A" COY

1ST CDN. PARA. BN.
9TH PARA. BN.

Benouville

"PEGASUS BRIDGE"

Amfreville

Gonneville-s-Mer

"A" COY

"V"

le Bas de Bréville

"A" COY

Château

Varaville

Bréville

Ranville

"N"

"B" COY

"C" COY

6TH AIRLANDING BDE.
5TH PARA. BDE.

le Mesnil

BRADBROOKE

Petiville

Flooded Area

R. Divette

Herouvillette

Bavent

TOSELAND

Robehomme

Escoville

Bois de Bavent

Bricquemille

Flooded Area

GERMAN COUNTER-ATTACK REPULSED

R. Dives

"K"

Touffreville

Bures

8TH PARA. BN.

Sannerville

2nd BATTALION
125th PANZER GRENADIERS
WITHDRAWAL

Troarn

0   1   2   3 km
0   1   2 mi

to Bellengreville
20 km

© S. Daniel, Starshell Maps, Prince George, B.C.

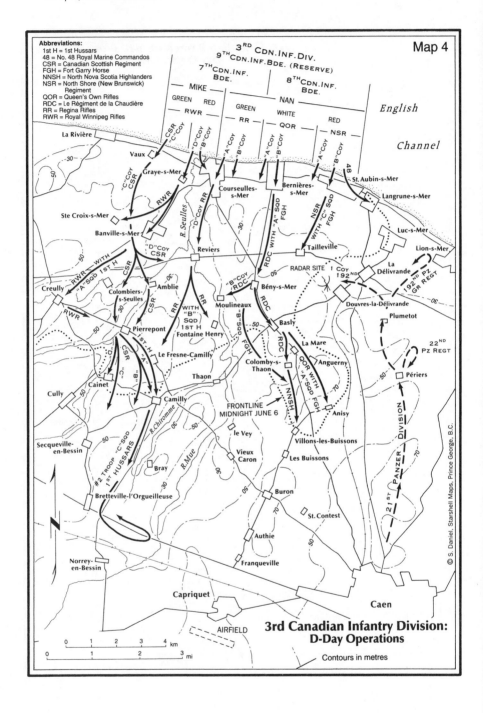

Abbreviations:
1st H = 1st Hussars
48 = No. 48 Royal Marine Commandos
CSR = Canadian Scottish Regiment
FGH = Fort Garry Horse
NNSH = North Nova Scotia Highlanders
NSR = North Shore (New Brunswick)
Regiment
QOR = Queen's Own Rifles
RDC = Le Régiment de la Chaudière
RR = Regina Rifles
RWR = Royal Winnipeg Rifles

Map 4

3rd Canadian Infantry Division: D-Day Operations

Contours in metres

© S. Daniel, Starshell Maps, Prince George, B.C.

Green On

I T WAS THE SILENCE. Major Lockhart Ross Fulton—"Lochie" to friends—knew intellectually that out there in the impenetrable blackness thousands of other ships surrounded the HMS *Canterbury* and all steered a precisely charted and timed course across the English Channel towards the coast of France. But he could neither see nor hear them. The only sounds were the gentle murmur of sea brushing past *Canterbury*'s hull, the throb of the ship engines, and the occasional soft-spoken conversation among the bridge crew. Yet in just a few minutes, the minute hand would sweep past midnight and the date would be June 6, 1944. The greatest armada in history was at sea. No navigational lights showed; the wireless radio was deathly silent. There was a dreamlike quality to standing here on the coastal liner's bridge at the shoulder of the ship's captain, sipping hot char and staring out at the blackness.

Fulton knew, though, that this was no dream. Nor was it another of the many amphibious and landing exercises that 3rd Canadian Infantry Division and 2nd Canadian Armoured Brigade had participated in since being selected a year earlier for a starring role in the invasion assault force. Come dawn, the major would be at the invasion's sharpest end when he took the Royal Winnipeg Rifles' 'D' Company ashore in the first assault wave.

Among the gear Fulton had lugged aboard was a large jute sack with its opening tightly closed and secured by a lock. Some hours earlier, when *Canterbury* had reached the designated point of no return, Fulton had opened the lock and emptied the sack's contents. This consisted of a stack of identical, highly detailed maps that showed where the Canadians were going to land. Until now, Fulton had been the only man in 'D' Company to know that the armada sailed towards the Normandy coast and a stretch of beach that was home to several insignificant seaside villages.[1]

As he handed the maps out to his young officers, Fulton knew that in a few short hours these place names would be entwined with Canada's history. But at this stage, his company and platoon commanders showed only scant interest in the identity of the villages previously known only by codenames. What did it matter that the village to the left of their landing beach was now labelled Courseulles-sur-Mer rather than Alba?[2] Of more importance was the fact that these maps accorded with those they had used earlier in the weeks and months of preparations for the invasion. There would, then, be no surprises now that they knew the ships were bound for Normandy rather than the Pas de Calais or other possible landing sites on the northwest European coastline.

It was also grimly ironic that the betting pool to which they had contributed nightly for weeks would go unclaimed because the winner was to be the one who correctly predicted the invasion point. Nobody had thought of Normandy. Who would be alive days from now when the fighting eased long enough for a new bet to be made and won?

Briefing finished, Fulton advised them all to "try and get a little sleep." But this proved advice he could not personally follow. Anticipatory adrenaline was starting to flow through his body, rendering the small cabin uncomfortably close. So he wandered up to the bridge and stared into the eerie darkness. It was a dirty night, with the seas tossed about by the trailing end of the great storm that had forced the invasion's postponement the previous night and for a time even threatened its cancellation.

Built for peacetime service shuttling passengers back and forth across the English Channel between Dover and Calais, *Canterbury* rode the seas with seasoned disdain. Fulton knew that would not be the case for the purpose-built flat-bottomed landing vessels designed to deliver troops, tanks, guns, and vehicles right onto the sand. For the thousands of men aboard those ships, the rough seas would have turned the crossing into a hellish test of endurance. He hoped the storm would soon abate and the Channel calm before they hove to off the French coast to board the small landing craft dangling in the davits mounted on the ship's main deck. The thought of running into shore and into battle with a company of men wretched with seasickness was worrisome.

Dawn and the beach dominated his thoughts. As midnight came and went, he was increasingly distracted to a point where he was barely aware of the nature of his conversation with the ship's captain. Instead, his mind reached out past the ship's rising and falling bow into the black night towards a Normandy beach codenamed Juno.[3]

IN ORDER TO BE HEARD over the howling whine of the AW41 Albemarle's two 1,590-horsepower piston radial engines, Lieutenant John Russell Madden had to bellow like some ornery track coach exhorting his team to greater effort. With the bomb-bay door behind him, Madden hollered for the nine other soldiers to get ready to jump. His ten-man stick, part of 'C' Company of the 1st Canadian Parachute Battalion, was to parachute into German-occupied France as the vanguard of the Allied invasion.

Struggling under the weight of more than a hundred pounds of equipment and parachute, the lieutenant could barely stand and it was impossible in the cramped, low-ceilinged aircraft to gain a fully upright position. That didn't really matter because all he had to do was pitch headfirst through the door in the bomber's floor and the rest of the section would follow. Madden wrestled open the steel bolts that held the door shut and then secured its heavy weight to brackets on the aircraft's side. Kneeling, hands braced on either side of the opening, the officer looked down upon a line of foaming surf rolling up against the Normandy coast. Then the plane was hurtling over a patchwork quilt of farmland at just five hundred feet of altitude—their assigned jump height. From points all over the compass, long streamers of tracer shells rose in lazy arcs as German flak batteries searched for targets.

Madden was searching, too; scanning the ill-lit ground below for any sign of recognizable landmarks that would tell him the plane was starting its run down Drop Zone V's less than two-mile length. Waiting, as well, for the warning order—the shout by the man behind him, who could see the red and green lights the pilot would use to signal the paratroops to start the jump process, that the red standby light had come on. Two minutes later, at 0020 on June 6, 1944, the green light should flash. Madden's cue to jump. All very precise, all timed to the second to ensure his stick landed directly on target. Then they would secure the drop zone for the following two battalions—one British, one Canadian—making up 3rd Parachute Brigade, which was to arrive twenty-eight minutes later.

The twenty-year-old lieutenant didn't see anything familiar, but it was damned dark down there. Mist or smoke drifted thick over the fields.[4]

Cold air turned into a gale by the wash of the propellers shrieked through the door and the din of the engines was deafening. "Green on!" Madden hesitated. That was wrong. Where was the "Red on" warning? Had he lost it amid the other racket? "Did you say Green?" he shouted.

"Yes, I said Green," the man snapped back.

Without further thought, Madden brought his arms in against his body and dove headlong into the darkness. Suddenly it was quiet. Just the quick rush of wind, the hard crack of the parachute opening above him, the rapid braking of his plunging descent towards earth. Madden had no idea what he floated down upon, for the ground was "covered with a sheen-like mist that shifted in mystical patterns to disclose doll-like farms." Seconds later, Madden landed "in soft pastureland."[5]

Within five minutes of landing, Madden had gathered in his parachute and located five of his men—those who had immediately followed him out of the plane. Of the last four men in the stick there was no sign. Nor was there any sign of the rest of 'C' Company. Two hundred yards away, a German flak gun hammered away at the dark sky. Madden stared skyward, straining to hear the sound of the Douglas c-47 Dakotas that were to bring in the rest of the battalion, hoping to see blankets of parachutes drifting down. But nothing happened. There seemed to be no Allied soldiers about other than his little six-man party. The lieutenant had the sudden apprehension that there would be no subsequent waves of paratroops. That once again, at the last minute, the invasion had been postponed. He had no way of knowing whether the rest of 'C' Company had been dropped or not. Certainly they weren't here—wherever here was. Given the confusion on board the Albemarle, it seemed fearfully possible that an order for the planes to turn around and abort had been missed.

"My God," Madden thought, "they've landed us and then decided not to go on with it. There's an invasion of just me and my five guys."[6]

PART ONE

THE ROAD TO OVERLORD

1

Maximum Force Needed

S TANDING IN A Normandy pasture with no other Allied troops at hand other than his five anxious Canadian paratroopers, Lieutenant John Madden had legitimate cause for concern. But not that the invasion of Normandy had been cancelled, as Operation Overlord was very definitely proceeding and the next twenty-four hours would prove the most decisive of the war. The invasion was a winner-take-all game with the jackpot to be won or lost on a single roll of dice. The Western Allies were gambling that they could win and hold a beachhead in France from which they could drive to the Rhineland and into Germany's heart—the most direct route to bring the war to a rapid conclusion. This was not, however, an impulsive or rash crapshoot. No previous military operation had been more carefully planned, more meticulously scripted in the form of time-tables and deployments, more intensely trained for, and more methodically launched.

Even as the last British troops had evacuated the beaches of Dunkirk on June 14, 1940, Britain's War Office had been consider-ing how continental Europe could be reinvaded and liberated from the German conquerors. This despite the fear of imminent invasion by Adolf Hitler's triumphant divisions massing on the opposite side of the English Channel. That threat had not yet slackened when the British Joint Planning Sub-Committee of the Chiefs of Staff presented Prime Minister Winston Churchill with a report on

October 5, 1940 that outlined the challenges Commonwealth forces would face in launching a cross-channel invasion. The prospects, the report stated, were bleak for the Commonwealth stood alone. Even should America weigh in against Germany, the logistical complexities involved in deploying modern armies meant "we can never hope to build up a very large force on the Continent."[1] Any landing was likely to be swept back into the sea by rapid deployment of nearby German divisions that would quickly outnumber and outgun the invaders. Hitler's Fortress Europe appeared unassailable.

Consequently, when the 15,911 men of the 1st Canadian Infantry Division arrived in Britain that December nobody was thinking of offensive operations. The immediate task was to transform an ill-trained and badly equipped volunteer civilian force leavened with a cluster of pre-war Permanent Force soldiers into an effective fighting division; one capable of defending Britain's shores from an invasion expected with the spring.

Germany's Luftwaffe, however, failed to gain air superiority over British skies during the aerial battle that raged from August 1940 to May 1941—a necessary precursor to any invasion. Then, on June 22, Hitler unleashed three million men against the Soviet Union on a front extending 1,300 miles from Finland to the Black Sea. Now the British planning staff considered a more favourable situation. Despite the stunning initial victories, those millions of German troops advancing into Russia were moving ever farther away from Fortress Europe's western flank and would not be easily recalled.

Meanwhile, the Commonwealth continued to strengthen and modernize its armies, navies, and air forces. By 1942, 500,000 Canadian soldiers were in Britain—a stunning achievement in mobilization by a nation of only 11.5 million souls. By then, too, American troops were starting to arrive. Japan's December 7, 1941 attack on Pearl Harbor had at last provoked the United States to declare war on fascism. On January 14, 1942, the British and American governments quickly agreed that "only the minimum of force necessary for the safeguarding of vital interests in other theatres should be diverted from operations against Germany."[2] The first priority for the Western Allies would be to defeat Hitler, with the war on Japan secondary.

But where should the first blow be struck? Although the British Joint Planning Staff had an operational plan called Roundup that envisioned six armoured and six infantry divisions assaulting the French coast somewhere between Dieppe and Deauville, the defending German forces were judged far too strong. Merely drafting the plan had convinced the British that such an invasion could only be delivered as part of "the final phase" of the war on Germany.[3] First the Third Reich's military machine must be greatly diminished through attritional battles fought elsewhere. Those other fronts, Churchill believed, were to be found in northern Africa and the Mediterranean. Only there did the British have sufficient military strength to quickly launch operations. And with the Russian army reeling in disarray back on Moscow, time was of the essence. If Russia capitulated, the Western Allies would face a potentially unwinnable war.

Furthermore, America's military might was still nothing more than potential. Like Canada, the U.S. had gutted its military during the inter-war years and had not seriously started mobilizing despite the gathering war clouds until Japanese bombers pounced on Pearl Harbor. Even the world's most industrialized nation could not whip into existence overnight a military force capable of the kind of amphibious invasion necessary to successfully breach the German defences on coastal Europe.

Curiously, this fact seemed to elude American military planners. While Churchill and his generals cautioned that an immediate invasion of France would be premature and destined to end in disaster, General George C. Marshall, Chief of Staff of the United States Army, recommended to President Franklin D. Roosevelt that the "first great offensive" be directed at northwest Europe.[4] Marshall wanted the quick, decisive results he thought could be achieved by a frontal attack across the English Channel—the shortest route to Germany—employing maximum strength and accepting the severe casualties that such a strategy would undoubtedly incur. If this invasion could not be immediately mounted, and Marshall recognized this was the case, then a series of limited cross-channel assaults should be undertaken in 1942. The Americans designated this strategy Operation Sledgehammer.

Meanwhile, Premier Joseph Stalin was demanding that his Western Allies do something besides talk and bluster. Germany's invasion of the Soviet Union had committed Hitler to a war on two fronts—always risky because it forced a division of strength and attention—but there was little happening on the western front to distract or weaken German operations against Russia. Northern Africa presented the most immediate front that could be opened against Germany with the military strength, resources, and capability that the Allies could rapidly assemble.

So it was that at the end of July 1942 the Americans reluctantly agreed to abandon Sledgehammer in favour of offensive operations in French North Africa, one of the Axis power's most far-flung outposts. Vichy France—a puppet regime established after the French surrender in 1940—had little military strength in the region and any invasion there would necessitate Hitler's countering it with German troops. The decision to undertake operations here represented a political victory for Churchill's favoured strategy of chipping away Germany's strength through operations in the Mediterranean, which he considered Europe's "soft underbelly." It also meant that there would be no invasion across the English Channel until 1943 at the earliest and more realistically, 1944.[5] It was going to be a long war.

EVEN AS MEDITERRANEAN OPERATIONS were initiated, Britain's Combined Operations Headquarters (COHQ), which included planners from all the armed services, started studying the tactical requirements for a successful invasion of northwest Europe. Various commando raids on the European coast were meticulously reviewed for the lessons that could be learned and applied to a larger operation. On March 28, 1942, a major raid had been launched against the U-boat pens at St. Nazaire and the facility considerably damaged despite heavy casualties to the attacking force. Emboldened by this raid's limited success, COHQ's commander Admiral Lord Louis Mountbatten decided to undertake a much larger-scale raid of Dieppe, a French resort town and port.

On August 19, 1942, a 6,000-strong Allied force that counted in its ranks 4,963 Canadians attempted to land on the beaches fronting

Dieppe. The raid, which marked Canada's combat debut in Europe, ended in disaster. The invaders were slaughtered on the beach. Only 2,210 Canadians returned to Britain, with 28 later dying of wounds. During the battle, 807 were killed and 82 of the 1,946 taken prisoner died in captivity.

For Canada, the raid was a grim tragedy that became immediately the source of an endless debate on its merits. But the planners at COHQ drew from the bloody failure a number of lessons that fundamentally influenced their strategy for the northwest Europe invasion. The rapid German reaction at Dieppe warned that any Channel port would be heavily fortified and manned by large numbers of German troops. They therefore abandoned the idea of launching an amphibious landing in close proximity to a major port, setting the wheels in motion to create temporary port facilities that could be established on landing beaches secured by the assault forces.

A vital lesson learned from Dieppe was that the landing force had been inadequately supported by naval and air force bombardment. "The need for overwhelming fire support, including close support, during the initial stages of the attack" was recognized as fundamental to winning a beachhead.[6] While battleships, heavy and light cruisers, and destroyers arrayed in sufficient number could smother the objective under a massive bombardment, these ships were unable to press sufficiently near to shore to provide "close support." Inevitably, they must cease firing for fear of striking the first assault waves just when their guns were most critically needed to keep the Germans cowering in their shelters. New ships capable of operating in extremely shallow waters would have to be developed. It was also deemed critical that means be found to unleash "the fire power of the assaulting troops while still sea-borne."[7] If the artillery, tanks, mortars, and heavy machine guns of the invading forces could bring their weapons to bear from the decks of special landing craft, the infantry could hit the beach supported by the same kind of overwhelming fire that would support them in a traditional land battle.

The Royal Navy decided to form a permanent naval assault force "with a coherence comparable to that of any other first line fighting formations."[8] Not only must the navy develop specially trained personnel capable of delivering troops safely onto a beach and then effectively supporting them, but the army must train its assault troops to work in close cooperation with the naval force. A team effort was required.

Some of these principles were put to the test during the invasion of French North Africa in November 1942. But it was the Sicily invasion of July 10, 1943 that served as a dress rehearsal, with heavy naval gunfire and aerial bombardment pounding the Italian defenders virtually senseless. Close support provided by a variety of special landing craft mounting heavy guns, rocket batteries, and mortars then denied them any respite before the Allied troops stormed ashore. Other purpose-specific craft made it possible to move infantry, tanks, and artillery quickly onto the beaches. The Landing Craft, Tank (LCT) was able to sail right up to the beach and drop a ramp, down which tanks trundled straight into the battle. Landing Craft Infantry, Large simultaneously put two hundred soldiers on the ground within minutes of dropping its ramps, although these craft were too bulky to be utilized in the first landing wave. That initial assault force went ashore in Landing Craft, Assault (LCA), flat-bottomed open craft capable of carrying a platoon and its equipment.

The landings in Sicily were a great success but the defenders were few and of poor quality. It was unlikely any landing in northwest Europe would face such half-hearted resistance. Still, the basic tactics and equipment were in place to make a landing feasible. There remained, however, the problem of determining where the invasion would occur, when, and who would be involved.

WITH THE INVASION of Italy, it was clear that the winds of war now blew more favourably for the Allies. Several months earlier, on February 2, 1943, the remaining 91,000 survivors of Generalfeldmarschall Friedrich Paulus's starving and exhausted Sixth Army had surrendered at Stalingrad. Their defeat followed an unparalleled, brutal six-month battle in which more than 200,000 Germans had perished amidst the ruins of the city. Such devastating casualties were impossible to replace. Then had come the destruction in May 1943 of the Afrika Korps during the battle for Tunisia, which marked the end of Germany's presence in Africa. Sicily had brought more German losses and the drain of strength continued in Italy as the Allies moved onto the mainland in September 1943. In Russia, the Germans faced one reversal after another. That Hitler had lost the initiative was clear. On both the Russian and Mediterranean fronts, Germany was fighting defensively. The heady days of blitzkrieg were over and the Germans were steadily, if slowly, being pressed back into Fortress Europe.

The invasion of Italy had secured a toehold inside that fortress but it was a tenuous one, proving difficult to expand. Despite attempts to achieve a breakthrough that would send the Germans reeling north and open the way for a drive into Austria—Churchill's vaunted back door into Germany—the U.S. Fifth Army, and British Eighth Army, which included in its ranks 27,000 Canadians, were able to advance only slowly and at the price of heavy casualties. To the east, the Russians faced a long, hard march to reclaim thousands of square miles of homeland before being in a position to start driving through Poland towards Germany.

As these events were playing out, the Allies realized the situation was so improved that an invasion of northwest Europe might be possible in the spring of 1944. The Combined Chiefs of Staff appointed British Lieutenant General Frederick E. Morgan to the position of Chief of Staff to the Supreme Allied Commander (COSSAC) and assigned him the duty of planning "a full scale assault against the continent in 1944 as early as possible."[9]

The rancorous Trident conference in May 1943, held in Washington, had seen the British and Americans sharply divided over the amount of resources and personnel that should be allocated to Sicily and following Italian campaigns. The Americans were as keen to limit these to mere holding actions as the British were to decisively drive Italy out of the war and develop Churchill's soft-underbelly strategy to break into central Europe. An uneasy compromise was reached whereby operations would be more vigorous in the Mediterranean than the Americans liked, while a cross-channel invasion was to be launched on May 1, 1944.

This invasion would be an all-out effort involving five infantry divisions in the first assault, two more quickly following, two airborne divisions landing inland of the invasion site, and twenty more divisions subsequently moving into the beachhead to undertake offensive operations to rapidly expand the lodgement. Even before the conference wrapped up, however, planners cautioned that there were not enough landing craft to make a five-division operation feasible. The plan was quickly altered so that the British would provide two assault divisions and one follow-on division and the Americans one assault division and one follow-on division.

Decisions made, the conference adjourned and Morgan got down to work. Under his direction, an integrated Anglo-American staff of officers drawn from all three services set about developing the specific invasion plan, codenamed Operation Overlord. Among these officers was Canadian Major R.A. Harris, who served as Morgan's Military Assistant.[10] Also stationed in Morgan's headquarters was a Canadian liaison officer, Major General G.R. Turner, whose primary responsibility was to keep First Canadian Army commander Lieutenant General Andrew McNaughton abreast of planning details. McNaughton was to be kept in the know not because he was the commander of First Canadian Army, but rather because he was also "the accredited military representative of the Canadian Government in the U.K." Turner's presence was not welcomed by the British Chiefs of Staff, but Morgan told his staff—British and American—that there was a "tacitly conceded" agreement to keep the Canadians informed of the developing invasion plan.[11]

On July 3, 1943, McNaughton was able to summon Lieutenant General Harry Crerar, then commanding I Canadian Corps, to inform him that 3rd Canadian Infantry Division would begin assault training in preparation for a possible role in the cross-channel invasion. Crerar's corps headquarters was to have responsibility for the division's "training and operations."[12]

Less than four months later, however, due partly to Crerar's persistent lobbying, I Canadian Corps was ordered to join the Eighth Army in Italy. This ended McNaughton's hopes of keeping the Canadian army overseas together as a cohesive force that would play a significant role in the invasion. Instead, on November 12, 1943, 3rd Canadian Infantry Division with 2nd Canadian Armoured Brigade attached came under command of the 1st British Corps "for operational direction and the training related thereto for the purpose of Operation Overlord."[13]

Meanwhile, plans for Overlord had been firming up quickly since the conclusion of the Washington conference. On July 15, 1943, Morgan had submitted his invasion plan to the British Chiefs of Staff and summarized it in a ten-point covering letter. First, he reiterated the task assigned and set out the primary challenges that must be overcome. The most critical of these was the need to rapidly "improvise sheltered anchorages off the beaches" through which reinforcements and supplies could flow to enable the beachhead's expansion. Of equal concern was the lack of sufficient and suitable craft. Increased production and reallotment of such craft from other theatres would be required. Furthermore, it might be necessary to postpone the date of the assault to allow the assembling of a suitably large flotilla.

A May 1 invasion, Morgan wrote, could be launched "only if we concentrate our efforts on an assault across the Norman beaches about Bayeux." It was here—midway between the two French ports of Cherbourg on the Cotentin Peninsula and le Havre at the mouth of the Seine River—that Morgan believed the Germans were least prepared to repel an invasion.

Finally, Morgan cautioned his superiors not to be lulled into over-optimism by the success of the Sicily landing that had occurred just five days earlier. The two operations, he said, "could hardly be more dissimilar. In Husky [codename for the Sicily invasion], the bases of an extended continental coastline were used for a converging assault against an island, whereas in Overlord it is necessary to launch an assault from an island against an extended continental mainland coastline. Furthermore, while in the Mediterranean the tidal range is negligible and the weather reasonably reliable, in the English Channel the tidal range is considerable and the weather capricious."[14]

THE BRITISH CHIEFS OF STAFF accepted the plan in principle and passed it forward for discussion by the Combined Chiefs of Staff at the Quadrant Conference in Quebec City on August 14, who granted approval the following day. It was recognized that a supreme commander must be appointed to oversee Overlord, but no decision was reached during the conference on who should fill such a post. The Americans did accept, however, British recommendations that Air Chief Marshal Sir Arthur Tedder be named Deputy Supreme Commander, that the naval commander should be Admiral Sir Charles Little, RN (soon replaced by Admiral Sir Bertram Ramsay, RN), and that Air Marshal Sir Trafford Leigh-Mallory, Fighter Command, RAF, should be air commander.

Recognizing that in the long haul the northwest Europe campaign would see more American than Commonwealth divisions employed, Churchill suggested that Roosevelt name an American to the supreme commander post. Roosevelt could not offer an immediate recommendation and would not do so until Christmas Eve, when he appointed General Dwight D. Eisenhower, then serving as Supreme Allied Commander, Mediterranean Theatre. During the course of the Sicily and Italian campaigns, Eisenhower had shown a talent for keeping a variety of prickly-natured subordinate officers at the army and corps levels working together despite differing nationalities and personalities.[15]

Eisenhower did not, however, get everything his way. When he proposed that General Sir Harold Alexander command the British Army Group, the British War Cabinet rebuffed this notion. Instead, they appointed Eighth Army commander General Sir Bernard Montgomery—precisely the man Eisenhower had hoped to prevent getting the appointment. The American general considered Montgomery abrasive, cocky to the point of conceit, and impossible to control. Because the British Army Group Commander also served as the operational chief of the landings, Eisenhower found the War Cabinet's decision difficult to swallow because Montgomery would have overall control over the invasion plan and its prosecution.[16]

During the Quebec conference, Churchill had been concerned that Morgan's proposal for Overlord was based on too limited an allocation of assault forces. He recommended that "every effort should be made to add at least 25 percent strength to the initial assault."[17]

Eisenhower was inclined to agree and Montgomery also didn't like the sounds of the plan. Arriving in London on January 3, 1944, Montgomery told Admiral Ramsay "that the assaults were not being made on a wide enough front, or with a sufficiency of force, and that it was necessary to extend them, both to introduce a greater number of formations on D-Day and also to accelerate the capture of Cherbourg."[18]

Montgomery set out a new landing scheme on February 1. Operation Neptune, as the naval and amphibious assault phase of the invasion was now designated, divided the landing sites between two armies. The Second British Army would go in on the left, with the First United States Army landing on the right. In the first assault, five British infantry brigades and three U.S. regimental combat teams would hit the beach. These units would be under the direction of five different divisions. Additionally, two airborne divisions would be dropped on the American flank during the night preceding the seaborne landings and another on the British flank. Here, the British 6th Airborne Division would carry out the airborne drop. This division's 3rd Parachute Brigade Group included the 1st Canadian Parachute Battalion. One of the British divisions engaged in the amphibious landing would be the 3rd Canadian Infantry Division. Because the addition of troops to the initial assault would require many more landing craft than currently available, the date for the invasion was pushed back to June 1, 1944.[19]

2

The Web-Footed Division

O N JULY 3, 1943, Lieutenant General Andrew McNaughton had informed 3rd Canadian Infantry Division's Major General Rod Keller that his command might lead the invasion onto one of the beaches. Keller had been promoted to divisional command on September 8, 1942, after fourteen months at the head of 1st Canadian Infantry Brigade. Major General George R. Pearkes and Lieutenant General Harry Crerar both thought he stood out from the small pack of senior Canadian officers to be considered. Pearkes praised Keller's abilities as a disciplinarian and trainer and described him as "young and energetic ... a forceful leader whose judgement can be relied upon."[1] On August 23, 1943, Crerar wrote that he considered Keller "in all respects, fit to command a division in the field. He has had considerable experience as GSO 1 [General Staff Officer Grade 1] of a division and is now commanding a brigade very successfully. He has strong military knowledge well above the average, and strong personality. He is young and energetic. I recommend him first in priority to command a division."[2]

Born on October 2, 1900, Keller was just shy of forty-two when his promotion to major general was approved. This made him the youngest Canadian to hold the rank. Although not quite five-foot-eleven and just over 170 pounds, his ramrod-straight bearing gave the impression that he was taller and more muscular than was actually the case. Born in England but raised in Kelowna, British Columbia,

Keller was passionate about swimming, hunting, and fishing. At an early age he had impressed adults and contemporaries alike with what seemed a natural military bearing. One childhood chum later told newspaper reporters that had his parents not called him Rod the contraction would certainly have been applied by his friends. "He always was straight as a stick," the friend said, "a born soldier."[3]

At seventeen, Keller fittingly enrolled in The Royal Military College of Canada. While he proved a marginal student academically, Keller impressed instructors with his strength of character and moral uprightness. It was these attributes that led to repeated declarations that he had the "makings of a fine officer."[4] In Keller's Christmas 1919 report, RMC Commandant Archibald Cameron Macdonell declared him of excellent character and a fine cadet. Macdonell did, however, "want him to be a little more cheery" and advised his parents to "tell him to smile under all circumstances."[5]

After graduating on June 24, 1920, Keller reported as a lieutenant in the Permanent Active Militia for duty in the Princess Patricia's Canadian Light Infantry stationed in Winnipeg. Despite the withered state of the peacetime Permanent Force, Keller's service with the PPCLI and on various military district staffs resulted in his selection to attend the prestigious British Staff College at Camberley in 1936. Attending either Camberley or the other British Staff College at Quetta virtually ensured a fast promotional track. Of the sixty-three Canadians to attend either college between 1919 and 1939, thirty-six ultimately reached brigade rank or higher.[6]

Now, having outstripped most of these men by gaining the coveted rank of major general, Keller seemed poised for an enviable military career. His Deputy Adjutant and Quartermaster General, Lieutenant Colonel Ernest Côté, considered Keller a "conventional tactician," but "very much a spit and polish officer who cut quite a figure in his battledress. We always kept a spare uniform for him, ironed and ready to go just in case." This degree of attention to appearances was equally reflected in his insistence that the division itself be well turned out. "He cared for his division and was sensitive to any slight on its reputation. He was a very proud man and always on top of the division's training."[7]

Underneath the polished facade lurked a troubled soul, which appearances occasionally hinted at. There was the fact that his round, perpetually ruby red face turned vivid purple when he became angered. And the raspy voice that could, again when angered, rip a man to shreds with scathingly brutal disapproval. Keller was seldom angry, however. More often than not he was cheerfully gregarious in the divisional officer's mess, not expecting to be deferred to and seeming to relish entertaining his officers with humorous stories that left them all laughing with genuine pleasure. But Keller's popularity as a raconteur could not hide from his staff officers the fact that he drank more than was common in an army much given to consumption of alcohol. A bottle of whisky a day was rumoured. And yet Keller was never seen to be drunk.[8]

Word of Keller's possible heavy drinking had reached Crerar even before he recommended the officer for divisional command. When Crerar confronted Keller directly about the matter, he was assured that the drinking was never overindulgent. Crerar accepted the officer's assurances without further remark.[9]

Not long after Keller's promotion, Captain Harold Bertrand Gonder of the Cameron Highlanders of Ottawa was appointed to be his aide-de-camp. Gonder had been born to missionary parents in China on May 19, 1909. He was sixteen when his family returned to Ottawa and, after spending one year in school, Gonder, like so many young men in the midst of the Great Depression, began drifting from job to job. He rode the freights from Toronto to Halifax and back to Ottawa, where he finally landed a position as a furrier. Bored by his work, he joined the Camerons as a militiaman on September 2, 1939. Eight days later, Canada was at war and Gonder quickly found himself promoted to the rank of sergeant. Two years after his enlistment, Gonder was sent to officer's training and soon after his return to the Camerons as a newly minted officer was appointed Keller's ADC. His job was to be Keller's shadow, ready to undertake any task.

Gonder came to respect the major general both as a man and an officer. Aware of the heavy drinking, he also noted its lack of effect on Keller's behaviour or appearance. The two spent many hours together travelling in staff cars from one meeting to another or to conduct troop inspections of the division's various brigades and battalions. Keller was a keen believer in the merits of formal inspections, considering that a well-turned-out regiment evidenced an intrinsic pride that would help it triumph on the battlefield. Before each inspection began, Gonder, drawing on his sergeant's experience, hastened down the lines of men while Keller engaged in pre-inspection formalities with the officers. He would encourage the soldier who was nervous of meeting the general, adjust the uniform of the mildly slovenly, and do his best to ensure Keller would be satisfied.

Normally during their journeys, the two men sat in the back of the car and enjoyed an amiable silence. Keller seemed to use this rare time of relative privacy, free of the ceaseless interruptions that typified the course of a divisional commander's day, for reflection. He would smoke his pipe with a thoughtful expression on his face. Gonder presumed that it was here the major general drafted many divisional training schemes and thought ahead to the division's amphibious assault. Upon arriving back at divisional headquarters, Keller would often proceed directly to his office and spend the next few hours locked away while he turned thoughts into orders or notes for discussion with his staff. Occasionally during their motorized rambles, Keller would become expansively conversational and engage Gonder in discussions that ranged far beyond military matters. But never did he speak of family or personal issues. His wife and two children were never mentioned. Nor did he ask Gonder a personal question.

Soon after becoming Keller's ADC, Gonder noticed that the man had one unusual eccentricity. Whenever a magpie crossed his path, Keller paused midstep, doffed his cap or beret, and then solemnly bowed to the bird. Should there be three birds, he bowed to each in turn. After witnessing this ritual repeatedly, Gonder worked up the nerve to ask its reason. "It's an old habit that we used to have, my father and I, in the Okanagan," Keller said. "My father always did that. He used to say that one was for sorrow, two for joy, three's a girl, and four's a boy." Understanding the roots of this oddity made Gonder think of the major general less as a stiff and soulless officer than as someone with a very human personality.

And then there came the night that Keller visited his old friend Brigadier Harry Foster, who was soon to take a short leave from 7th Canadian Infantry Brigade to command the Canadian forces involved in the recapture of Kiska Island off Alaska from Japanese forces. This was no formal visit, so Gonder remained outside Foster's office to allow the senior officers to talk without inhibition. Finally, just after midnight, the door opened and Keller emerged. Gonder was shocked to see that both Keller and the brigadier were unsteady on their feet. He hastened to Keller's side and stayed with him as they walked slowly and with exaggerated care to the staff car. Gonder noted that several officers and men, returning from evening passes in town, were going past and he could sense their eyes falling on them.

As soon as they were in the car and it had exited the base gates, Keller said in the most vicious tone Gonder had ever heard from him: "Captain Gonder, report to me in my quarters at 0715 hours this morning." Until then, he had always called Gonder by his first name. Worried about what sin he had committed, Gonder reported precisely at the prescribed time. Keller stood behind his desk, uniform immaculately pressed, showing no sign of effect from the night's drinking. "I cannot bear to have any of my men see me while I am inebriated," he growled. "You permitted that to happen last night. I will not tolerate it. Never allow me to get in that condition again. If ever you suspect that I'm on my way to losing my control and my dignity and the appearance that every commander should have, I want you to come up to me and say, 'Sir, I think it's time to go home.' And you will find that I won't argue and I will thank you and I will come."

Keller was good to his word, for on two occasions Gonder somewhat nervously advised the major general in a soft whisper that he should go home. Keller immediately thanked his host or hostesses, bade farewell to the other guests, and walked with great poise and dignity to his car. "Thank you, Hal," he would say as they settled in the car. Ever more respectful, Gonder freely admitted that he would give the major general everything he had in the way of loyalty and service.

By convention, the tour of an ADC was limited and Gonder's tour ended shortly after Keller was alerted to his division's possible role in the invasion. Normally, an ADC is appointed to a staff officer position, a prospect Gonder dreaded. It was this fate that hung over the officer when Keller summoned him to his office in the late summer of 1943 and reminded the captain of this tradition and the fact that he knew of no ADC who had not gone on to staff work. "But I know one now and that's you," he said softly. "You're not made for staff duty. You're made to be with your men. You would like to go back to your men, wouldn't you?"

"Yes, Sir," Gonder responded.

"I'll arrange it," Keller said.

Gonder was immediately posted back to the Camerons. Thereafter he saw little of Keller except during the inevitable inspections when Gonder would be one of those officers standing in line and hoping his men were satisfactorily turned out. "Hello, Hal," Keller would say briskly and continue down the line without further sign of familiarity, which was what Gonder preferred. He wanted neither to have Keller look down his nose at him nor make any kind of patronizing fuss over him. They were both just soldiers doing their duty.[10]

AS OF JULY 3, 1943, the primary duty of every soldier in the division was to learn his role in carrying out an amphibious assault landing, a task complicated initially by a total lack of any landing craft. In their absence, Keller issued orders for the battalions to conduct mock landings from the inside of "craft" that were no more than lines of tape staked out on the ground to the exact dimensions of Landing Craft, Assault (LCA). Nets and ladders were fixed to cliffs and the men climbed down these to simulate descending the scramble nets used to disembark from larger transport ships into LCAs.[11]

The relentless pace of training was physically and psychologically demanding. Posted to the North Nova Scotia Highlanders 'C' Company on July 27, 1943 as a platoon commander, Lieutenant Jack Mersereau Veness was immediately cast into a regimen of running his platoon through a seemingly endless gauntlet of mock assaults and obstacle courses. Route marches were common. During one twenty-four-hour exercise, the North Novas marched forty-two miles while carrying full pack loads along a route that required the men to climb two-hundred-foot cliffs, swim a river in full uniform and gear, and end the ordeal with a display of marksmanship on a firing range.[12]

August and September saw individual battalions dispatched to the Combined Training Centre at Inveraray in Scotland. Here, actual landing craft combined with the frequent use of live ammunition made the exercises all the more real. One week, the North Novas suffered a man hurt or killed on every single day. Veness had a close call when the man crawling behind him accidentally discharged his rifle and the bullet tore through the sleeve of the officer's jacket and grazed his arm.[13]

During the Royal Winnipeg Rifles' stay, the tough conditions of Inveraray were further compounded by a curious ration order issued by acting commander Brigadier Church Mann—standing in for Brigadier Harry Foster while he was involved in the Kiska operation. Having just taken command of the Winnipegs' 'D' Company, Major Lochie Fulton was dismayed to come off the field soaking wet and frozen through, only to find that there would be no hot meal. Instead, the men were made to subsist on Spam sandwiches because Mann believed operating field kitchens during extensive field exercises was too difficult. Fulton decided that, while Mann might be a good staff officer, he should never have been given command of troops, for the man obviously had no idea how dramatically such basic comforts as a hot meal or the lack of it can influence morale.

Not only the endless rain ensured that the soldiers were soaked day and night. Although the flat-bottomed LCAs were designed to get right up on a beach for a foot-dry landing, this seldom proved the case, thanks to rocks or the seabed slope. When the ramp in the front dropped, Fulton and his platoon would charge out and inevitably plunge into waist-deep water so cold it shocked the breath out of them. When the battalion moved into the Highlands for maneuver exercises, their vehicles bogged down in the soft heath. Then, while trying to seize a point of high ground in a mock assault, a two-inch mortar salvo fell short, killing two of 'D' Company's men. When the three-week training session at Inveraray came to a close, Fulton and his men were "quite happy to leave there." But the young officer recognized that the training would stand them in good stead during real combat.[14]

Queen's Own Rifles Sergeant Dave Kingston would have concurred. The twenty-two-year-old Torontonian had never experienced such realistic training. Near the end of the QOR's Inveraray training, commander Lieutenant Colonel J.G. "Jock" Spragge gathered the men together. "Today and tomorrow we're going to do something entirely different," he said. "'A' Company is going to defend this hill and 'B' Company is going to attack. Difference is that both companies are going to use live ammunition. Tomorrow 'C' Company will defend this hill and 'D' Company will attack, both using live ammunition. The idea is you'll get used to these bullets whizzing by you." Then the roles would be reversed, with the defending companies taking the turn as attackers.

A platoon sergeant in 'C' Company, Kingston and his men took up their positions in slit trenches on top of the hill, with the officers marching back and forth just below the crest behind them so they were not exposed to the incoming rounds 'D' Company was firing. "Remember, tomorrow you're going to be down there coming up that hill, so aim high," the officers shouted repeatedly. Kingston and his men blazed away, bullets and tracers buzzing overhead as 'D' Company threw a steady rate of fire back while clawing a path up the virtually sheer hill. Kingston was relieved no casualties were suffered during the exercise, but the value of the lesson was clear in the way the men resolutely pressed on with their assigned tasks during all subsequent live fire drills.[15]

It only failed to rain one day while the QOR were in Inveraray, but the men ended up soaking wet anyway. Lance Corporal Rolph Jackson's platoon was loaded into an old landing craft and taken half a mile out to sea. When the vessel halted in the rolling swells, its crew settled down with their bagged lunches and the officer in charge breezily told the infantrymen that their lunch awaited them back on shore. All they had to do was swim with their full battle kits back to the beach. Groaning under the weight of forty-pound packs and weighed down awkwardly by their weapons, the men piled over the side into the icy water and swam shoreward. Some soldiers didn't know how to swim and even a number who did found the weight of gear and waterlogged uniforms too much. Men faltered and were only saved from drowning by the last-moment arrival in a rowboat of British commandos, who fished those in trouble from the sea.[16]

THE EXERCISES AT INVERARAY presented the armoured and artillery regiments opportunity to test various unique techniques and equipment for use in establishing a beachhead. This was particularly true for the artillery regiments, which were to bring their guns into action while still on board specially prepared Landing Craft, Tanks pressing shoreward close behind the initial landing forces. British and Canadian gun experts thought that firing artillery from the decks of ships would be either impossible or doomed to wild inaccuracy. Brigadier P.A.S. "Stanley" Todd, 3 CID's commander of artillery regiments, believed otherwise. So did many of his subordinate gunners.

Among these was Major James Douglas Baird of the 13th Field Regiment, Royal Canadian Artillery. During the exercises in Scotland, the thirty-six-year-old officer from Red Deer, Alberta acted as the regiment's fire control officer. Each of the regiment's batteries was allotted two LCTS, each capable of accommodating four 25-pounders, and told they were going to learn how to fire the guns accurately from offshore against targets on the invasion beach. To keep the guns steady, they were lashed to the deck by wrapping a U-shaped cable around the wheels and then secured with special bolts to mountings welded to the steel decking. As only the wheels were fixed, the gun crews could still drag the gun around by the trail to bring the barrel to bear on the target. In very short order, the gunners were dropping shells within three hundred yards of their targets.[17]

While such accuracy was impressive, the exercises raised an issue that threatened to scuttle the entire plan for using ship-based artillery. Once the infantry was as little as a thousand yards inland, it was imperative that the gun regiments be quickly landed on the sand to support the advance. Unbolting the guns from the LCT decks, however, proved a laboriously slow task and then it proved impossible to swing the trails on the narrow ships in order to hitch them to the towing tractors for offloading. Each gun had to be manhandled muzzle first down the landing ramps. Todd considered solving the problem by doubling the number of each regiment's guns—one set to be lashed to the LCT decks for firing offshore and the other limbered up on other LCTs for quick unloading—but rejected this solution as there simply were not enough guns available. Nor were there enough spare LCTs.

Todd and his staff decided to set the 25-pounders aside and re-equip the division's artillery regiments with a self-propelled gun that could be shackled with chains to the deck during the firing phase and then simply driven off the LCT under its own power on landing. This plan was quickly approved and in early September the regiments began receiving allotments of American Priests, an SPG that mounted a 105-millimetre howitzer onto the chassis of an outmoded M3 tank from which the turret had been removed. The gun crews set to work mastering not only how to fire new artillery pieces but also how to drive the machines. It soon became evident that the Priest gave the gunners greatly increased mobility, which should enable them to better keep pace with the advancing tanks and infantry during the hoped-for rapid breakout from the beachhead.[18]

Major Baird became an immediate fan of the Priest. The 105-millimetre gun fired a heavier shell and was only slightly slower to reload than the 25-pounder. Weighing twenty-five tons, the SPG was so heavy it remained steady on the ship deck and the shackle chains served to prevent the steel tracks side-slipping on the steel decking in rough seas. The most important strength of the Priest, though, for the ship-to-shore bombardment phase, was that the gun was provisioned with seven alternate weights of charges, as opposed to the three that were standard to the 25-pounder. This meant the gunners could engage targets at a greater variance of ranges without radically adjusting the angle of the gun barrel—improving accuracy when firing on targets at either short or long range.[19]

Still, Todd and his staff remained unsure that the shore bombardment scheme was viable because of the risk that the shellfire might fall on the infantry as they scrambled out of the sea onto the beaches. To ensure accurate gunnery, a new gun control system had been devised in Scotland that entailed a Forward Observation Officer (FOO) travelling in a Landing Craft Infantry, Small to within a thousand yards of shore. From this close vantage, he would radio range corrections and concentration adjustments back to the Fire Control Officer (FCO), aboard a motor launch running towards shore on a course that parallelled that of the LCTs upon which his regiment's guns were loaded. Such a system enabled the guns to begin firing ten thousand yards offshore because the FOO could see the fall of shot and then radio necessary corrections to the gunners, who as yet would be unable to even see the shoreline.

While the theory was sound, reality was bedevilled by a serious glitch. The motor launches were equipped with radar necessary to fix their distances from shore. But these radar sets emitted a signal that entirely disrupted the wireless sets being used to communicate with the FOOs. All the FCOs, like Baird, could hear were great bursts of unintelligible static.

Todd was not about to let a communication problem derail a sound and necessary application of the division's artillery. He also knew that unless reliable communications could be assured, the guns were firing blind and such artillery support was of little use. Todd asked Major H.S. Patterson, commander of the Royal Canadian Signal Corps section supporting 3 CID's headquarters, to find a solution. Patterson was at first nonplussed. The radar emitted interfering signals that easily jammed the amplitude modulation radio sets used by Commonwealth troops. This was the crudest of the three possible modulation systems that radio communications could utilize and highly susceptible to interference problems. The most sophisticated form of wireless used phased modulation, but this technology was still in its infancy and no military sets existed.

That left the third type of modulation. The U.S. Army had frequency modulation wireless sets and Patterson knew these systems were less prone to jamming by either manmade or natural sources, although they had a limited broadcast range. He borrowed an American No. 509 wireless, mounted it in a motor launch, and found it worked like a charm. On water, where there were no obstructions to block transmissions, the set's range was between seven and eight miles—far beyond the ten thousand yards he required. And, unlike

the British No. 38 set whose crystal drifted notoriously off its designated frequency net, 509 crystals were extremely precise. Patterson
knew the various artillery regiments scattered in four-gun groups
over a large number of LCTs would have to net their radios together
days before the actual amphibious landing and then go into absolute
wireless silence for security purposes. Any crystal drift could mean a
failure of communication just when the guns were supposed to begin
firing. When Patterson reported his findings, Todd immediately secured permission to equip the division's artillery regiments with the
necessary number of 509s.[20]

By the end of September, the division was concentrating around
Portsmouth. They moved into a training schedule that involved working closely with a naval assault force designated Force J, composed of
many ships that had been involved in the Dieppe landings. These
ship and crews had been kept together in the aftermath of the failed
raid to provide a laboratory for developing and testing combined operation techniques. It was around this nucleus of experienced sailors
that the landing force that would support 3 CID was formed.[21]

The division also married up here with 2nd Canadian Armoured
Brigade, whose three regiments were to provide tank support. The
brigade was seriously handicapped by a critical shortage of the type of
tank it was to take into combat. Despite an agreement among the Allies in summer of 1943 to adopt the use of a single battle tank in
order to maximize production and supply efficiencies, the supply of
these tanks was lagging far behind requirements. Consequently, it
was not until January 1944 that 2 CAB received its first ten American-
designed Shermans. While the tankers waited anxiously for the rest
of their tanks to arrive, they had to train for an amphibious landing
with Canadian-made Rams or British Valentines. The undergunned
and lightly armoured Valentine had been declared obsolete in 1942
and production of the Ram had ceased in July 1943.[22]

Dieppe had grimly demonstrated that infantry landing on a beach
alone were easy prey for defenders sheltered in concrete pillboxes
and other fortified positions, who could rake the exposed attackers
with machine-gun, mortar, and artillery fire from a position of relative safety. Lieutenant General Frederick Morgan, Chief of Staff to

the Supreme Allied Commander, and his staff were determined that an armoured regiment would set down on the beach alongside each infantry brigade to immediately destroy the beach fortifications with direct fire from the tanks' main guns. In the Canadian case, the 7th, 8th, and 9th Canadian infantry brigades would be supported respectively by the 1st Hussars, the Fort Garry Horse, and the Sherbrooke Fusiliers.[23]

Attempts to land tanks directly on the heels of the infantry had failed miserably at Dieppe. Many landing craft were sunk before reaching the beach and those tanks that were successfully disembarked either fell quickly to the fire of antitank guns or had tracks broken by the stony beach. The latter difficulty could be avoided by landing only on sand or pebble beaches, but how to land tanks in sufficient numbers on a hotly contested beach remained a seemingly insoluble problem. It was simply too easy for antitank guns mounted in fortified positions to pick off tanks trundling down the ramps of LCTs like ducks in a row. Fortunately, a solution to the conundrum soon presented itself in the form of a tank capable of "swimming" ashore under its own power. Known as the Duplex-Drive tank, it was part of the growing inventory of unique purpose-specific tanks being created by the 79th British Armoured Division under the command of the eccentric inventor and tanker, Major General Percy Hobart.

One of Hobart's "Funnies," as the division's oddball-looking tanks were collectively known, the DD tank was rendered buoyant by means of a collapsible canvas screen fitted to the hull just above the running gear. Attached to the screen were thirty-two regularly spaced tubes of four-inch diameter. When injected with compressed air, the tubes expanded like sausages, pulling the attached screen upright, with the result that the tank became completely encircled by a canvas ring steadied not only by the inflated tubes but also by eight metal braces bracketed to the hull. The screen provided sufficient displacement to keep the tank afloat even in relatively rough seas. Two propellers powered by the tank engines were mounted to the base of the rear of the hull and provided propulsion sufficient to give the tank a six-knot top speed. As the canvas screen extended a foot higher than the turret, the driver was unable to see where he was going, so the tank commander provided steerage from atop the turret with a crude but effective rudder that could be pushed to the right or left.[24]

The 1st Hussars and Fort Garry Horse had been selected to support the initial assaulting infantry brigades, and each was to have two of its three squadrons equipped with DD tanks. The crews from these squadrons received their nautical training at Great Yarmouth under the tutelage of Hobart's tankers and several British submariners. Corporal Jim Simpson, a crew commander in the 1st Hussars' 'B' Squadron, was struck by the intense secrecy that surrounded this training. Although the twenty-five-year-old, who had enlisted only three days after Canada declared war on Germany, was a seasoned tanker, he had never seen training like this. Normally, because tank operations at night were extremely rare, training was a daylight affair. Fear of the top-secret tanks being detected by German reconnaissance planes, however, resulted in the tankers being ordered to take the DD tanks out on the water only at night.

Although the DDs were seaworthy, they were easily swamped. The slightest damage to the screens by enemy fire or battering by heavy surf could cause the tank to founder and sink like a stone before the crew could safely bail out. To ensure the tankers were able to avoid being entombed in a watery grave, they were taught to escape from a tank turret stuck at the bottom of a twenty-foot-deep shaft into which thirty thousand gallons of water was pumped through two high-pressure pipes. Three crewmen at a time were each equipped with a Davis Escape Apparatus—standard evacuation equipment for British submariners—and put inside the turret with instructions to make their way to the surface once the tank was submerged.

It took only seconds for the fast-flowing stream of water to fill the turret, making it essential for the crewmen to remain calm and do precisely as they had been instructed. When Simpson's turn came, he moved with careful deliberation as the water gushed through gaps in the turret's steel skin. The mouthpiece and nosepiece of the escape vest had to be fitted with precision to prevent salt water entering his mouth or nose and causing a life-threatening choking fit. Once the oxygen flow valve was turned on and he could breathe comfortably, Simpson dropped down to the bottom of the turret. Here the three men waited for the tank to finish flooding. Then, one after the other, they slowly and carefully wormed up past the many sharp edges that jutted out from equipment in the tight confines. The first man in line opened the hatch and led them out into the shaft, where the increasing rate of oxygen flow entering the vest provided sufficient buoyancy to carry them to the surface.

Often men panicked during the escape and lost their mouthpiece, nosepiece, or both. They hit the surface spitting and coughing, usually hysterical with fear. But the training officers kept them at it until everyone knew what to do in the event that his tank sank off the shores of France.[25]

The DD tank was not the only specialized armoured vehicle the Canadians received from Hobart's strange collection. There was also the Crab, which had a rotating cylinder mounted on its front to which long flailing chains were attached that literally churned up the ground ahead of it to detonate mines. A turretless Churchill tank chassis provided the platform for the Armoured Vehicle Royal Engineer (AVRE). This versatile device mounted a short-barrelled 12-inch demolition gun called a petard, which fired a 40-pound, square-shaped round nicknamed a "flying dustbin" for destroying fortifications or breaching obstacles such as concrete walls. Additionally, an AVRE could carry bridging such as fascines—bundles of rods for filling ditches—or short lengths of girded ramps able to bear forty tons that could be winched into position using a 30-foot cable mounted to the chassis. The Armoured Ramp Carrier, known as the Ark, bore two foldout steel ramps that could be dropped to create a bridge, with the Churchill tank upon which they rode forming the centre support. On the back of the Bobbin was a 110-yard spool of sections of coconut husk carpet attached to bamboo poles that could be unravelled and spread over mud or deep sand so tanks and trucks could cross without becoming bogged down. Because these tanks were so highly specialized, all but the DDS were crewed by 79th Division personnel seconded to the assaulting divisions of the Second British Army. When the Funnies were offered to the Americans as well, their commanders scoffed at the utility of the strange vehicles and decided to use only the DD tanks in their assault.

By contrast, Keller noted in a report that as a result of the various exercises it was "apparent that special assault equipment was necessary," and that through Hobart's Funnies "this was indeed provided." His soldiers, he added, were, through "patient trial and experiments," learning to waterproof everything from their rifles to wireless sets. Vehicles such as jeeps and trucks were fitted with tall air intake and exhaust stacks that would allow them to continue running while entirely submersed. As one training exercise followed another, Keller described his division "as being 'web-footed.'"[26]

It was also a division with a headquarters staff frantically doing their all to plan for every eventuality that might arise in a massive invasion operation unlike any ever undertaken in military history. In November 1943, Don Mingay was promoted from his position as second-in-command of the Essex Scottish Regiment and posted to 3 CID as a lieutenant colonel to be Keller's General Staff Officer, Grade 1. When Mingay reported to Keller, the general did not deign to rise from his chair. "Mingay, I didn't ask for you. I don't know anything about you. You have not had any experience and I will give you one week to satisfy me that you can do the job or back you go to where you came from. You are excused."

Saluting smartly, Mingay turned sharply on his heel and marched out of the office. He quickly learned of Keller's drinking habits and his lack of interest in the operational side of the division's management. Mingay's first task was to gather a planning staff, but he also recognized an immediate problem within the division over communication between the administrative and operational wings of the headquarters staff. Simply put, "they hardly ever spoke to one another."

The simple solution to this, Mingay decided, was for him to move his desk right into Lieutenant Colonel Ernest Côté's office so the two divisional wings were sitting shoulder to shoulder. When this proved a workable idea, the two men directed all their subordinate staff to link up with those carrying out parallel tasks and work together.[27] It was several weeks after his arrival at the division that Mingay realized Keller must be satisfied, for the general had not followed through on his threat to sack him after a week's probation.

[3]

Learning New Skills

LIEUTENANT PETER HINTON had received his watch-keeping ticket in late summer 1943 while serving as a sub-lieutenant aboard the Bangor-class minesweeper HMCS *Kelowna* steaming up and down the British Columbia coastline. A short time later he received orders posting him to Falmouth, England. There, in the fall of 1943, the twenty-three-year-old was awestruck to be given his own command. Admittedly, Landing Craft Infantry, Large 262 was a rather modest ship, but still the burden of command rested heavily on the sailor, who had only ten months of sea experience.[1]

Like the twenty-nine other LCILS that were evenly organized into three Canadian flotillas, LCIL 262 had seen hard service in the Mediterranean since being first used for the invasion of Sicily. Twenty-four had sailed under the U.S. flag and the other six with the Royal Navy. Shortages of replacement parts and proper tools combined with the engine and ship maintenance inexperience of their American and British crews had reduced the craft to "a shocking condition" by the time they passed into Canadian hands.[2]

When Royal Canadian Navy flotilla maintenance crews and locally hired dockyard navvies attempted to effect repairs, the task was complicated by the sheer volume of shipping that plugged Britain's repair dockyards. Such facilities "were already hard pressed with landing craft by the hundreds, and tools and spares were still in short supply,

46

and such vital items as tachometers and temperature gauges were scarcely obtainable."[3] Some of the craft were in such desperate condition maintenance officers were unable to guarantee the flotilla commanders that they would even be seaworthy in time for the invasion.[4]

While LCIL 262 was undergoing repairs, Hinton and his twenty-two-man crew squeezed aboard to familiarize themselves with the vessel. The lieutenant was confident that 262 would be ready in time for any invasion, but was less confident in his own ability. And then there was his crew, of which only a quarter had ever been to sea. Neither coxswain nor chief motor mechanic had sea experience.

The LCILS were odd vessels, designed to be both seaworthy and capable of a beach landing. Unlike smaller landing craft, they sported a proper bow, but were flat-bottomed to enable a run onto a beach. Drawing only two feet of draft forward and five feet aft, they were 158 feet long and 23 feet, 3 inches wide at the centre. Two sets of quad General Motors six-cylinder diesel engines powered the vessel to a top speed of nineteen knots, but it cruised comfortably at fifteen knots. Each LCIL could carry about two hundred soldiers, who disembarked down two narrow ramps extended well ahead of the bow from the ship's starboard and port sides in order to enable the troops to get ashore dry-footed.

Equipment aboard was basic. Hinton noted that there was "no echo sounder, no radar, no direction finding gear. Navigation was strictly by eyeball, magnetic compass, and sextant. Luckily we didn't ever need to use the sextant as the only one onboard was pinched by the dockyard navvies before we left Falmouth."[5] The craft was armed with four Oerlikon anti-aircraft guns, twelve rifles, and two revolvers. Standing on LCIL 262's bridge, watching the maintenance workers banging away at his ship, Hinton felt growing pride in his ship and the "great bunch" of men that formed his all-Canadian crew.[6]

LCIL 262 was deemed ready shortly after New Year's for sea trials. A tug pulled the craft out of its berth, tightly wedged between two other ships. For the next few hours, LCIL 262 "shot around the harbour without bumping into anything," Hinton later recalled. "When we headed back we were supposed to meet up with a tug to shoehorn us back into our berth because everything was just jammed with ships." But the tug failed to show. Tired of waiting, Hinton decided he and his crew were up to the challenge of docking under their own steam. "Full of confidence and enthusiasm that only age and lack of experience could generate, I came into this narrow U-shape of two long jetties ready to do a 180 degree turn in order to tuck in bow out, which we all had to do. What I didn't know is that in any breeze it was virtually impossible to turn without losing way—that is, you couldn't turn the ship with the screws. Very rapidly we landed on the rocks at the end of the U, much to the amusement of the navvies who were eating their lunch in the sun. I looked around and all my sailors had gone below, much ashamed. But we weren't harmed and were soon towed off by the tug and put in our berth."[7]

Mock landing exercises followed. There was nothing fancy about the procedure—the LCILs just drove straight for the beach on a flooding tide at twelve knots. When the craft was about a hundred yards from touchdown, a large catch anchor was dumped off the stern. Then the craft skidded onto the beach and the ramps were extended to offload the troops. Although the intent was to enable the soldiers to make a dry landing, the pitch of the seabed fronting most beaches normally caused the LCIL to bottom out short of dry ground. Consequently, first to go down the ramps were two or three sailors who waded ashore, dragging with them long ropes secured to the end of the ramps. The disembarking soldiers, heavily encumbered with combat equipment, could use the ropes to steady themselves as they struggled through the usually hip-deep water to reach shore. The craft got off the beach by riding the rising tide while the crew winched it back out to sea by reeling in the catch anchor's chain.

THE THREE LCIL FLOTILLAS were just a small portion of the ships the Royal Canadian Navy contributed to the massive armada assembling in the ports of southern England. At least some Canadian ships were to play a part in virtually every aspect of the invasion, which would involve the greatest concentration of vessels ever assembled. Total naval ships numbered 5,420, to which a further 1,256 merchant and private vessels were added, for a total of 6,676. Of these, the Royal Canadian Navy provided only 121, with total crew complements of 9,269. Scattered among the vast Royal Navy contingent of ships and crew was an additional 511 RCN personnel.

Although the number of Canadian sailors and ships was small in comparison to the American or British commitments, the various RCN roles in the invasion were of pivotal importance to the success of the landings. Many thousands of ships would not be directly involved in either the immediate assault landings or the essential follow-up phases of the first two days. Of the RCN contingent, however, 102 would be so engaged—consisting of LCILS, Landing Ships, Infantry (Medium), minesweepers, destroyers, frigates, corvettes, and motor torpedo boats (MTBS). The total number of ships drawn from these classes, from all Allied naval services to be involved in Operation Neptune, was 570, so Canada was providing 18 per cent of such vessels.

Many ship classes, of course, were not included in the RCN's inventory. These ranged from massive battleships to the minute Landing Craft, Assault that would run many of the troops, including Canadians, onto the beaches. The total number of vessels to be involved in the actual assault numbered 1,850, of which the RCN share constituted 5.5 per cent of the whole.[8]

Originally, some RCN ships had not been assigned a role in Operation Neptune, but with General Bernard Montgomery's January decision to land five divisions on as many separate beaches, the ship requirement suddenly increased. A critical shortage of minesweepers was immediately recognized by the British Admiralty, so on January 16 it formally requested that the Canadian government place sixteen Bangor-class minesweepers under Royal Navy command.[9]

Bangors came in two models, the larger at 180 feet long by 28.5 feet wide and the smaller at 162 feet by 28 feet. Maximum displacement was 672 tons. Both models had an eighty-three-man crew and a sixteen-knot top speed. As the Germans had laid few mines off Canada's Atlantic coast, these ships had mostly been converted for use in anti-submarine patrolling and the crews had little or no minesweeping experience. The ships had also been stripped of winches and other minesweeping gear to accommodate extra depth charge weaponry.

As the British Admiralty wanted the vessels in England by the end of February, a frantic refit was undertaken at Halifax to ready the Bangors for the new assignment. In addition to reinstalling minesweeping equipment, the ships were outfitted with better and more numerous armaments to increase their survival odds during operations close to an enemy coast defended by powerful coastal batteries. The original light 4-pound bow gun was replaced with a 12-pounder. For anti-aircraft defence, two 20-millimetre Oerlikons were positioned either side of the bridge with a power-driven twin Oerlikon located aft.

The pace of the refit was badly slowed when the minesweeping equipment contracted from one of the two Canadian manufacturers was found to be inadequate. Most sea mines consisted of a weight linked to the explosive by a long chain, so that the weight rested on the seabed, holding the explosive charge stationary and submerged a short distance under the surface. Minesweepers cleared such minefields by reeling out from stern-mounted winches long wires fitted with cutters to sever the chain connecting the charge to the weight. The minesweeping wires were extremely heavy and at full extension placed tremendous strain on the winch—a strain that one manufacturer's winch system was incapable of supporting. By the time the flaw was discovered, half the ships had already been fitted with the defective equipment and were deemed unreliable. So, although RCN command had assured the British Admiralty the ships would be "efficient and fully worked-up" before they sailed for England, this would not be the case.[10]

While the refit was underway, the crews learned new combat skills. Aboard HMCS *Bayfield,* Able Telegraphist Stan Richardson was introduced to the Oerlikons on January 31. The twenty-year-old from Powell River and his shipmates spent the next few days either firing the guns or studying aircraft recognition manuals to enable them to distinguish between friendly and enemy planes. On February 8, *Bayfield* started loading up for sea duty. Richardson's job that afternoon was to stow dozens of crates of Coca-Cola and cigarettes below decks. The next day it was depth charges and ammunition. Valentine's Day was spent performing minesweeping trials at sea.

After two days of such practice, the ship's crew turned to live gunnery drills followed by an evening of shore leave. Richardson immediately headed for Lohney's Restaurant where he "had a sirloin steak and all the trimmings! Who knows," he confided to his diary, "it may be my last meal in Canada."[11]

Before hoisting anchor, a formal inspection by Halifax harbour's commander was preceded by a day of ship cleaning. Allowed to go ashore a final time that evening, Richardson lost his wallet on a streetcar, only to find it turned in later for safekeeping at the Nova Scotia Power Supply office. Wallet retrieved, he paid a barber for a one-inch-long brushcut, took in a couple of movies, and bunked for the night at the YMCA. Late the next afternoon, *Bayfield* received its final inspection and, at 1500 hours on February 18, "led the *Mulgrave, Georgian,* and *Thunder* through Halifax Boom Defense and Gates. So I took my last look at Canada through a porthole before going on watch. I must say I am sure glad to leave Halifax. I must have the wandering itch or something, but I sure like to see new countries."[12]

Over the following three days, the rest of the minesweepers put to sea in divisions of four ships a day. They took an indirect route past Newfoundland and then south to the Azores before turning north towards Plymouth, England, because the ships had insufficient fuel storage capacity for a direct cross-Atlantic passage. Each four-ship convoy steamed directly into the maw of an endless series of gales. Alternately plowing through ice or heavy seas, the small ships started taking damage.[13] On February 20, Telegraphist Richardson fretted that the ice building up on the ship was rendering it hazardously top heavy. "We are bouncing around at 45 degree angles," he wrote. "All china dishes have been smashed in the mess."[14] *Bayfield* spent the following night in St. John's and then sailed towards Horta in the Azores. The ships slammed head-on into a gale on February 23, against which they could make only six knots.[15] "Looked out portholes, but could only see masts of other ships once in awhile. Wave after wave went clear over the whole ship."[16]

Bayfield started taking water forward, while *Thunder* developed a serious condenser leak and started to give way. The struggling *Bayfield* took her in tow. In the following convoy, the flotilla flagship

Caraquet was towing *Vegreville*. *Bayfield* was first to limp on a high tide into Horta on February 29. The Portuguese pilot put aboard *Mulgrave* to guide the ship into harbour made a navigating error that put her aground and caused serious damage. While the rest of the sweepers soon set out on the final leg of the voyage, *Mulgrave* stayed behind awaiting an oceangoing tug that could tow her to Plymouth for repairs. She would not reach the final destination until March 22.

By then, the rest were heavily engaged in minesweeping exercises. The Commander-in-Chief of Plymouth harbour, whose command the ships came under, had quickly realized that the Canadian Bangors were far from ready to assume operations in hostile waters and instituted a rigorous training plan, nicknamed "Pious Dream." Each training phase was designed to last a week, but this schedule had to be abandoned as the ships—particularly those fitted with the deficient winch systems—were beset by equipment defects. Finally, it was decided that the ten most reliable ships would form a single flotilla, while the remaining vessels beefed up understrength British flotillas.

Caraquet became the flotilla flagship, with Acting Commander H.G. "Tony" Storrs in command. *Bayfield* was among the ships assigned to the flotilla. By March 27, the Canadian flotilla swept a dummy minefield in rough seas, cutting a total of ninety-four mines, of which all but one lost in heavy fog were successfully destroyed. The Admiralty staff reported being satisfied and deemed the flotilla fit for operational service.[17]

In addition to the minesweepers, the British Admiralty had requested that the RCN select several corvettes and two Canadian National Railway fast liners for participation in Operation Neptune. As the corvettes could make the Atlantic crossing quickly, they would not be required until almost the last minute. The liners, which had been converted shortly after war broke out into Armed Merchant Cruisers and were currently undergoing conversion to Landing Ship Infantry, Medium, were given sailing orders in late December 1943. With the refit at Burrard Dry Dock in Vancouver far from complete, *Prince David* and *Prince Henry* set out just after New Year's Day on an almost month-long voyage to Britain.

Prince David arrived at Clyde on January 28 and "was at once besieged by the staff of the Rear Admiral, Landing Ships Unallocated who came aboard to see what she needed and what Canadian LSIS were like." They were greatly impressed by the cafeteria-style mess. Equally impressive were the bunks, which a report written after the inspection described as "tubular steel frames stretched with canvas and slung in layers from stanchions so that they could be folded down out of the way when not required." This system was deemed far "more comfortable . . . and slightly more economical in space than the hammocks and messing plan in RN LSIS."[18]

On February 3, *Prince Henry* arrived. Dockyards were so in demand, however, that the two ships were not able to enter John Browns Yard at Clydebank for completion of their refits until February 22. More than one hundred modifications and equipment installations were required to ready the ships for their new role. Two twin Oerlikons were mounted on the flag deck's forward wings, encryption machines were added to the signals room so the ships could serve a headquarters function, and various advanced radar systems were fitted into the chart room. More mundane equipment, such as a loud hailer system, was also installed. These ships would not carry the troops directly to the beach. Rather, eight LCAS mounted in davits on the main deck would run the infantry ashore by companies.

No sooner had this refitting operation got underway than severe labour unrest struck the shipyards. Strikes and slowdowns were common throughout the spring of 1944. Consequently, the work on *Prince Henry* and *Prince David* proceeded sluggishly. The former was only ready for trials on April 10 and the latter three days later. Trials were cursory, for on April 18 both ships sailed for Cowes on the Isle of Wight where Force J's ships were concentrating.[19]

WHILE THE MINESWEEPERS and LSIS were sailing from Canada to Britain and completing their refits, most of Force J had been conducting increasingly complicated mock invasion exercises. Some of these focussed purely on the naval aspects of the plan, but more often they were carried out in tandem with 3 CID units. For Brigadier Stanley Todd, the divisional artillery commander, Exercise Savvy on February

12 was the most pivotal. Included in Savvy was an artillery firing demonstration from the decks of ships that was performed under the watchful eyes of Montgomery, King George VI, and a miscellany of other dignitaries and high command staff. With the new communication systems in place, the firing accuracy proved such that Montgomery readily agreed to the technique being incorporated into the division's assault plan. This brought much relief to Todd's staff, who had feared the entire scheme they had laboured long and hard over might be shelved.[20]

Between the larger exercises, navy and army units engaged in weekly schemes that focussed on mastering one specific skill. For Force J, "there were numerous LSI, LCI, and LCA flotilla manoeuvring, beaching, night navigation, signals and firing exercises."[21]

Along with General Dwight D. Eisenhower and Prime Minister Winston Churchill, Montgomery was again present during Exercise Trousers. The codename "gave staff signals officers plenty of scope for fun with such code signals as 'Trousers Down,' 'Trousers Up,' 'Trousers Wet,' and 'Trousers Torn,' meaning to [respectively] start or stop loading, or postponement or cancellation of the exercise." Exercise Trousers was conducted over several days in mid-April and involved ships from the entire invasion force attacking a series of beaches near Portsmouth.[22]

On April 12, Lieutenant Peter Hinton's LCI L 262 and eleven other craft of the same type drawn from the three Canadian LCI flotillas put their assault troops dry-footed on a stiff gradient beach under the watchful eye of the assembled dignitaries. "To our delight," he later recalled, "Monty detached himself and strode down the beach and I thought he was going to give us some inspiring message, but all he did was stop, unbutton his fly, solemnly urinate, button his pants up, and return to the group. I always thought it might have been editorial comment on our performance."[23]

But that performance was becoming ever more polished. All that remained was one final full-dress rehearsal—Exercise Fabius. On May 4, Force J and all elements of 3 CID carried out a full-scale landing exercise. So extensive was the lead-up that rumours circulated wildly the night before that this was to be the real thing and they were bound for the French coast. Force J sailed from the assembly ports "in daylight and, in bright moonlight with a calm sea, spent the night on an excursion 25 miles into the Channel southeast of the Isle of Wight."[24] The waters through which the ships passed had been sporadically mined by German aircraft and there was the constant threat that lurking German motor torpedo boats, called E-boats, might pounce out of the darkness. Ahead of the main body of ships, a flotilla of British minesweepers cleared away the first threat, while destroyers and cruisers guarded the flanks against possible E-boat incursions. Shortly after dawn, Force J hove to off a long beach ten miles east of Portsmouth in Bracklesham Bay.

During the disembarkation of troops from Flotilla 262, of which Hinton's LCIL 262 was part, a dangerous groundswell broke the grip of several heavily laden British soldiers from the steadying lines and the men quickly drowned. Hinton considered their deaths a bitter lesson in how "not to do things." But he also thought it inevitable "that there was going to be a casualty rate with training."[25]

Becoming a training casualty seemed an all too likely possibility to Royal Winnipeg Rifles' Major Lochie Fulton during Fabius. Standing on top of a Duplex-Drive tank turret, watching 1st Hussars 'A' Squadron commander Major Dudley Brooks steer the tank in an ungainly manner towards shore, Fulton feared the contraption would sink any moment. As Brooks tried to keep it running true, the tank tossed back and forth in the current and waves slopped sporadically over the canvas screen. Fulton was uncomfortably aware that, having been tasked to accompany the tank ashore as a familiarization exercise, he had not been provided with a life jacket.

There was another worrisome problem. The scheduled bombardment of the beach by the guns on the ships had passed and all shelling had ceased. But, as yet, the flotilla of rocket ships that was to smother the beach with explosive charges had failed to fire. "You better slow down, Dudd," Fulton told Brooks, as they closed on the shore. "Those rockets haven't fired yet and there's no place in that tank for me."

Brooks replied that the tank had only one speed and given the increasingly rough waters he was going to have to land or risk being swamped. As the tank rumbled out of the sea onto the sand, hundreds of rockets started to whoosh towards them. Fulton yelled at Brooks to stop the tank and jumped down on the sand, throwing himself between the tracks. Rockets were exploding all around and making a hell of a noise. But when they finished exploding, Fulton crawled out from under the tank and saw no sign that they had caused any real damage. On D-Day, he suspected, the rockets would again be all flash and noise with little useful effect.[26]

Despite various glitches and delays, the Canadian assault battalions did get ashore quickly during Fabius and proceeded to conduct a mock breakout from the beach. The North Shore (New Brunswick) Regiment pushed inland, captured several vital bridgeheads, and by evening was dug in on its assigned objective. The next morning, the battalion loaded onto the backs of supporting Fort Garry Horse tanks and pushed well out ahead of the rest of the division to seize a key tactical feature. On May 6, Fabius concluded, with the umpires, who had been monitoring and assessing the performance of the North Shores, deeming that the battalion had successfully completed all its tasks.[27] The question left to ponder, for all but the senior commanders in the know, was the degree to which Fabius mirrored the plans for the invasion itself. By early May, there was no question that the invasion of northwest Europe was imminent.

[4]

Death or Glory

WHILE FORCE J AND the 3rd Canadian Infantry Division trained for the amphibious invasion, the Western Allies were engaged in an intense air campaign intended to smooth the way for the landing forces by weakening Germany's ability to defend the French coastline. This campaign started in late 1943 within days of the appointment of Air Marshal Sir Trafford Leigh-Mallory as Air Commander-in-Chief of the specially formed Allied Expeditionary Air Force (AEAF). Leigh-Mallory answered directly to General Dwight D. Eisenhower and was given operational command of the Royal Air Force 2nd Tactical Air Force, the U.S. 9th Air Force, and the squadrons of the Air Defence of Great Britain.

The fifty-one-year-old Leigh-Mallory had joined the Royal Flying Corps in 1916, won the Distinguished Service Order while commanding an aerial reconnaissance squadron in 1918, and had been commanding 12 Group—a RAF fighter unit—when World War II broke out. His handling of the group's fighter wings during the Battle of Britain helped turn the tide against the Luftwaffe. By 1942, Leigh-Mallory headed up RAF Fighter Command and came from that illustrious posting to the AEAF.

At first, AEAF operations were hampered by the continuing commitment of medium and heavy bombers and fighter escorts, particularly those of the U.S. 9th Air Force, to Operation Pointblank—a massive raiding program intended to destroy Germany's aircraft factories and oil refineries. Operation Pointblank's chief advocate was Lieutenant General Carl Spaatz, commander of the U.S. Strategic Air Force, who argued against shifting squadrons to Leigh-Mallory's control.

As the invasion date neared, however, the Combined Chiefs of Staff acknowledged that Pointblank was failing to achieve its purpose, while air operations against coastal defensive and communication targets desperately needed to be beefed up if they were to prove effective. Consequently, in March 1944, they directed that Operation Overlord "should have priority over Pointblank and that the direction of strategic air forces should pass from the British Chief of Staff" to Eisenhower. This gave Leigh-Mallory a free hand to direct all British and American bomber forces against targets at will.[1]

The most effective support the air forces could "give the Army during the preparatory phase," he believed, "would be by attacking the enemy's rail communications, with the object of so disorganizing his railway system that he would find it difficult to supply his divisions in northern France when the fighting started and still more difficult to bring reinforcements into the lodgement area."[2] Dubbed the Transportation Plan, this facet of AEAF operations was given planning priority. But other targets could not be ignored. Leigh-Mallory knew that to protect the invasion fleet and troops once they landed on the beaches the Allies must have complete air superiority. He therefore had to hit hard at German air bases within striking range of the invasion beaches in an attempt to smash the Luftwaffe. The same held true for German combat vessels lurking in Channel ports along the French and Belgian coast. Finally, almost daily photo-reconnaissance missions were required to gather intelligence on German dispositions and other information vital to the invasion planning.[3]

The U.S. 9th Air Force had 2,909 operational aircraft, while the RAF and RCAF counted an additional 2,768, for a total of 5,677. Not all of these were combat planes; there were 1,090 transport planes, 154 artillery observation aircraft, 219 reconnaissance planes, and 1,133 gliders. While the gliders and transport planes were to play a pivotal role in the planned landings of airborne troops on the night preceding the amphibious landings and the reconnaissance planes would perform vital intelligence-gathering tasks, that left just 3,081 fighters and bombers to conduct the AEAF's offensive plan.[4]

Six Canadian squadrons that had arrived in Britain only in mid-March were among the RCAF units tasked to the AEAF—Nos. 438, 439, 440, 441, 442, and 443. The first three squadrons were equipped with Hawker Typhoon fighter-bombers. Designed to serve as both a low-altitude bomber and a fighter plane, the Typhoon could carry two thousand-pound bombs and had four 20-millimetre machine guns mounted in its wings. Rocket rails could replace the bomb racks— making the Typhoon a particularly deadly threat to tanks, artillery, and transport vehicles.

Conducting a rocket attack against a German tank required significantly different skills than dive-bombing a bridge, however, and switching bomb racks for rocket rails was a six-hour job. For these reasons, each Typhoon squadron was specially trained to work either with bombs or rockets. The three Canadian squadrons formed 143 Wing, RCAF commanded by Wing Commander R.T.P. "Bob" Davidson. Originally from Vancouver, Davidson had gone to Britain and joined the RAF in 1937. He had seen combat in skies over Greece in 1940 and 1941, tangled with Japanese Zeros in a Hurricane fighter at Ceylon the following year, and been flying Typhoons since April 1943 in Britain. Davidson's Distinguished Flying Cross citation stated that he "displayed extreme keenness for ops (operations)."[5] It was a keenness that he had at first to keep in check, as replacement aircraft were in such short supply that all Canadian and British Typhoon squadrons were held back to preserve their numbers. Leigh-Mallory's staff believed "the primary role of Typhoon fighter/bomber squadrons will be attacks in close support of our ground forces using bombs or RP (Rocket-Projectiles) and cannon."[6]

Squadrons 441, 442, and 443 were equipped with Spitfire Mark IXs and formed 144 Wing, RCAF under the command of the British flying ace Wing Commander J.E. "Johnnie" Johnson. This new-model Spitfire mounted two .303 Browning machine guns in each wing, could exceed four hundred miles per hour as well as climb and turn nimbly, and easily matched any Luftwaffe fighter. Designed primarily as a fighter, the Spitfire could be fitted with bombs. The

Spitfire squadrons' primary role was "day fighting" and their second-ary role "ground attacks using bombs and/or guns; bombing attacks are to be carried out by dive-bombing."[7]

Johnson's three Canadian squadron leaders were all combat veter-ans. Twenty-six-year-old George Hill of Pictou, Nova Scotia held a Distinguished Flying Cross and had downed his first German during the massive aerial battle of the disastrous Dieppe raid. He had gone on to rack up thirteen more victories while flying in North Africa. Frankly outspoken, Hill commanded 441 Squadron. Also holding a DFC, Brad Walker had served a tour in Britain and then commanded a squadron in the Aleutians. At Digby, he took the helm of 442 Squadron. Pushing thirty, almost ancient in the fast-reflex world of fighter pilots, Wally McLeod had chalked up thirteen victories, prima-rily during the defence of Malta. Johnson considered the tall man from Regina to be an instinctive "killer" and was glad they were com-rades rather than foes.[8]

Flying Officer Gordon F. Ockenden was assigned to McLeod's 443 Squadron. Although the squadron quickly started flying missions, it also spent a good amount of time "under canvas," a nickname for establishing ad hoc airstrips. The idea was to prepare the squadrons to support the expected rapid advance of Allied troops beyond the invasion beachhead. To move all the personnel, equipment, mess and hangar tents, plus accommodation tents, required about two hun-dred trucks. By the time the lead elements of the convoy had arrived at the designated location—usually nothing more than a farm field or meadow large and level enough to fly fighters off—an advance party would have prepared a strip to receive the squadron's eighteen planes. Ockenden, a twenty-year-old from Vermilion, Alberta, would set his Spitfire down on the new field and then pitch in alongside the mechanics, armourers, cooks, and other personnel that constituted a squadron in setting up the new facility. A few days later, they would be on the move again.[9]

The wing's first combat mission at the end of March was part of 2nd Tactical Air Force's attempts to gain air superiority by attacking Luftwaffe airfields. Squadrons 441 and 442 struck a field near Dreux, France. Shortly after takeoff, Johnson's plane developed radio trouble and he was forced to abort, leaving Wing Commander E.P. Wells as-suming command. From a position well to the west of the airfield, the approaching Canadian pilots could see a large cluster of twin-engine aircraft with no sign of any pilots trying to get them airborne. Before the Germans discovered their presence, Wells told 442 to maintain altitude to serve as both a decoy and to provide cover in the event that enemy fighters appeared. He then led 441 in a screaming dive out of the sun towards the parked aircraft. "The squadron," Wells reported, "dived very rapidly to ground level on the south side of the airfield and made an extremely fast run across it at about 400 miles per hour, each pilot selecting his target on the run in. The Spitfires continued low down and fast for a couple miles after the attack, then pulled up fast and reformed without any difficulty."[10]

The Spitfires were created for this kind of strafing attack and this was the type of flying for which the pilots were specifically trained. The first time Wing Commander Johnson saw his "lean Spitfire with two bombs hanging on its slender wings, I decided that I was never going to be crazy about this phase of our work. The Spitfire seemed intolerably burdened with her load, and the ugly, blunt bombs were a basic contradiction of all [its] beauty and symmetry."

Johnson asked McLeod what he thought. Ever the scrapper, McLeod allowed that he would rather see two "decent long-range tanks to hang under the wings" instead of the bombs because that would allow them to "go to Berlin with the Yanks and get stuck into some real fighting."[11]

Aesthetics aside, there was another problem. When fitted with two five-hundred-pound bombs, the Spitfire frames were stressed by the weight and there was no type of bombsight or other aiming de-vice. Aim directly at the target during the dive and the bombs, falling away on a line of flight different from the descending plane, struck short. Wing Commander Hugh Godefroy, one of the most veteran and respected RCAF fighter officers, was commanding 127 Wing when his squadrons had to begin experimenting with the dive-bomb-ing. "The target was to be approached at eight thousand feet," he later wrote. "When it was opposite the wing tip, the aircraft was to be turned and dived at an angle of sixty degrees holding the bead of the gun-sight on the target. At three thousand feet a gradual pull-out was to be executed and on the count of three, the bomb was dropped."

That was the theory, but Godefroy discovered "that this technique of dive-bombing was extremely inaccurate. One could only guess at what was a 60° dive. Without dive brakes, Spitfires dived so fast that the hands of the altimeter went around in a blur. Pulling out at exactly three thousand feet with the use of an instrument that lagged was impossible."[12]

Not surprisingly, accuracy was negligible. Normally, the targets were missed by anywhere from seventy to three hundred yards. Yet the dive-bombing missions were of critical importance in isolating the invasion battlefield from German attempts to bring in reinforcements. Targets were road and railway bridges, viaducts, and communication hubs. The pilots and staff planners viewing the results of the training attacks fretted that the Spitfire and Typhoon dive-bombers would present little more than a nuisance to the Germans.[13] But the training continued, with all concerned hoping the pilots could sharpen their skills enough to do some good on the bombing front while continuing to conduct ongoing combat missions over the continent.

Finally, on May 8, with the pace of attacks on the northwest Europe transportation system quickening, Davidson's 143 Wing drew a dive-bombing mission. The morning dawned bright and clear, but a heavy white frost coated the ground as nine Typhoons from 438 Squadron formed up on the runway at Manston. Davidson was in command. Theirs was a top priority target, the Douai railway yards— twenty miles south of Lille, in northern France. Just as the planes were to take off, Davidson's Typhoon developed a problem and he had to quickly exchange it for another. The Typhoons achieved complete surprise, sweeping down quickly to drop their bombs before any anti-aircraft guns could be brought to bear. "Results were very good," recorded the squadron diarist, who also noted that this was the deepest penetration the squadron had made into enemy territory. As the squadron raced home, Davidson's engine stalled while still over France. Unable to get the temperamental 24-cylinder Napier Sabre engine going again, he was last seen by the other pilots in the raiding party gliding towards earth. Davidson managed a dead-stick landing unscathed and was quickly scooped up by the French Resistance. (He would emerge in September 1944 when Allied troops marched past his hiding place.)[14]

ALLIED FIGHTER SQUADRONS found it difficult to lure Luftwaffe fighters into the skies for head-to-head combat throughout early 1944. Just as the Allies desperately sought to destroy German planes before the invasion, the Luftwaffe attempted to preserve its dwindling forces for that decisive moment. To force the Luftwaffe into battle while simultaneously crippling northwest Europe's rail system, the size and pace of Ramrod missions was stepped up. These missions sent bombers, heavily protected by fighters, against important ground targets that the Germans could not easily allow to be destroyed. In April and May, railroad bridges, tunnels, marshalling yards, and rolling stock were given special attention.

Sometimes the Luftwaffe took the bait, other times not. On March 27, four separate Ramrod missions pounded marshalling yards from Belgium to southern France and attacked coastal gun batteries along the French coast. The next day, Ramrod 804 sent a massive force of bombers to savage the Nantes-Gassicourt railroad line and the Creil marshalling yards, with flights of Canadian and British fighters hovering protectively overhead. At the same time, RAF Typhoon squadrons, also protected by fighters, dive-bombed V-1 launch sights along the coast and other targets near Caen. Both days, the Luftwaffe stayed on the ground.[15]

On May 21, with the invasion fast approaching, Ramrod 905 launched seventeen hundred planes, including four hundred RCAF and RAF fighters, into northwest Europe to devastate the railway network and force the Luftwaffe to fight. Five of the nine Spitfire squadrons were RCAF—402, 403, 416, 421, and 441. Wing Commander Johnson led one three-squadron group, while Wing Commander Lloyd "Chad" Chadburn commanded another. Hailing from Aurora, Ontario, Chadburn had won a DFC in the battle over Dieppe and was one of the RCAF's most respected wing commanders. After grouping over Hawking, the strike force roared across the English Channel and Belgian coastline to hit targets around Brussels and throughout northwest France. While the bombers slammed marshalling yards, the fighters raced down to strafe trains caught on the move.

German anti-aircraft batteries defending the marshalling yards hurled up massive volleys of flak, and every train jumped by the fighters proved heavily protected by flak and machine-gun batteries mounted on flat cars or freight-car roofs. While the raid reportedly destroyed 159 locomotives, only three of these fell prey to the strafing fighters that bore the brunt of Allied losses. Twenty-one fighters and twenty pilots, including four Canadians, were reported missing or dead at the end of the operation. The Luftwaffe again refused the fight.

Not so the next day, however, when just eighteen Spitfires from Chadburn's 416 Squadron swept across the Channel to pounce rolling stock. Finding the trains less heavily protected by flak batteries, the Spitfires destroyed four locomotives before coming across an airstrip from which German fighters were scrambling. At the end of the ensuing low-level melee, five Canadians each claimed a kill. Three of the pilots, Flight Lieutenant Patterson, Flying Officer McFadden, and Pilot Officer Palmer, witnessed their kills hit the earth. But the scrap was more chaotic for flight lieutenants Mason and Forbes-Roberts. After snapping a quick burst at one German fighter, Mason found another had jumped his tail. As he yanked his plane into a hard evasive turn, Mason saw the plane he had fired on struggling "to level out at tree-top level [before going] down into a large field at over 250 mph. I was right on the deck behind him and he did not come up from the field. I was unable to see him crash as the other aircraft was breaking into me." Palmer supported his claim, having "observed an aircraft crash in a field, with a little smoke or dust rising from it but not being on fire." Forbes-Roberts, meanwhile, had pounced on a German fighter just lifting off the runway. When his opening machine-gun burst scored a small strike, Forbes-Roberts loosed a second burst of machine-gun and cannon fire that also struck home before flashing by the German plane and losing sight of it. Patterson, however, saw a German plane go into a spin about five hundred yards from his position and at an altitude of only five hundred feet, while Palmer spotted a parachute drifting down near the airstrip. Forbes-Roberts was consequently credited with a kill.[16]

Downing five fighters in a single day was a significant achievement for any Allied squadron operating in northwest European
skies in the first part of 1944. So seldom did the Luftwaffe venture
out to fight that between November 1943 and D-Day all Canadian
Spitfire squadrons could claim only fifty-six victories—fourteen
being downed by 401 Squadron.[17]

More successful were the Canadians who stalked their prey by
night. There were four such RCAF squadrons in Britain: 406, 409,
410, and 418. The first three were night fighters, generally defending
the skies over the United Kingdom. No. 418 Squadron was trained
and equipped as an intruder unit, venturing under cover of darkness
into German-occupied territory.

Early in January, the Luftwaffe had launched a last-gasp terror
bombing campaign against London to retaliate against the massive
day and night bombing raids of Berlin during the same period. At
the end of February, these sporadic raids shifted away from the
British capital to ports and shipping to disrupt the Allied invasion
buildup. Even though the German pilots attempted to sneak into
British skies by trailing in the wake of Allied bombers returning
from night raids on the continent, the night fighters usually intercepted them. By the end of May, the Luftwaffe had lost 329 bombers
and had failed to seriously crimp the invasion preparations.[18]

While the Canadian night fighter defence squadrons had been
knocking down Luftwaffe bombers, the intruder squadron claimed
the greatest number of kills of any Canadian squadron. Led by thirty-
three-year-old Wing Commander Paul Yettvart Davoud, who had
been born in Provo, Utah but immigrated to Canada in the 1930s to
fly for Canadian Airways, the squadron had been re-equipped in early
1944 with the Mosquito. Versatile, fast, and incredibly nimble for a
two-engine plane, the Mosquito packed enormous firepower, with
four 20-millimetre Hispano cannons slung under its body and four
.303 Browning machine guns mounted in the nose. For bombing
missions, it could carry four five-hundred-pound bombs. Mosquitoes
had a two-man crew, the pilot and a navigator. Often referred to as the
"Wooden Wonder" because the light plywood construction rendered
it difficult to detect with radar, the Mosquito had enormous range for

such a small craft. It was capable of flying 1,860 miles and was originally designed to strike targets deep inside Germany and then to use its superior speed to dash home before the Luftwaffe and flak units could respond. In a string of intruder raids during the first five months of 1944, 418 Squadron proved that the Mosquito was an unparallelled night fighter. By the end of May, it reported fifty-five air-to-air kills and the destruction of forty-six more planes caught on the ground.[19]

As May closed, Leigh-Mallory rightly claimed that the Luftwaffe in northwest Europe was so shot up that it posed little threat to the gathering invasion forces. He estimated air-to-air combat losses to the Germans inflicted by AEAF aircraft operating from bases in Britain between November 1943 and the invasion, at 2,655. No reliable estimate of planes destroyed on the ground was possible because many had been destroyed by high-level light and medium bomber strikes, but such losses were believed to greatly exceed the air-to-air kill total.[20]

In the three weeks leading up to D-Day, Leigh-Mallory had directed increasing numbers of bombers to carry out strikes to eliminate or neutralize all airfields that lay within "a radius of 150 miles of Caen. The primary object of these attacks was to destroy the aircraft repair, maintenance, and servicing facilities and thereby cause the maximum interference with the operational ability of the German Air Force."[21]

To keep German intelligence guessing as to where the landings were to occur, the same intensity of operations had to be carried out against airfields throughout western France, Belgium, and Holland. So while forty airfields within the Caen radius were selected for destruction, an additional fifty-nine elsewhere were designated as priority targets. Ninety-one of these ninety-nine airfields were subjected to bomber strikes that dropped a total of 6,717 tons of bombs. In the aftermath, Leigh-Mallory's staff determined that the attacks "accomplished the desired object of placing the enemy under the same handicap as the Allied fighters by forcing them to operate from airfields a long way from the assault area."[22]

Airfields were not normally the prime focus of bomber operations. There remained the transportation system, with thirty-seven railway targets ranging from marshalling yards to key bridges designated for destruction. Twenty-two of these were judged at the end of May to have been "sufficiently damaged to require no more attention" during the initial invasion period. Another fifteen were "severely damaged." A German report intercepted by Allied intelligence confirmed the success, with the author gloomily judging the entire transportation system linking France to Germany "most seriously crippled."[23]

ALTHOUGH CURRENT TECHNIQUES had proven effective against many targets, the Allies were soon to unveil several new means to destroy targets previously immune to bomber or fighter-bomber attacks. Flight Officer Donald Harry Cheney of Ottawa had been flying Lancaster heavy bombers in 630 Squadron, RAF in late April 1944, when ordered one morning to report immediately to Air Vice-Marshal Sir Ralph Cochrane. A staff car with driver and guard waited to whisk the twenty-four-year-old officer to his meeting with the commander of No. 5 Group, Bomber Command. Cheney's "heart just absolutely turned to an ice cube. What in the name of heaven have I done?" he wondered.

Soon Cheney was being ushered into an office situated in a country home so sumptuous and comfortable that it was hard to believe this was the headquarters of a man who regularly sent hundreds of bomber crews to wreak destruction over the night skies of continental Europe. "Good morning, Cheney. I'm very happy to meet you," the air vice-marshal said as he stepped from behind a great desk to shake the young flyer's hand. After offering Cheney a cigarette and lighting it for him, Cochrane gestured to a chair.

Sensing Cheney's continuing anxiety, Cochrane said, "Now, I want you to completely relax. I have something that I want to discuss with you and I will not ask you to give me an answer right away, but I will expect an answer in twenty-four hours." Had Cheney ever heard of 617 Squadron? the air vice-marshal asked.

"Yes, Sir, I certainly have. That's the Dam Buster squadron, the Death or Glory Boys."

Cochrane grinned at that. "Well, you have a very good record of finding targets, in getting through, in completing your missions, and getting home even with an engine short and so on." He noted that Cheney had twenty missions under his belt, as did his crew. "We think that you might be good material to bolster this squadron. We are going to be developing some very interesting new techniques. You will learn more in due time about the new developments that are coming and new targets that are coming, but you would be, if you agree, assigned to special work which will have great bearing on the outcome of this war. That will be all, thank you. I have other things to attend to." Cochrane reminded Cheney that he needed an answer the following morning.

After getting permission from his squadron commander to open the sergeant's mess early, Cheney gathered his seven-man flight crew together to discuss the proposition over drinks. His was a smorgasbord crew, with Cheney the only Canadian, the flight engineer and navigator both Scottish, the bombardier Welsh, radio operator and rear gunner English, and the mid-upper gunner Australian.

"Now it comes to a vote," he said. "If we're going to go to this squadron the likelihood is that we'll finish our tour there unless we come a cropper. It's a wonderful squadron. Air Vice-Marshal Cochrane told me that the squadron commander, Wing Commander Leonard Cheshire, is probably the finest bomber pilot in the world and as brave as a lion. So we have an opportunity to make a very, very significant contribution to the war."

Cheney did not state the two conflicting concerns each man must wrestle with before voting. On the one hand, the crew was living on borrowed time. They were engaged in a continuous run of night missions over Germany. It was common to fly as many as three missions against Berlin a week. Or a raid might take them to the Ruhr, where the factory cities bristled with anti-aircraft defences and swarms of night fighters, or any of several equally heavily defended cities in the heart of the Reich. Endless nights of tedium sporadically broken by stretches of terror as the sky around the Lancasters lit up with incendiaries and flak and the flashing cannon of attacking night fighters. Bombers fell, the formations closed to fill the gaps, bombs were dropped, and the long return flight began. So far they had been lucky.

Twenty missions and all still alive. Such fortune was rare and could not be trusted to continue.

But 617 Squadron had come by the Death and Glory Boys nickname honestly. On May 16, 1943, in a spectacular raid, nineteen Lancasters attacked and breached three important Ruhr valley dams. Eight of the bombers were shot down and 53 of 133 crewmen died, while another three were taken prisoner. The squadron went on to complete one special raid after another against targets in Italy, France, and Germany. Six months after their combat debut, only six of the crews from the first raid survived.

When Cheney asked each man in turn to cast a vote, the majority opted to join 617 Squadron. "Okay, we're going to get a chance to do something different, interesting, and probably daring," he said.

Their first challenge proved to be finding the new squadron's airfield because No. 5 Group's bases were so closely packed that the perimeter lights of one strip often overlapped another. After initially bouncing down at the wrong base, Cheney thought he had found the correct one but requested that the tower crew flash a green Aldis signal lamp as confirmation before he shut down the engines. "Do you see the light?" the traffic controller asked.

"Yes, I see the light," Cheney replied and realized immediately that he was damned to eternal ribbing. It started immediately. "Hear that," one of his crew said. "Skipper's seen the light." A second later, "I heard it too. Cheney's seen the light."[24]

Cheney's crew was immediately set the task of learning the art of pinpoint bombing. Tossing a bomb within fifty yards of a target from an altitude of 17,500 feet was the goal they strove towards, no easy task with a heavy four-engine bomber. Cheney's Lancaster was the Mk III variant manufactured in Canada. Powered by four 1,390-horsepower Packard "Merlin 224" engines, weighing 68,000 pounds, it could range over 2,250 miles at a cruising speed of 210 miles per hour and a maximum altitude of 24,500 feet. The Lancaster was designed for high-altitude bombing and armed to defend itself without fighter protection. Nose, belly, and mid-upper gun turrets were fitted with twin .303-calibre machine guns, with the tail turret mounting four

.303 machine guns. Its payload could be a single 22,000-pound bomb or 14,000 pounds of smaller bombs.

Cheney and his crew carried out mock attacks with six bombs. And finally, after many days of trying, they scored a direct hit and began steadily narrowing their average margin of error below the fifty-yard range to between thirty-five and forty yards. The training officer told the newly promoted flight officer that he was doing well, but had to sustain that average for at least seven days straight before the crew would be put on the operational flight roster.

The importance of pinpoint accuracy became clear one evening in late May when a number of flatbed trucks arrived with what looked like giant cigars hidden under a covering of canvas. When the truck was unloaded at the bomb dump, its cargo proved to be the biggest bombs any of the squadron had ever seen. The new bombs were nicknamed Tallboys. Weighing 12,000 pounds and loaded with 5,600 pounds of Torpex (torpedo explosive), they had specially angled fins that produced a rapid spin and when dropped from an altitude of at least twenty thousand feet reached supersonic speed. Spin and speed combined to enable the bomb to penetrate the earth to two hundred feet before exploding with enough force to create a massive crater up to a hundred feet around. The shock waves created by the explosion radiated outward with earthquake-like violence that collapsed structures well beyond the explosive ring. So powerful was the bomb's striking force that it could penetrate sixteen feet of concrete. This was the new device Air Vice-Marshal Cochrane had said was in the works. Within a week, Cheney and his crew were routinely dropping dummy Tallboys within thirty yards of the aiming point and were added to the operational flight roster. In late May, they learned their first combat mission would be on the night of the invasion itself. But rather than attacking targets with the ordnance the squadron had nicknamed the Earthquake Bomb, they would be carrying out a vital mission of deception.[25]

[5]

The Intelligence Fog

IT WAS WHAT BOTH SIDES frantically sought to gain and to deny the other: intelligence, a commodity arguably more valuable than a great army's firepower. Without it, an army fought clumsily and blind. Supreme Headquarters, Allied Expeditionary Force (SHAEF) was determined to retain the initiative in the intelligence battle. With each passing day in May, although a wider net of ever less senior officers was given detailed information to prepare for the forthcoming invasion, only a small number were let in on the secret of where and when it would occur.

Not knowing where the invasion would fall, the Germans were forced to defend a coastline stretching from Norway to the French-Spanish border. And SHAEF did all it could to prevent Hitler's Oberkommando der Wehrmacht (Armed Forces High Command) from narrowing the threatened front through two elaborate deceptions, Fortitude North and Fortitude South. Fortitude North was a relatively modest affair intended to convince OKW that a series of raids on Norwegian ports from Scotland was in the works. Ignoring evidence of a massive Allied buildup in England, the German naval command took the bait offered by Fortitude North. On March 5, 1944, an encrypted message from Oberkommando der Kriegsmarine (OKM) reported the arrival of six British divisions in Scotland for operations "of limited scope" in central or southern Norway. Duly intercepted by the Allied Ultra intelligence unit that was reading most of the top-secret German high command codes sent via enigma machines, the message was welcome news for SHAEF, as were subsequent intercepted messages that showed OKM still clung tenaciously to this expectation well into May.[1]

While the Wehrmacht's top naval officers prepared to intercept convoys bearing phantom British divisions towards Norwegian fjords, the rest of the German high command was little fooled by Fortitude North. But Fortitude South was a different matter altogether. Launched in late 1943, this elaborate deception plan aimed to convince the Germans that an entirely fictional First United States Army Group (FUSAG) commanded by General George S. Patton was mustering between Kent and Sussex to invade France's Pas de Calais. Thousands of tanks, artillery pieces, trucks, and other equipment constructed out of plywood, cardboard, and cloth were cleverly placed to create the illusion of an attempt at secrecy and camouflage while ensuring German spies and reconnaissance flights would detect their presence. Several real divisions were also shifted to give a more realistic appearance. In April, 11 Canadian Corps moved its headquarters and staff a few miles north of Dover to Eastling Wood while 2nd Canadian Infantry Division encamped on Dover's outskirts. There followed a number of high-level and ostentatiously exaggerated inspections of the town and these units by senior Allied commanders that German intelligence was unlikely to miss. This included a major tour of Dover on May 23 by General Bernard Montgomery in the company of First Canadian Army commander Lieutenant General Harry Crerar and 11 Corps' Lieutenant General Guy Simonds.[2]

Carefully leaked intelligence reports suggested FUSAG would fall upon Pas de Calais in July. It was hoped that OKW would consequently see the Normandy landings as a weak feint designed to soak off divisions from Pas de Calais to bolster the Germans defending the beachhead. In this event, the Germans would likely hold their divisions at Pas de Calais and at least some of the mobile Panzer divisions concentrated inland in place until the Allied Normandy force was consolidated and readily able to repel any counterattacks.

In coded messages intercepted by Ultra between January 9 and March 23, 1944, various references were made to General Patton and FUSAG. But the context was so vague Allied intelligence officers were unable to tell if the Germans were fooled or not. Although Ultra was proving invaluable in other theatres of the war, it was of less utility in northwest Europe. Senior commanders, such as Oberbefehlshaber (Commander-in-Chief) West Generalfeldmarschall Gerd von Rundstedt, seldom communicated with OKW through coded messages as it was entirely possible to report by telephone.[3]

Despite this handicap, the Allies did know that German high command was both uncertain and divided in opinion regarding the likely invasion site and how to respond. While there was no shortage of senior officers voicing strong opinions, none had sufficient authority to develop a defensive strategy on his own initiative. That authority rested with Adolf Hitler, who in December 1941 had appointed himself not only titular head of the entire Wehrmacht but also of the Heeres (Army). Prompted largely by his innate distrust of senior army officers, this decision put Hitler in the peculiar situation of holding two positions at different levels within the German command chain. So ultimately, Hitler, while figuratively waving the baton of an Oberkommando des Heeres (Supreme Commander of the Army), was subordinate to and answerable only to himself in the role of Oberster Befehlshaber der Wehrmacht (Supreme Commander of the Armed Forces).[4]

In fact, the senior German command system, wrote Generalleutnant Hans Speidel, who served as Generalfeldmarschall Erwin Rommel's Chief of Staff at Army Group B, "corresponded neither to the timeless laws of warfare nor to the demands of the hour or of reason."[5] Instead, the supreme navy, air, and army commanders held equal authority, operated independent of each other and reported directly to Hitler, first through the offices of OKW's Operations Chief, Generaloberst Alfred Jodl, and second through Hitler's Chief of Staff, Generalfeldmarschall Wilhelm Keitel. While this system ensured that no major military action proceeded without the blessing of Jodl, Keitel, and Hitler, it greatly hobbled interservice coordination and planning.

But the command structure was even further confused by Hitler's insistence that the individual operational theatres be similarly structured. In theory, OB West Generalfeldmarschall von Rundstedt commanded northwest Europe, but neither the commanders of the region's air arm, Luftlotte 3, nor its naval arm, Marinegruppe West, were answerable to him. They were considered merely "assigned" to OB West and reported directly to OKW. Then there was the Nazi Party's SS units formed by and firstly answerable to Reichsführer Heinrich Himmler. Adding to the confusion, the primary unit responsible for coastal defence construction—Organization Todt—was controlled by Reichsminister for Armament and War Production Albert Speer and carried out its work "on orders from the Führer."[6]

As Speidel ruefully noted, this tortured system "led not only to a confused chain of command, but to a command chaos."[7] In December 1943, Army Group 'B' Commander, North, Erwin Rommel strode into the midst of this mess on a special "Führer mission" with orders to assess the western front from Denmark to the Alps, including the entire northwest European coastline and that of the Mediterranean. The Afrika Korps hero embarked on this duty with the support of a group of staff officers designated as Army Group B. His instructions were to report directly to Hitler or to OKW and merely keep von Rundstedt informed of his activities.[8]

Everything Rommel saw on the French coast left him dismayed. While the major ports had been transformed into heavily defended fortresses that would doom any amphibious landing to a Dieppe-style disaster, the open countryside beaches were extremely vulnerable. Many concrete gun emplacements and bunkers had been constructed to cover these beaches all along the coast, but there was no consistency in their strength and the defending troops were so dispersed that reinforcements could not be quickly shifted to danger points. "The battle for the coast will probably be over in a few hours," Rommel gloomily told Hitler on the last day of December, and noted that a successful defence would hinge on the ability to quickly bring up reinforcements from inland.[9]

Hitler agreed. For weeks he had harped almost daily at OKW

briefings that the coming invasion "will decide the issue, not only of the year, but of the whole war. If we succeed in throwing back the invasion, then such an attempt cannot and will not be repeated within a short time." A victory like that would enable the Germans to transfer divisions from central Europe to Italy and Russia, where Hitler hoped to fight the advancing Allied armies to a standstill. Hitler believed two static fronts could be held indefinitely. But he warned that if a third front was opened in France, "we can't win a static war in the long run because the matériel our enemies can bring in will exceed what we can send to that front. With no strategic reserves of any importance, it will be impossible to build up sufficient strength along such a line. Therefore, the invader must be thrown back on his first attempt."[10]

Little came of these surprisingly prescient conclusions until mid-March, when Hitler gave Rommel operational command of the anti-invasion forces from the Dutch-Belgian border south to the mouth of the Loire River at St. Nazaire. Two German armies defended this coastline. The northern sector south to the western flank of the mouth of the Seine was guarded by Fifteenth Army, while Seventh Army took over from there south to the Loire River. Although officially subordinate to von Rundstedt, Rommel never hesitated to bypass the chain of command by going directly to Hitler.[11]

For his part, von Rundstedt carried on as best he could. The sixty-eight-year-old came from a long line of Prussian officers and had been soldiering for fifty years. His was the military background most distrusted by the Nazis, and von Rundstedt's contempt for Hitler went unconcealed. He and Rommel immediately clashed over strategy, but it was soon clear which of the two men was in charge. "As Commander-in-Chief West," von Rundstedt later grumped, "my only authority was to change the guard in front of my gate."[12]

Rommel set to with a verve that contradicted his growing pessimistic outlook. He was convinced Allied air superiority would make it impossible to move Panzer divisions from strategic points of concentration inland to reinforce the beach defenders. Arguing that the only possibility was "to resist the enemy in field positions, which had to be constructed for defence against the most modern weapons of war," he had 4 million mines sown on the beaches facing the English Channel by May 20, 1944.[13] This was a mere smidgen of the 200 million mines Rommel really thought necessary to be effective. Furthermore, the existing minefields were laid in a thin band along the beachfront, whereas he wanted them to extend between five and six miles inland so the invader was paralyzed long enough for strong counterattacks to be organized.

He also sought to prevent the Allied landing craft getting onto the beaches by installing a maze of obstacles extending twelve hundred yards into the sea. Approached from seaward, the obstacles consisted first of rows of wooden or concrete stakes behind which ramps built of logs or steel rails had been driven into the sand facing outwards and propped up to form a six-foot-high barrier. Then came lines of pyramid-shaped obstacles formed by bolting three concrete, steel, or wooden bars together, amongst which were liberally sprinkled so-called Hedgehogs—sections of heavy angle-iron bolted together to form an X-shape. Most of these obstacles had mines attached.[14]

The Germans had long accepted that airborne troops would be dropped to secure the flanks of the amphibious landings and disrupt counterattacks. So Rommel had ten-foot stakes driven into the ground at intervals of a hundred feet in the fields situated close to the beaches that presented likely landing sites. Each stake was to be mined and linked to the others in a field by wire, rendering the landing site impossible for gliders to use and perilous for parachutists. The air-landing obstacles were nicknamed "Rommel's Asparagus." While successful in getting vast numbers of Hedgehogs and Asparagus obstacles erected by the end of May, few of the latter had been mined or wired.[15]

Plagued by shortages of Todt troops, the Germans often dragooned the local French populace into constructing many of the defensive systems. Throughout the spring of 1944, men like twenty-year-old Roger Chevalier spent as much time planting Rommel's Asparagus as crops in the fields. Chevalier worked as a farmhand near Anguerny, which was west of Caen and about six miles in from the Normandy coast. As a young boy, Chevalier had lost his parents after his mother ran away with another man and his father blew his head off with a shotgun. Raised in an orphanage at Falaise, Chevalier had struck out on his own in his teens and eked out a living as a farmhand. Shortly after the occupation, he had married and now had a young daughter.

For the Norman farmers, the German occupation was more hardship than repression, for other than being forced to participate in the increasingly regular work parties and having food they produced routinely requisitioned without payment, they were left to live as they always had. Grudging acquaintances were even struck. In Chevalier's case, a German soldier once approached his home on the farm and asked if he had any eggs. As Chevalier and his wife kept many chickens, they had an abundance of eggs, and as the German was asking rather than demanding, he gave the man a half-dozen. From then on, the German came once a week for eggs and the two men would chat in pidgin French interspersed with the odd word of German that Chevalier had picked up.

Chevalier had never considered there would be any benefit in the relationship for him until one day when he had business in Douvres-la Délivrande. Although less than three miles from Anguerny, this village lay within the coastal security zone that the Germans had established and into which access by French civilians was carefully controlled out of fears of sabotage. Such anxieties were greatly heightened at Douvres-la Délivrande because of the presence of a nearby Luftwaffe radar station. When Chevalier attempted to pass through the roadblock checkpoint that controlled access from the interior to the coastal area, the German soldier checking his papers found them not in order because his signature on the identity card looked somewhat different from that on his pass. Chevalier was immediately detained for questioning by the Gestapo. While the terrified young man was waiting for the dreaded Nazi police to be called, the German to whom he gave eggs every week happened along. "I know this man," he told the guards. "He's no terrorist." Chevalier was released.

While not a member of the French Resistance, Chevalier was not above doing what he could to hamper the German war effort, however.

When he and the other farmers around Anguerny were rounded up and made to dig the holes in which Asparagus poles were planted, Chevalier carefully dug his only as deep as required to enable the pole to remain upright. This way, he figured if a planted field did end up being used by Allied gliders or paratroops, the Asparagus obstacles would topple under whatever weight was placed on them and might not hamper the landings. The tactic worked well and was one adopted by most of the impressed French workers until one day a German soldier pedalled into a field in which they were completing planting of a cluster of Asparagus. When the soldier propped his bike against one of the poles, it keeled over. "Sabotage, sabotage," the soldier screamed at the Frenchmen. The next day they were forced to replant the Asparagus and this time a German soldier methodically measured each hole's depth before the log was emplaced.[16]

While Rommel could draw on the French populace to enable him to plant more defensive obstacles, he could do little to alter the fact that there were too few troops to adequately guard the entire coastline—something he was forced to do because the invasion could fall anywhere. He inclined to agree with von Rundstedt and okw that the Allies would either come at Pas de Calais to seize Calais or the stretch of beaches between the Somme and Seine estuaries, with the intention of capturing le Havre. German reasoning here was logical. An invasion in either region would entail a short crossing for the invasion fleet, seek the capture of a major port, and establish the invaders dangerously close to Germany's industrialized Ruhr valley.[17]

As for the Seventh Army's zone, the only rational objective was Cherbourg on the Cotentin Peninsula, with the probable landing site being the relatively calm waters of the peninsula's eastern coast. While there was some fear of a landing in Normandy, the beach region between "the Orne and Vire rivers was declared unsuitable for landing operations by both the navy and Fifteenth Army."[18] This area was therefore initially given no special priority for fortification.

That all changed, however, on May 2 when Hitler suddenly read a series of intelligence reports indicating major concentrations of British and Canadian troops in southeast England and of U.S. troops in Wales. Although okw was dubious, Hitler ordered that the divisions defending Normandy and Brittany be immediately reinforced with anti-aircraft and antitank weapons. OKW Operations Staff Officer General der Artillerie Walter Warlimont was among the officers disinclined to credit Hitler's instinct "but he kept harping on it and demanded more and more reinforcements for that sector."[19]

Not only the intelligence reports guided Hitler's thinking. He assumed the Allies must seek to establish a stable front while they massed troops and supplies for a major breakout offensive, which necessitated their capturing intact a major port. With Cherbourg on its northern shore, Hitler believed "there was no better place on the whole coast than the Cotentin peninsula for this purpose." To capture Cherbourg, the Allies would have to use both Cotentin's relatively few suitable eastern beaches and those close by in Normandy if they were to put sufficient force on the ground quickly enough to transform the peninsula into a fortress before the Germans counterattacked.[20]

On May 8, von Rundstedt learned from German agents in Britain that the Allies were ready to launch their invasion and would commit an astonishing twenty divisions to the first wave.[21] German estimates of Allied divisions available for the invasion and immediate exploitation inland were ever more wildly exaggerated. Speidel believed there were sixty to sixty-five divisions available, all "armoured, mechanized, and motorized."[22] The appointment in March of Lieutenant General Harry Crerar to command First Canadian Army had been noted. German intelligence postulated that he commanded a total of five infantry and three armoured divisions. These "highly-rated Canadian formations are to play a role in the forthcoming operations," one report warned. That there were only three Canadian divisions in Britain evidenced how badly German intelligence gathering capability had gone awry.[23]

Intelligence staff could only suggest that the landings would fall somewhere "between Boulogne and Normandy."[24] On May 8, however, Luftlotte 3 concluded a photo-analysis based on spotty reconnaissance flights over the southern coast of England and reported that troop concentrations indicated the invaders would attack between le Havre and Cherbourg. Intercepted and decoded immediately by Ultra, the report sent a shiver through SHAEF. There came a collective sigh of relief shortly thereafter when Luftlotte 3 extended the possible landing zone all the way east to Dieppe.[25]

With Hitler hectoring him at every turn, Rommel raced to harden the Normandy defences. But neither he nor von Rundstedt would divert all resources and reinforcements in that direction on the basis of a hunch. Although more beach and Asparagus obstacles were installed, progress was slow due to shortages of manpower and material. Three infantry divisions defended the Normandy beaches. From Cherbourg east down the Cotentin coast to the Vire estuary stood the 709th Infantry, with the 352nd Infantry holding the beaches east of here to the village of Asnelles-sur-Mer, beyond which the 716th Infantry's line extended to Franceville-Plage on the immediate east side of the Orne.

These divisions were deemed incapable of repelling a determined invasion force, but Rommel hoped they might delay it until nearby Panzer divisions could launch a decisive counterattack that would throw the enemy into the sea. To position such divisions close to the threatened Normandy coast, he moved the 12th ss Panzer (Hitlerjugend) Division to a point fifty miles inland between Elbeuf and Argentan. The Panzer Lehr Division was farther back again to the east in the vicinity of Seventh Army's headquarters at le Mans. On May 6, the 21st Panzer Division moved close to Caen with some of its highly mobile and elite regiments spread out across a sector about five miles inland from the beaches.[26]

These dispositions were the best Rommel could put in position in May. Lacking definite proof that the invasion would fall here, okw and von Rundstedt resisted any further requests for additional divisions. The Allies enjoyed such mastery of the English Channel's skies and waters that reconnaissance flights were limited to quick dashes along the coast to photograph "possible points of embarkation" and German naval vessels seldom approached the British coastline at all. Left guessing, the Germans could only remain thinly spread, trying to defend the entire French coastline. It was a strategy that prompted Rommel's chief of staff, Generalleutnant Hans Speidel, to remember Frederick the Great's admonition that "He who will defend everything defends nothing."[27]

IF THE GERMANS SUFFERED from a paucity of adequate intelligence, the Allies wallowed amid riches. Between April 1 and June 5, the Allied Expeditionary Air Force (AEAF) photo-reconnaissance units flew 3,215 missions in an attempt to meet what Air Marshal Sir Trafford Leigh-Mallory described as each particular service's "own requirements and individual problems" that "only photographic reconnaissance could hope to solve.... The variety, complexity and moreover, the detailed accuracy of the information gathered and assiduously collated was of great importance in the preparatory phase of the operation."[28]

To prevent the Germans from predicting where the Allied interest truly lay, the entire coast from Holland to Spain was subjected to equal numbers of reconnaissance intrusion flights. This entailed gathering vertical and oblique photos of "beach gradients, beach obstacles, coastal defences and batteries.... Obliques were taken at wave top height, three to four miles out from the coast, in order to provide the assault coxswains with a landing craft view of the particular area to be assaulted or likely to be their allotted landing spots. Then obliques were flown 1,500 yards from the coast at zero feet, to provide platoon assault commanders with recognition landing points. Further obliques were taken again at 1,500 yards from the shore, but at 2,000 feet to provide, for those who were planning the infantry assault, views of the immediate hinterland."[29]

Inland terrain was similarly treated "so that infantry commanders could pinpoint themselves after they had advanced. Again, it was necessary to photograph hidden land behind assault areas, so that the infantry commanders would know the type of terrain behind such obstructions as hills or woods."[30] The bridges over waterways and banks they stood upon were photographed from every angle so engineering units could prepare proper bridging materials to replace these crossings if the Germans destroyed them. Prospective drop zones for airborne landings were similarly scrutinized in meticulous detail. And, of course, enemy troop dispositions were constantly monitored.

It was a terrifically tasking operation. The RCAF's 400, 414, and 430 fighter-reconnaissance squadrons of the 39 Reconnaissance Wing flew seven hundred of the total missions—many directly over the Normandy beaches and around the cities of Caen and Bayeux. Often a Mosquito or Spitfire returned empty-handed because the plane developed mechanical trouble and had to abort, or problems with the cameras produced no usable photos, or, more often, cloud or fog obscured the targets. Of 142 missions flown in May by 414 Squadron, only 90 were deemed successful and 8 partially so.[31]

As May progressed, the photos updating the Normandy beaches caused concern. General Dwight D. Eisenhower noted that these "pictures were studied and one of the disturbing things these continued to show was the growing profusion of beach obstacles, most of them under water at high tide."[32]

Further down the command chain at 3rd Canadian Infantry Division Headquarters, Major General Rod Keller and his staff waded through an endless flow of intelligence reports, appreciations, and organizational instructions from above to weed out what was useful. The same process went on at the 1st Canadian Parachute Battalion HQ and that of Force J. From these headquarters, relevant information funnelled down the pipeline and was filtered into ever smaller packets. Never had a military operation of such enormous scale been so meticulously scripted.

Keller never let the swarm of information detract his troops from the central goal. The division and the naval crews responsible for landing them were a team, he said. Every step was to be taken to ensure "the highest team spirit was engendered in the assault force, not, repeat not, in water-tight compartments, such as infantry, artillery, naval crews." Instead they were to follow "the principle that all teams assist other teams, with the objective first, that every fighting soldier be landed with his arms, ammunition, and equipment on the enemy's shores, and secondly, that he get across the beaches *quickly* to the designated objective or objectives."[33]

In early April, the Canadians established a special HQ on the Isle of Wight to precisely plan the landings. This necessitated Keller and his staff being joined by two senior staff officers and the intelligence officer from the three infantry brigades and 2nd Canadian Armoured Brigade. Over a five-week period, these officers finalized the details for the Canadian D-Day landing and subsequent push inland.[34]

More than one Canadian staff officer was driven into a fury when he reported a major weakness in Second British Army's overall plan to the headquarters staff of Second Army Commander General Miles Dempsey only to have the concern dismissed as unwarranted. The division's General Staff Officer, Lieutenant Colonel Don Mingay, soon realized that "all their senior planning staff were regular Sandhurst trained officers, who didn't really have too much confidence in the judgement and capabilities of the Canadian volunteer planning officers."[35]

Generally, though, Lieutenant Colonel Ernest Côté, who controlled the division's administrative arm, believed the planning and training directly benefited from the British Second Army hierarchy and above that of SHAEF staff. "There was always," he recalled, "lots of directions and regulations. What we had to furnish in paperwork, plans and action was, though new to most of us, very clear in our minds for we received our orders from above and they were clear. Sometimes we didn't obey all the orders we received or produce all the paper our superiors wanted to read, but the hierarchy worked well to keep us at our level on the straight and narrow. So it's not surprising that we developed quickly. We developed expertise quickly for we were young, energetic and adaptable and because when we made a mistake or forgot something our higher headquarters and to some degree our brigades would point this out to us. I never remember our headquarters being at a loss as to what to do in a given situation. We were young and relatively new to the game of war, but we did our best."[36]

The supporting fire promised for D-Day particularly troubled Lieutenant-Colonel John Craig of the divisional staff. He felt it was far too weak and overlooked a number of concrete bunkers that were certain strongpoints from which the Germans could bring fire to bear on the landing force. Craig took his concerns to Mingay, who managed to get the fire plan strengthened by haranguing as many British staff officers as he could for as long as possible. It was at moments such as these that the steel in Mingay's character exhibited itself to best advantage. Côté noted often how, whether it was in his dealings with Keller or superiors at Second Army HQ, the operations staff officer "always held his ground and never took guff."[37] Finally, Mingay was promised more naval guns to bring fire to bear on these targets.

In fact, he won such a major reallocation of guns that instead of the original scheme to allocate just sixteen four-inch guns to support the Canadians, they would go ashore after a barrage by 198 guns firing from destroyers, cruisers, and battleships. There would also, of course, be the 105-millimetre Priests of the four Canadian artillery regiments and some of the tanks from 2 CAB firing off the decks of their landing craft.[38]

The quantity of detail these staff officers waded through sometimes drove them to distraction and various spoofs circulated that reflected in tone, if not conclusions, the legitimate briefing papers. One such document landed on Mingay's desk. Awash in official paper, he found the hefty "Operation 'Overboard' Appreciation" allegedly produced by the offices of U.S. Stupid and British Most Stupid amusing enough to pass on to Craig and some other HQ staff officers. The prime objective of this operation, the document stated, was "to provide some employment for a very great number of officers."

Of the forthcoming assault, it pronounced that "any length of beach is too short to take the number of vehicles belonging to the number of divisions that will be necessary to assault such a length of beach." That said: "Unless immediate steps are taken to construct sufficient beaches in this country which can be towed across the channel already assaulted, no assault can take place."[39]

But, of course, the assault was to happen and it was increasingly difficult to balance the requirement to keep the landing sites secret against the need to provide sufficient intelligence to enable junior officers to successfully carry out specific missions. Time was needed for each unit commander to develop a thorough operational plan, so vital information had to be released at a rate sufficient to ensure the invasion forces were not left groping through an intelligence fog of their own making.

Despite the codenames and other attempts to keep the landing site a secret, many young officers who were not supposed to be in the know had accurately pinpointed where they were going. Navy

Lieutenant Russell Choat twigged to the truth after two beach landing exercises on the English coast near Poole. Born in Maple Bay on
Vancouver Island, Choat had been a teenager attending school in
England when the war broke out. An attempt to return to Canada in
1940 aboard the liner *City of Benares* ended tragically when a
German U-boat sank the ship shortly after it sailed. He was one of
the few survivors. Stuck back in Britain, the seventeen-year-old
joined the Royal Naval Volunteer Reserve in early 1943 as an ordinary seaman. He was soon selected for officer training and in April
1944 was posted to the Landing Ship, Infantry *Llandovery Castle* as
the navigator and boats officer of a flotilla of eighteen Landing Craft,
Assault crewed by Royal Marines. This ship was part of Force J and
would be landing Canadian infantry on D-Day.

As the Marines had little experience in boat navigation, Choat
was to be in the lead LCA in the centre of the line to make sure the
flotilla landed in the right place. During practice landings near
Poole, he decided there must be a reason they landed on the same
beach in two separate exercises. Fetching an atlas of the French
coast, Choat and another flotilla officer carefully studied the coastline
and determined they would be landing in Normandy very close to
Caen. Shortly after mentioning his hunch to some of the Marines,
Choat was summoned before the Marine captain commanding the
flotilla and accused of having somehow acquired restricted intelligence documents. He told the captain that his conclusion was
nothing more than an educated guess. The captain told him to keep
his guesses to himself.

Choat was certain he was right and hoped the Germans were not
similarly astute. It seemed a pretty easy deduction. Soon, however, he
had even more confirming evidence. As the flotilla navigator, Choat
was given a mosaic of photos taken at sea level that showed the beach
just as it would appear from the deck on an LCA on the run to shore.
The clarity of the photos and the detail they captured stunned the
young naval lieutenant. Pointing to a large two-storey house that
seemed to stand directly behind a seawall, the briefing officer said
that was Choat's aiming point. He was to put his LCA on the sand
directly in front of the building.[40]

Each extended briefing of officers was parsed out only as the intelligence staff decided knowledge was critical to unit preparations. So it was not until late May that Choat received the photos needed to familiarize himself with the landing point. But 3 CID's battalion commanders and their second-in-commands had received very similar intelligence three months earlier because they had to work out assault plans at the company, platoon, and even section levels. Even here, the intelligence materials provided "existed in a vacuum, divorced from identifiable localities" with names of towns replaced by codenames.[41]

Nearly every evening after dinner, Canadian Scottish Regiment commander Lieutenant Colonel Fred Cabeldu and Major Cyril Wightman slipped off to a closely guarded tent to study the bogus maps of their assigned beach by candlelight. Drawn to a scale of 1:25,000, the maps were "complete with tinted contours and an overprint of enemy defences."[42] Every road, track, copse of wood, hedgerow, and building extending from the beach inland to the final objectives was represented. Supporting the maps were an ever growing number of photographs. But the intelligence tool Wightman found most useful was one whose appearance had solved a mystery that had teased his thoughts for almost two years.

In 1942, Wightman had received orders to round up all the carpenters in the battalion for a special assignment. As the CSR hailed from Victoria, a good number of men had worked in the building trades erecting houses of wooden construction. So he quickly gathered in just under fifty men and off they went, never to be seen again. Then an intelligence officer showed up in April with a carefully constructed model of the beach with precise wooden replicas of all the buildings behind it that would be attacked on D-Day. The intelligence officer confided that the CSR carpenters had been involved in constructing these models. To ensure the carpenters had no idea what they worked on, they had been widely scattered. Some had remained in Britain, while others returned to Canada. One man might have been working in a little room in Vancouver and another in a shop area near Tofino. They received photos and drawings of a specific building and made a model of it that was then sent to the intelligence officers, who painstakingly situated each structure correctly on the overall model.

Wightman and Cabeldu studied that model again and again, considering the fields of fire that Germans in the window of one house might bring to bear on their men. Obvious strongpoints were identified and plans made to secure them. With each passing evening, the two men thought themselves that much closer to ensuring the battalion's part in the assault succeeded. They also believed the intense training over the past five years had honed 3rd Canadian Infantry Division into the finest combat unit in the Canadian or any other Allied army—a feeling shared by the majority of the division's troops and officers.[43]

[6]

Spoiling for a Fight

ALTHOUGH 3RD CANADIAN INFANTRY DIVISION'S confidence in its fighting prowess ran high, it could never match that of the nation's small force of paratroopers, who considered themselves Canada's elite unit. They were like airborne soldiers everywhere in this sentiment. Such a sense of superiority was inculcated into the soul of every army's airborne troops in order to give them a distinct edge in battle over ordinary soldiers. The decision to form the 1st Canadian Parachute Battalion with a total allocated strength of 26 officers and 590 other ranks was made by National Defence Headquarters, Ottawa (NDHQ) on July 1, 1942 in an attempt to catch up with the other Western Allies.[1]

As early as December 1940, the British War Office had decided to form a "special service battalion" that would function rather like the light cavalry of past wars. When the British briefed Canadian Brigadier M.A. Pope on the idea, the liaison officer duly reported back to NDHQ that the force would be tasked to "seize bridge crossings, defiles and aerodromes well in advance of the slower-moving main body of the army."[2] In November 1941, Britain's War Office authorized an expansion of this airborne force to a full division in an attempt to match the Germans, who had made highly effective use of such troops during the invasions of France, Greece, and Crete.

While the Canadians were still considering the merits of forming a parachute unit, a Saskatoon Light Infantry officer, Lieutenant Colonel G.F.P. Bradbrooke, was busy completing training with the British paratroops at Royal Air Force's Ringway Parachute Course. By the time NDHQ made its decision, the Canadian officer had his paratrooper wings and was almost immediately tipped to command the new battalion. Although his given names were George Frederick Preston, friends called him Brad and anybody else was expected to stick to the initials in written correspondence or his rank and last name in verbal address. The slender Bradbrooke had been an accountant before the war.[3]

As Bradbrooke could not immediately return to Canada from Britain, Major Hilton Proctor assumed temporary command of the battalion, only to discover that the Parachute Training Centre being constructed at Camp Shilo in Manitoba would not be completed for some months. Accordingly, the first volunteers from the other ranks underwent basic parachuting instruction at Fort Benning, Georgia, where the Americans were training their own airborne divisions, while the majority of officers—drawn from units in Britain—were trained at Ringway.[4]

The primary purpose of airborne troops was to drop behind enemy lines and sow havoc there until relieved by advancing friendly forces. They must bring all supplies with them and be highly self-reliant, as access to supporting firepower would be greatly limited. Every volunteer was carefully assessed for suitable levels of physical conditioning, self-motivation, and quick-wittedness. The minimum age was eighteen and the maximum thirty-two. Nobody could weigh over 220 pounds and recruiters looked for men "with a history of participation in rugged sports or in a civilian occupation or hobby demanding sustained exertion."[5]

Many were rural boys—loggers, farmers, ranchers, and miners—seasoned by the hard-scrabble struggle to survive the Great Depression. Boyd Anderson, Jim MacPherson, and A.J. "Scotty" MacInnis fell into this group. They hailed respectively from a ranch in the Wood Mountains of Saskatchewan, the deep timber country near North Bay in central Ontario, and the mines of Cape Breton.[6]

But there was also Lorne Whaley, a United Church minister's son, who thought becoming a paratrooper would prove to the world he "wasn't a sissy."[7]

Among the officers were several athletes. Major Jeff Nicklin was a Winnipeg Blue Bombers offensive and defensive end before the war, while Captain Fraser Eadie had declined a spot on the Chicago Blackhawks to enlist in the army. While the men came to respect Nicklin, few liked him. Bellowing like a gridiron coach, he harangued them to ever greater exertion and never considered a job well done. Eadie was as strict but his wry sense of humour made him more popular.

Like Nicklin and Eadie, Lieutenant John Madden was a Manitoban. He had joined the Canadian Officer Training Corps at the University of Manitoba at age seventeen and a year later volunteered for the Winnipeg Rifles. The moment Madden heard of NDHQ's decision to form a parachute battalion, he volunteered, and returned from Britain as part of the first batch of officers sent directly to the battalion.

Madden went through jump training at Fort Benning alongside the last draft of recruits to arrive there. The course lasted four weeks, with the first week dedicated to physical training that included hours of exercises followed by route marches in the sultry Georgia heat. Week two brought more of the same, but with some hand-to-hand combat training mixed in. The third week concentrated on the techniques of jumping and handling parachutes, including parachute jumps from the top of a 250-foot steel tower. Then came the graduation week of five actual airborne drops with ever decreasing altitudes until the last was carried out from planes flying at just 800 feet. This, however, was still double the altitude at which they might be required to jump into combat.[8]

Whenever possible, off-duty hours were spent in Phenix City, Alabama across the Chattahoochee River from the base. The place teemed with smoke-filled bars, honkytonks, and strip joints where hookers gathered, the booze flowed, and fists were thrown as easily as the insults that the Canadians traded with their American comrades-in-arms. One of Madden's men was knifed to death in a barroom brawl over some slight that nobody could remember after the event.

Another needless tragedy had struck early in 1943 when the first graduates had undertaken a demonstration jump intended as a publicity stunt for the new battalion. First out of the plane had been Major Hilton Proctor, whose parachute had no sooner opened than he was clipped by the wing of a plane carrying several newspaper photographers trying to capture close-up photos of the officer. Details of the accident were quickly hushed up, but it was a sobering reminder to the battalion of how vulnerable paratroops were during the drop to earth.[9]

On March 23, 1943, the training at Fort Benning concluded and the battalion headed for Camp Shilo, opening shop there on April 15. Fort Benning had been tough, but training at Shilo proved tougher as a final effort was made to weed out any but the best and most determined troops. The pace of physical conditioning, jump training, and weapons and explosive practice was gruelling. New recruits arrived and many washed out, suffering the humiliation of being returned to their former units. So, too, did some of the Fort Benning graduates. The failure rate was almost 60 percent.[10]

Bradbrooke was on the scene by then and made a reputation as a tough disciplinarian little interested in getting to know the men he commanded. Formal, distant, and possessed of an accountant's fussy concern for administrative detail, he seemed more at home in his office than out on the training ground. Madden considered him a competent peacetime officer but worried about how he would perform in combat.[11]

WHILE THE PARACHUTE BATTALION had been training, NDHQ had been considering the merits of a request that it be added to the roster of 6th British Airborne Division. On April 7, 1943, NDHQ agreed. Three months later, 31 officers and 548 other ranks departed Halifax for overseas service. While this brought the battalion almost to its recommended strength (slightly increased from the originally envisioned size), almost the same number still needed to be trained and sent along to serve as reinforcements. Probable casualty rates in battle were expected to run far higher than that of regular infantry battalions and might well reach 50 per cent. Therefore, it was deemed necessary to have a reinforcement pool almost equal to the size of the battalion to draw upon in order to quickly return the unit to its normal strength.

On August 11, the battalion moved into Carter Barracks at Bulford Camp in Wiltshire and was formally designated as part of 3rd Parachute Brigade of the 6th Airborne Division, along with 8th and 9th British Parachute Battalions. The brigade commander was thirty-two-year-old Brigadier James Hill, a Sandhurst graduate from a long military line. He had narrowly escaped from Dunkirk, volunteered for the paratroops in late 1941, led the 1st British Parachute Battalion in North Africa, where he was grievously wounded, and was only allowed to stay in the service by signing a waiver disclaiming any right to a military pension. Standing six-foot-two, Hill had the stature and bearing of a soldier.[12] He also had the instincts and immediately struck the officers and men of 1st Canadian Parachute Battalion as a competent leader. Madden thought him "a tremendous man, absolutely fantastic."[13]

The Canadian paratroops were immediately plunged into a new training regimen for the full division's apparent role in a drop behind enemy lines to support an amphibious invasion. There would be two primary tasks: to seize ground inland that dominated the beachhead and to hold it until relieved in order to block any counterattack attempts directed towards the beaches.

A comprehensive training syllabus was followed to get the Canadians up to snuff. Through to the end of October, the emphasis was on training special weapon platoons in the operation of specific types of weaponry and the junior officers in field tactics. There were three special platoons—a heavy machine-gun platoon, a mortar platoon, and a Projector Infantry Antitank (PIAT) platoon. While these troops learned their specialist trades, the other personnel drilled endlessly to even further raise their physical fitness levels and shooting ability. "Airborne troops in action," read one training directive, "would not have an unlimited supply of ammunition, and every shot fired must find its target."[14] In late November, the Canadian battalion average marksmanship ratings were reported to be well below the other two battalions of 3rd British Parachute Brigade.

Hill assigned a British staff sergeant to work with the Canadian battalion at rectifying the problem. The sergeant immediately insisted that every man spend a minimum of six to eight hours a week on the gunnery range. Bradbrooke backed him up, declaring that "skill and efficiency in the handling of all weapons must reach and will reach a higher standard than any arm of the service."[15] Mostly those weapons were the standard Lee Enfield rifle, the Bren gun, and the light Sten submachine-gun. But there were also hand grenades, PIATS, light mortars, and other odds and sods that could be used by troops dependent on their feet to get wherever they needed to go after a parachute drop.

Having been trained in the American style of parachuting, the Canadians also had to adjust to the British system. One aspect that caused much concern was the British insistence on jumping without a backup reserve chute that could be deployed if the main chute failed to open. There was also a kit bag attached to the soldier's leg by a rope that was uncoiled to its full twenty-foot length just before landing. Ideally, the kit struck the ground first and served as a brake to soften the force of the landing, but if it was released prematurely the bag could act like a pendulum and set the parachutist spinning wildly so that his fall to the ground was uncontrolled.

On October 13, 1943, a first group of sixty-four Canadians jumped with forty pounds of mortar parts and other equipment loaded into kit bags. Nobody was injured and Brigadier Hill, who had attended the demonstration, was satisfied with the way the men handled themselves. The other troops were soon put through similar test jumps.[16]

Route marching in the perpetually cold and rainy fall weather ceased to be anything but a demanding routine. Fifty miles in eighteen hours was the objective. By October 21, the Canadians were matching the other battalions of 3rd Parachute Brigade in stride, both on the march and in marksmanship. Hill granted the brigade a ten-day leave—the first the Canadians had received since their arrival. To ensure the men could spend the leave pleasurably rather than shunting for hours and even days from one rail siding to another en route to London, Hill arranged for a connector train to speed the battalion from Bulford to Andover. From here, a fast train provided a quick link to London. Most of the men caught these trains but others headed for Scotland or off into the countryside for a quieter and less expensive time away from the base than could be had in the capital.

Being able to arrange this special transport for his Canadian troops greatly pleased Hill, but ten days later he was cursing under his breath after a local stationmaster angrily stormed into his office. Two Canadian paratroops en route back from London on a night train, the man reported, had slithered onto the top of a passenger car and worked their way up to the locomotive. They had then dropped two grenades down the funnel, disabling the engine. Unable to identify the culprits, Hill had to let the matter rest. But it reminded him that the Canadian battalion seemed to be "always spoiling for a fight."[17]

This wasn't necessarily a bad thing in a paratrooper. He thought that the Canadians nicely rounded out the fighting abilities of his three battalions. The 8th British Parachute Battalion pulled off its missions through the sheer grit of its troops and officers, scoffing at even the slightest suggestion that a carefully executed plan might be useful. On the other hand, the 9th prided itself on professionally implementing meticulous operational plans that were rigidly followed without thought to on-the-spot modifications to meet unexpected developments. Hill thought the Canadians balanced the best features of these disparate approaches and would prove excellent in combat as a result.[18]

FOLLOWING THE LEAVE, the pace of training accelerated yet again, with the emphasis on exercises shifting from small platoon or company tasks to battalion-scale night operations. The umpires for Exercise Schemozzle on the night of November 8–9 scattered the men from two platoons in each battalion randomly over the nearby countryside to simulate what might happen if planes failed to drop everyone on the drop zone. Despite the resulting confusion, the main body of the Canadian battalion and even some of its "lost" paratroops managed to reach their forming-up point just before dawn in time to capture their assigned objective on schedule. Although the exercise was successfully concluded, some officers grumbled afterward that it was very unrealistic to think that any of their transport planes would fail to drop troops anywhere but on the designated drop zone.[19]

More exercises followed, with each throwing the battalion into mock combat situations likely to be encountered during the invasion. Counterattacks were met and repelled, bridges were seized and wired for destruction, roads mined, and artillery batteries attacked and silenced. "By the end of the year the battalion," read one report, "was perfecting methods of movement across country by day in the face of enemy opposition and a drill for attacking defended features and battery positions by night."[20]

On January 20, 1944, came Exercise Manitoba. "The idea behind this exercise," Bradbrooke wrote three days before, "is to drop the complete fighting personnel of this unit on one dropping zone in the shortest possible time with a rapid clearance of the dropping zone of all personnel." The drop was to be made from planes of 38 Group, Royal Air Force, which would drop the battalion during the invasion. Over a span of just fifteen minutes, five hundred men jumped from fifty airplanes. Watching from the drop zone, Canadian war artist Lieutenant G.C. Timming was amazed how quickly the ground became "covered with gold, green, red, and blue blobs of the deflated chutes. Some men landed on farms, on rooftops, some in trees from which the chutes were later torn by main force by the RAF men. On landing the men rushed on their containers, took out packs and Bren guns, and ran under cover as much as possible to the agreed rendezvous. At no time were more than a few men discernible on the field although 500 or more had dropped that afternoon."[21]

Exercise Co-Operation simulated an attack by 6th Airborne Division on a section of French coast, with the Canadians to seize a height of land and repel a counterattack by the U.S. Parachute and Airborne Light Tank Squadron, which was playing the role of enemy. At 1700 hours on February 7, the battalion jumped with full battle equipment in the kit bags attached to their legs, while the heavy weapons, mortars, and machine guns were dropped in separate containers. While only a few men were injured in the jump, there was extensive damage to equipment, resulting from the parachute-dropped containers breaking open on impact and a number of kit bags also splitting apart. Despite these problems, Hill was pleased with the Canadian performance. "If they continue to make progress ... at this rate they will soon be the best jumping exponents in our Airborne Corps and I should very much like to see them achieve this end for themselves," he wrote.[22]

Suddenly, in May, all parachute jumping was forbidden to prevent jump-related injuries and deaths. Everyone knew the suspension meant the moment of battle must be very near.[23]

On May 24, 1st Canadian Parachute Battalion received orders at reveille to move by truck to a security transit camp. Lieutenant Sam McGowan told his men that in three hours they were to be on the parade ground with nothing but their combat gear. All spare kit, he said, was to be packed, labelled, and left on the foot of their beds for storage by the quartermasters "until we get back from wherever we're going."[24]

Corporal Dan Hartigan and the rest of his platoon were ready to go ninety minutes later, so they killed the remaining time by smoking and trying to guess where they might be heading. At the parade ground, the men were issued ammunition, had their gear inspected, and then were loaded into transport trucks. As the long convoy wound its way across the English countryside, Hartigan's platoon passed the hours playing craps on a blanket one of the quartermasters had thoughtfully tossed in the back of the truck for use as a rolling mat. Eventually, the trucks passed through a gate and entered a tent encampment in a large field encircled by a single strand of waist-height barbed wire.

As the men climbed down from the trucks, a sergeant bellowed into a megaphone: "You are now in a place called a security transit camp. Here you are going to learn the best kept secrets in the world. Anyone who places a foot beyond that single strand of barbed wire will be shot without being challenged. Your best bet is not to go within a hundred feet of it," he warned.[25]

The paratroops assembled on the parade ground before a makeshift stage that Bradbrooke and his headquarters staff mounted a few minutes later. With a flourish, the lieutenant colonel pulled a canvas cover off a large map showing the south England coast and the French coast, with the English Channel in between. Bradbrooke confirmed that the paratroops would soon be leading the invasion forces into France and said he would tell them more that evening.[26]

During the evening briefing, Bradbrooke gave a general outline of the invasion plan. On the western flank, General Omar N. Bradley's First United States Army would establish a beachhead on Cotentin's east shore near the city of Varreville and another between the Drôme and Vire rivers. Meanwhile, on the eastern flank, General Miles Dempsey's Second British Army would seize a long beachhead extending east from Port-en-Bessin to Cabourg at the mouth of the Dives River. This beachhead would be expanded inland on the first day to encompass the cities of Bayeux and Caen.

In the American sector, 4th Infantry Division would establish the beachhead on the Cotentin Peninsula with a landing on a sheltered beach codenamed Utah, while 1st Infantry Division, reinforced by the 116th Regiment of 29th Infantry Division, set down in front of the town of St. Laurent-sur-Mer on Omaha. In the centre of the whole front, the British 50th Division would land immediately east of Arromanches on Gold Beach and drive inland to Bayeux, linking up with the Americans en route. East of the 50th Division, the 3rd Canadian Infantry Division and 2nd Canadian Armoured Brigade would attack Juno Beach, and on their left, the British 3rd Division would strike Sword Beach at Lion-sur-Mer and break through to Caen by the afternoon. The flanks of the invasion force would be secured by airborne landings, with the U.S. 82nd and 101st Airborne Divisions dropping at the base of the Cotentin Peninsula to isolate Cherbourg, while the 6th British Airborne dropped east of the Orne River and seized crossings over the Caen Canal.[27]

The battalion intelligence officer Lieutenant R.D.J. Weathersbee added that 6th Airborne's specific tasks would be to capture several bridges and hold them until relieved, while destroying several others to deny their use to the enemy. Wrecking parties would also knock out several communication installations, German strongpoints, and some coastal gun batteries that could threaten Sword Beach.[28]

It was 3rd British Parachute Brigade's job to block several possible routes that German counterattacking forces could use to reach the beaches from the east. Six bridges crossing Dives and its tributary, Divette, would have to be blown and blocking forces set up on several roads. The brigade was also responsible for destroying a coastal battery at Merville on the mouth of the Orne River.

Knocking out the Merville battery and denying the Germans use of the roads north of it fell to 9th Parachute Battalion, while 8th Parachute Battalion would blow all bridges in the southeast part of the sector. First Canadian Parachute Battalion would meanwhile operate in a roughly triangular area marked at its apexes by the villages of Robehomme, Varaville, and le Mesnil. Inside this zone, they were to destroy a bridge and an enemy headquarters at Varaville, another bridge at Robehomme that crossed a wide ditch, protect 9th Battalion's attack on the Merville battery from any Germans moving in from the south, and seize and hold a vital road junction. Le Mesnil crossroads, as this road junction was known, stood on top of the narrow le Plein–Bois de Bavent ridge, a 180-foot-high strategic feature that separated the Orne and Dives valleys. Securing the thickly wooded ridge would prevent its use as a German observation post. The same height advantage had led Brigadier Hill to select the crossroads on the ridge for his brigade command post.

'C' Company would jump ahead of the rest of the battalion, secure the drop zone, and then carry out the attack on Varaville. After destroying the Robehomme bridge, 'B' Company would establish a holding position in this area to check any German attempt to attack the airborne division from the east flank. 'A' Company, meanwhile, would cover 9th Battalion's attack on the Merville battery and then move to seize le Mesnil crossroads.[29] Weathersbee concluded by saying that specific details of these operations would be set out in company-level briefings and then further broken down by platoons and individual sections.

A smiling and unusually animated Bradbrooke wrapped up by saying, "You're going to be surprised and happy when you learn all the things you are going to do on this operation. Believe me, there will be a part for every soldier here. Get a good night's sleep and good luck!"[30]

To Die Gloriously

THROUGHOUT SOUTHERN ENGLAND, soldiers by the thousands were either moved to security compounds or awoke one morning to find their base transformed into a virtual concentration camp. Since April 5, the Regina Rifle Regiment had been in Hiltingbury Camp, Camp 7, Block C (c-7)—part of a great tent city that sprawled over most of Hiltingbury Common six miles north of Southampton. On May 25, American soldiers with orders to allow nobody in or out sealed the entire camp.

Only ten days earlier, the only people in 3rd Canadian Infantry Division who had known the precise location of the invasion had been a mere handful of Major General Rod Keller's divisional staff officers. On May 15, however, the veil of secrecy had been lifted for the brigade and battalion commanders and their second-in-commands during a day-long briefing session held in the great dining hall of Cranbury House—the large estate housing Keller's headquarters.[1]

Major John Clifford Cave, the Sherbrooke Fusilier Regiment's thirty-six-year-old second-in-command, had never seen so much senior brass gathered in one place. The tobacco smoke–filled room was crammed almost to overflowing.[2]

First came a general appreciation of the overall invasion plan, with the division's intelligence officer using a large map to detail the passage of the invasion fleet from England to the five beaches in

Normandy. Then a new map was undraped that showed Juno Beach and the inland countryside. The beach was a five-mile strip of low, flat sandy coastline running from the seaside resort of St. Aubin-sur-Mer in the east to the Château Vaux about a mile west of the mouth of the River Seulles. Fronting the beach were the villages of Bernières-sur-Mer about two and a half miles west of St. Aubin-sur-Mer and the small fishing port of Courseulles-sur-Mer on the eastern bank of the Seulles River. Tucked slightly inland on the western bank of the river was the hamlet Graye-sur-Mer. River Seulles widened just behind its mouth to create several basins that offered good shelter for fishing boats.[3]

In several places, a series of rocky ledges normally submerged during high tide extended as far as a mile out to sea. On the west bank of the Seulles, the beach at low tide was a half-mile deep and backed by a deep swath of ten-foot-high dunes. Between Courseulles and Bernières it was mostly sand broken by a few rocky outcrops. Both villages were well protected from storms by concrete seawalls the assault forces would have to breach.[4]

Next, Lieutenant Colonel Don Mingay took the stage to explain the operational plan. Two infantry brigades, each supported by an armoured regiment and two regiments of artillery, would comprise the assault wave. Tanks and infantry would hit the beach together, with the artillery providing covering fire. The Royal Winnipeg Rifles strengthened by a Canadian Scottish Regiment company would land west of the River Seulles, while the Regina Rifles touched down in front of Courseulles. The rest of the Canadian Scottish Regiment would form 7th Canadian Infantry Brigade's reserve. Supporting these landings would be the 1st Hussars Armoured Regiment and the 12th and 13th artillery regiments. On the left, 8th Canadian Infantry Brigade would put the Queen's Own Rifles on the beach in front of Bernières while the North Shore (New Brunswick) Regiment swept into the western outskirts of St. Aubin. The Fort Garry Horse would be in support along with the 14th and 19th artillery regiments—the latter seconded to the division from 2nd Army Group, Royal Canadian Artillery. In reserve here would be Le Régiment de la Chaudière.[5]

Immediately after the assault force secured the beach, Mingay explained, the reserve regiments would land. Then the two brigades would launch a four-phase drive inland. Phase I was simply to occupy Vaux, Graye-sur-Mer, Courseulles, Bernières, and St. Aubin. In Phase II, 7 CIB would secure crossings over the River Seulles and advance to Creully—a medieval castle town about six miles inland—while 8 CIB would take up a parallel position on a low ridge extending north to south from the village of Basly through Anguerny to Anisy. These were the division's intermediate objectives for the day. For Phase III, 9th Canadian Infantry Brigade, having landed while the two leading brigades pushed inland, would pass through 8 CIB and seize the villages of Authie, Ardenne, Carpiquet, and the strategically vital Carpiquet airport. Simultaneously on the right, 7 CIB would wheel to the southeast from Creully to occupy the ground between Putot-en-Bessin, Bretteville-l'Orgueilleuse, and Norrey-en-Bessin. This would put the two leading brigades astride the Caen-Bayeux Road—Objective Oak—by evening. Phase IV was simply to reorganize here and dig in.[6]

Because of a significant gap on the left flank between the Canadians and the British division on Sword Beach, No. 48 (Royal Marine) Commando was placed under Keller's command. Its four hundred-strong force of five fighting troops and one heavy weapons troop armed with mortars and medium machine-guns would land on the division's eastern boundary and capture Langrune-sur-Mer while another commando unit drove over from Sword to link up with No. 48.[7]

Opposing the Juno Beach landing would be the 716th Infantry Division's 736th Grenadier Regiment, most specifically its 2nd Battalion beefed up by elements of the 441st East Battalion (comprised of eastern European conscripts and volunteers). The intelligence officer described the 716th as "a low category division of two regiments of infantry and one regiment of artillery [equipped with] two field and one medium battery. All personnel are trained in coast defence although the better trained have been transferred to field divisions. The remainder consists of young soldiers, men of older classes unfit for service on the Eastern Front and men who have been wounded and are only slightly disabled. In comparison with a first class field infantry division its fighting value has been assessed as 40 per cent in a static role and 15 per cent in a counterattack. The division should be up to strength in personnel (13,000) and equipment, and is probably over-strength as it has been reported that non-German soldiers, Russians, Mongols, etc. have been seen in the divisional area."[8]

Although the opposing regiment was considered of poor material, it was dug in behind a maze of beach obstacles and enjoyed excellent fields of interlocking fire from a complex of fortified strongpoints. These strongpoints consisted of concrete pillboxes with adjacent open machine-gun pits. In key points, 75-millimetre guns had been positioned inside casemates or open emplacements to add to the direct defensive fire. All obvious routes by which infantry and tanks could move off inland from the beach were covered by at least one strongpoint, and all the strongpoints were well protected by minefields and barbed wire entanglements.

Reconnaissance photos had identified at least nine strongpoints on Juno Beach, with two particularly formidable positions on either side of the river mouth by Courseulles and one each at Bernières and St. Aubin. Ranging between two thousand and three thousand yards back of these, the reconnaissance photos showed that the Germans were well along in construction of a system of dugouts thought to contain heavy mortars and machine guns. Although some positions had been identified, intelligence staff had only a slight idea of the number of German artillery batteries deployed well back of the beach that could be brought to bear on the landing force. Most of these were 75-millimetre batteries, but at least a few 88-millimetre guns had been detected. There was also a battery of four 105-millimetre guns within direct fire range of the beach.

Once the strongpoints were overwhelmed, the 716th Division was expected to pose little further threat to the landings, but in short order the Canadians could face counterattacks by two armoured divisions positioned within easy striking distance of Juno Beach. The 21st Panzer Division, under Generalleutnant Edgar Feuchtinger, was just eight hours away in the area of Falaise. Almost wiped out in Tunisia at the end of the African campaign, this division had been rebuilt with young and well-trained soldiers. Farther east, near the Seine estuary, the 12th ss Panzer (Hitlerjugend) Division was comprised of untested but fanatical Hitler Youth. Its officers and non-commissioned officers, however, were all veterans and many had seen service on the Eastern Front. The 12th ss could easily be on the scene the day after D-Day (D+1).[9]

The briefing ended with discussion of a subject that had been worrying everyone in the room—estimates of probable casualties. They were told that 21st Army Group Headquarters predicted that 9,250 of the 70,000 British and Canadian soldiers landing on D-Day would be dead, wounded, or missing by day's end. Of these, 3,000 were expected to have drowned. The Canadian forces, including 1st Canadian Parachute Battalion, landing on D-Day would total about 15,000. By simple averaging, Canadian casualties were expected to tally 1,982 men, almost 15 per cent of the landing force lost in a single day.[10]

It was a sobering thought and one that Mingay again explained a few days later to a group of about thirty Canadian journalists who would accompany the division to Normandy. Mingay walked the reporters through the same thorough brief that had been given to the officers, including illustrating the operation on a series of highly detailed maps. When Mingay told the reporters of the estimated casualty projections, the room grew quite still. Then *Montreal Gazette* correspondent Lionel Shapiro stood and asked Mingay "what plans had been made to withdraw if the landing was unsuccessful?" Mingay, who was sitting on the edge of a desk at this point of the briefing, responded: "There are no plans for withdrawal. If it fails the Allied cause will be in real jeopardy." Shapiro was incensed, accusing Mingay and the entire Allied planning staff of being "stupid, incompetent." Mingay sharply retorted that they "were taking no chances that anyone in the organization would even contemplate anything but success." The invasion force either succeeded or died on the sand.[11]

THAT THE ENGLISH CHANNEL might be running red with blood as the assault ended in failure was a distinct possibility. And even if it succeeded, the likelihood of personal survival was by no means guaranteed, as soldiers, sailors, and airmen alike learned when the bleak casualty projections were revealed during ensuing briefings. During several brigade and battalion level briefings, Captain Peter Simonds of the Royal Canadian Corps of Signals noted the general reaction. "Some," he later wrote, "remembered that the estimated 500 casualties for Dieppe had run to about seven times that figure and decided, on this basis, that they had just about 'had it.'" Yet they seemed strangely unfazed. Simonds was "downright alarmed as well as forced into admiration at the carefree, relaxed manner with which they approached their ordeal. Frankly, I would have liked to have seen this splendid cross-section of young Canadian manhood outwardly place a higher value on their own useful lives and well-being."[12]

When Major Roger Rowley briefed the Cameron Highlanders of Ottawa, which, as the division's heavy weapons battalion, would be landing in scattered units alongside the rest of the division's battalions, Simonds was taken aback by the man's casual dismissal of their chances. Rowley reminded Simonds of Errol Flynn, both in his appearance and cavalier style. "You might as well face the facts, men," Rowley said, "that you stand a good chance of being killed. So what? It's a damned sight better to die gloriously writing one of the greatest pages in history than to die twenty years hence lying in a drunken stupor in a gutter with the rats eating off your red nose." Expecting outrage at such flippancy, Simonds was surprised when the men instead "burst into a gale of appreciative laughter. They felt just like [Rowley] about the whole affair—they were in it to the finish, come what may. Nowhere else have I seen anything approaching the devil-may-care exuberant morale and spirits I encountered . . . with the 3rd Canadian Infantry Division."[13]

Not everyone appreciated the manner in which briefing officers warned of a possible slaughter. In late May, a Royal Navy Commander briefed the 31st Canadian Minesweeping Flotilla's ship captains aboard HMCS *Caraquet.* Lieutenant Commander James Green, captain of *Wasaga,* was deeply disturbed by the man's cold-blooded manner. First, he dismayed the captains with the news that, instead of clearing the invasion route for Force J's crossing to Juno Beach, the

Canadian flotilla was now to sweep the lanes ahead of the American force sailing to Omaha Beach.

He followed up this bad news by saying that the minesweepers leading the way into the beaches were particularly vulnerable to being crippled by shore battery fire and could expect heavy losses among their crews or even the disabling of their ships. In the latter event, he warned, the damaged vessel would immediately be blown out of the water so it would not get in the way of the landing craft carrying troops and equipment to the beaches.

Briefing over, the ship captains proceeded to *Caraquet*'s quarter-deck to await boats that would take them back to their respective ships. For a time, nobody spoke and Green noted each man's grim expression. Finally, one officer dug a set of dice out of a pocket, knelt down, and rolled them on the deck. A rough, hard crap game ensued with every man throwing in pound notes without the slightest care if they were lost. At first, Green raked in the loot, then he fell into a losing streak that continued until his wallet was emptied.[14]

Shortly after the briefing of the ship captains, Royal Canadian Navy Vice Admiral Percy Nelles addressed the crew of *Caraquet*. Among those assembled was Stoker 1st Class George Irwin, who listened to Nelles calmly explain that the minesweepers were expected to suffer 75 per cent losses. As *Caraquet* would be in the lead, the vice admiral fully expected the ship and its entire crew would be lost. For that reason, he offered everyone in the crew a chance to stand aside without fear of penalty. They would merely be confined ashore until the invasion was launched and then reassigned to other duties. No one took the offer up.[15]

WHILE FEW FALTERED, a good number flinched when told the precise nature of their assignments. Rifleman Hugh Lamb of the Queen's Own Rifles' 'A' Company discovered he was to be the third man off his Landing Craft, Assault. He was to dash across the sand to the concrete seawall and blast a hole in the tangles of barbed wire on top of it with a bangalore torpedo. During landing exercises, the rifleman raced towards imaginary concrete seawalls with his hollow explosive-filled pipe on a shoulder and imagined what it would be like on the real day. Germans dug in behind the wire, ripping away with machine guns, and him running straight into their fire. Lamb saw himself dead, his wife left without a husband, his son orphaned.

He had married young, at seventeen, on August 7, 1939 and promised his wife that despite having spent four years in the militia he would not enlist until they were settled. For the first year, he and his bride were too poor to live on their own, so each lived separately with their respective parents in Mississauga. Then their son came along and Lamb found a job as an apprentice carpenter with a sash-and-door company in nearby Georgetown, where the young couple set up a home. But on January 3, 1943, Lamb and his brother went to the local RCAF recruiting depot to enlist. When his brother was rejected, however, the two walked over to the army depot and enlisted there, with the idea that they wanted to stay together.

Little concerned with the desires of two brothers, the army promptly split them up. Lamb's militia experience was such that he fast-tracked through training at Camp Borden and was sent overseas just six months after his enlistment. At Aldershot, he asked to join the Queen's Own Rifles for no better reason than he liked their dress uniforms and knew they were Canada's second-oldest regiment. Surprisingly, the army actually gave him the requested assignment.

But Lamb didn't want this current assignment. He searched desperately for any way short of desertion to avoid carrying that bangalore torpedo and found his opportunity when a call went out for volunteers to the pioneer platoon. Despite the fact that the platoon was nicknamed "the suicide squad," Lamb figured his survival odds were better in its ranks than being the third man out of that LCA. To his relief, he was accepted.[16]

SOUTH ENGLAND LITERALLY seethed with men and equipment as the month of May drew to a close. Ships clogged every port and it was the rare open field not cluttered with tents or vehicles. Every day, more ships steamed into the harbours until eventually they overflowed so that vessels were sent to any sheltered anchor point along the coast or around the Isle of Wight. The destroyer HMCS *Algonquin* steamed out of a clinging night fog into brilliant morning sunshine at Portsmouth on May 27 to find the sea "a mass of shipping of all types." Eventually, Captain Desmond W. Piers tracked down an oiler to refuel. When that was completed, the destroyer was conducted to an anchorage off Seaview on the Isle of Wight. It was 2230 hours when the *Algonquin* dropped anchor alongside HMCS *Huron* and the other ships of 26th Destroyer Flotilla.[17]

Until being ordered south to join the invasion fleet, this flotilla had been part of the Home Fleet based at Scapa Flow, Scotland, serving primarily as escorts for convoys sailing to Russia or launching fast raids on German shipping in Norway. When the flotilla started practising shore-bombardment techniques in the late spring, however, Piers had realized they were to be part of the forthcoming invasion. This was a complex new form of gunnery to learn, as it combined the use of radar and visual tracking both from the destroyer itself and from spotting craft offshore to bring accurate fire down on beach targets. Then there was the added complication of firing indirectly on invisible inland targets with fire direction provided by officers operating alongside the advancing troops. That the invasion was imminent was rammed home when *Algonquin*'s gunnery training became so intense that for the better part of ten days "the hands were continuously at action stations for up to fifteen hours at a stretch and every form of action organization was tested."[18] This training ceased on May 25 and after a quick resupply the flotilla sailed south.

After many dreary months in Scapa, southern England in springtime seemed a paradise. Piers, who was nicknamed the "Smiling Tiger" because his smile never reached the eyes that seemed to be constantly alert for any dereliction of duty, had joined the navy in 1931 at age seventeen and took command of *Algonquin* in the early part of 1944. He was a strict disciplinarian, who would never hesitate to break a subordinate officer's career if he deemed it necessary, but would surely do so in a polite and friendly manner. On Sunday, May 28, Piers took a break from his duties and went ashore with another ship's captain. "All the things we missed at Scapa were here," he later wrote, "trees in full foliage, gardens in bloom, people bathing on the long sandy beaches, everybody enjoying the lovely summer sun. At this point war seemed very far away."[19]

The war was, however, very close, as the vast armada of assembled shipping standing off the beaches attested. Piers quickly found it difficult to cut himself free for shore visits as each day was eaten up "reading the unbelievable amount of Operational Orders that are necessary for such an operation as this. However the instructions are very clearly laid out and it is easy to find any information required."[20] The masses of documents were supplemented by various briefing sessions as the destroyer captains learned their role in the invasion. *Algonquin* would at first protect Major General Rod Keller's 3rd Canadian Infantry Division headquarters aboard HMS *Hilary* during the channel crossing and then bombard targets on Juno Beach. That *Algonquin* would be supporting Canadian troops delighted Piers and his crew. On June 2, when *Algonquin* returned from a night patrol in the channel and entered Portsmouth harbour to hook up with an oiler, Piers saw troops everywhere going aboard landing craft and realized the invasion was imminent.[21]

LOADING THOUSANDS of soldiers and their mass of weaponry and vehicles onto ships was a vast logistical undertaking. The first Canadians entered "the sausage machine" on May 30 just a few days after the division was equipped with new battle dress uniforms and assault helmets specially designed for the Commonwealth invasion forces. With a less distinctive brim than the traditional piss-pot "Tommy" helmet, the new model fit more snugly and was wrapped with camouflage netting into which twigs and leaves could be woven to break a man's outline. The new battle dress jerkin was touted as being "waterproof, gas proof, rat, mouse, and louse proof," wrote the North Shore Regiment's Catholic padre, R. Miles Hickey. It was also thick, coarse, and heavy. Hickey found his could stand on its own without collapsing, "like the old time starched dresses of years and years and years ago."[22] They were also liberally supplied with pockets, into which most of the men stuffed extra magazines of ammunition.

When the soldiers moved out of the security camps to board the trucks that would carry them to the ships, each man carried only his battle kit. Still, they were staggering under the weight. Stormont, Dundas and Glengarry Highlander Private Danny Darling weighed his gear load and discovered it tallied seventy-eight pounds. His kit was basically the same as every other Glen carried. He "carried two Bren gun magazines, two No. 36 grenades, one No. 75 anti-tank grenade, two smoke grenades, one No. 69 grenade and three bandoliers of rifle ammunition, besides socks, towel, gas cape, respirator, ground sheets, a small collapsible bicycle, two 24-hour ration packs and a commando knife."[23]

Troops in the 7th and 8th Canadian Infantry Brigades were spared the weight of the folding bicycle with which some 9 CIB soldiers were equipped. This brigade's three regiments would land on the heels of the assault brigades, whereupon some infantry companies were to immediately assemble the bicycles and then breezily pedal along country roads to Carpiquet airfield with their company commanders riding along on small James motorcycles. In the absence of the weight of the bicycles, most of the assault troops opted to pile on more ammunition and grenades, fearful of running out at a critical moment. Captain Ronald Shawcross of the Regina Rifles noted that each man in 'A' Company generally carried 150 rounds of ammunition for their Lee Enfield rifles as well as several magazines for the Bren guns. At the time, it didn't strike him as excessive. He had burdened himself with a rifle and stuffed his pistol inside his tunic, figuring that waving a pistol around would only mark him as an officer to any German sniper.[24]

For the infantry, the entire process of assembling kit and moving down the pipe to the ships proved an orderly undertaking. But the tankers of 2nd Canadian Armoured Brigade were left fretting until virtually the last moment as to whether they would have enough tanks for everyone. During the training phase, the three regiments had been equipped with outmoded Rams and Valentines, with a complete changeover to Shermans promised by the end of April. In the end, even as the squadrons were being ordered to ready for shipboard loading, the Shermans were just arriving. These tanks were a mixed bag of diesel-powered Sherman IIIs and Sherman Vs equipped with Chrysler gasoline engines. Many, particularly among the Sherman IIIs, were in poor condition.[25] Those sent to the 1st Hussars had come direct from long service at a firing range, where the guns had fired off ten thousand rounds each. The morale of Lieutenant Bill McCormick's 'C' Squadron troop crashed the moment the men saw the tanks they were to take into combat. He scrounged a can of paint and dressed up the interior of his Sherman, but there was nothing to be done about one of the three tanks that had an engine in such bad shape it was unable to keep up even during column marches around the camp. McCormick managed to wangle a replacement, which proved to have an unfixable chronic fuel leak. When yet another replacement was provided, the gun muzzle was found to have a bad burr that affected its accuracy, but the crew managed to file the steel edge smooth. With two extra tanks fit only for the wrecking yard, teams of 2 CAB's Royal Canadian Electrical and Mechanical Engineers (RCEME) Workshop and regimental fitters cut their tracks into pieces and welded these to the fronts of many Hussar tanks to strengthen the armament of the thin-skinned Shermans.[26]

A 2 CAB report noted "that it was only thanks to Trojan work by [these personnel] that the regiments were able to go into battle with more or less 'battleworthy' tanks."[27] Fort Garry Horse commander Lieutenant Colonel Ronald Morton worried that the delay in delivery meant that 'A' Squadron, which was not equipped with Duplex-Drive tanks, had almost no opportunity to learn how to operate the new tanks before the invasion itself. He was even more concerned about the reconnaissance troop, which received its light turretless Stuarts, known as Honeys, so late that the crews' first chance to drive them was en route to the loading docks.[28]

The Canadians moved from the camps to marshalling points near the ports of Southampton and Portsmouth, where they were divided into specific loading complements for each vessel. In the marshalling areas, each soldier was handed a small pack of French currency, a Mae West lifebelt, pills to prevent seasickness, and, should the pills fail to work, a vomit bag.[29] Many factors beyond maintaining unit integrity determined who was assigned to which ship. Weight factors had to be considered, as did each vessel's scheduled approach to the beach and its means for disembarking troops. Detailed manifests drafted to control the process proved their worth as the loading proceeded with few glitches or last-minute changes.

On Landing Ship, Tank 155, Fort Garry Horse Major E.M. Wilson was the senior army officer and therefore commanded all army personnel aboard. In addition to his tankers, there were sixteen additional units. These included some British airborne engineers, Royal Canadian Army Service Corps personnel, medical staff, and heavy anti-aircraft gunners. "The staff work behind the successful marshalling and embarkation of a force this size," wrote the Fort Garry Horse war diarist, "staggers the mind."[30]

Not everything proceeded without mishap. When engineers started backing a group of heavily loaded twenty-ton trailers aboard LST 155 on June 3, one gathered such momentum going down the ramp that the eight-wheeled monstrosity plunged overboard with its tractor dragged helplessly along. Although much of the equipment was damaged, nobody was injured.[31]

There were disruptions to the carefully drawn manifests that also had nothing to do with loading procedures. On June 3, the 1st Hussars Regiment's 'C' Squadron and Regimental Headquarters tanks lined up on a street next to the Southampton docks to load on several Landing Craft, Tank. Trooper Ralph Burley was loitering beside the tank in which he was a gunner when a group of the regiment's officers came up and one announced, "This tank won't go in on D-Day." Burley and his mates were dismayed. They had been working towards this moment for years and now were to be denied a role. The officer curtly informed them that the tank would be shuffled over to join the regiment's rear echelon elements as a security detail and would land well after the invasion.

No sooner had Burley absorbed this unwelcome news than the squadron's sergeant major approached Burley. "You're not getting off that easy," the man said. "You're going with Lieutenant Irving. He's going to be on a landing craft with two 17-pounder Shermans mounted on the bow and you're going to be ammunition detail. You and three other guys." The twenty-one-year-old Torontonian joined

Lieutenant Fleming Ladd Irving's party on an LCT and found the two tanks chained down on the vessel's bow. Irving told the four men they were to pass ammunition stored behind the tanks up to the loaders while the gunners engaged a fortification next to Courseulles-sur-Mer that was protecting a German gun. The lieutenant explained that the ammo-passing detail was necessary so that when the tanks finished the fire mission they could immediately land with still full ammunition racks.[32]

British tank specialists had developed the 17-pounder Sherman Firefly to give Commonwealth armoured regiments a tank capable of winning head-to-head shootouts with the German Tiger and Panther V tanks. With a muzzle velocity of 2,900 feet per second, its armour-piercing rounds had almost twice the penetrating power of the Sherman's standard 75-millimetre gun. Whereas only the occasional fluke round from a 75 would pierce the thick hide of a Tiger or Panther, a hit from a Firefly meant an almost certain kill. The 17-pounder barrel was much longer than the 75-millimetre, however, giving it a distinct profile that was hard to camouflage. Being the new star in the Allied armoured parade, the Fireflys allotted to 2 CAB regiments were usually commanded by troop leaders and, because of the late delivery of these tanks, the average crew had only been able to fire six test rounds before marshalling for loading. They would have to learn the strengths and limitations of the new gun in battle.[33]

With D-Day scheduled for the morning of June 5, most of the division was well along in the loading process by June 2. Some of the assault infantry companies were berthed aboard former passenger liners (Landing Ship Infantry, Large) that were well equipped with kitchens and sleeping quarters below deck, such as the *Canterbury* that Major Lochie Fulton's Royal Winnipeg Rifles 'D' Company boarded. But the armoured regiments that would be involved in the initial assault and the artillery regiments that would be firing from ship decks were loaded onto flat-hulled LCTs lacking accommodation areas. These tankers and gunners found whatever clear spaces they could beside their tanks or guns and bedded down on the hard steel. Still, nights were warm and days sunny, so the men were content.

They sunbathed, wrote letters, and gambled. Officers threw in the occasional route march up and down the docks to keep their troops limbered up.

June 4 dawned windy but clear. The 1st Hussars were ushered off their boats and marched up and down the docks for several hours.[34] Many craft were already at sea, having sailed the day before to anchorages in the Solent. *Canterbury* and *Laird Isle*—the latter carrying 'B' Company of the Royal Winnipegs—had sailed from Southampton into the Solent on June 3. 'A' and 'C' companies, along with a reserve company of the Reginas, were already anchored nearby, having sailed on *Llandovery Castle* the previous day.[35]

As the morning progressed, the weather began to turn. Clouds moved in, the temperature dropped, a strong northwest wind came up, and light showers fell. The sea in the Solent grew rough. Despite the worsening conditions, *Llandovery Castle* and many other ships weighed anchor on schedule and started creeping slowly into the English Channel. Lieutenant Russell Choat, the navigating officer for the Landing Craft, Assault boats that would take the soldiers onto the beach from the ship, worried that the appalling sea conditions would result in some of the smaller vessels being lost during the crossing. Then late in the afternoon, with the ship about eight miles out, a radio signal ordered the ship back to harbour. The invasion was cancelled.[36]

For the ships like *Llandovery Castle* that were equipped with radios the order was immediately acknowledged and acted upon. But many vessels, such as Landing Craft Infantry 262 and the rest of the LCIs of the 262nd LCI Flotilla, had no radios. Lieutenant Peter Hinton, commanding LCI 262, saw large vessels on every side of him suddenly swing about while his twelve-ship flotilla plodded onward. Then a destroyer swept past with its signal light madly blinking the order to turn back. Hinton brought the helm about. During the brief but chaotic return voyage, Hinton witnessed several collisions, including one between a heavy cruiser or battleship and a Landing Craft, Tank that threw up "a great shower of sparks from the LCT."[37] From his vantage, it looked as if the LCT had been sliced in two, but there were no ships reported lost that day.

As the returning ships approached the English coast, all semblance of order was lost and "a massive traffic jam ensued." The LCIS finally struggled back into Southampton harbour and tied up in the berths they had departed only hours before.[38] Sailors and soldiers were left to speculate whether the invasion would happen at all.

THAT DECISION WAS CAUSE for heated debate at Supreme Headquarters, Allied Expeditionary Force. Either the invasion went ahead on June 6 or it must be postponed until June 17 at the earliest, and the meteorologists were predicting that the weather would only worsen as the month progressed. In fact, they were predicting the stormiest June of the century. Because of the vast array of obstacles planted below the high-tide line it was critical the invasion be launched when high tides coincided with first light. The door on the first such period in June was fast closing and would shut entirely on June 7, with the next favourable period beginning June 17 and lasting only until June 21. But during that period there would be no moon, while on the night of June 5–6 the moon would be full, illuminating the channel for the crossing and assisting the air force in locating their bomb targets and paratroop drop zones.[39]

On the evening of June 4, General Dwight D. Eisenhower and his commanders-in-chief met in the library of Southwick House in Portsmouth, SHAEF headquarters since May 29. SHAEF Chief Meteorological Adviser, Royal Air Force Group Captain J.M. Stagg, was grim. "No one could have imagined weather charts less propitious for the greatest military operation in history as those we had before us," he later wrote. There did, however, appear to be a slight chance the weather would clear sometime late on the 5th and remain so at least through the morning of June 6. After that, the forecast grew worse by the day. That was the best Stagg could offer Eisenhower.[40]

The supreme commander looked to the others. His army commander, General Bernard Montgomery, had been willing to go on June 5 despite the weather conditions and vehemently opposed further postponement. Admiral Bertram Ramsay and Air Marshal Trafford Leigh-Mallory were both hesitant, with the latter gravely worried about the likelihood that air operations would be impossible or difficult because of heavy cloud.[41] Leigh-Mallory's enthusiasm for Operation Overlord had been waning steadily as the launch date approached.

Perhaps more than any other commander-in-chief, the air marshal feared disaster. Only the week before, he had argued for cancellation of the airborne operation because the heavy casualties in planes and men predicted for the initial drop was unacceptably high. And there was the probability that the airborne divisions would face annihilation if the amphibious landings failed or the beach assault forces were seriously delayed in reaching them. Eisenhower had remained resolute that the airborne plan must be carried through despite the risks. The role these divisions would play in screening the beaches from immediate counterattacks was critical to success.

Leigh-Mallory again leaned towards cancellation. He suggested the decision be delayed until early in the morning to give the meteorologists more forecasting time. Eisenhower said they would reconvene at 0415 hours. Stagg consulted a clutch of weather forecasters by telephone conference at 0300 hours and was presented with a host of wildly diverging predictions. By the time some consensus was agreed upon, he had to dash directly to the library.

Eisenhower and the rest looked sombre when he rushed in. Stagg told them there would be fair weather throughout southern England during the night of June 5 and that this front should last "into the late forenoon or afternoon of Tuesday [June 6]. Visibility would be good, wind force 3 mostly and not exceeding force 4 to 5 along the Normandy coast."[42]

Again Eisenhower polled his commanders. Montgomery was impatient to get on with it. Ramsay deferred to Leigh-Mallory. The air marshal pondered a moment and then slowly stated that although the conditions were poor he was willing to proceed. Eisenhower nodded and then said: "I don't see how we can possibly do anything else."[43]

PART TWO

BATTLE FOR THE BEACH

[8]

No Bands or Cheering Crowds

AT 0455 HOURS ON Monday, June 5—less than fifteen minutes after General Dwight D. Eisenhower decided to launch Operation Overlord—Commodore G.N. Oliver and Major General Rod Keller, both waiting anxiously aboard HMS *Hilary*, were ordered by Supreme Headquarters, Allied Expeditionary Force to set sail.[1] The commanders of Force J and 3rd Canadian Infantry Division immediately released their own orders to ensure that all ships were fully loaded and ready to head for Normandy in accordance with a complex schedule of timed departures based on the speed of each class of vessel.

Aboard Landing Ship, Infantry HMS *Brigadier,* anchored off the Isle of Cowes, North Shore (New Brunswick) Regiment's Roman Catholic Padre Miles Hickey anxiously watched a bleak dawn break. Whitecapped waves whipped hard by a strong wind pitched the large ship from one side to another and Hickey worried that the invasion would again be cancelled or delayed. Going below, he found the officers' quarters packed with men tensely awaiting the verdict. He imagined every one of the thousand soldiers crowded into the ship's berths was waiting with bated breath. A short while later, Major G.E. Lockwood, the North Shore's second-in-command, walked in and said simply, "It's on." An audible sigh of relief passed through the room and young men turned to each other and grinned or shook hands.

Although it was less than twenty-four hours since Sunday Mass, Hickey held another service in the early afternoon and thought every Catholic soldier and sailor aboard attended. Aware that many of the kneeling soldiers were undoubtedly receiving their last Holy Communion, he put his heart and soul into delivering the service and thought he had never done better.[2]

"Church services are held on practically all craft," the 19th Field Regiment, Royal Canadian Army war diarist noted.[3] The Canadian Scottish Regiment's Protestant chaplain, thirty-two-year-old Anglican Reverend Robert Lowder Seaborn, managed to hold individual services aboard the three ships over which the Canadian Scottish Regiment was scattered. Then, like thousands of other Canadian troops aboard the ships, he wrote letters home—two, in fact, both to his wife, Mary Elizabeth, called Betty.

"I can't help being proud to be in on this show with such a grand lot of men," he wrote. "They are so steady and trustworthy and ready for the job they have to do.

"If anything should happen to me," he added with palpable reluctance, "so that I don't return, it will bring so much sorrow and pain to you, such added burdens with Dickie and John and Jane dependent on you. But you will work your way through it and come out stronger and steadier, with your faith tried and tested and not found wanting."[4]

In his later letter, the chaplain added, "Don't think of this as an 'in case' letter, because it isn't. It's just to write you tonight while I have the opportunity and to let you know that I am well and happy and quite content to be here—not to say a bit excited. . . . Always remember that no news is good news."[5]

Seaborn's attempt to reassure his wife while also bracing her for the worst was common to the letter writers. It fell to the platoon officers to read their men's letters to ensure no military secrets were betrayed. Queen's Own Rifles Lieutenant John D. McLean found that most said little more than "good night and good luck." But one soldier apologized to his mother so heartrendingly for every misdeed, whether real or imagined, and then emotionally thanked her for raising him so well. Disturbed by the morbid tone, McLean visited the man in his bunk to cheer him up. The soldier grimly predicted his death in the morrow. McLean countered that if he survived the letter would only cause his mother undue anguish. But the soldier refused to take back the pages or to write another version. Finally, he consented to McLean's holding the letter and mailing it only in the event of his death. Back in his own quarters, the officer carefully tucked the letter inside the palm-sized edition of the New Testament that he carried in the left breast pocket of his battle jacket. He then joined the other platoon officers from 'B' Company in a game of hearts and quickly lost all his French francs to Lieutenant Hank Elliot.[6]

Always a good time-killer during the long periods of waiting that were a soldier's lot, gambling helped many pass the tedious hours until their ship sailed. Equally popular, and not merely a diversion, was the cleaning of weapons and final adjusting of gear. Then there were assigned tasks that rammed home the imminence of approaching combat, such as the need for the troops in the infantry battalions to prime their grenades.

Despite the fact that a first round of seasickness pills was distributed in the morning, most of the men were not bothered by the ship motion as long as the vessels remained at anchor, so much thought was given to last meals before entering a combat zone. While those troops aboard the former ocean or channel liners dined well on food whipped up by the ship cooks, the LCIS and LCTS lacked kitchens, so the men aboard them had to break open composite ration boxes and scour them for the tastiest offerings.

In the early afternoon, the slower LCTS, LCIS, and LSIS weighed anchor. The craft bearing the Highland Light Infantry sailed at 1330 hours with the war diarist noting: "There were no bands or cheering crowds to give us a send off on the biggest military operation in history. A few dockworkers silently waved good-bye. Friends called farewell and bon voyage from one craft to another. A few craft blew their whistles and up on the bridge Sagan the piper played 'The Road of the Isles.' The 9th 'Highland' Brigade was on its way."[7]

They sailed into the midst of a vast armada of ships jockeying for position and also into a rising wind that "tossed the tiny craft about like straw—necessitating a second issue of pills." At 1600 hours, the ship bearing the Highland Light Infantry was deemed far enough out to sea for the true invasion maps to be broken out and distributed to the officers. A briefing of the troops ensued, but the war diarist thought it good that—except for the true names of objectives being provided—the plans remained unchanged, "as many were too seasick to evoke much interest. As night bore down the sea got worse. Many spent the night on the deck in a driving rain—just to save time. Others lay below in a miserable heap and evoked the gods that be to do their worst as nothing could be any worse. Few were interested in eating that night—a sure proof of their misery. Those leaning over the rail lost complete faith in the effectiveness of seasick pills—and that's not all they lost."[8]

First Hussars tanker Lieutenant Bill McCormick's troopers had a cooker set up in the front of their LCT and were trying to concoct a stew for dinner. But once the ship rounded the Isle of Wight and entered the English Channel, every fifth wave broached the bow, swamping the flame. Anyone trying to relight it ended up drenched. Finally, McCormick told the men to forget about the cooker and make do with cold rations. Finding anywhere dry to sleep was impossible. When darkness fell, the lieutenant bedded down on his tank's back deck.[9]

Rifleman Jack Martin was particularly susceptible to seasickness. His cross-Atlantic voyage as a replacement bound from Halifax to Britain in April 1942 had been horrible, as had all amphibious exercises since. This voyage, however, seemed even more hellish. Martin and his mates were mortarmen in the Queen's Own Rifles Support Company's No. 3 Platoon, which was to land after the battalion's initial assault companies and follow the advance inland in their Bren carriers. Being mechanized meant crossing the channel aboard an LCT rather than a more comfortable and seaworthy liner. With a following wave pitching up the bow as the last one lifted the stern, the flat-bottomed craft seemed to literally buckle inward at the centre every few seconds. The deck was awash with several inches of saltwater. "I'm going to be awfully sick," an increasingly queasy Martin warned a nearby sailor. The man looked at him pityingly and then said, "Listen, why don't you lay up on the gunwale by the ramp door and then if you have to be sick just let it go overboard." Martin took his suggestion and was repeatedly ill, but also found the air fresher than down on the deck and imagined he might live after all. But, God, he wanted to get on that beach and off this damned sea. Dying could be no worse.[10]

Aboard Landing Craft Infantry, Large 262 Lieutenant Peter Hinton thought the stiff southwesterly wind hammering the invasion fleet was undoubtedly the cause of the "most massive case of seasickness in history." When he went below to check on the North Nova Scotia Highlanders jammed in the tight troop spaces below decks, he found the conditions "ghastly." But there was nothing he could do to lessen their misery except keep his craft plodding eastward into the gathering night.[11]

FIVE MILES AHEAD of the main armada, 255 Allied minesweepers and dan-buoy layers divided into ten flotillas were clearing wide channels within which the invasion forces were to travel in closely organized columns. That German-laid minefields existed along "the whole length of the Channel south of latitude 50° N to within ten miles of the French coast" was known, but intelligence had been unable to accurately pinpoint precise locations. Consequently, the largest minesweeping operation in history was required to ensure that the invasion fleet approached the Normandy coast unscathed. Initially, the invasion fleet was broken into five columns with one bound directly towards each landing beach. Upon reaching the German minefield zone, each column would split in two, with ships capable of twelve knots entering one swept channel and those able to achieve only five knots the other.[12]

Sixteen Canadian minesweepers were involved in the sweeping operation. Ten comprised the 31st Minesweeping Flotilla under command of Acting Commander Tony Storrs, while the six others had been divvied out among three British flotillas. The thirty-seven-year-old Storrs was worried sick that his flotilla might stray off course and cause the American ships following closely behind not to draw up precisely in front of Omaha Beach. Accurately navigating a course across the channel in darkness with a strong cross-tide that was attempting to shove the vessels sideways posed a formidable task, particularly as minesweeping flotillas were highly unwieldy. Taking up position on the extreme starboard boundary of the channel, Storrs's ship, HMCS *Caraquet*, led the formation. Eight hundred yards astern of *Caraquet* and two hundred yards to port followed *Fort William*. Maintaining the same distances and bearings from *Fort William* was *Wasaga*. Then came *Cowichan, Minas,* and *Malpeque*. Known as a 'G' Formation, this positioning of the minesweepers enabled each leading ship to cover the one behind with its sweeping wire, while ensuring that the entire breadth of the designated channel was swept.

Sailing astern of *Fort William* was the British armed trawler *Green Howard*, which dropped dan buoys fitted with a flag and a battery-powered light. Each light was spaced a mile apart and served to indicate the outer starboard perimeter of the channel to the following fleet. Astern of *Malpeque*, *Bayfield* performed the same function on the port flank. To the rear of the actively sweeping ships trailed *Milltown, Blairmore,* and *Mulgrave*—serving as reserve vessels in the event that one of the others suffered an equipment breakdown or was damaged by enemy action and needed to be replaced. Another British trawler, *Gunner,* was also present as the reserve dan layer.[13]

Were he forced to rely purely on standard navigational skills, Storrs knew some off-course drift would be inevitable. Fortunately, he had the help of a top-secret electronic gadget of which there were supposedly only ten in the entire world—one mounted in the bridge of each minesweeping flotilla commander's ship. Known as QH2, the device measured the differing pulse rates transmitted from three transmitting stations and presented the information on a cathode ray tube scope. When the readings were plotted on a special chart that provided the transmitter coordinates, it was possible for Storrs to accurately maintain his course. Or so he hoped. The final confirmation would come only when his ship neared Omaha Beach, for standing off its shores was a midget submarine that would flash a recognition beacon as the sweepers drew near. Finding the midget where it was supposed to be would tell him he had maintained the proper course.

Storrs did not wish to think about what it would mean if the midget were not to be seen.

Because *Caraquet* was stationed on the tip of the 'G' Formation, it was the only minesweeper in the flotilla that faced real peril during the channel crossing. To provide some measure of protection, a small British motor launch preceded its passage, but the launch's sweeping wire was too light to be effective and would only serve to provide a last-minute warning should mines be encountered. It was going to be a nerve-wracking night, but so far, except for a brief calamity as the flotilla had left harbour, things seemed to be proceeding like clock-work.[14] As the ships had weighed anchor, HMCS *Wasaga,* standing on *Bayfield*'s port bow, suddenly went full astern instead of full ahead and backed into *Bayfield* with a mighty crash. Although *Wasaga* suffered no more than a bend in her port quarter, *Bayfield*'s stern plate broke above the water line and two holes opened below. At first, it looked as if the ship might not be able to sail, but her engineer officer and his crew managed to shore up the broken bulkhead and then rig collision mats over the holes in her bow. *Bayfield* soon caught up to the rest of the flotilla and the operation got underway on schedule.[15]

"We have a big hole in our bow and shipped quite a good deal of water, but nevertheless this is it," Telegraphist Stan Richardson wrote in his diary on June 5. "Closed up to battle stations at I PM and wore our anti-flash gear, tin helmets, life-jackets, and gas masks. Also given Field First Aid Kits and RCN ration tins. No sleep for any-one. Laid red-lighted Dan Buoys every eight minutes. Transports rendezvoused with us at II PM."[16]

By late evening of June 5, the weather had cleared, although the sea continued to be whipped into high waves by the hard wind. In Weymouth Harbour, HMCS *Camrose* remained at anchor, for its part in the invasion was not to take place until June 7, when the small corvette would escort two tugs towing the decrepit French battleship *Courbet* to the Normandy coast. The *Courbet* was not bound for battle. Rather, it was to be sunk as part of a breakwater to shelter one of two artificial harbours the Allies planned to begin constructing immediately after the invasion beaches were secured. The fact that the Allies were capable of building such harbours, known as Mulberries, was a closely guarded secret. As long as the Germans believed the Allies could only bring major volumes of reinforcements and supplies ashore through an existing French port, the probability of an invasion at Pas de Calais would continue to be suspected and the Normandy landings hopefully dismissed as a feint.

The Mulberries were essentially a prefabricated harbour, the components of which could be towed across the channel and then linked together like pieces of a Meccano set. Each Mulberry consisted of 146 concrete caissons that were two hundred feet long but varied in size according to the depth of water in which they were to be sunk. The smallest displaced 1,672 tons of ocean and the largest 6,044 tons. Attached buoyancy chambers rendered them light and floatable for the cross-channel crossing to their deployment position, whereupon the chambers would be flooded to sink them in place on the seabed. Once the Mulberries were in place, fifty-eight blockships—including *Courbet*—were to be sunk to provide 24,000 feet of breakwater to shelter the vulnerable harbours from damage by gales.

Whereas the Mulberries would provide an immediate point for rapid offloading of troops and supplies, the Allies had developed another means for feeding the insatiable appetite the invading armies would have for fuel. Codenamed Pluto, the fuel-delivery system consisted of ten pipelines that were to be laid across the channel from Sandown Bay on the Isle of Wight to Querqueville, west of Cherbourg, as soon as the French village was captured by American troops. In the meantime, four pipelines would be laid in two sectors fronting the invasion beaches to an offshore mooring point sufficiently deep to accommodate a large fuel tanker. The tanker would hook up to one of the pipelines and be able to pump its load ashore at a rate of six hundred tons per hour.[17]

Leading Signalman I.J. Gillen had learned the role *Camrose* was to play in protecting *Courbet* for its passage to the Normandy coast and the reason for it on June 4. Until then, the Canadian sailors had been baffled as to why their fast fighting ship was playing nursemaid to a barely seaworthy ship clearly overdue for the scrap yard. *Courbet* had in fact been only recently raised from a watery grave, having been scuttled in a French African port at the time of the French surrender to Germany. Having been mostly submerged for several years, the mark of the waterline could still be detected on the 22,000-ton ship's towering foremast. *Courbet* remained a rusting hulk with the barrels of her formerly large main guns hacked off at the turrets.

Standing on the *Camrose*'s deck looking over at the "dead ship," Gillen suddenly heard a great roar of engines at 2340 hours. "Out of the dusk, over the hills they came," he later wrote, "flying low—bombers, troop transports, gliders in tow, in groups of 35 to 50. Each plane was burning red and green side lights, white light in tail, and bright white Morse light under the fuselage. The combined effect of these made each group look like a cluster of brilliant jewels floating through space. Hour after hour, through the night, they roared off into the darkness; and the sight of them, the thought that here was history being made, found most of us with little to say."[18]

PRECISELY TEN MINUTES before Leading Signalman Gillen spotted the aircraft passing overhead, 'C' Company of 1st Canadian Parachute Battalion had lifted off from Harwell Field aboard fourteen bombers as part of the leading wave of planes headed for Normandy. Each Albemarle carried a ten-man stick. The paratroops were so heavily laden with equipment they could hardly manage more than an awkward waddle, and finding a comfortable sitting position in the cramped bomber had proven impossible. The authorized kit weight, including parachute, was seventy pounds. But most of the men had increased this by an average of 50 per cent. Sewing extra pockets onto the outside legs of their pants and to the front of the British-issue Denison camouflage smocks made it possible to double the allotment of ammunition and grenades—running out of ammunition being the soldiers' greatest fear. Some had also stuffed the fabric kit bag with additional munitions despite warnings that this could result in the twenty-foot-long rope connecting the paratrooper's leg to the lowered kit during the descent snapping under the increased weight.[19]

With the men so overloaded, the Albemarles struggled off the runways with difficulty. Corporal Dan Hartigan aboard the second plane aloft had listened anxiously to the straining engines as the plane clawed its way up to the designated cruising altitude. Once it levelled off, the men started checking each other's kits one last time to make sure everything was properly stowed. "Get it fucking done and be fucking careful, too," Sergeant Harvey Morgan bellowed. Particular care was taken to ensure that primed explosives were positioned well clear of anything that might hook a detonating pin when the jump time came. "No accidents, please!" Morgan added in a mocking tone.[20]

Hartigan had never seen a wilder looking group of men than his fellow paratroops this night. Everywhere you looked there were rifles, Bren guns, stubby-looking Sten submachine guns, and sheathed fighting knives. Coiled and attached to their web belts was a six-foot-length of rope with a toggle on one end. All exposed skin had been blackened with charcoal, and burlap rags were tied into the camouflage netting of the helmets to break the distinctive outline. Inside the space between the head harness and the helmet the men had jammed spare cigarette packs or, for those intent on using every available square inch as a munitions dump, small plugs of plastic explosive.

The corporal was glad his mates looked tough and ready. He figured they needed every bit of grit and a healthy measure of luck to boot if they were going to get through the coming night alive. As he understood it, an attacker should have three-to-one odds in his favour to have a good chance of victory. Yet every briefing had predicted the paratroops would be fighting at one-to-one odds.[21]

Equipment check concluded, Hartigan wormed awkwardly into the bomber's tail section where a Plexiglas window in the floor offered a view. No sooner was he in place than the bomber bumped upward on a pocket of air, a telltale sign it had just passed from landward out over the sea. Below, the white cliffs of Dover seemed so close he might be able to touch them. Then the plane dropped almost down onto the water and skimmed along the surface to escape detection by German radar. Hartigan was awestruck to be looking up at the

great chalk cliffs for a few minutes before being swallowed by darkness. To the southeast, the moon gleamed bright and sky and sea
seemed to meld into a uniform midnight blue.[22]

Farther back in the bomber column, Lieutenant John Madden
pondered the events of the Catholic Mass he had attended earlier.
Prior to the service, each paratrooper had been issued with packets of
condoms for no better reason Madden could determine than that
German paratroops had carried such things when they jumped on
Crete. Once the Catholic paratroops had gathered in a large marquis
tent to take Holy Communion from the 3rd Brigade's Irish padre, the
man "started fulminating about how we would go to meet our deaths
having in our pockets the means of mortal sin. When we got up and
marched out at the end of the service the ground was littered with
discarded safes. The men, in their very suggestible state, had discarded them and I was one of those who put the means of temptation
aside."[23]

Perhaps, he thought, it was that same suggestible state that had
turned a small incident on the flight line into something that continued to trouble his mind. As Madden had been preparing to climb into
the Albemarle, Lieutenant Colonel G.F. Bradbrooke came up. "Good-
bye, John," he said simply, and then walked on down the flight line.
Madden wondered why Bradbrooke had picked this occasion to
address him by his given name for the first time.[24]

FLIGHT TIME TO Drop Zone V was ninety minutes and 'C' Company
had been allowed an hour's head start on the rest of 1st Canadian
Parachute Battalion, which would take off from Down Ampney Field.
By the time the battalion arrived over the Drop Zone, 'C' Company
was to have it secured and the pathfinders from the British 22nd Independent Parachute Company—jumping alongside 'C' Company—
to have it marked with Eureka beacons that emitted both a light and
radio signal to guide the planes in.

At 2325 hours, thirty-nine C-47 Dakotas lifted off, carrying 725
troops. Not all of these paratroops were Canadian, for Brigadier
James Hill's 3rd Parachute Brigade Headquarters' Company and
some ancillary British troops were also jumping onto Drop Zone V.

Three of the planes towed gliders carrying jeeps and trailers filled with ammunition and signals equipment.[25] Including the men from 'C' Company, well ahead in the Albemarles, 27 officers and 516 Canadian other ranks were bound for the night drop into Normandy. Also headed for Drop Zone V were 540 men of British 9th Parachute Battalion and eleven Horsa gliders loaded with jeeps, demolition charges, and other heavy equipment that had departed from other airfields.[26]

The Albemarles bearing Company 'C' approached the Normandy coast in the company of 1,135 Allied bombers sent to attack ten German coastal artillery batteries capable of firing on the invasion beaches. By bombing the batteries in tandem with the drop of the leading parachute companies, Allied planners hoped the Germans would remain unaware that an assault by airborne troops was underway until the entire 6th British Airborne Division was on the ground and closing on its many objectives. No. 6 Group, Royal Canadian Air Force, flew 230 of these bomber sorties, with their primary targets the batteries situated east of Sword Beach at Merville, Franceville, Houlgate, and Longues. Scattered low-lying cloud obscured the targets, but the crews wanted to believe their explosives fell on target. In reality, however, most landed well wide of the mark. The Merville Battery was merely shaken, at Longues only one of four guns was silenced, and the other two batteries were untouched. The Luftwaffe offered no resistance against the massive raids and anti-aircraft fire claimed only one Canadian crew.[27]

While most of Bomber Command was raiding vital strategic and tactical targets, 617 Squadron—the Dam Busters—engaged in a complicated deception mission, codenamed Operation Taxable, intended to dupe German radar operators into believing an Allied invasion fleet was bound for Pas de Calais. RCAF Flight Officer Donald Cheney was piloting one of the squadron's Lancasters that departed the English coast shortly after midnight and followed a precise course towards a potential landing beach lying between le Touquet just south of Boulogne and Fécamp to the northeast of le Havre. Several planes flew in a well-spaced line at a precise altitude of three thousand feet and a speed of 116 knots. Crammed into every available inch of space inside the planes were bundles of various shapes and sizes of long silver foil strips known as Window or Chaff. When dropped, Window confused radar detection equipment, making it impossible for the Germans to tell whether the signals they were picking up were real or phantom ships.

Each Lancaster had twice its normal complement of crew members because of the difficulty manhandling the Window bundles in the tight confines over to the flare chute, through which one bundle after another was launched in a continuous stream into the night sky. Also aboard was an airman designated a Window Master, who used a chart to determine which type of bundle was to be cast out at a specific point in the flight. As the planes drew ever closer to the French coast, the Window bundles grew larger and were composed of wider strips in order to simulate the greater radar profile an approaching convoy of ships would radiate as it drew nearer. The stream of Window had to be constant or an alert radar detection technician might note the brief gap in detected signal and realize this was a ruse rather than a real invasion fleet. The requirement that the plane maintain precisely the same altitude and speed throughout the entire two-and-a-half-hour flight was so demanding for pilot and co-pilot that two of each were aboard. At the halfway point, Cheney and Flight Engineer Sergeant J. Rosher were to hand off to their counterparts.

At a designated point off the French coast, the planes banked to port and retraced their path while still releasing less heavy Window bundles to produce a less strong signal and maintain the illusion of a convoy still closing on the coast at a speed of 8 knots. Following in Cheney's wake was another Lancaster that replaced his plane at the front of "the convoy" while the Canadian pilot flew back towards England and then looped back along the original flight path while continuously launching Window. During each subsequent rotation, the planes flew closer to the French coast and turned back on themselves farther away from England so the Window signal appeared to have a tail as well as a head.

When it came time for Cheney and his co-pilot to hand off to the other flight deck team, the flight officer could hardly lever himself out of the seat, his muscles were so stiff and fatigued. His men were also beginning to reel with exhaustion as they dragged thousands upon thousands of pounds of Window to the launcher. When the mission ended and the planes returned safely to England, most of the men could barely walk.

Cheney had no way of knowing if the deception worked, but he thought the entire operation brilliantly conceived and executed. He was particularly proud that it had been three RCAF officers in the squadron—Don Maclean, Hugh Monroe, and Danny Walker, the 617's navigation leader—who masterminded the plan.[28]

Also in the air this night was twenty-four-year-old Flight Lieutenant Thomas G. Anderson of the RCAF's 418 City of Edmonton Night Intruder Squadron. He had lifted off from a base at Holmsley South in Hampshire piloting a Mosquito MK VI that packed a payload of fifteen thousand pounds in bombs. Anderson's navigator was Flight Officer Frank Cadman. The two men had flown twenty-four missions together—mostly attacks on German airfields scattered across France, Germany, Belgium, Holland, and Denmark. All but 5 of the 92.5 hours flying time racked up on these missions had been under the cloak of darkness.

Their mission was to patrol the area of the airborne drop zones and bomb or strafe any searchlights or flak positions discovered—normally targets they went out of the way to avoid in order to escape detection by the enemy. But having been personally briefed by Brigadier General Paul Williams, who commanded the American troop-carrier contingent carrying U.S. Airborne troops into Normandy's airspace, Anderson and Cadman so recognized the mission's importance that they "might well have flown to hell for him."

Soon after arriving in the assigned patrol sector, Anderson's Mosquito ran into a hornet's nest of flak streaking up at it from several anti-aircraft batteries. At least one shell hit the plane hard, but no serious damage was noted. The two spent another thirty minutes searching for enemy targets. After locating and strafing several flak guns, the two flyers decided that at least one 20-millimetre gun position had been destroyed. They had failed, however, to identify a target worthy of the bomb load.

Normally such explosives would have been dumped over the Channel during the return flight, but the water below their plane was so choked with ships sailing towards Normandy they could identify no safe place over which to jettison the bombs. Deciding they must land with the bombs aboard, Anderson returned to base. As the Mosquito touched down on the runway, the starboard undercarriage leg, which, unknown to them, had been badly damaged by the flak, collapsed and the plane crash-landed. Neither Anderson nor Cadman were injured, but as they crawled out of the wreckage the Mosquito started to burn. Remembering the fifteen-thousand-pound bomb load, the two men "ran like hell" away from the wreckage. Moments later, a crash tender arrived and its crew put out the fire, but the plane was damaged beyond repair.[29]

WHETHER SUCH DECEPTIONS as Operation Taxable confused the Germans as to the timing and location of the invasion was something Allied intelligence was unable to establish through its Ultra intercepts or other means. In fact, neither Generalfeldmarschall Gerd von Rundstedt's headquarters staff nor that of Generalfeldmarschall Erwin Rommel had any suspicion an invasion was underway until the first paratroops started landing. No warning orders had been issued and Operation Neptune's vast armada closed on the Normandy coast without detection—in large part due to bombing attacks against several coastal radar stations and the massive Window operations that created a virtual box of screening chaff around the ships. Remarkably, the heavy bombing raids against coastal batteries and radar stations in Normandy combined with the unusual disruption of clear radar reception in the English Channel failed to trigger any alarms.[30]

So sanguine were the Germans that Seventh Army convened a much-delayed map exercise in Rennes, Brittany on June 5. Most divisional and regimental commanders were present for the exercise, which dealt with a theoretical repelling of an invasion by airborne forces.[31] Rennes was about two hundred kilometres from the Normandy beaches and a good three-hour drive away. Missing from the exercise was Generalleutnant Edgar Feuchtinger, who had slipped away from 21st Panzer Division headquarters to spend the night in Paris with a female friend. Accompanying him to Paris was the division's senior staff officer, which left Hauptmann (Captain) Eberhard Wagemann as acting divisional commander. Also absent was ss Generaloberst Josef (Sepp) Dietrich, who commanded 1st ss Panzer Corps. He was on leave in Brussels.[32]

For his part, Rommel had deemed it safe to travel on June 5 to Germany with two purposes in mind. He wanted to press Hitler to post more Panzer divisions to Normandy and also planned to attend his wife's birthday at their home near Ulm.[33]

Although the Germans appreciated the possibility of an invasion sometime during favourable tide conditions of June 4–7, the adverse weather had convinced their intelligence and meteorological staff that the night of June 5–6 would pass without incident. This assurance had been passed to all divisional commands and from there down to the various regimental headquarters. Major Hans von Luck, commander of the 21st Panzer Division's 125th Panzer Grenadier Regiment, had received an "all clear" order on June 4 for the next two days and no revisions were issued on June 5. The thirty-two-year-old von Luck had his headquarters in a poorly furnished house on the edge of the village of Bellengreville, just outside of Vimont to the east of Caen. Throughout the day, there had been rain and high winds. He "did not anticipate any landings, for heavy seas, storms, and low lying clouds would make large scale operations at sea and in the air impossible."[34]

Since the division's reformation in Rennes on July 15, 1943, von Luck had been at pains to ensure his regiment retained a battle-hardened edge despite soft duty on the French coast. Many of his men were combat veterans who had escaped from Tunisia when the 21st Panzer Division and the rest of the Afrika Korps had been virtually destroyed. The division had been bulked up with a hodgepodge of troops transferred from other units during its reformation. Most of these soldiers were castoffs that other unit commanders had been only too happy to be rid of. Despite this reinforcement, each regiment had only sufficient manpower to form two battalions rather than the authorized strength of three.

The regimental commanders, including von Luck, had been hard at work trying to fashion an effective fighting force through a relentless regimen of combat training and battle exercises. In addition to honing the men's fighting skills, the major believed such exercises bolstered morale—although he had to admit the cushy life in Normandy was equally good for morale, particularly the regular access to "butter, cheese, *crème fraîche* and meat, as well as cider."

Midnight found von Luck at a table covered with maps and papers rather than edible delicacies. The documents related to an exercise his 2nd Battalion was just concluding between the communities of Troarn and Escoville, about seven miles from the coast. To the east, this area was bordered by a marshy swamp created when the Germans flooded farmland adjacent to the River Dives by breaching its banks just before its mouth at Houlgate. The canalized section of the River Orne and parallel-running Canal de Caen, which provided access by ship from the coast to Caen, formed the area's western boundary.

The regiment's 1st Battalion was scattered by companies into holding positions closer to Bellengreville. This battalion was "equipped with armoured personnel carriers and armoured half-track vehicles." Although he expected no attack this night, von Luck had earlier issued a standing order that "in the event of possible landings by Allied commando troops, the battalions and companies were to attack immediately and independently."[35]

Just after midnight, the major "heard the growing roar of aircraft, which passed over us. I wondered whether the attack was destined once again for traffic routes inland or for Germany herself. The machines appeared to be flying very low—because of the weather? I looked out the window and was wide-awake; flares were hanging in the sky. At the same moment, my adjutant was on the telephone. 'Major, paratroops are dropping. Gliders are landing in our section.'" Immediately, von Luck put the regiment on alert, instructed the commander of 2nd Battalion to "go into action wherever necessary," and alerted divisional headquarters, only to learn that both Feuchtinger and his senior staff officer were absent. Hauptmann Wagemann had no new orders for von Luck, but reiterated a standing Seventh Army order that the Panzer divisions were not to get tangled into combat engagements without first receiving clearance from von Rundstedt's headquarters. This order was to prevent the mechanized divisions becoming entangled in actions against diversionary forces and being unavailable when the major invasion happened.

The major desperately wanted to immediately counterattack what he recognized as the beginning of the invasion, but without authorization from divisional command he could only manoeuvre his regiment to effectively engage the paratroops that were moving in his direction. He hoped in that way to at least button them up until orders were issued that would allow the 21st Panzer Division to crush the paratroopers entirely.[36]

Von Luck knew the fight for Normandy was on.

[9]

Stick to the Objective

A FEW MINUTES BEFORE midnight on June 5, the pilots of the Albemarle bombers bearing 1st Canadian Parachute Battalion's 117 men of 'C' Company throttled back and the lead man in each stick began unbolting the hatch. Aboard the bomber that was second in line, Corporal Dan Hartigan pulled the hatch back and saw water shimmering in the moonlight off to his right. This must be part of the flooded farmland adjacent to the River Dives, he realized, and the dark rectangular shapes neatly dividing the water into regular sections must be the hedgerows used by Norman farmers to mark their field boundaries. The positioning of the flooded fields reassured Hartigan that their plane was on course and should any moment pass over the lock-gates of the Canal de Caen preparatory to a swing eastward for the final approach to Drop Zone V, southwest of the village of Varaville.

Behind Hartigan, Private Gilbert Comeau patted a pocket of his smock only to discover he had forgotten his cigarettes. Turning to Private Bill Middleton, he pleaded, "Jesus, gimme a cigarette, Middy." Middleton told him he was nuts and would blow them all up if he lit a cigarette inside the bomber. "I don't mean for now," Comeau yelled back over the roar of the engines and the wind blasting through the hatch, "but I'm crackin' and I want it for the first chance I get when we're on the ground."

Jerking off his helmet, Middleton fished a pack of Sweet Caps from under the lining and passed it to Comeau. "Here, take the whole damn package for good luck. You might need it. And if you live long enough to smoke 'em all, you might stand a chance of coming back."[1] Then the red warning light blinked on and Hartigan, number two in the jump line after Corporal Myles Saunders, fixed his eye on the display in readiness to tap Saunders on the shoulder the moment it flashed from red to green.

At six minutes before midnight on June 5, the red light in the lead bomber winked out and the green one came on. Privates Peter Bismutka and H.B. "Sinkor" Swim plunged shoulder-to-shoulder into the night sky, moments later becoming the first Canadians and among the first Allied troops to touch down in Normandy.[2] The entire stick cleared the Albemarle in twenty seconds and landed close together right on the drop zone.

Instead of landing mere seconds later just a short distance away, Hartigan's stick were still aboard the plane waiting for the jump light to come on. When it did, however, Private Middleton shouted in the corporal's ear: "Okay, Hartigan, I'm right on your back, see you on the lower deck!" Hartigan threw himself out of the plane and as the static line yanked the parachute canopy open had an immediate sensation "of absolute, irrevocable commitment—no going back!" A feeling of almost giddy exhilaration washed over him. "Oh, my God, what have I done?" Hartigan moaned and started whispering the Lord's Prayer while at the same time reflexively responding to his training by looking around carefully to get oriented. Some way off, Hartigan spotted what he thought must be the J-shaped hedge where the company was to rendezvous near the Grand Château de Varaville. No sooner had he fixed that detail in his mind than, "slashing through the outer limbs of an apple tree I slammed into the plank back door of a Frenchman's house, landing flat on my buttocks on his stoop." There was no response from inside to his literally dropping in on the homeowner's doorstep.[3]

Close by, Middleton whacked into a large deciduous tree. Parachute tangled in overhead branches, one foot jammed and bent at a ninety-degree angle against the trunk by the joint of a branch, the private dangled helplessly. With each passing second, the trapped ankle became more badly swollen, making it increasingly difficult to wriggle free. Middleton would remain pinned there until being spotted and taken prisoner by some Germans on June 7.

Saunders, Hartigan, and Middleton were the only men in the stick to make dry landings. The other seven floated down into the flooded country and were left struggling for their lives in the mucky morass under the weight of equipment and collapsing parachute canopies. Everyone in the stick was badly scattered, groping individually through the black night towards the drop zone. What had seemed a perfectly executed jump had quickly deteriorated into chaos.[4]

Hardly any planes were releasing their sticks over Drop Zone V. During the channel crossing, the Albemarles had maintained a loose formation, but the moment they crossed the coast German anti-aircraft guns had opened up with streams of fire and the planes scattered. When tracers started cracking past the plane carrying Captain John P. Hanson, 'C' Company's second-in-command, just fifteen feet to the right, the pilot "immediately swung left and we were thrown violently about. When we sorted ourselves out I could see that we had changed our direction and the coast was on my right. We swung inland further down the coast, resulting in my stick being dropped about ten miles off the DZ."[5]

Hanson landed in waist-deep water. After struggling out of his parachute harness, he looked and saw an aircraft with one engine on fire passing overhead. The captain followed the stricken Albemarle's passage inland for about ten miles before it nose-dived to the ground. Hanson hoped the Canadians aboard had managed to jump safely before the plane crashed.[6]

Sergeant W.R. Kelly, an exceptionally strong miner from Kirkland, Ontario, had ended up near the base of a dead tree with his legs entangled in the parachute lines so that he hung upside down with his head submerged in an icy pool. Having strapped eighty pounds of gear to his body, he was unable to right himself. Every measure of his great strength was required just to perform a slight neck crunch to free his head from the water for a few precious seconds in which to suck in fresh drafts of air. Just as Kelly's strength was failing and he became resigned to drowning, some men from his stick arrived and cut him free.[7]

Due to a mix-up in the light sequence on Lieutenant John Madden's plane, the officer and five of his men had landed on the west side of the River Orne only about 1,200 yards from the beach.[8] When it came Private Nelson MacDonald's turn to jump as number six, he inadvertently kicked the hatch partially closed, blocking the exit. In the seconds it took to frantically pull the hatch open and then twist his body out into the night, he worried the plane would carry him too far away from the front of the stick to link up with Madden. Drifting down, MacDonald watched the muzzles of anti-aircraft guns flashing in the distance and their tracers arcing into the sky. MacDonald's fears of being separated from the leading element of the stick proved unfounded, for he managed to locate Madden and the others within minutes of landing. Of the four men who should have jumped right after him, however, there was no sign.[9]

Unknown to MacDonald, after he wriggled through the hatch, the door had banged completely shut. While the remaining paratroopers aboard wrestled it open, the pilot circled back around to what he thought was the same point where the front of the stick had jumped. But he was miles off course and the last four men went out over the flooded area east of the Drop Zone. Two drowned and the other two were taken prisoner.

Intent on rejoining the battalion, Madden led his men at a creeping pace on an eastward track that also drew away from the beaches. Everywhere the paratroops turned, more German positions materialized out of the darkness, necessitating long delays as the men crawled around or between them. According to the divisional plan, a glider assault force was to have captured two bridges—one over the River Orne and the other the Caen Canal—that 3rd British Infantry Division coming off Sword Beach would use to link up with the paratroops. Madden estimated his position at about two miles from where the bridges crossed the waterways at the village of Bénouville. If the

glider force was successful in capturing the crossings, Madden would
be able to use them to get east of the Orne and link up with the Canadian battalion. Even though it would surely take hours of travelling
through enemy-occupied territory Madden never questioned his re-
solve to reach Varaville without delay. Paratroops, particularly the
officers, were relentlessly indoctrinated "to stick to our objective" no
matter what.[10]

STICKING TO THE OBJECTIVE was what Major Murray MacLeod intended, regardless of the fact that only sixteen other men from 'C'
Company had so far joined him at the J-shaped hedge rendezvous
point. A former bank teller from New Glasgow, Nova Scotia, MacLeod
was reputed to be the battalion's most resourceful and professional
company commander. This night, MacLeod had the good fortune to
be among the few paratroops actually landed in the right place. As he
had headed for the rendezvous, however, the bomber force attacking
Merville Battery overshot its target and loosed its ordnance onto the
drop zone and the surrounding countryside over which his company
was strewn. Several bombs struck the field right around MacLeod,
hammering him into the ground with massive concussions. When
the bomb drop ended, he staggered to the hedge, arriving there at
0030 hours. After telling the other paratroops who had assembled
there that he was suffering from severe internal pains in his chest
and stomach, MacLeod started laying out how 'C' Company's greatly
diminished ranks would carry out the assigned mission.[11]

His immediate concern was that in just thirty minutes the
remainder of 1st Canadian Parachute Battalion, the entire British 9th
Parachute Battalion, and the headquarters of 3rd Parachute Brigade
were to descend on a drop zone that was anything but secure. Smoke
and dust kicked up by the misplaced bombs had created an unnatu-
ral and impenetrable haze that hung thickly over the ground. While
the British pathfinders had dropped on target, they reported that
every one of their Eureka signal sets had broken on impact. That
meant the pilots bringing the next wave of parachutists in would
have to find the drop zone through dead reckoning, for nobody on

the ground could create any form of lighting for them. Lighting signal fires was ruled out because they would be sure to draw Germans like flies and likely be impossible to see from the air through the smoke and dust, anyway.

At the southern extremity of the drop zone, the village of Petiville was reported as sheltering several machine-gun positions, while to the east Varaville housed an artillery headquarters and right next to the nearby Grand Château de Varaville was a 75-millimetre gun position. Until these positions were wiped out, any further landings were in jeopardy. There was also a signal post and a small bridge over the River Divette, just east of Varaville, that were to have been blown up by 'C' Company within thirty minutes of landing.

The bridge had been tasked to Madden's platoon, but he and his men were among the missing. So too were all of MacLeod's other officers except for Lieutenant H.M. "Chuck" Walker. Deciding to ignore the signal post, MacLeod told Sergeant Gordon Davies to take one man with him and see what could be done about wrecking the bridge. He then ordered Walker to rush the houses at Petiville that faced the drop zone with just three men. That left an eleven-man force to tackle Varaville.

Spreading into a thin line, this main element of paratroopers swept towards the village, their immediate rally point the front of the château's grounds. With the clock ticking down to the moment the rest of the assault force would arrive, stealth was forsaken for speed. Private Peter Bismutka, MacLeod's runner, made certain to stick close to his commanding officer. Halfway to the objective, Bismutka stumbled upon six paratroopers, all still dazed and shocked after narrowly escaping being blown to bits by the bombers. MacLeod quickly turned them around, adding their number to his advancing line.

Reaching the château grounds without incident, the small force discovered that the château itself had been converted into a barracks. Although empty, many of the bunk beds inside were still warm to the touch. As MacLeod finished checking out the main building, Walker's party returned from the dash to Petiville to report that the houses there had been empty but showed signs of recent occupation. MacLeod quickly regrouped his men and they started advancing by bounds towards the château's gatehouse, with one team moving while the others provided covering fire. They moved cautiously but steadily along a wide driveway bordered by tall Lombardy poplars towards the yellow two-storey building. Meeting no resistance, they quickly occupied the building and again discovered in the rooms up- stairs recently vacated bunks.[12]

From the upstairs windows facing a road that bordered the estate grounds, MacLeod studied a nearby fortified trench system and large concrete emplacement surrounded by barbed wire. Somewhere inside that defensive work MacLeod knew was a 75-millimetre gun position, but it was impossible to make out its precise location. From the bed count in the château and gatehouse, the major estimated that the fortification was defended by between eighty and ninety-five Germans.

There was no way that just twenty lightly armed paratroops could overwhelm such a heavily defended position. Although their field kits had contained heavier weaponry, such as bangalore torpedoes, Bren guns, and PIATs, most of this equipment had been lost when the ropes attached to the men's legs had broken under the added weight of the extra ammunition they had added to the kits. Any who had suc- cessfully landed in the flood zone with kit intact had ended up aban- doning it to avoid drowning. Besides their personal weapons—either a Sten gun or rifle—the paratroopers had only one PIAT gun and an assortment of grenades.[13]

MacLeod decided their only option was to set up a perimeter around the gatehouse and prevent the Germans in the fortification from sallying out to attack the drop zone until he was reinforced and could take the offensive. He directed Walker, with twelve men, to oc- cupy a shallow ditch facing the fortification and, leaving Privates H.B. "Sinkor" Swim and Fred Rudko to guard the gatehouse's entrance- ways, went upstairs to observe the gun position with Private G. Thompson in tow. A few minutes later, Lieutenant Walker, having got his men into their positions, joined the upstairs group. The two officers peeked out of a window just in time to see a bright muzzle flash in the German position, followed a second later by a terrific explosion on the ground floor. Flying chunks of brick and plaster sprayed the two men guarding the doors there and the air filled with such thickly choking plaster dust they had to stagger outside to prevent being suffocated.

Now able to plainly see the 75-millimetre gun protected by a concrete emplacement, MacLeod sent for Corporal W.E. Oikle and told him to take a crack at knocking the German weapon out by firing on it from the second-storey window with his PIAT. When Oikle's first round fell short, he started the awkward and slow process of reloading. Private Bismutka suddenly burst into the room with news that fifteen more men had arrived. He was just finishing his report when a high-explosive shell ripped through the wall, flying shrapnel filled the room, and the explosion detonated Oikle's supply of PIAT bombs with devastating effect.

Lieutenant Walker and Oikle died instantly. MacLeod and Bismutka were gravely injured. At first thinking himself unscathed, Thompson looked down at the broken rifle cradled in his arms to see part of one hand was missing.[14] With the lower half of MacLeod's face torn away, it was clear the officer was dying. Bismutka's situation was equally desperate.

It was just after 0100 hours. Sergeant M.C. "Mosher" MacPhee, now the senior ranking soldier, took charge while medical aide Private William Ducker raced through a hail of machine-gun fire to reach the gatehouse in order to help his injured comrades. One by one, the medical aide carried MacLeod and Bismutka back through enemy fire to the château, where he had established an ad hoc aid post. For his actions in trying to save the two men, Ducker was later awarded the Military Medal.[15]

The sound of many planes throttling back their engines overhead announced the imminent arrival of the rest of the paratroops, but there was nothing the small force could do to help with the landing besides what they were already doing—keeping the Germans at the gatehouse bottled up. MacPhee frantically reorganized to mix the newly arrived men in among the survivors of the original force, with orders to fire only at targets they could see in order to save ammunition. Targets proved few and far between, though, for after hitting the gatehouse with the two 75-millimetre rounds the Germans seemed content to hunker in their holes rather than taking further offensive action.[16]

THE REMAINING ELEMENTS of 1st Canadian Parachute Battalion, the British 9th Parachute Battalion, and the headquarters of 3rd Parachute Brigade ended up scattered as badly as 'C' Company. In fact, all of 6th British Airborne Division was badly dispersed. So were the two American divisions when they landed on the opposite side of the invasion beaches at the base of the Cotentin Peninsula. An unknown number of British and Canadian paratroops drowned in the flooded area and many others barely escaped its icy waters. Most who did reach firm ground had either lost or been forced to abandon their heavier equipment. Of the twenty-six C-47 Dakotas carrying Canadian paratroops, nine dropped their sticks over the flooded zone. Five more planes gave the jump signal over Breville, a village two and a half miles west of Drop Zone V, and two (including Madden's) ended up on the west side of the River Orne. Most of the other sticks were scattered so widely afield it proved impossible after the fact to accurately determine their drop locations.[17]

While the deliberately flooded ground posed great hazard to the paratroops, dying in a watery pool or deep bog was possible anywhere in the valley between the River Dives and River Orne. Where the Germans had breached the Dives, the adjacent fields had been transformed into shallow lakes but water also flowed westward from these areas across the fields to fill the numerous irrigation ditches and shallow depressions to the brim. The water table also rose, so that the fields were dotted with freshly formed marshy bogs. It was into this quagmire that 6th British Airborne Division had been cast and the Canadians had the worst luck of all.[18]

The Dakota pilots crossed the coast and entered a maelstrom of anti-aircraft fire as the fully alert German gun crews threw up everything they had. When the pilots zigzagged wildly to dodge the rising streams of fire, the paratroops were tossed about in the back like ten-pins and many were unable to follow their mates out after the green light was switched on. Hoping to salvage the situation, the pilots often ordered the men remaining aboard to wait until they made another pass over the same spot the first cluster had jumped onto. Few managed to accurately locate this position and one stick after another was widely dispersed.

Other planes took direct anti-aircraft hits and the men inside had to jump for their lives. The plane bearing a stick composed of many of the battalion's headquarters people, including Regimental Sergeant Major W.J. Clark, Padre George Harris, and Private Tom O'Connell took a direct hit in its left-wing engine. As flames started engulfing the wing and the plane nosed towards the ground, the paratroops took to the silk. O'Connell and Harris jumped so close together their parachutes tangled and the two men plunged towards the earth under largely collapsed canopies. Panicked, O'Connell thrashed wildly about in an effort to pay his field kit out below him so that he would not be crushed by it when they hit ground. Speaking almost into his ear, a voice calmly said, "Take it easy, old man. Whatever you do, take it easy." O'Connell calmed instantly at the padre's softly spoken advice and even as the two men crashed down through some trees managed to assume the correct landing position. The force of the impact knocked the private unconscious. He did not awaken until about noon on June 6 and was saddened to find Harris lying dead beside him. Their two parachutes were twined together like a rope and it was a wonder they had managed to slow the men's descent at all. Had it not been for Harris's calming counsel, O'Connell believed he would surely have died.[19]

After O'Connell, Harris, and twelve other men had bailed out of the stricken plane, the flight crew managed to bring the fire under control and stopped the remaining soldiers from jumping until they made another pass over what they believed was the drop zone. The plane was dangerously low when Private Harvey Minor of the battalion's antitank platoon jumped. A few seconds later, he "somersaulted through some low trees and landed in water."[20]

Minor cut himself free of entangling parachute lines with his commando knife and wallowed to dry land. After wandering alone for a while, he heard a man coughing and shortly came upon RSM Clark. Eventually, they rounded up the other four men who had jumped with them. "We were in terrible country—crisscrossed by canals but not flooded—nothing like the flooded canals around the Drop Zone."[21]

Medical Officer Captain Colin Brebner was in another plane that had to keep five of its men aboard for a second pass after the first fifteen jumped. Brebner went out in the second group and after a fifteen-second descent ended up dangling about thirty to fifty feet off the ground with his parachute completely entangled in the upper branches of a large elm. His parachute lines stretched twenty-two feet from the silk canopy to his shoulders and the tree trunk was at least twenty feet away with no intervening branches. Brebner's field kit was filled to bursting with vital medical supplies and he was unable to release it, but the weight prevented his climbing up the lines to free the canopy or to swing in a wide enough arc to grab hold of the tree trunk. Then his parachute straps started slipping up his body until they snagged on the holster of a 45-calibre pistol he was technically prohibited by the Geneva Convention from possessing. Brebner realized that there was only one way to free himself and that was to hit the quick release button on his chest and fall out of the parachute harness. But the fall was likely to kill him.

Brebner hesitated, but kept thinking of the fact that he was the battalion's only doctor and might even now be badly needed to save Canadian lives. Positioning his body as trained for a hard landing, he hit the release button, wriggled free of the straps, and the next moment was knocked unconscious. It was still dark when he awoke later and he was relieved to discover his legs could still move. Then he felt the smashed bones in his left wrist. That was okay, he thought, for he could conduct surgery one-handed. Rolling over, he levered himself to his feet with his good hand and took a step, only to fall hard on his back. Brebner knew instantly that his pelvis was broken and he was helpless.[22]

A half-hour later, Brebner's batman, Private Bill Adams, appeared. Brebner by now had a pretty good fix on his probable location and was able to direct Adams towards the battalion headquarters' rendezvous point. Ignoring the man's protests that he could not leave the doctor behind, Brebner ordered Adams to load up with all the medical supplies he could carry and take them to the battalion. After Adams left, Brebner tried to inject himself with a morphine syringe but was unable to break the seal because of his useless left wrist. He gritted his teeth and waited to be rescued.[23]

DESPITE LANDING KNEE-DEEP in a marsh near the River Dives, Lieutenant Colonel G.F. Bradbrooke reached the battalion's main rendezvous site near le Bas de Bréville, southwest of the Varaville–le Mesnil road, in good time. He found Major Jeff Nicklin already there along with the battalion's signals officer Lieutenant John Simpson and intelligence officer Lieutenant R.D.J. Weathersbee. Also present were about seventy-five paratroopers, of whom only a third were Canadian. The rest were a mixed bag of Brits from the 8th and 9th battalions and an antitank detachment of the Oxford and Buckinghamshire Light Infantry. The latter had been landed by Horsa glider and were still equipped with their gun and a good supply of ammunition.[24]

Hearing gunfire from the direction of Varaville, Bradbrooke told Weathersbee to take two men and find out what was happening there. He then told his second-in-command Major Nicklin that the rest of the force would advance on le Mesnil crossroads.[25] Lieutenant Simpson and a small party of men were sent to destroy the signal exchange building that had been one of 'C' Company's uncompleted assignments. Simpson quickly returned to report that the building had been abandoned and the equipment easily destroyed.[26]

As Bradbrooke set off with his main force on a slow and cautious march towards the crossroads, more British and Canadian paratroops filtered in to bulk its strength. Such intermingling of battalions was commonplace as lost men bungled into each other in the inky blackness and decided to stick together at least until they reached a recognizable landmark.

Corporal Dan Hartigan had been searching for an opening in an impenetrable hedgerow when suddenly an ear-splitting whistle warned him that one of the bombs overshooting Merville Battery was about to land right on him. Hartigan dropped flat against the base of the hedge and the bomb exploded on the other side directly opposite. He was stunned by the blast and completely buried under two inches of mud. After frantically freeing himself, the corporal discovered the blast had so badly concussed all his joints and muscles that his limbs jerked spasmodically every few moments. The pervasive nature of this condition earned him the nickname "Hopalong."

After staggering along the hedge in a barely conscious state for a few minutes, he felt something running down his face and wiped away blood dribbling out of his mouth and nose. Despite his condition, Hartigan was sufficiently lucid to feel sure that the J-shaped hedgerow was only a few hundred yards away if he could just find a way past the impenetrable hedge. Finally, he came to a gate and started climbing over it to get to the other side. As he swung over the top, someone poked him in the rear with the point of a bayonet and growled, "Punch."

"Judy, you dumb bastard," Hartigan yelped, and scowled down at his friend Private Eddie Mallon. The private was bomb happy, too. What had seemed a promising route to the rendezvous point came to nothing. Hartigan realized they were wandering in circles about the time they neared a paved road and another Punch-Judy challenge. This time, it was a 9th British Battalion lieutenant wandering lost with six of his men. The officer ordered the Canadians to fall in and follow him towards where he hoped the 9th Battalion was rallying for the attack on the Merville Battery. By now, Hartigan could hear gunfire coming from Varaville and insisted that he and Mallon's duty was to go there. The lieutenant finally shut the two men up by telling them he was in command and they would do as told.

At 0230 hours, the party arrived at the rally point and the lieutenant reported to Lieutenant Colonel Terence Otway, who was forming up only 150 men to carry out the attack that was to have been mounted by the entire battalion. Otway, frantic with anxiety at possibly failing to complete the vital mission on schedule, ripped into the lieutenant that the two Canadians were of no "bloody use" to him and should be sent "back to where they bloody well came from." Hartigan was initially infuriated by the commander's apparent disdain, but then realized the attack on the battery had been meticulously planned, with every soldier repeatedly drilled on his precise role. That plan was now in tatters and Otway and his men were going to have to improvise—not 9th Battalion's strength.

Somewhat sheepishly, the lieutenant set a course for Hartigan and Mallon to follow that would take them back to Varaville and sent them off, but it would be dawn at the earliest before they could cover the distance that now lay between them and 'C' Company's objective.[27] Behind them, at 0250 hours, they heard the sounds of the 9th Battalion going into the attack and the gunfire quickly drowned out the lighter and more distant sounds of shots coming from the southeast where the Canadian battalion was fighting.*

FOR THE MANY PARATROOPS wandering in small packs or alone through the countryside, the approach of dawn promised a chance to get their bearings, link up with comrades, and complete missions. A critical target for the Canadians was the Robehomme Bridge spanning the River Dives. Its destruction was one of 'B' Company's tasks, specifically that of No. 5 Platoon commanded by Lieutenant Norm Toseland. As soon as the officer landed, he had set about gathering as many of his men as possible while trying to puzzle out in which direction the bridge lay. At 0200 hours, Toseland, with about ten men from his platoon and a mix of the same number of British paratroops, encountered a young French girl riding a bicycle along the road they followed. Sergeant Joe LaCasse flagged the girl down and asked her to show him on a map where they were located in relation to the bridge. Jumping off her bicycle, the girl led the paratroops across a field to the river and then pointed the bridge out in the distance.

Toseland and his group arrived at the bridge to find Major Clayton Fuller already on the scene. The major had landed squarely in the

---

* Against heavy odds, the British paratroops successfully overran the battery but lacked the demolitions (these had been lost in the jump) to demolish the guns. They were, however, able to temporarily disable them. But the cost was high. Only eighty men were left and twenty-two had been taken prisoner.

river itself, but managed to swim ashore. Neither he nor any of the men with him had any explosives and so they were simply attempting to prevent the Germans using the bridge until a demolition team arrived. Toseland canvassed the men in his group and scrounged together sufficient plastic explosives to lay charges under the bridge girders, but the resulting blast failed to sever the span. The blast did, however, serve to guide about thirty more paratroopers to the position. Among these was Captain Peter Griffin, who took over command of the group from Toseland. Although Major Fuller was the senior officer present, he had no intention of hanging about long, as his assigned task was to get to where 'B' Company was supposed to rally at le Mesnil crossroads. The presence of additional paratroops, however, gave Griffin and Toseland sufficient strength to establish a strong defensive position around the bridge. At about 0600 hours, Captain A.J. Jack of the Royal Engineers arrived with enough explosives to finish the demolition.[28] Twenty minutes later, he had the bridge nicely wired with dynamite and turned to Griffin. "It's your bridge," he said. "Would you like to light the fuse?" Griffin did and the bridge was quickly ripped apart.[29]

Sometime before the Robehomme Bridge was blown, Sergeant Gordon Davies and the man sent with him by Major MacLeod to destroy the crossing of the Divette near Varaville succeeded in their task. When the men dug in at the château's gatehouse heard the explosion, a cheer went up. There was precious little else to give the men cause for joy. Just before dawn, Captain John Hanson had arrived in time to hold Major MacLeod's head in his lap as the man died. Private Bismutka, MacLeod's loyal runner, succumbed shortly thereafter. Hanson assumed command, but could do nothing to shift the impasse between the Canadians and the Germans beyond the gatehouse. So he had everyone maintain the positions set out earlier by Sergeant MacPhee.[30]

Meanwhile, 'C' Company's Lieutenant Sam McGowan and a group of men had entered the village of Varaville en route to the château, but stumbled into two sections of German infantry. A sharp firefight ensued, in which McGowan's men were able to deny the Germans access to the village. The lieutenant had his men dig in around the village's church and established an observation post in the steeple. Although successful in driving the Germans back, McGowan's party soon drew heavy mortar and artillery fire and started to take casualties. Their hold on the village was tenuous at best but McGowan determined to hang on.[31]

Not far away, Lieutenant Colonel Bradbrooke was still pushing his force up a road towards le Mesnil crossroads, but being greatly held up by snipers firing from various houses bordering the road along the way. Each sniper had to be cleared out by an attack on the house, with the British six-pounder antitank gun snapping out shells in support. Bradbrooke realized it would be well into morning before his men reached the crossroads.

And far away to the west of the River Orne, Lieutenant John Madden's seven-man party had made scant progress inland from their starting point only 1,200 yards from Sword Beach. No sooner had they set out than Madden was forced to take evasive action to avoid being discovered by German infantry that must have seen their parachutes during the descent and were now actively searching for them. Consequently, they were still close to the coast when the massive pre-invasion naval and aerial saturation bombardment of the beaches opened at 0500 hours. Suddenly the countryside around them seemed to erupt. The men dived into any available depression and cringed as the air sang with shrapnel and the ground violently trembled. Hell had come to Normandy.[32]

[10]

All Aflame

T HE SMALL SHIPS of the 31st Royal Canadian Navy Minesweeping Flotilla were in the vanguard of the invasion fleet approaching Omaha Beach when the mighty guns of the American, British, and French battleships and cruisers loosed their first salvoes. As it had throughout the long night's operation, Acting Commander Tony Storrs's *Caraquet* led the formation. The pace of the ships was measured, their course necessarily unwavering despite the fact that they now parallelled the French coast, with *Caraquet* just two miles offshore. Broadside to the shore, Storrs knew the ships surely presented tempting targets for any German shore batteries still unscathed from aerial bombardment.[1] In front of their respective sections of beach, all ten of the sweeper flotillas conducted the same final mission—clearing the sea that the LCAS and LCTS bearing the assault troops to the beaches must travel.

Seaward, the predawn darkness was rent by main-gun muzzle flashes from the U.S. battleships *Texas* and *Arkansas,* the British cruiser *Glasgow,* and the French cruisers *Montcalm* and *Georges Leygues.*[2] Shells shrieked over the minesweepers. It was impossible to see where individual rounds fell, for the coastline was smothered in smoke and flame raised by the naval bombardment and the exploding bombs dropped by rank after rank of Allied bombers. Aboard *Bayfield,* Telegraphist Stan Richardson scribbled in his diary: "The French coast only two miles off all aflame."[3]

As *Caraquet* started to come about to lead the flotilla back out to sea, its sweeping wire snagged on the seabed and Storrs ordered it cut loose. Close behind, *Fort William* tangled its wire on a buoy marking the mouth of Port-en-Bessin harbour and had to abandon it. Normally, the crews would have endeavoured to recover the wires, but their orders were to clear the way for the Allied assault ships already steaming down the now clear channels. When the last minesweeper in the formation completed its pass, the flotilla broke apart, with each ship moving independently towards a rendezvous point well offshore where they were to anchor and await further orders. *Fort William* and *Mulgrave* were approaching the line of ships bombarding the shore when a shore battery countered with a salvo of its own. One heavy shell, more than capable of mortally wounding a small minesweeper, exploded "less than 100 yards away" from the two vessels. Then the cruiser *George Leygues* blundered towards *Minas* and the small ship only narrowly avoided being sliced in two by the battleship's towering bow through a hard evasive turn to starboard. At the same time, *Fort William* had to duck to one side to avoid colliding with a Landing Ship, Tank already steaming towards the beach.[4]

Despite these moments of brief alarm, all the minesweepers safely extracted themselves from the beach area and soon arrived at the rendezvous point. The Canadian skippers had been warned they would probably suffer heavy casualties completing their missions and that critically damaged ships would be sunk without hesitation or consideration for the lives of the men aboard to prevent a dead vessel hampering the assault ships approaching the beach. But the minesweepers had gone in and come out again without a single ship or even sailor scratched. And they had cleared the way for the rest of the invasion fleet to bear down with its might of men and arms on Normandy.

ALTHOUGH THE HEAVIER warships kicked off the naval saturation bombardment of the Normandy coast at 0500 hours, the invasion fleet's seventy-five destroyers kept silent—conforming to an order to hold fire until forty minutes prior to when the Allied troops in their assigned sector were to hit the sand. Before Juno Beach, the larger ships blazing away consisted of the British battleships *Ramillies* and *Warspite*, the heavy cruiser *Jamaica*, and twelve light cruisers. Among the destroyers assigned to Juno were two Canadian V-Class Destroyers, *Algonquin* and *Sioux*.[5] During the channel crossing, *Algonquin* had served as the escort for Force J's command ship *Hilary*, but upon arriving at the latter ship's holding position nine miles offshore at 0600 hours Captain Desmond Piers ordered the destroyer to steam shoreward. All around the speeding destroyer, large LSIS were lowering small flotillas of troop-loaded LCAS, and swarms of LCTS and LCIS jockeyed into formation for the run to shore. Piers estimated that there "were hundreds of craft of every description within range" and thought it unbelievable that the German shore guns kept their silence.

Algonquin and *Sioux* now spearheaded the invasion force, plunging through the heavy seas towards the beach while the landing craft remained miles offshore. Overhead, the low, heavy cloud cover that had prevailed through the night appeared to be thinning. Through the gaps, Piers glimpsed waves of U.S. Eighth Air Force B-17 Flying Fortresses and other heavy bombers streaming in to strike the coastal defences. Over a thirty-minute period prior to the assault forces reaching the beach, 1,365 American bombers were to dump 2,796 tons of ordnance on selected targets spread along the coast, adding further to the destruction already wrought by RAF Bomber Command during the night.[6]

Because of the remaining low cloud cover, however, the accuracy of the American bombardiers—little trained in blind-bombing techniques used by Bomber Command during its nighttime raids—was hit and miss.[7] Three miles offshore. *Algonquin* turned broadside to the beach and its four 4.7-inch single guns opened fire on a battery of two 75-millimetre guns believed hidden between some seashore houses immediately west of St. Aubin-sur-Mer. The ship's gunnery officer, Lieutenant V.M. "Corkey" Knight, found it difficult to accurately direct the fall of shot against the target because of obscuring clouds of smoke and dust raised by the exploding bombs. "God damn Air Force is messing up our target again," a ship's officer scrawled in

Algonquin's log. One concentration of bombs fell into an area of forest behind *Algonquin*'s target and when the smoke cleared all Piers saw remaining was "just a few shredded tree trunks."[8]

About a mile and a half east of *Algonquin*'s position, *Sioux* ranged in on two large buildings near Langrune from a distance of 10,000 yards offshore. Each building was believed to conceal a 75-millimetre gun. *Sioux* fired its first salvo against this target at 0705 hours. Fifteen minutes later, after loosing five salvoes, the gunnery officer ordered the fire shifted to another target because the houses were "now quite obliterated by smoke." Six minutes later, the ship's 4.7-inchers launched into an eight-minute continuous bombardment of a fuel tank standing just off the beach. When this was burning fiercely, the guns swung back onto the original target for "good measure."[9]

Over by St. Aubin-sur-Mer, *Algonquin* was happily creating mayhem. Figuring two houses facing the beach were likely candidates for sniper positions, Piers ordered them blasted into rubble. When Chief Engineer Johnny Lloyd came up to the bridge, Piers suggested he pick out a target. Lloyd pointed to what "looked like a summer hotel right on the beach. We blew it to smithereens," the ship's captain wrote happily afterward. "Pleased with the progress of the battle, 'Chief' cheered us on and went back to tell the boys in the Engine Room how things were going!"[10]

Piers remained baffled as to why not a single German gun tried to take the destroyers on. Nor did any shore guns direct fire towards the assault craft now beginning to head in to the beach. It was broad daylight and any element of surprise the Allies might have enjoyed was clearly past. Every German in the area had to be awake and scrambling through dust, smoke, and continuing explosions to his assigned position. He kept expecting "a nasty surprise in the form of some new German secret weapon" to explain the lack of response from shore, but nothing materialized. *Algonquin* and *Sioux* continued firing on possible enemy positions while the landing craft streamed past them and pressed hard for the beach.

EIGHT BRITISH AND ONE Free French destroyer had joined the two Canadian destroyers in the Juno Beach shore bombardment. And in the last thirty minutes before the first troops reached landfall, a range of smaller craft added their guns to the beach drenching. Seven Landing Craft, Gun (Large) mounted with 4.7-inch guns worked the shore over from a closer range than the destroyers could manage, as did eight Landing Craft, Tank (Rocket). Fitted with more than a thousand explosive rockets released in twenty-six salvoes, the LCTRS were to saturate the beach just minutes before the landing. There were also six shallow-draft Landing Craft, Support (Large) equipped with six-pounder antitank guns engaging suspected enemy strongpoints at close range and six Landing Craft, Flak providing anti-aircraft protection.[11] Aboard several LCTS were two squadrons of Centaur tanks armed with 95-millimetre main guns crewed by marines of the 2nd Royal Marine Armoured Support Regiment. The marines were to support the infantry by "beaching their LCTS as violently as possible and opening fire from the craft themselves" five minutes before the infantry's LCAS reached the sand.[12] Once the beach was cleared of enemy, the Centaurs would roll off the LCTS and join the advance inland.

Added to this naval firepower were sixteen LCTS on which the four Canadian artillery regiments had fixed their 105-millimetre Priest self-propelled guns. Each LCT carried four SPGS of a single artillery troop, its radios, jeeps, and Bren carriers—everything the unit needed to be fully operational once it disembarked on the beach. Also joining the vessel-based shelling contingent were the two 1st Hussars 17-pounder Firefly tanks commanded by Lieutenant Ladd Irving of 'C' Squadron. These were to knock out a fortification near Courseulles thought to be immune to destruction by the less accurate naval and aerial bombardment. With all this massive weight of gunnery protecting the 187 ships in Force J and blasting the beach, Piers thought the only thing hampering an easy landing for the assault force was the weather. Although the destroyers and larger ships were barely affected, the rough seas tossed the smaller craft about like corks and some were straining engines to the limit just to maintain a shoreward course.[13]

Because of the heavy seas, Force J's commander, Commodore G.N. Oliver, pushed the scheduled touchdown back ten minutes for each of Juno's two sectors. This meant that the landing time—designated H Hour—for Mike Sector would come at 0745 rather than 0735 and at 0755 in Nan Sector. Mike encompassed a relatively narrow beach frontage stretching eastward from Juno's most westerly boundary before Vaux to the western edge of Courseulles-sur-Mer, with Nan extending from there to St. Aubin-sur-Mer. Both beach sectors were further subdivided into zones. Moving west to east, Mike was divided into Mike Green and Mike Red, while Nan was divided into Nan Green, Nan White, and Nan Red. Each zone marked the landing boundary of one assaulting infantry regiment.[14]

Oliver's decision to delay the assault meant that the Canadians, always scheduled to carry out the last Allied landing, were to be later yet. The nature of the low shelving beach, with its many rocky outcroppings that were only submerged enough between mid- and high tide for landing craft to cross without bottoming out, had necessitated the initial delay. It had been hoped to place the assault forces on the sand immediately in front of the German beach obstacles and let the troops thread through them on foot or in their tanks. The engineers would then land immediately behind the leading troops and clear lanes through the obstacles for use by the follow-on forces.[15] But with H Hour now to come at a later point in the tide cycle, "the landing craft would be obliged to touch down in the middle of the obstructions designed to destroy them."[16]

The decision also necessitated hasty redeployment of the artillery regiments' LCTs to adapt their firing run to match the new time sequence. Each field regiment formed up parallel to the others in a double rank, with three LCTs forward and three back in a staggered formation to ensure that every gun had a clear field of fire even when the muzzles were almost fully depressed. This formation ensured that the ninety-six guns of the four regiments could all blaze away unhindered. The 12th Field and 13th Field regiments ranged on Mike Sector, while the 14th Field and 19th Army Field regiments turned their attention on Nan Sector. The 14th Field faced Bernières-sur-Mer and the 19th Army Field St. Aubin-sur-Mer.[17]

Earlier trials had revealed that the LCTs, with their flat bottoms and relatively light construction, were too unstable to provide a steady gun platform while holding a fixed position off the coastline. The only way to keep the guns on an accurate firing line was to steam towards the target at a steady course and speed. Consequently, the original plan called for the Canadian SPGS to start firing for effect from a range of nine thousand yards offshore and to cease fire when the range closed to two thousand yards. Firing was to commence thirty minutes before H Hour and last twenty-five minutes. This meant that the craft would be closing on the beach at a rate of about a thousand yards every five minutes. Each gun crew was to shoot three rounds during each two-hundred-yard interval, for a total expenditure of 105 shells per gun. Once the craft reached the two-thousand-yard range, they were to turn hard about and assume a holding pattern until the infantry and tanks had managed to render the beach safe for the landing of artillery. At H Hour plus 75 minutes, the 12th Field Regiment was to disembark from its LCTS on Mike and the 14th Field Regiment on Nan. The other two regiments would follow respectively at H Hour plus 120 minutes.[18]

As plans are wont to be, this one was very orderly and precise, but made no allowance for the effect of rough seas. Aboard the LCT carrying 12th Field Regiment's 16th Battery, Corporal Fred Rogers, the battery headquarters radio signaller, "was tired, sick, and hungry. The barge was buckling, bending, creaking, and groaning. Water was coming over the sides." The twenty-two-year-old from Windsor, Ontario was particularly concerned about all the water slopping around because stacked on the craft's deck were six hundred rounds of high-explosive ammunition packed in cardboard cases. Those cases now looked saturated with salt water.

Playing centre in a bucket brigade, Rogers stood on a narrow platform jury-rigged to the back of one of the SPGS, so that he could pass shells handed to him by a man on the deck over to the gun loader. To meet the three-rounds-per-200-yard fire rate, the shells had to be passed up at a steady pace. But as the man down on the deck tried to break the carton open at its seams, the cardboard turned out to be so mushy from seawater that he was unable to achieve a clean opening. Precious seconds were wasted as he and the other men on the deck raced about locating jackknives to cut the carton tops off.[19]

Over in the fire-control motor launch out front of 13th Field Regiment's LCTS, Major James Baird's radio was buzzing with demands from the Forward Observation Officers aboard LCAS carrying the infantry towards shore that the bombardment begin immediately. The infantry LCAS, they reported, were taking fire from the beach that the artillery could suppress. Baird quickly hoisted a blue signal flag that directed the guns to start ranging on the beach with smoke shells while still 14,000 yards out, well back of where these first ranging shots were to have originally been fired.[20] As the FOOS radioed in adjustments, Baird ordered the necessary line and range corrections. Once he heard the shot was falling on target, Baird ordered fire for effect at a range of about 11,000 yards.

With the motor launch closing on the beach at a steady six knots, Baird was able to determine with the ranging radar the artillery flotilla's precise distance from shore. He could then accurately direct a steady lowering in the elevation of 'B' Troop's gun barrels every two hundred yards to ensure the fire fell "just where the grass starts to grow on the beach."[21] When the LCTS reached the two-thousand-yard range, Baird signalled empty guns, ordered the craft to come about, and led them back to sea to await their turn to land on the beach. Baird thought the effect of the bombardment on the Germans must have been "devastating."[22]

Aboard the Force J and 3rd Canadian Infantry Division command ship Hilary, Major General Rod Keller agreed. The supporting artillery, he wrote, "put on the best shoot they had ever done."[23] Few of the men comprising the ninety-six gun crews had any time to reflect on whether the shoot was successful or not. Their immediate concern was to dump all the spent brass, shredded cartridge cases, and other waste generated so that the SPGS would be free to disembark from the LCTS when their turn to land came. Chucked overboard with the rest of the rubbish were dozens of unfired rounds that had been scattered across the LCT decks in the course of the artillery shoot.[24]

Like the other regiments, 14th Field had been ordered before embarkation to harness a string of land mines like a girdle around the circumference of its SPGS, to be handed over to the engineers for use in clearing beach obstacles once the gunners reached shore. As the

regiment's LCTs had closed on the coastline during the bombardment run, however, a few stray German shells exploded nearby in the
water. Bombardier Okill Stuart of Montreal realized that if a piece of
shrapnel struck a mine, they would be blown sky-high. In September
1939, Stuart had been happily preparing to attend Oxford University
but the war scuttled that plan and he returned to Canada to enlist. On
his father's advice, Stuart had declined an invitation to apply for a
commission and instead was soon applying his prowess in trigonom-
etry as assistant to the 14th Regiment's surveyor and gun positions
officer. Stuart didn't need to do any calculations on his trusty slide
rule to determine the mathematical probability that they would all die
disastrously if the mines were still aboard when they made the final
run right up to the beach into the face of enemy fire. Without seeking
clearance from the regiment's commander, Lieutenant Colonel H.S.
Griffin, the men aboard Stuart's LCT cut the mines free and dumped
them over the gunwale.[25]

On the LCT carrying 'C' Troop's 66th Battery of the 14th Field,
Lieutenant W.D. Peter Cox was as alarmed by the mines hanging on
his SPGS as Stuart, but it never occurred to him as troop leader to
order them thrown off. Besides, every available spare inch of space
inside was crammed with the crew's shells and spare ammunition
they were carrying for the infantry regiments, so the mines were only
one hazard among many. In addition, neither he nor his gunners had
been able to bear the thought of getting rid of the ammunition left
from the seaboard shoot. Instead, thinking it might come in handy,
they piled it into the SPGS so thickly that they were left sitting on
shells—although this raised them so high that each man towered
above the armoured hide that was to provide protection from German
small-arms fire.[26]

WHILE THE LCTs bearing the artillery regiments were coming about,
other LCTs carrying the squadrons of the Fort Garry Horse and 1st
Hussars armoured regiments equipped with Duplex-Drive tanks
were closing in. These were to have launched their loaded tanks
seven thousand yards offshore, so the Shermans could reach the
beach ahead of the infantry assault regiments and provide covering

fire for their landing. Also preceding the infantry regiments were to have been two groups of British mechanized troops aboard LCTS that were to run up onto the sand and drop their vehicles. The Centaurs of the 2nd Royal Marine Armoured Support Regiment composed one of these groups, while the other was the 5th Assault Regiment Royal Engineers, equipped with Armoured Vehicles Royal Engineers (AVRES) and armoured bulldozers. The former regiment would back up the Canadian DD tanks with their own powerful guns, while the latter cleared beach obstacles and cut escape routes from the beach inland.[27]

Even before dawn, it had become evident to the naval officers controlling the landing schedules that the rough seas were going to disrupt the timing. While the meteorologists aboard *Hilary* reported waves averaging three to four feet and a wind blowing out of the northwest at only Force 4—about eighteen miles per hour—no allowance was made for offshore swells that effectively doubled the wave heights. Furthermore, as the waves broached the rocky shoals lying off the beach, their height increased dramatically. There was also a strong starboard cross-current that threatened to push the landing craft well east of their assigned touchdown points.[28]

Recognizing that the seas were stormier than any of the DD squadrons had encountered during training, the flotilla officers controlling their deployment sought the opinion of the tank commanders on whether a launch should even be attempted. The Fort Garry Horse senior squadron commander, Major William Roy Bray, suggested the decision be postponed until the LCTS were between three thousand and two thousand yards offshore.[29] Major J.S. Duncan and Major Dudley Brooks of the 1st Hussars looked into the "churning and choppy sea ... [and] replied that it was too rough."[30] The LCTS with the tanks bore on towards shore. As for the British engineers and marines, some of their vessels had fallen out of the convoy inadvertently during the channel crossing and were still hastening to catch it up, so it was impossible for them to precede the infantry's arrival on the beach.

Well ahead of the LCTS bearing the DD squadrons was the one with the two 1st Hussars 17-pounder tanks mounted on its front that were commanded by Lieutenant Irving and tasked with firing on the fortified gun position near Courseulles. Standing behind the tanks in readiness to hand ammunition up to the loaders, Trooper Ralph Burley and three other Hussars tried to ignore the icy seawater sloshing around their ankles. The LCT was heaving in the swells, making it hard for the men to keep their balance. During the crossing, some of the tankers had tried cooking up some food with a propane burner, but Burley had been too seasick to eat any. Everyone was seasick now and the run towards shore was a misery.

Then the two tanks opened fire with a deafening crash that set Burley's ears ringing despite an earlier attempt to protect his eardrums by wrapping a scarf around his head. Burley and the others formed a chain and started passing shells to the gun loaders. Coming up from a crouch while passing one round up to the man on the back of the tank, Burley struck his forehead on a bracket bolt mounted on the tank and opened an inch-long gash above one eye. Blood blinded him and the trooper was gripped by a convulsive fit of vomiting. Frantically swiping the streams of blood from his eyes so he could see enough to handle the shells, attempting to ignore the vomiting attacks, Burley kept passing the ammunition.

Because the shells were being manhandled through the hatch in the top of the turret, the tank crew commanders were forced to use periscopes to direct the guns onto the target. Halfway through the shoot, one periscope lens became so covered with seawater that the crew commander was no longer able to see through it. "Somebody get up here and wipe off these periscope sights," he bellowed. Burley's crewmate, Trooper Harold Newburgh, jumped to the task by straddling the 17-pounder's muzzle and reaching up from this position to wipe the periscope lens clean with a rag. Just as he finished the job, the gunner accidentally triggered the gun. When the badly dazed Newburgh returned to the deck, Burley saw that the man's eyebrows had been blackened and singed by the muzzle blast.

Although the LCT carried two hundred rounds of loose ammunition for use in the firing mission, Irving ordered ceasefire after each tank had fired only about thirty rounds.[31] Then the LCT broke off its advance and swung back out to sea.

Behind it, the LCTs carrying the DD tanks were doing likewise, even as the squadron commanders still wrestled with whether to launch or, instead, have the LCTs land the tanks directly on the beach. Able to make better time in the rough seas than the LCAs, the LCTs had closed on the beach so far ahead that they risked touching down at 0725 hours—twenty minutes earlier than the infantry. The flotilla officers therefore ordered them to come about in a wide circle to the right that would bring them back in fifteen minutes to the possible launch point three thousand yards out. At that time, the flotilla officers would decide whether a launch was to proceed or not. While a direct landing would avoid the risk of DD tanks being swamped or capsized, it would greatly increase their danger of being lost by the sinking of the LCTs or destroyed on the beach in clusters by concentrated German antitank fire. Whatever the choice, their new landing time was to be 0740 hours for Mike sector and 0745 for Nan—five minutes ahead of the scheduled touchdown for the infantry on Mike and ten minutes ahead of that for Nan.[32]

As the LCT carrying Bombardier Okill Stuart reached its holding position offshore, the young bombardier was struck by the deafening noise around him. From near the beach, the rocket ships were unleashing salvoes that shrieked ashore with a "swish, swish, swish" sound. Then "you heard, 'chug, chug, chug' [and] found it to be the noise of the 16-inch shell from a battleship, so far to the rear that you could not see it. Something different was happening everywhere—all with a bang!"[33]

11

Roll Me Over, Lay Me Down

BERTHED AS THEY had been aboard the seafaring passenger liners converted into Landing Ship, Infantry rather than the smaller LCTs and LCIs, the infantry of the leading assault wave had enjoyed a more comfortable night than most other soldiers in the Canadian invasion force during the storm-tossed channel passage. Still, the troops had been so keyed up that few slept and the poker games in the smoke-filled holds played on. Men smoked cigarettes, cursed their luck when the cards failed them, or roared in triumph when the dice rolled right. Those who declined gambling concentrated on cleaning weapons and gear, writing final letters, or chatting quietly with friends about what the coming day might bring. Reveille came between 0300 and 0400 hours, with breakfast soon served. Food quality varied in accordance to each ship's mess facility. For the Royal Winnipeg Rifles, it meant nothing but tea and a cold snack.[1] The Queen's Own Rifles fared well as the cooks heaped the plates with eggs cooked sunny side up, fried bacon, and thick slices of white toast.[2] Any man desiring a tot was allowed "a . . . shot of good old navy rum."[3]

Similar fare without the rum ration was offered the Canadian Scottish Regiment, but Captain H.L. Alexander of 'C' Company noted that "breakfast was a meager affair for most."[4] Having observed the churning seas, most of the men ate sparingly because they knew the LCAS would be hard tossed in the rough seas despite also knowing "it would be the last proper meal for a couple days."[5] The Canadian Scottish aboard the Royal Canadian Navy's *Prince Henry* were each given "two hard-boiled eggs and cheese sandwich as extra ration" courtesy of the ship's crew, who had saved the food from their own previous day's lunch and this morning's breakfast. The battalion's second-in-command, Major Cyril Wightman, thought it a gesture typical of the crew and skipper Captain Val Godfrey, who he considered "a grand man."[6]

No sooner had the Canadian Scots of 'B' Company and the Headquarters Company on *Prince Henry* finished stuffing the lunch ration into their already overloaded packs than the ship ceased steaming towards the Normandy coast. It was 0605 hours. Godfrey ordered three short blasts on the ship's whistle to signal the other LSIs that they were at the assigned disembarkation point and dropped anchor. The LSIS stood in an almost perfect line twelve thousand yards off Juno Beach, with each ship spaced one thousand feet apart.[7] The thirty-nine-year-old Wightman, who had initially joined the Victoria-based regiment in 1924 to fill a spot on its rugby team and then taken an officer's commission four years later, "was tense, overly tense, almost to the point of speechlessness."[8] But like everyone else, he filed to his assigned LCA. Each LCA complement numbered between thirty and forty, most comprised of a single platoon. Reverend Robert Seaborn moved along the boat deck and said "a little prayer to each little group before they went over the side" into their assault craft.[9] Then he walked over to where Wightman stood to take his place among the men assigned to that LCA. At 0645 hours, with the battalion's pipers playing "cheerfully in the bright morning," 146 Canadian Scots embarked in seven LCAS. "As the troops left," noted a naval report, "they gave three rousing cheers for the *Prince Henry*, which her ship's company heartily reciprocated."[10]

Only one company of the Canadian Scottish Regiment was part of the first assault wave—Major Desmond Crofton's 'C' Company. This company would land on the extreme western flank in Mike Sector Green to protect the right flank of the Royal Winnipeg Rifles by taking out a fortification dug in on the beach in front of the Château

Vaux and then securing the estate itself. Immediately to 'C' Company's left in Mike Red, the Winnipeg's 'D' Company under Major Lochie Fulton would land, while Captain Philip Edwin Gower's 'B' Company secured the left bank of the River Seulles. On 'B' Company's right flank in Nan Green, 'A' Company of the Regina Rifles would set down in front of Courseulles-sur-Mer, with 'B' Company coming ashore to the immediate left. Major Duncan Grosch commanded 'A' Company and Major F.L. Peters 'B' Company. Supporting the 7th Canadian Infantry Brigade regiments were the Duplex-Drive Shermans of the 1st Hussars, with 'A' Squadron backing up the Winnipegs and 'B' Squadron the Reginas.

Left of the Reginas in Nan White, the Queen's Own Rifles would assault Bernières-sur-Mer, with 'A' Company on the right and 'B' Company left. Major Hume Elliott Dalton commanded 'A' Company, while his brother Major Charles Dalton, six years older than Elliott, led 'B'. The thirty-three-year-old Charles had joined the Queen's Own Rifles Cadet Company in 1925, followed by his brother a few years later. The two siblings were extremely close and were also popular with their men. Both were handsome, looked perfectly cast in the dashing young officer role, and played the part as if born to it. But they were also competent leaders who led from the front.

That two brothers would lead both Queen's Own Rifles assault companies had been determined purely by chance when the battalion's four company commanders established the order of landings with a coin toss. Aboard ss *Monowai,* a New Zealand liner, the two brothers had stood together as they waited for the order to board the LCAS. Realizing that he might never see his brother again, Charles tried to think of some meaningful parting words. Elliott, too, wondered what to say. Finally, when the order to embark came, Charles simply said, "I'll see you tonight." The two men shook hands and walked briskly to their boats.[11]

Also taking to LCAS were the men of 'A' and 'B' companies of the North Shore (New Brunswick) Regiment that were to attack Nan Red. Major John Archibald "Archie" McNaughton commanded 'A' Company. At forty-seven, he was older than most company commanders. Leading 'B' Company was Major Bob Forbes. 'A' Company was to set down immediately west of St. Aubin-sur-Mer and pass through an open gap between this town and Bernières-sur-Mer on the right while 'B' Company pushed directly into St. Aubin.

Supporting the Queen's Own Rifles and the North Shore Regiment were respectively 'B' Squadron and 'C' Squadron of the Fort Garry Horse. Major Jack Meindl commanded 'B' Squadron and Major William Roy Bray 'C' Squadron.

SOME LSIS HAD THEIR assault craft slung in a single rank of davits. This enabled all the troops to simply climb aboard their respective LCAS and be lowered on cables to just a few feet from the water and then released. Major Lochie Fulton's 'D' Company of the Winnipeg Rifles departed the liner *Canterbury* in this manner. On other LSIS, such as *Llandovery Castle,* the LCAS hung in tiers so that it was possible only for the lower rank to be boarded directly from the boat deck. Once these craft were dropped, the upper tier was lowered with only its boat crew aboard. The soldiers then climbed down scramble nets cast over the ship's side and jumped into the LCA—no easy task for men burdened with heavy packs and weapons even in calm water. On June 6, the LCAS were pitching up and down violently in five- to six-foot swells and bouncing hard off the sides of the LSIS.[12]

One of the first infantry casualties was probably Winnipeg Rifleman Andrew G. Mutch. He was on board a 'D' Company LCA that had been damaged by a large wave just as it cast free of its LSI. With one engine knocked out, it was struggling to make way forward as wave after wave broached its side, threatening to swamp the little craft. Drenched and scared, the soldiers aboard were all desperately seasick. About two miles out, Rifleman J.H. Hamilton noticed that Mutch had crawled up on the gunwale in order to be sick. Seeing a large wave bearing down on them, he lunged for the man but was too late to prevent him being washed overboard. The rifleman went under the surface and did not reappear.[13]

Aboard *Monowai,* 'B' Company of the Queen's Own was lowered to the water in ten LCAS and then 'A' Company scrambled down the nets to jump into their craft. Charlie Martin, 'A' Company's Company Sergeant Major, watched anxiously as the men boarding the LCA he commanded made the slow and awkward descent. Each man had to pause, clinging to the net, to measure the moment he should jump into the LCA. This was just as it yawed against the LSI's side. A mistimed leap could easily drop a man between the two craft so that he would either be drowned or crushed between the two hulls. The loading was taking longer than scheduled and the naval officers in the LCA and on the boat deck shouted at the soldiers to pick up the pace. Finally, everyone but Martin was aboard. After one final look around the boat deck to ensure no equipment had been forgotten, Martin turned to see the LCA crew already casting off. Clambering down the net, the CSM jumped towards the departing boat but landed on the gunwale and would have fallen back into the sea had not two of his men pulled him inside.

Martin took up his assigned position directly behind the drop ramp. On his right was No. 9 Platoon's sergeant, Jack Simpson. Before being promoted to CSM, No. 9 had been Martin's platoon. Almost every man on the LCA had enlisted in 1940 at about the same time as Martin had. They had trained together for almost four years for this moment. Simpson was a good friend of Martin's and a competent sergeant, who also had a brother over in another LCA carrying No. 7 Platoon ashore.

Milling around in the rough seas, the LCAS circled the LSIS as they waited for the order to head for the beach. Martin wondered what caused the holdup.[14] Every extra minute spent aboard the LCAS added to the numbers of men becoming violently seasick. Aboard the LSIS, most of the soldiers had been okay, but being pounded about in the smaller craft was making dozens of men ill.

Rifleman Bill Bettridge started throwing up the steak and eggs he had eaten for breakfast just minutes after he jumped into Martin's LCA. One of 'A' Company's two snipers, the twenty-three-year-old from Brampton was tough as nails on land but now he was so sick he worried about being useless when they finally reached the beach. Bettridge filled his brown plastic vomit bag and those of several of the unaffected men around him. Bettridge looked up from his hunkered position of misery at the sound of a rocket ship loosing off hundreds of charges just as an Allied P-51 Mustang fighter flew directly into the salvo's path. The plane disintegrated. Bettridge realized with a kind of grim awe that he had just witnessed a man die.[15]

In another LCA, Lance Corporal Gerry Cleveland of Yarmouth, Nova Scotia was in the middle row just behind the door, with his platoon section of the North Shore's 'A' Company in a line behind him. They were supposed to sit like kids on a toboggan on the bench that ran down the centre, but everyone was standing and craning to see the beach as well as to help their queasy stomachs. The men on the benches running along the sides were also standing rather than sitting, with their backs against the armoured hull. "We'd be on top of a wave and could look down and see an LCA in a trough. The next thing you'd be down in the trough looking up and there was water on either side of you way up there high above," Cleveland later recalled. Although raised in a town where fishing was the economic mainstay, Cleveland's family had been dairy farmers. He knew nothing of the sea. To his untrained eye, the waves seemed thirty to forty feet high and terrifying.[16]

WITH THE INFANTRY heading shoreward, the moment of decision arrived for the flotilla officers commanding the launching of the Duplex-Drive squadrons of the Fort Garry Horse and 1st Hussars. Deciding that the sea was too rough, the officer controlling the Fort Garry Horse tankers ordered the LCTs to take these Shermans to within a few hundred feet of shore and let them swim from there.[17] When the LCTs carrying the 1st Hussars were about three thousand yards from the beach, however, their flotilla commander told 'A' and 'B' squadrons to launch.

Aboard the four LCTs bearing 'A' Squadron's nineteen tanks, the Down Ramp Order bells rang and Major Dudley Brooks radioed for the crew commanders to launch their Shermans. German artillery and mortar rounds were splashing into the water all around the closing LCTs as the Hussars' tankers fired up their engines and deployed the canvas screens. In the LCT farthest to port, Lieutenant H.K. "Kit" Pattison rolled off the ramp and bobbed down into the water—the Sherman settling nicely so that it looked like nothing more than a large rectangular canvas dinghy with three-foot-high sides making its way shoreward. Just as his tank took to the sea, however, the chains holding the door level to the waterline were shot away, preventing the other tanks from launching safely in deep-water conditions. The LCT on the starboard flank was also unable to disembark its tanks due to a mechanical failure with the ramp. Both of these LCTs made for the beach in order to disembark their tank complements onto dry land.[18]

Meanwhile, Lieutenant William Little, commander of 'A' Squadron's No. 5 Troop, launched off another LCT. Waves immediately broached the canvas screen and two of the Sherman's five engines sputtered and died. Corporal Jim Paisley, the driver, assumed water had shorted out some electronics. Bursts of machine-gun fire tore through the screen just above the water line, but the tank remained buoyant.[19]

Back on the LCT from which Little's tank had just launched, the remaining two tanks in his troop were still waddling towards the ramp when a nearby rocket ship fired a salvo. Trooper Stan "Fish" Seneco, the driver of Corporal Harv Stanfield's tank, watched with growing horror as the salvo pushed the rocket ship back with such force that a small tidal wave was created. Seconds later, that wave smashed into Little's tank and demolished the canvas screen, causing it to immediately sink. To Seneco's relief, all five tankers soon bobbed to the surface, but then a spray of blood spurted out of Trooper G.H.S. Hawken's body and the man, who had only recently joined No. 5 Troop as a reinforcement, sank below the surface and did not reappear.[20]

Deciding to delay launching the tanks still aboard the LCT until it was closer to shore, the naval commander ordered the craft to steam past the survivors of Little's tank. Although there were numerous small rescue power launches nearby, none attempted to pick up the four men because priority was given to saving fully intact tank crews for delivery ashore. Finally, when one launch passed close by at about 1000 hours, Little threatened its crew with his pistol, with the result that the men were picked up.[21]

While 'A' Squadron managed to launch only ten of its nineteen DD tanks, all of 'B' Squadron got away. Lieutenant Bruce Deans immediately reported complete engine failure and ordered his tank abandoned as it foundered. Major J.S. Duncan tried to form the remaining tanks in a line for a kind of six-knot cavalry charge to shore, but the heaving seas left each tank crew fending just to keep afloat and heading roughly towards assigned touchdown points. Sergeant Léo Gariépy was about thirty yards off Duncan's port side when the strut holding up one of his rear sections of canvas broke. Gariépy's crew prevented the screen's total collapse by hastily wedging a fire extinguisher between it and the tank hull. Small-arms fire from the beach showered the tank. Then two great pillars of water shot up around Duncan's tank and it just disappeared. Gariépy noted that "there were only four heads in the water." Duncan and his crew, save Trooper R.E. Tofflemire, who drowned, were later rescued by an LCT and returned to England. Looking over his shoulder and seeing the other tanks still churning towards the beach, Gariépy led the way in.[22]

MIXED IN AMONG THE DD tanks were the LCAS bearing the Royal Winnipegs and Regina Rifles. Standing in the front of his assault craft, Major Fulton thought, "there was all the noise in the world" around him. Fulton was watching the beach, trying to pick out through the smoke and dust cloaking it where his landing point was situated. The major wanted 'D' Company's headquarters section to set down precisely in order to ensure that he could effectively gain immediate control over his platoons. Suddenly something started whacking against the steel hull of the LCA and with a start Fulton realized it was German small-arms fire. "Then you'd see a big spout of water come up and it dawned on me it was artillery fire and this wasn't going to be a surprise. The Germans were awake and waiting for us."[23]

Off to the east, the Queen's Own Rifles and North Shore regiments were well ahead of the Fort Garry Horse squadrons that were to have preceded them to the beach because of the time lost when it was decided not to launch the tanks until they were almost ashore. CSM Charlie Martin was shocked to discover, as the LCAS carrying the two assault companies drew closer to the beach, that the great armada standing off Normandy was no longer visible nor were there any aircraft overhead. All he could see were the regiment's ten little boats formed in a line across a 1,500-yard front. Ahead, the houses and buildings of Bernières-sur-Mer were visible. No fire was coming from the German fortifications. In fact, for a few minutes a deathly quiet prevailed that added an eerie sense of unreality. As the LCAS closed on the beach, they started moving farther apart, each making for an assigned landfall point. To Martin's right, he could see a concrete breakwater and line of rocks jutting out into the water. Suddenly, a single machine gun opened up from shore and a piece of metal chipped off the LCA by a bullet slashed Rifleman Cy Harden's cheek open. A sailor quickly slapped a bandage on the wound and shouted, "If that's the worst you get, you'll be lucky."[24]

While the Germans defending Bernières-sur-Mer held fire until the Queen's Own had practically touched down in order to avoid betraying their positions, those at St. Aubin-sur-Mer opened up with everything they had while the North Shore Regiment was still well out. In Lance Corporal Gerry Cleveland's LCA, the men were still gawking at the beach, trying to make out their objective among the row of shell-battered houses that were visible through the drifting smoke, when machine-gun rounds started hammering the ramp in the front. Everyone sat down quick to get below the protection offered by the armoured gunwales.[25]

Lieutenant Charles Richardson's platoon of 'B' Company had treated the initial run in as nothing more serious than another training scheme. His men were in high spirits, nobody suffering sickness despite the rough seas, and loudly singing bawdy popular songs. "Now, this is number one, and the fun has just begun. Roll me over, lay me down, and do it again," they belted out lustily.[26] Before they could break into the chorus of "Roll Me Over," an armour-piercing round sliced through the front of the lca and a chunk of shrapnel struck Private P. White in the chest, knocking him sideways but only winding the man. There was a deathly silence. Richardson looked at the thirty-nine men under his command and the expressions on their faces told him that they now understood this was serious business.[27]

That war was no laughing matter had been rammed home to Richardson by the drowning death of his older brother, James Stanley Richardson, in a tragically ill-conceived demonstration exercise on July 2, 1942, when twenty officer cadets attempted to swim Ottawa's Rideau Canal. Intended to promote the newly declared Army Week, the swim was attended by National Defence Minister J.L. Ralston and attracted hundreds of onlookers. The young men had dropped into the canal burdened by full battle gear, including forty-pound packs and rifles. No safety precautions were in place to rescue any of the cadets who should falter during the twenty-yard swim. Many ran into difficulty and five were fished unconscious from the water. Two of these, James Richardson and Raymond Lawton Roberts, died. Richardson had been just shy of his twenty-second birthday.[28]

The younger Charlie had been a lance corporal at the time with no ambition to enter officer training. Following his brother's death, however, he was encouraged by senior North Shore officers to take the admission tests and become what Jim no longer could. Deeply affected by his brother's death and by that of a close cousin, Marvin Black, who had fallen during the Commonwealth defeat at Hong Kong in December 1941, Richardson agreed. He rejoined the North Shores as a lieutenant just a few months after Doug Black, Marvin's brother and a tail gunner in an RCAF bomber, was shot down and killed over Belgium. Doug had been his age, Marvin the same age as Jim, and the two Blacks as close as his own brother. Richardson grimly decided in the aftermath of these tragedies that, as the war had taken the other three, it surely wasn't "going to take the whole four of us.... I had the feeling I was going to come through." But it was hard to be confident of personal survival when suddenly there were German shells whistling right over his head as he hunkered down in the LCA and anxiously waited to hit the beach.[29]

On the North Shores' right flank, Lance Corporal Gerry Cleveland had a Bren gunner, Private Gilbert Duke, stick the muzzle of his weapon through an open slot next to the front ramp so he could fire back at a German MG that was raking the craft with bullets. They were about two hundred yards from touchdown and the little LCA's engine strained forward under full power. Tracers from the German gunner flicked overhead in clusters. "Fire! Fire!" Cleveland yelled at Duke, but the man just stood there with the butt of the Bren in his shoulder as if paralyzed.[30]

Down the entire length of Juno Beach, German fire was thickening, making it abundantly clear that the massive naval, artillery, and aerial bombardment had failed to even dent the beach defences. Queen's Own Rifleman Doug Hester turned to his comrade Doug Reed as their LCA approached the shore and said, "There's the church. I thought it wasn't supposed to be there." The steeple, which dominated the shoreline, was to have been blown off to prevent its use as an observation and machine-gun position. It stood defiant, showing nothing more than a couple of superficial shell scars on its exterior. Then the two riflemen saw the five pillboxes positioned on the seawall, each spitting tracer fire their way, and knew a tough job lay ahead.[31]

An after-action analysis of the bombardment by the Royal Navy gloomily concluded that only 14 per cent of 106 German positions targeted by naval guns were put out of action and most of these fell prey to the close-range fire from the destroyers. The Combined Operations Headquarters Special Observer Party concurred. "All evidence shows that the defences were NOT [emphasis theirs] destroyed." Most of the fire had been widely scattered and the bombs dropped during the aerial bombardment were found to have largely landed well inland. However, a great deal of explosives had struck the towns indiscriminately. St. Aubin-sur-Mer's foreshore buildings were determined to have been 90 per cent destroyed, most totally collapsed by shell strikes. The remainder of the town had suffered damage ranging between 30 and 40 per cent. Bernières-sur-Mer and Courseulles-sur-Mer were more fortunate, but those buildings still standing were capable of being used as defensive positions. As for the rocket fire, it was found to have been more noise and bluster than useful. It was hoped rather forlornly that the entire massive bombardment might at least have served to dampen German morale and in that way made the going easier for the assault forces, but there was no hard evidence to support this.[32]

Also unscathed were the obstacles barring access to the beach. Royal Canadian Navy Lieutenant Russell Choat had cast off from the *Llandovery Castle* with a platoon of Regina Rifles aboard his LCA, which was part of the 557th Landing Craft Flotilla, Royal Marines. The eighteen LCAS were arrayed in three rows of six craft each, with Choat as the navigation officer in the centre of the second row, from which position he could control the move to shore. When they had started the run in, the beach had been so wreathed in smoke it had been hard for Choat to detect the beachfront hotel in the centre of Courseulles that was his aiming point. But as they drew closer he had no problem matching it to the recognition photos memorized during ceaseless hours of training. His goal was to hit the beach right in front of it.

There was a surprising amount of fire coming his way and the Reginas were crouched right down for cover. Choat and his coxswain didn't have that luxury. They hunched behind the thin armoured screen and struggled to keep the LCA on track in the rough seas. The lieutenant thought the man in the most dangerous position was actually his engineer, who had to sit right between the two Ford v-8 engines that powered the craft and monitor their operation. If the LCA hit a mine, the explosion was predicted to tear the bottom out of it and rip the two engines free of their moorings so that the man would likely end up with a massive engine crushing his lap. Choat was actually surplus to the craft's operation, there only to control the flotilla's navigation. On most of the other LCAS there was just the coxswain and engineer.

The LCA was only one hundred yards from touchdown when a 40-millimetre shell "knocked a small hole in the bow just where the ramp hinged with the main hull," Choat later recounted. "This effectively forced water through the hole at greater volumes than would be normal and the boat started to sink." The LCA pressed on, settling as it did, to within twenty yards of the beach when it lost way. Choat ordered the Reginas off. The soldiers piled down the ramp into waist-deep water and started sluggishly wading towards shore under the weight of their gear. Choat and the marines shut down the engines, then jumped into the water and sloshed towards the dubious safety of land.[33]

NOT ONLY THE INFANTRY LCAS were struggling to get ashore, the DD tanks of the 1st Hussars were still battering their way in against the might of the unrelentingly rough seas. The winds continued to howl and the waves battered the canvas screens with punishing blows. Nineteen-year-old Trooper Bill Bury was the co-driver in Sergeant James Malcolm "Ace" Bailey's tank, which had launched from the same LCT that had carried Major Duncan and the rest of 'B' Squadron. The Hamilton-born Bury was seasick, as were the rest of the crew. Fearing the waves were going to break the struts holding up the screens, Bailey ordered Bury, gunner Al Williams, and loader/ operator Larry Allen to come out of the tank and support them. But when they were a few hundred yards out, machine-gun rounds started ricocheting off the water around them and the three men jumped back inside. Bailey dropped down into the turret and used a periscope to look over the top of the screen so that he could continue steering the tank in the right direction. Suddenly, the tank's treads were churning on sand and the crew knew they were ashore. Almost immediately, Bailey ordered the tank halted and the screens dropped to enable the main gun to be used against enemy targets.[34]

Fortuitously, the tank had grounded right between two concrete pillbox positions that had been constructed so their firing ports looked down the length of the beach rather than out to sea. This enabled them to fire on anything trying to cross the beach to reach Courseulles-sur-Mer and also rendered the positions virtually impervious to any seaward shellfire. Each pillbox was armed with a small artillery piece and a machine gun, so they could smother the beach with withering fire. The Germans inside either pillbox, however, were unable to bring these guns to bear on Bailey's tank.

Trooper Williams started blasting away at any German targets Bailey identified. Every time Trooper Allen fed another 75-millimetre round into the breech, the stench of cordite and smoke filling the turret caused him to throw up because of the lingering effect of his seasickness. Everyone in the tank was so focussed on bringing effective fire down on the Germans, they failed to notice that the tide was rising around them until water gushed into the engine compartment and drowned several of the motors. Then Bury reported that water was rising in the driver and co-driver compartments. When Bailey ordered the tank moved further up the beach, the still functioning motors proved too gutless to power the thirty-five-ton Sherman out of the mushy sand. They were stranded, but decided to stay inside the tank and keep firing the gun until the seawater threatened to drown them all.[35]

Bearing down on the beach nearby was the LCT with the ramp that had earlier lost its lift chains. Suddenly, this boat struck a mine that ripped a hole in its bottom and set it listing hard to port. Sergeant F.B. "Sailor" Kenyon managed to launch his tank off the damaged ramp, but shrapnel shredded parts of Corporal Harv Stanfield's screen and the moment his tank hit the water it began sinking. His driver, Stan Seneco, frantically tried to get out of his compartment's hatch but the Davis Escape Apparatus made him too bulky to get through it. He dropped back into the compartment, ripped the escape vest off, and then floated to the surface. A non-swimmer, Seneco clung grimly to the top of the tank turret, which for the moment was still above the surface and seemed to be kept buoyant by some of the screen's inflated tubes.

Beside him, loader/radio operator Trooper Nicholls suddenly cried out, "I forgot to turn the radio off." The man dove headfirst through the turret hatch into the completely flooded tank interior and returned a moment later to report that he had been successful in his mission. Nobody had the heart to tell him it had been a pointless thing to do, for it was part of their training to never leave the tank unmanned with the radio on, running down the batteries.

Looking to shore, Seneco saw Corporal J.M. Kay's Sherman still in the water and almost on the beach when its DD screen started deflating.[36] Shot in the stomach on the run in, Kay had initiated the deflating process prematurely. Within seconds, the tank was swamped and the rising tide forced the crew to bail out.[37] As the men climbed out of the turret, German machine guns opened up from three sides. Seneco watched helplessly as bullets cut Kay, Trooper E.S. Sinclair, and Trooper J.L. Jackson "to ribbons."[38] Trying to avoid the bullets, Trooper J.W. Forbes was smashed into an obstacle post by waves and suffered back injuries that paralyzed him. The driver, Corporal Stephen

Runolfson, managed to help Forbes ashore and then went back into the sea repeatedly to rescue other wounded men in danger of being drowned. He was awarded the Military Medal.[39]

Despite the heavy gunfire striking the water around Stanfield's half-sunken tank, Trooper Oscar E. Smith and Seneco decided to risk inflating the dinghy strapped on the Sherman's hull for fear they would otherwise drown. As Smith climbed aboard the bright orange dinghy, a wave suddenly swept it away. Seneco was dragged along clinging to its side for a bit but then lost his grip. He was left struggling to keep afloat, waving his arms and legs ineffectually in the rough seas. For some reason Seneco could never later explain, he paused in his struggles to carefully remove his pistol from its holster and stow it inside his jacket next to a thick wad of cash he had won off the other men in poker games during the crossing to Normandy.

Stanfield obviously remembered the cash, too. He started yelling to Seneco, "Throw your money back. Fish, throw your money back." Seneco knew that Stanfield thought he was going to drown any moment and, being a poor swimmer, was unable to do anything to rescue him, so he didn't even think the corporal callous. Just as he was on the verge of sinking forever under the surface, a Davis Escape vest with "Fishey" written on it floated up and, hardly believing his good fortune, the trooper wrapped his arms around it. Floating on the current, Seneco drifted in front of the beaches until finally another tanker on one of the LCTs standing offshore was able to come over and rescue him in a dinghy. The rest of the crew managed to get safely ashore.[40]

Following close on the heels of the 1st Hussars DD tanks was the LCT carrying Lieutenant Irving and Sergeant Lamb's 17-pounder Sherman Fireflies that had been tasked with knocking out a fortification in Mike Sector. Although the other LCTs carrying 'C' Squadron tanks were not scheduled to land until forty-five minutes after the first assault wave, this one was to go in early to get the two heavy guns into action. Trooper Ralph Burley and the rest of the ammo passing party were huddled down behind the protective cover of the tanks and LCT's armoured hull because of the heavy small-arms fire striking the craft. On the bridge, one of the Royal Navy sailors was returning fire with a pintle-mounted 20-millimetre machine gun. When Burley looked up to see how the man was doing, he was no longer visible and the weapon was burning. He thought German bullets must have hit it.

The front ramp dropped and Burley could see the shore coming up fast. "What's that sticking out of the water near shore?" Burley shouted to one of the sailors. "Looks like bulrushes to me."

"Bulrushes be damned," the man bellowed. "They're mines on cedar posts."

That should make it pretty exciting, Burley thought, as the LCT started weaving through the obstacles. He could hear posts scraping against the sides of the craft, but no mines exploded. Then the LCT bottomed out and the signal was given for Irving and Lamb to disembark. The tanks rolled out into water only three feet deep and Irving yelled over his shoulder how happy he was with the nearly dry landing as the two Shermans barrelled onto dry ground and headed up the beach.

As the LCT started backing out to sea from the beach, Burley caught sight of scattered infantry running across the sand but he could no longer make out the two Fireflies and the only DD tanks visible were a couple in the surf that appeared to have been swamped. When the ramp was back up, Burley glanced over the side of the LCT and saw some bodies wearing tanker overalls floating in the water nearby. He recognized one that was face up as a friend. Although Burley was aware he would soon be reassigned to another tank and rejoin the regiment in the battle lines, he was not sorry to be granted a short reprieve from the beaches of Normandy.[41]

12

Merry Hell

"**O**UR ENGINES ARE wide open and we'll take you in as far as we can," the flotilla commander of the LCAS carrying the Royal Winnipeg Rifles 'B' and 'D' companies yelled in Major Lochie Fulton's ear. Bullets ricocheted off the hull with a hard clattering rattle, loud as hailstones striking the tin roof of a prairie shack. The LCA grounded with a hard lurch that threw the heavily burdened soldiers up against the ramp in a crush. As the men behind stepped back to give those closest to the front breathing room, the ramp dropped open. Fulton immediately led his men forward and with one great charging stride went off the end of the ramp into water he expected at best would only reach the top of his boots. Plunging up to his waist, the major barely kept from sprawling onto his face in the icy sea. A glance over his shoulder confirmed that the LCA seemed pretty well high and dry, so Fulton guessed it must have hung up on a shoal that the craft's commander mistook for the beginning of the beach.

The quick backward glance assured him that 'D' Company's headquarters section was hot on his tail. During the exercises they had always dashed like Olympic sprinters out of the water and up the sandy beaches, but in the heaving surf Fulton managed what seemed little more than an old man's shuffle. Bullets struck the water around him, leaving little circular rings like a stone does when skipped. Fulton had the fanciful notion that despite the weight of his gear and the waist-deep water, he might step over the skipping rounds and thus avoid being hit. Some of his men were suddenly pausing and then just slumping into the water as if they had tripped or sought to sit down for a moment's rest. "My gosh," Fulton realized as one man went down, "he's been hit." They had been ordered to leave those who fell, told their job was to get across the beach to the cover of the dunes. The order was ignored. One man after another paused to grab a wounded buddy and drag him to shore. Suddenly the water was only knee deep and then, splashing free of the sea, Fulton was dashing faster than he ever had in the exercises through streams of tracer fire ripping down the length of the beach.[1]

Rifleman J.H. Hamilton was the second man in his section aboard the LCA that had lost an engine during the run in and had a man swept overboard. The current had pushed the struggling craft well away from the rest of 'D' Company, so that it hit the beach in the middle of a gap between the Winnipeg Rifles and where the Canadian Scottish Regiment's 'C' Company was landing on the far western flank of Juno Beach. Rifleman Philip Genaille was pressed up against the ramp in front of Hamilton when it dropped. A single tracer round marking the approach of a burst of machine-gun slugs arced out from the beach towards them and Genaille suddenly grunted as the burst tore his stomach apart. The man fell dead. Hamilton stepped over him and charged for the sand dunes. The hot blast of an explosion struck him from the side, followed by the piercing agony of a chunk of shrapnel lodging in his right nostril. Hamilton staggered to the cover of a dune, collapsed, and passed out.[2]

Officers compiling regimental, brigade, and divisional records later tried in vain to determine precisely when the first assault waves landed on Juno Beach in an effort to verify who landed first. The subject would remain cause of endless debate among 3rd Canadian Infantry Division veterans. Normally, such details could be reconstructed and confirmed from the radio logs of regimental and brigade communications. But reporting such a detail as the time feet hit the sand had been of scant importance to assault wave commanders trying to keep their men from being slaughtered on a beach raked by gunfire and exploding shells. Either radios were ignored during the long deadly minutes of the fight to establish a Canadian toehold in Normandy or the messages sent were wildly inaccurate.

That the entire assault wave hit the beach later than scheduled is certain. In Mike Sector, the 7th Canadian Infantry Brigade and 1st Hussars were, according to the rescheduled plan, to touch down at 0745 hours with the tankers arriving some minutes earlier. Yet it was not until 0758 that Major F.L. Peters, commander of 'B' Company Regina Rifles, tersely radioed to regimental headquarters the code-word Popcorn. This meant that from his LCA—still running towards the beach—he had observed some of 'B' Squadron's DD tanks churning up the sand ahead of him.[3]

According to the Royal Winnipeg Regiment's war diarist, however, the two leading companies of his battalion beached at 0749 hours—the earliest recorded landing time—and were completely ashore just seven minutes later. He also remarked on the DD tanks and the Armoured Vehicles Royal Engineers (AVRES) "being late." Bolstering 'D' Company's strength was the regiment's pioneer platoon, while 'B' Company was strengthened by 'C' Company's No. 15 Platoon and two sections of No. 6 Field Company, Royal Canadian Engineers.[4] Using demolitions, the engineers were to open up lanes through the beach obstacles to enable the following 7 CIB units to come ashore more easily.

'C' Company of the Canadian Scottish Regiment was also under Winnipeg Rifles' command, with the task of securing Château Vaux. Coming into shore, the LCAS carrying this company managed to weave between the obstacles fitted with mines without mishap and dropped their ramps within six feet of the sand. As the ramp dropped in front of him, Lieutenant Roger Schjelderup "could see the open grey beach with not a person in sight. We were the first to land and over the beach somewhere was the enemy. There was machine gun fire coming from the left front as we disembarked at the double. So skillful had been the landing that we were able to leap ashore without getting our feet wet."[5]

Schjelderup's No. 13 Platoon had to cross the beach and cut a path through barbed wire in order to take out a concrete pillbox containing a 75-millimetre gun and several machine guns. Sited to the west of the company's landing area, it was ideally positioned to cut the assaulting Canadian Scots to pieces. Yet as Schjelderup led his men in a charge towards the fortification, no machine-gun tracers or muzzle blast from the gun came from the narrow slits of its firing ports. The machine guns firing from the left flank of the beach exacted a toll in dead and wounded but Schjelderup's men raced on without hesitation. When the leading section reached the pillbox, only a handful of German corpses and some abandoned equipment was discovered inside. The fortification had been one of the few destroyed by the naval bombardment.[6]

While No. 13 Platoon secured the pillbox, Lieutenant F.G. Radcliff's No. 15 Platoon worked slowly through tangles of wire to come up on the château from the left. The large building was located in a wooded park that would have been pleasing to the eye were it not concealing coveys of German snipers and machine-gunners. Shot twice while still in the wire, Radcliff fell mortally wounded. Sergeant T.D. Carney took over.[7] When several scattered machine guns opened up from a height of ground right of the château, Lieutenant D.A. "Sandy" Hay ordered his No. 14 Platoon to clear them out. Corporal W.G. Ritchie was killed leading his section in a brave dash towards the position. The marksmanship of Private B.M. Francis, a native Indian from British Columbia, finally broke the German resistance when he dropped several snipers with single, well-placed shots. Francis killed one enemy with a snapshot from the hip at a range of fifty yards. Shortly afterward, Francis fell prey to another sniper's bullet, but not before the high ground was won.[8]

No. 15 Platoon, joined by Schjelderup's men and Major Desmond Crofton's HQ section, managed to clear the woods around the château by having the majority of the men lay down withering fire to force the Germans in one position to take cover while a section overran them. Another section would then leapfrog the first while its advance was similarly covered. Despite heavy casualties, the Canadian Scots soon had the château surrounded. Crofton ordered two men carrying flame-throwers "to burn the place down if there was too much opposition in the building," but two grenades thrown through windows convinced the enemy inside to surrender.[9]

Crofton sent Schjelderup to clear the remaining woods south of the château through to a grain field. Encountering more snipers, a stiff fight was needed to finally eliminate "a lot of pockets of enemy resistance." The company consolidated about 1,400 yards off the beach on the edge of the field. It was not yet 0830 hours.

Leaving the men to dig in, Crofton conducted a reconnaissance to the eastern edge of the wood to see if the other Canadian Scot companies had landed yet, for they were to come up on his rear and carry the battalion's advance inland. There was no sign of the battalion, but he was alarmed by what he did see. Just off to his left, immediately east of Graye-sur-Mer, the Little Black Devils, as the Winnipeg Rifles were nicknamed because their regimental crest included a wicked-looking little devil waving a spear, were being cut to pieces. And inland to the south, a large force of German infantry was mustering in the villages of St. Croix-sur-Mer and Banville-sur-Mer for an apparent counterattack on Graye-sur-Mer and possibly Courseulles-sur-Mer. Crofton realized "that this area of the beachhead was in danger of being overrun by the enemy." He sent a runner back to 'C' Company with orders for the artillery and naval Forward Observation Officers, who had accompanied the Canadian Scots ashore, to immediately join him on the edge of the wood with their radiomen in tow. Crofton planned to saturate the assembling force with fire from the navy's destroyers and then throw his troops between any counterattacking force and the beach in order to give the Winnipegs time to win their fight for the sand.[10]

FROM HIS POSITION INLAND, Crofton was unable to see all of the beachfront being assaulted by the Little Black Devils. With the château's woods blocking his view immediately to the north, the major could only see 'B' Company's landing area and the length of beach beyond that was under assault by the Regina Rifles. Therefore, he was unaware that 'D' Company, landing directly in front of Graye-sur-Mer, had met only slight opposition in its dash to the sand dunes and were now sheltered there from the crossfire ripping the length of the beach from a German pillbox positioned at the mouth of the River Seulles.

Looking back to the waterline, Major Lochie Fulton was relieved to see Major Dudley Brooks of the 1st Hussars 'A' Squadron "coming out of the water with four tanks that had made it to shore." Running over to the Shermans, Fulton shouted up to the tank officer. "Dud, I think there's nothing but minefields and wire in front of us. We've got to blow that up to get through. But I think 'B' Company needs a lot more help than we're going to need, so go help them."

Hearing several explosions behind him, Fulton turned in time to see that one of his platoons had already blasted a route through the wire with bangalore torpedoes and the other two platoons were following the first through the gap in the tangles of wire. Without waiting for Brooks to respond to his suggestion, Fulton dashed to regain control of his company's advance.[11]

Some of Brooks's squadron was already locked in a bitter fight alongside 'B' Company. Of the ten tanks that successfully launched from the LCTs, only seven had reached the beach. Those landing in 'B' Company's area came under immediate fire from a number of German artillery pieces positioned in concrete fortifications. Captain John Wilson "Jake" Powell was still weaving his tank through a maze of beach obstacles fixed with deadly antitank Teller mines when an armour-piercing shell from a 50-millimetre gun sliced halfway through his Sherman's main gun and ripped a gouge out of the turret's side. With the main gun rendered useless, his only hope was to charge out of the water in a direct line towards the gun position in the concrete fortification and engage it with his co-axial machine gun. Another shell rang off the tank's hull and shrapnel wounded Powell in the hand, but he still managed to retain control of his tank as it closed on the fortification and killed the crew with the machine gun—an action that earned him a Military Cross.[12]

On Mike Sector's extreme left flank, 'A' Squadron's Lieutenant Red Goff led his No. 3 Troop up onto the beach in front of a point where the River Seulles bent back on itself in a slight oxbow before emptying into the sea immediately west of Courseulles. Across the river, a narrow neck of land was consequently bordered by water on three sides, so that it appeared to be an island to the tankers.

Dug into the sand on this ground, a concrete fort housed a 75-millimetre gun that opened up on the tanks as they waded across the river towards it. One shot from the German gun knocked out Corporal H.A. Pockiluk's Sherman and several machine guns hosed the crew as it bailed out. Pockiluk, Lance Corporal I.A. Lytle, and Troopers W.F. Hackford, R.F. Moore, and H. Osborne were all killed. The remaining two tanks, noted the Hussars' regimental historian, quickly knocked out the gun "with a vengeance and slaughtered mercilessly the machine gunners who were raking the beaches from the shelter of buildings."[13] With the antitank guns silenced, the surviving tanks of 'A' Squadron turned to help 'B' Company tackle the German infantry still fiercely defending the beach.

For the men of 'B' Company, even getting ashore had been a dreadful task, for their LCAs had sailed into heavy machine-gun, shell, and mortar fire while still seven hundred yards off the beach. Facing them were five "large reinforced concrete blockhouses about 30 feet square with numerous machine-gun positions between them in concrete strongpoints amongst the sand dunes."[14] The LCA carrying Rifleman Jake Miller's platoon dropped them about fifty yards offshore into water chest deep. All around him, men were being cut down by bullets and disappearing beneath the waves. Just short of the sand, Miller's platoon commander, Lieutenant Rod Beattie, collapsed in calf-deep water with a bullet in his spine. Miller flopped on his stomach in front of the lieutenant and started firing his rifle towards a pillbox aperture, only to have a German gun there fire back with a round that painfully grazed his left side. Then a mortar bomb exploded on his right and shrapnel sprayed him. One chunk, larger than the rest, lodged in his right knee.

Rifleman Emil Saruk raced across the open beach to the pillbox and slipped stealthily out of sight behind it. A few seconds later, the gunfire from the position abruptly ceased. Miller figured the twenty-seven-year-old soldier had managed to get in through a back door to kill the Germans inside.

As Miller started crawling painfully out of the water, Lieutenant Beattie called out, "Jake, don't leave me." Miller "crawled back and tried to drag him away from the water's edge. With the wet sand and all, I was unable to pull him away from the incoming tide. Bill Walsh, our platoon Sergeant, was still up and around. I hollered at Bill to help Rod to higher ground. Sgt. Walsh just picked Rod Beattie up like a child and carried him to the shelter of the sand dunes." When Miller and some of the other men in the platoon reached the pillbox, they found Saruk's body lying behind it and a cluster of dead Germans within.[15]

In a nearby machine-gun pit, twenty-six-year-old Corporal John Klos was discovered with his hands locked in death around the throat of the gunner he had strangled. Next to the two men lay the corpse of the German loader. Badly wounded in the stomach and legs by a machine-gun burst coming off an LCA, Klos had somehow managed to reach the offending gun position and kill its crew.[16]

Following close behind the LCAs that had landed 'B' Company was an LCT loaded with two armoured bulldozers manned by Royal Canadian Engineers and a section of the Winnipeg Rifles mortar platoon, consisting of two Bren carriers each carrying a 4.2-inch mortar and towing an ammunition trailer. The driver's compartments on the bulldozers were protected by a cage of one-inch-thick protective armour. These big machines were positioned one behind the other in the front of the LCT, with the carriers in single file behind. When the craft reached the beach obstacles, it was to drop the bulldozers, which would then clear a path through to the shore to make future landings less hazardous and complicated.

For their part, the mortar section was to rush ashore, set up its mortars, and start firing high explosive and smoke rounds to cover the work of the engineers and the landings by the next infantry wave. Rifleman Jim Parks, who had joined the army in 1939 at the tender age of just fifteen by lying to the recruiting officers, was startled to see the beach defences still very much in action. As the sailors started lowering the front ramp, a 75-millimetre armour-piercing round ripped through it and ricocheted off the lead bulldozer's blade. Shards of steel lashed one of the sailors, but the man continued calmly winding the ramp down despite being seriously wounded.

As the two bulldozers disembarked, they sank right to the bottom of the driver's compartment, and Parks realized the water here must be close to twelve feet deep. Yet the carriers were only waterproofed to operate at a four-foot depth. Panicked by the shell hit, the boat captain was loudly yelling at the mortar section's commander, Sergeant Tommy Plumb, to get the carriers off. At the harried sergeant's signal, Rifleman Carl Wald obediently drove his carrier and trailer off. Both promptly sank from sight. The driver and the rest of the men aboard grabbed hold of various compo-ration boxes to keep from drowning and were swept away on the current.

When Parks and the men on the second carrier said they would disembark only if the LCT was taken closer to shore, the boat captain screamed that he had gone in a bit closer and that would suffice. Recognizing the futility of further argument, the mortarmen loosened their equipment belts in case they needed to quickly shed their weight and drove off the ramp, only to have their carrier also sink like a stone. Parks, grateful that he was an excellent swimmer, wriggled out of his equipment belt and started breaststroking for shore. But the tall waves kept washing over his head. Parks had swallowed a lot of salt water and was growing disoriented, when he was relieved to feel his feet touch firm ground. Stumbling out of the shallows, Parks passed several wounded men lying face down in the water. He dragged one of them along with him out of the water and then went back and one by one fetched the others up onto the beach without checking whether they were dead or not. The soldier thought it possible that he might make a mistake if he tried doing that and leave a wounded man to drown.[17]

The beach itself was strewn with bodies. Others hung in the wire fronting the pillboxes. But there were also riflemen out past the wire who had almost reached the line of fortifications, and he saw other soldiers moving into the large wire tangles. To his right was a pillbox that had already been silenced. Parks and another man decided to carry Lance Corporal William John Martin, one of the men he had fished from the water, over to its protective cover. Shot in the lung and groin, Martin was in a bad way. Bubbles of blood dribbled with every ragged breath out of his mouth. After setting him down inside the pillbox, Parks bent to hear Martin's whispered words. "Hold me,

I'm cold," the man said. "Hold me, I'm cold." Parks gently took the soldier in his arms like he would rock an infant. A few minutes later, Parks realized Martin had stopped breathing. Laying Martin's body in a corner, Parks returned to the shoreline and began pulling other bodies of men from the sea in the hope that at least one might still be alive.[18]

Standing tall on the beach so his men must see him and completely disregarding the fact that by doing so the officer betrayed his status to any German, Captain Phil Gower directed 'B' Company's attack on the fortifications. Having lost his helmet, the bareheaded officer strode along the beach gathering men into effective fighting sections and then sending them against specific German machine-gun and rifle positions in coordinated attacks. One after another, the enemy positions fell, but the cost was high. When the last fortification was silenced, Gower had only twenty-six other ranks fit for duty. All his platoon commanders were either dead or wounded. Gower won the Military Cross.[19]

AS HAD BEEN THE CASE for the Winnipeg Rifles, the assault companies of the Regina Rifles faced profoundly differing levels of resistance during their landing on Nan Green. 'B' Company under Major F.L. Peters met little opposition in front of the eastern outskirts of Courseulles-sur-Mer. Its biggest obstacle was the seawall, which proved too high for the men to clamber over. Finally, a Sherman from the Hussars growled up and blasted a section of the wall apart, enabling the men to gain hand- and footholds in the shattered masonry and dirt behind to climb onto the promenade and then rush into the town. Moving house to house, 'B' Company started rooting the Germans out of the eastern side of Courseulles.[20]

'A' Company, meanwhile, had set down right in front of Courseulles-sur-Mer and plunged into a bloodbath. Facing them was a gun emplacement with four-foot-thick walls of reinforced concrete that contained an 88-millimetre gun flanked on either side by heavy machine guns in concrete bunkers. Major Duncan Grosch had just emerged from the surf when his right leg buckled and he pitched in agony onto the sand with a machine-gun round in his knee. All around, the men of his company were crying out in pain. Many were falling dead. When his radio signalman's corpse sloshed up against him, Grosch realized that either the rising tide would drown him if he stayed put or he would likely catch a fatal bullet. The major started crawling across the sand. Ignoring the burning agony of his knee, every inch gained was won through sheer willpower. Finally, the pain overwhelmed him and Grosch used the vial of morphine given to company commanders to sedate himself. As he waited for the drug to take effect, Grosch felt water tugging at his boots and realized the tide was again threatening to drown him. He crawled higher up the beach, hoping to get above the high-tide mark. After gaining little more than a yard or two, the morphine kicked in and, as the pain subsided, the exhausted officer rolled onto his back, no longer caring about the rising water. Then two men grabbed either arm and dragged him to the dubious safety of the seawall. Drifting in a drugged haze, Grosch dimly realized that his war was over.[21]

While the major's test of battle had ended in seconds, Captain Ronald Shawcross, Grosch's second-in-command, now had to save what was left of the company. The twenty-eight-year-old Regina-born officer had joined the regiment in 1936 as a private and risen from the ranks. Aboard his LCA, the six men in the front two rows had been instantly shot down when the ramp dropped. Shawcross grabbed each man and pulled him back into the LCA to save them from drowning and then ran ashore behind the rest of his platoon. Mortar rounds blasted the beach as one man after another fell, bodies ripped by shrapnel. Realizing that it was only one mortar firing, Shawcross timed how many seconds passed between the arrival of each round. Then he sprinted towards the beach wall, dropping a mere second before the next round exploded. Reaching the wall unharmed, the captain was dismayed to see that only four of his men had made it through the enemy fire. The survivors huddled under the wall's protective cover.

Shawcross started frantically trying to gain the attention of the Shermans milling about on the beach, which were firing at random targets without any obvious purpose besides creating havoc. Grosch had assigned the captain the job of ensuring the tanks coordinated their actions to help the infantry get forward. To this purpose, he had been given a yellow-painted map case that he was to carry slung over his back to act as an identifying marker. But none of the tankers paid any attention to him, no matter how obviously he turned his back their way. Frustrated, Shawcross yanked the strap holding the case around, only to see that the yellow case had been shot cleanly away. The captain abandoned any idea of trying to work with the tanks. To run back out onto the beach to the Shermans would be plain suicide.

Most of the company that remained was strung out along the seawall, pinned down by the heavy fire coming from fortifications positioned right in front of houses lining the promenade. Double aprons of barbed wire and machine guns positioned to fire in fixed lines down the length of the wire stood between the Reginas and these pillboxes. When one man tried to pick a way through the wire, he was instantly shot to pieces. The Reginas were stuck.[22]

Meanwhile, Lieutenant Bill Grayson, an 'A' Company platoon commander from Regina, had found a gap in the wire and managed to reach the cover of one of the houses facing the sea. From the back of the house, the officer could see one of the gun emplacements down a short alley from his position, but the alley was blocked by barbed wire and covered by an MG42 machine-gun position. Getting past this obstacle seemed impossible until the officer realized that the Germans manning the gun fired their bursts according to some methodical time sequence rather than seeking out particular targets. Once he timed out the sequence, Grayson waited for a burst to finish and then dashed madly towards the fortification, only to become entangled in the wire with no hope of fighting free before the next scheduled burst arrived. He braced his body for the impact of bullets as the second hand on his watch swept up to the designated time, but nothing happened. Realizing the German crew must have needed to change ammunition belts or clear a jammed round, Grayson tore himself free of the wire without regard for the wicked barbs slashing his flesh and clothes. Dashing to the pillbox, he flung himself against its concrete side for cover, unhooked a grenade from his webbing, and chucked the explosive through an open aperture. When it exploded, Grayson kicked in the back door and stepped in with his pistol at the ready.

He was in time to see some Germans scrambling out another door. As he raised his gun to fire after them, the last man in the line turned and rolled a potato-masher type grenade across the floor. When the explosive skittered to a halt between Grayson's legs, he scooped it up and hurled it out the door behind the fleeing Germans. Once the grenade exploded, Grayson set off in pursuit, zigzagging through a trench system that led to the main pillbox housing the 88-millimetre gun. The lieutenant peered cautiously through the doorway leading inside and was greeted with shouts of "Kamerad, Kamerad." He beckoned with the pistol and thirty-five Germans emerged with arms held high. The main defensive position was taken.[23]

With the 88-millimetre and the machine guns immediately around it silenced, Shawcross was able to get the attack going again. Realizing that trying to cut or pick a path through the wire was futile, the captain told the men to jump over it. By ones and twos they rushed the wire and dived over, rolling on the other side back to their feet, and then piled into the German trench system. Shawcross led them in a bloody chase as they overran one cluster of Germans after another. When the fortifications were cleared, 'A' Company moved into the streets of Courseulles to start clearing houses. The captain knew it would be slow work. The entire company numbered only 28 men out of approximately 120 that had approached the beach little more than a half-hour earlier.[24]

DESPITE SHAWCROSS'S FRUSTRATION with the tankers, 'A' Company's costly victory in front of Courseulles may well have been lost without the uncoordinated assistance provided by the 1st Hussars. When Sergeant Léo Gariépy's tank landed right in the thick of the action, he had immediately loosed five rounds from the 75-millimetre gun at a pillbox. Then he advanced fifty yards and fired another five rounds at it. No fire was returned after that, so he "engaged machine-gun nests dotting [the] beach which were playing merry hell along the water line."[25]

Other tanks closed on the guns firing from pillboxes that covered the length of the beach. A 50-millimetre gun position later found to have more than two hundred empty shell casings scattered around as evidence of its ferocity of fire was silenced "by a direct hit which penetrated the gun shield, making a hole 3-inch by 6-inch." An 88-millimetre gun dug into a position alongside the River Seulles was also silenced by fire from the Hussars, as was a nearby 50-millimetre gun that was holed at short range by a Sherman.[26]

In Sergeant "Ace" Bailey's disabled tank, the situation grew critical during the midst of the fight for control of Nan Green. Trooper Bill Bury advised Bailey that the tidewater in the driver's compartment was up around his neck. "We have to get out of here," he said. Agreeing, Bailey climbed out of the turret hatch to make way for the rest to evacuate. When they had dropped the canvas screens, the tank had been little more than 50 yards from shore in relatively shallow water. Now the beach was 150 yards away and the hull completely submerged. Heavy waves were rolling over the turret. Everyone but Bury joined Bailey outside. They clung to a pile of duffel bags stuffed with the crew's personal effects, which had been secured to the tank hull behind the turret, and floated in the water, keeping the turret between themselves and a German machine gun that was firing their way. Grabbing the handles of the 50-calibre machine gun mounted on top of the turret, Bury started ripping off bursts at the enemy gun crew's position. Bailey yelled: "You're drawing fire on us. Stop shooting the guns." Bury did as ordered and abandoned the tank, but thought he had been close to eliminating the threat.[27]

With the tide still rising, the crew decided to try for shore. Loader Larry Allen pointed out how any infantrymen or tankers floating in the water who were not obviously dead were being fired on by German snipers intent on finishing them off. Their only chance, he said, was to play dead and let the rising tide carry them in to the beach. The men set off singly, letting the sea take them. Allen went last, floating off as the tank completely submerged. He loved swimming and believed he could get ashore safely by keeping underwater most of the way. Almost immediately a wave lifted him, sweeping him more than thirty yards towards the beach in a matter of seconds. "One more like

that and I'm home free," he thought. Allen dog-paddled, waiting for
the next wave. This time, however, as he "rode up the side of the wave
it broke and rolled me over and over as well as down. I was bursting
for air, and then I saw the lighter water above me and realized I was
nearing the surface. As I broke through the air, I gulped and gasped
just as the next wave broke over me and I took in salt water. As I tum-
bled towards the bottom of the channel, I strangled on the water."[28]

Seeing Allen caught by the surf, Bury fought his way over to the
man. "Come on, Larry, I'll help you," Bury said.

"Just leave me. I've had it," Allen moaned.

"No, you haven't. You're going in with me," Bury replied and
pulled Allen close to him as the waves swept them in among a cluster
of obstacles. The two men bounced off one obstacle after another and
Bury was worried they would trigger a mine. He grabbed hold of
an X-shaped steel obstacle and balanced on a crossbar, still clinging
to the semi-conscious Allen, to recover his breath. When he felt
stronger, Bury kicked off again and this time the waves carried the
two men in to shore. Gunner Al Williams was already ashore and the
two men dragged Allen out of the surf. Then Bury made for a pillbox
that had by now been knocked out by the infantry. Inside he found a
pile of German clothes in a corner. Bury was soaking wet, shivering
with cold. Stripping off his sodden uniform, he dragged on a pair of
German pants and hobnailed boots. Under his overalls, Bury had a
blue turtleneck sweater that he left on. Realizing he didn't look much
like a Canadian soldier, Bury tried to improve the effect by putting his
dripping black tanker's beret on. Then he carefully hung up his uniform to dry and sat down for a rest. He had lost track of both Williams
and Allen and had no idea what had happened to Sergeant Bailey or
the tank's driver.[29]

UP ON THE BEACH, the Royal Canadian Engineers' AVRES had
landed and were trying to bridge an antitank ditch in front of
Courseulles that blocked the tanks from pressing into the town to
help the infantry. Some of the LCAS from the two Regina Rifle companies making up the second wave were also arriving. The beach was
anything but safe, though, when the men of 'C' Company and 'D'

Company landed. Rifleman Chan Katzman of 'D' Company jumped off an LCA into waist-deep water and with another man started lugging a six-foot long bangalore torpedo towards shore. The soldier on the front of the torpedo let it go and took off for dry land. Katzman tried to drag the torpedo along for a moment by himself but was unable to make any headway, so he abandoned it.[30]

Around him, the company was meeting disaster. Two LCAS slammed into mined obstacles and most of the crew and soldiers aboard were killed by the explosion or drowned. Only forty-nine men from 'D' Company managed to get ashore.[31] Among the dead was its commander, Major J.V. Love.[32] When Katzman got ashore and saw how many of his buddies had been killed or wounded, he went wild. Seeing some prisoners being marched along the beach, he ran over and "was going to shoot them, but CSM Bruce McConnell stood in front of me and said I'd have to shoot him first because we didn't shoot prisoners." A chastened Katzman backed down and was grateful to the sergeant later. Heading towards the other side of the beach, however, the rifleman was shot in the leg.

He made his way to where some other wounded had been gathered, along with a number of German prisoners. Katzman spoke Yiddish and could make out one German soldier declaring that he was a medic who would like to treat the wounded prisoners. The rifleman was having none of that when Canadians were waiting for medical officers to arrive, so he told one of the other soldiers to point his rifle at the German and then told him in Yiddish to either treat the wounded Reginas or be shot. Katzman was his first patient and the rifleman credited that medical aid with probably saving his leg from having to be amputated.[33]

While 'D' Company had been almost wiped out, 'C' Company under Major C.S.T. "Stu" Tubb had landed on the eastern flank behind 'B' Company virtually without incident. The company swept into Courseulles and cleared its assigned area of the town with equal ease. As Tubb's men completed this task, Lieutenant Colonel F.M. Matheson and his regimental headquarters section arrived and set up in a house secured a few minutes earlier. The remnants of 'D' Company, now commanded by Lieutenant H.L. Jones, set out for their immediate objective of a bridge crossing over the River Rue. This was two miles inland beside the village of Reviers. It was 0930 hours and behind them 'A' Company's mauled ranks were still fighting to secure their designated sector of Courseulles that bordered the port on the western flank.

Despite their small numbers, Shawcross thought the operation was going pretty well, with the last buildings in sight, when they suddenly started taking fire from houses behind, back almost on the beach. The indefatigable Lieutenant Grayson grabbed three men and rushed back to find the pillbox there reoccupied by Germans armed with a heavy machine gun. When they were fired on, however, the ten enemy soldiers promptly surrendered. Grayson nosed around and discovered more Germans emerging from a tunnel that they were using to infiltrate behind the Canadians. A short firefight ensued in which several Germans were killed before twenty-five more surrendered. This action, combined with his earlier heroics, won the lieutenant the Military Cross, and put paid to the German hold on Courseulles.[34] But it was clear that gaining control of beaches where the defenders' fortifications were based in seaside buildings was a costly business. This was a lesson also learned the hard way by 8th Canadian Infantry Brigade when the Queen's Own Rifles at Bernières-sur-Mer and the North Shore (New Brunswick) Regiment at St. Aubin-sur-Mer were caught in a cauldron of fire.

13

The Real Thing

LANCE CORPORAL GERRY CLEVELAND of the North Shore (New Brunswick) Regiment's 'A' Company went into chest-deep water at 0810 hours. Tracers zipped overhead as he blundered towards shore. The two- and three-storey houses facing the beach seemed to hide swarms of machine guns and snipers, all firing directly at the men in the water. Yet, surprisingly, nobody off Cleveland's LCA was hit. "They were bad shots, firing over our heads." A high concrete wall lined the beach in front of the scattered buildings, which lay on the western outskirts of St. Aubin-sur-Mer. To the left of the last house, however, a fifty-yard-wide gap was plugged with barbed wire entanglements. On the other side of this opening, more wall stretched the length of St. Aubin proper.[1] Clearing the houses to the right of the gap was 'A' Company's first task, then they were to link up with the Queen's Own Rifles landing at Bernières-sur-Mer to the west of the North Shores.

Lieutenant M.M. Keith was one of the first men ashore, rushing ahead of his men towards the cover of the seawall. Somebody stepped on a mine that exploded with terrible fury, killing Sergeant Hugh McCormick, Lance Sergeant Pat Walsh, and Corporal Albert Savoy instantly. Fearing the base of the wall was sown with mines, Keith broke to the left so that his platoon drew up in front of the gap and ordered Private Gordon Ellis to open a lane through the wire with his bangalore torpedo. The man shoved the long, explosive-filled pipe into the tangled snarl, lit the fuse, and dashed back to where the lieutenant was crouched out of the torpedo's explosive range. The ensuing explosion was far greater than expected, for the charge also ignited a large buried mine. Ellis was killed and Keith badly wounded. The wire obstacle was, however, ripped open.[2]

Seeing the wire had been breached, Cleveland dashed through and continued into the group of houses without mishap. Machine-gun and sniper fire crackled, forcing the men to stick close to the walls for protective cover. Firing from the upstairs levels, the Germans had excellent fields of fire, whereas the Canadians could not effectively return fire without stepping well out into the open streets. A Bren gunner in Cleveland's section dodged bravely into the centre of a street and ripped the upstairs windows of a house with bursts of fire to keep the Germans ducking while the rest of the section broke into its ground floor.[3] Grenades and rifle fire forced the defenders back from the top of the stairwell, enabling the men to gain the landing there and then clear the rooms with grenades, rifle fire, and bayonets.

Cleveland and his men cleared several houses this way before pausing in an opening between buildings to regroup. The rest of 'A' Company had also managed to come through the gap and was fighting by platoons for control of the row of seaside homes. Cleveland's Bren gunner squatted suddenly as if spying out a target the lance corporal was unable to see through all the smoke and confusion of gunfire and exploding grenades. As he moved to look over the man's shoulder, a mortar or artillery round crashed down. Shrapnel tore into the calf and ankle of Cleveland's left leg, and Privates George McLeod and Alfred Blanchard fell dead to the ground. Everyone dived for cover as the mortars bracketed the area. When the mortar fire lifted, the survivors in the section took off to attack another house, leaving Cleveland to make his way back to the beach. He hobbled through the gap and flopped down against the seawall.[4]

While 'A' Company battled for control of the houses west of St. Aubin-sur-Mer, 'B' Company tackled the town proper. Lieutenant Charles Richardson's platoon was first onto the beach, landing on the company's right flank, with Lieutenant Gerry Moran coming up quickly on his left. Touching down to the rear of the leading companies was Lieutenant Paul "Bones" McCann with Major Bob Forbes and his headquarters section. McCann's platoon was to provide a base of fire support while Moran and Richardson got into the town.[5]

In addition to machine guns and snipers in the houses, 'B' Company faced a major concrete strongpoint that had "exceptional command of the beach" with a 50-millimetre gun, several machine-gun nests, and three 81-millimetre mortars.[6] Not only were all the casemates here constructed of thick reinforced concrete, but steel doors and shutters protected the doors and apertures. A system of deep entrenchments provided the Germans excellent fields of fire towards every possible avenue of approach and further contributed to the strongpoint's formidable strength. Approximately a hundred Germans were defending the position.[7] Housed in a large underground barracks beneath the strongpoint itself, the Germans were able to move from one firing position to another via a series of tunnels that also provided access to surrounding houses. Totally unaffected by either the aerial bombardment or naval gunfire that was to have reduced the strongpoint to a smoldering ruin, the Germans covered the beach with withering fire the moment the North Shores closed on the sand.[8]

Mortar rounds and shells were exploding all along the beach as Richardson led his men out of the water. Right in front of him stood the hulking concrete pillbox housing the 50-millimetre gun. Machine-gun fire kicked up the sand as the platoon dashed for the dubious protection of the seawall and the houses.[9] Armed with nothing heavier than Bren guns and two-inch mortars, the platoon was in no position to take on the pillbox with a direct assault, so Richardson attempted to flank the position by leading his men in among the houses.

Down the beach, Lieutenant Moran discovered that the seawall sheltered his platoon from the fire coming out of the houses but offered no protection from the Germans shooting from the strongpoint because it jutted out over the wall. His men were bunching up and the situation was only going to worsen as 'C' and 'D' companies were already unhorsing from their LCAS and wading in. Wanting to get the platoon moving, Moran stepped out into the open on the beach and started yelling orders while waving his arms. He never finished issuing the commands, as a sniper immediately shot him in the left arm. The bullet ripped through his arm, entered his chest under the armpit, and exited out the centre of his back. As the impact spun him around, a mortar bomb exploded and the concussion slammed the officer flat on his face. Trying to lever himself up, Moran discovered his left arm was useless. Someone pulled him back down and he passed out.[10]

From a spot near the wall, Captain Bill Harvey, 'B' Company's second-in-command, realized that the attack on the strongpoint was faltering. A Bren gunner in front of him was cut down by enemy fire but, quickly scooping up the weapon and its ammunition, another soldier put it back into action. Harvey "could see the way in which the enemy had arranged his field of fire and had all the approaches covered with machinegun fire. Snipers were cleverly located and could move underground from one point to another." The Germans were exacting a bloody toll. Within minutes, Harvey saw two more Bren gunners fall. Then both his radio signallers were killed. His No. 18 radio set also abruptly stopped working. Harvey realized that the North Shores needed tanks badly if the battle for the strongpoint was to be shifted in their favour, but the Fort Garry Horse squadron was not yet ashore.[11]

German machine-gun and shell fire still smothered the beach. When Chaplain Miles Hickey and Medical Officer John Aubry Patterson started wading through the water alongside 'C' Company, a soldier next to the priest was shot down. Hickey "dragged him ashore, and there in that awful turmoil I knelt for a second that seemed an eternity and anointed him—the first of the long, long list I anointed in action." Between the wall and sea, many North Shore soldiers "lay dead or dying. It was our duty to get to them, so, with our stretcher-bearers and first aid men, Doctor Patterson and I crawled back again across that 50 yards of hell."[12]

As Hickey reached a group of three wounded soldiers, a shell landed in their midst killing them all, but leaving the chaplain unharmed. Suddenly several Duplex-Drive tanks waded ashore from LCTs that had unloaded them about a thousand yards from the beach.

"The noise on the beach was deafening," Hickey later wrote, "you couldn't even hear our huge tanks that . . . were crunching their way through the sand; some men, unable to hear them, were run over and crushed to death. A blast shook the earth like an earthquake, it was the engineers blowing the wall. All the while enemy shells came screaming in faster and faster; as we crawled along, we could hear the bullets and shrapnel cutting into the sand around us; when a shell came screaming over, you dug into the sand and held your breath, waited for the blast and the shower of stones and debris that followed; then when it cleared a little, right next to you, perhaps someone you had been talking to half an hour before, lay dead. Others dying, might open their eyes as you reached them. By the little disc around their neck I knew their religion. If Catholic, I gave them Extreme Unction with one unction on the forehead, but whether Catholic or Protestant, I would tell the man he was dying and to be sorry for his sins, and often I was rewarded by the dying man opening his eyes and nodding to me knowingly."[13]

Hickey saw two men, struck by mortar fragments, stumble into the middle of a minefield before collapsing. Without hesitation, the chaplain dashed into the midst of the mines, applied first aid to the wounded soldiers, and then brought them out of the minefield to safety. For this and other courageous acts in succouring the dying and wounded on the beach, Hickey was awarded the Military Cross.[14]

Major Ralph Daughney, 'C' Company's commander, dashed from one platoon to another getting them organized and headed off the sand. Dogging his heels with a No. 18 set strapped on his back was radio signalman Private Joe Ryan. When the two had gone off the ramp of an LCA together, the water had only come up to the six-foot-one officer's waist, but the five-foot-four Ryan had "damned near drowned with water up to my chin." Soldier, radio, and all his other equipment, including a rifle, had been thoroughly soaked by the time he reached shore. Ryan had been scared coming in on the LCA, calming himself with silent prayers, but the beach was even more terrifying. Men were down or falling all over the place, with other soldiers vaulting over or around them in a desperate attempt to gain the seawall.[15]

A steel ramp that a party of engineers braced against the wall pro-vided a rapid means for most of 'C' Company to quickly get over the wall and in among the houses. Daughney and Ryan came up on the street fronting the seaside buildings right behind the leading pla-toons. From buildings to their left, German machine guns were firing, the MG42's cyclic rate so fast that each burst sounded like someone tearing a sheet apart with demonic force. Daughney grabbed the radio handset to call for fire from a destroyer, only to dis-cover the set's battery was dead. With a sickening sense of personal failure, Ryan realized that in the confused scramble to board the LCA he had left the spare battery on the LSI. The company was incommu-nicado and there was nothing he could do to rectify the situation.

Daughney used runners to control the movement of his company, working it towards a church in the heart of the town that was a main objective. The men were breaking into buildings and rooting out snipers and machine-gunners, but no sooner was the job declared finished than other Germans sprouted up in nearby houses, requiring a new round of fighting. Finally, they reached the church and in an intense melee managed to clear a nest of snipers out of the steeple.[16]

The North Shore attack was by now badly behind schedule and, al-though the town itself was slowly falling, the strongpoint remained intact. Lieutenant Richardson's platoon of 'B' Company was com-pletely stalled short of the position, pinned down by German ma-chine-gun and mortar fire. When Richardson sent Private Harry Blakely to summon help, the man ran through a storm of machine-gun fire and reported the situation to 'B' Company's Major Bob Forbes. The officer said tanks would soon be rushed to Richardson's aid and he must hang on until they arrived. Sprinting through the same hail of fire, Blakely carried the report back to his platoon com-mander. The private won the Military Medal for this action.[17]

'C' Squadron of the Fort Garry Horse had run into difficulties get-ting its tanks ashore. Sergeant M.L. Murphy's Sherman sank on the run in and he and Trooper F.R. Gordan drowned. When Sergeant P.C. Parkes was killed by sniper fire while manning the tiller of his DD tank, his loader/operator Lance Corporal R.J. Stevenson took over, only to die himself in a rain of bullets. Another tank was flooded and sank. Sergeant J. Martin of No. 4 Troop rolled his tank up on the beach, only to have it set afire by an exploding shell. Backing the tank up into the sea drowned the fire but also flooded the engine compartment. Stranded in the water, Martin and his crew stayed with the tank, firing high-explosive rounds against suspected German targets until a 75-millimetre armour-piercing round wrecked the gun barrel.[18]

Having lost four of his squadron's tanks getting ashore, Major William Bray formed up the remaining sixteen along the beach and waited impatiently for engineers to clear a lane through a minefield blocking the only vehicle route leading into the town. Finally, at about 0900 Bray's patience snapped and he led the tanks into the minefield. Mines disabled three Shermans, but the rest entered St. Aubin and scattered in troops to assist the North Shores.[19]

Coinciding with the landings of the Fort Garry Horse had been the run in to the beach of 19th Army Field Regiment, Royal Canadian Artillery aboard four LCTs. The 63rd Battery landed to the west of the town and just two hundred yards in from the waterline arrayed its Priests in a line to start blasting rounds into St. Aubin. The 99th Battery quickly joined the 63rd on the gun line, but the third battery—the 55th—ran into problems when the LCT carrying one of its troops lost its rudder to a German shell and was stranded offshore until repairs could be effected. It would not land until mid-afternoon. The second troop and the 19th's Regimental Headquarters, meanwhile, disembarked easily enough from LCTs, only to get jammed up in front of a blocked beach exit. Before the exit could be cleared, a German mortar scored a direct hit on one of the self-propelled guns. When the Priest blew up, fire spread from it to another SPG and a Bren carrier, both of which were laden with explosives. Pandemonium broke out as men abandoned nearby vehicles for fear of being caught in a chain reaction of explosions that could spread through the SPGs, carriers, and half-tracks that had all been jockeying for a position to get through the beach exit once it was opened.

Realizing disaster would only be averted if people took a hand in moving the remaining vehicles out of harm's way, Gunner Harold

Chaplin—already suffering from shrapnel wounds inflicted when the mortar round hit the first SPG—boarded a half-track filled with explosives. The gunner sat calmly behind the wheel while a carrier behind him was moved out of the way and then backed the half-track to safety. Once in the clear, Chaplin drove to the regiment's gun position west of St. Aubin. By this time he was so weak from loss of blood, he had to be lifted bodily from his seat. Chaplin's actions earned a Military Medal.[20]

Meanwhile, one of the Fort Garry Horse tank troops had managed to extricate Lieutenant Richardson's infantry platoon from its difficulties, but not before seventeen infantrymen were killed or wounded. Richardson gathered the survivors together and crouched down beside Lieutenant McCann to plan a coordinated attack on the strongpoint, supported by tank fire. Before the attack started, however, the North Shore's battalion commander, Lieutenant Colonel Donald Buell, arrived on the scene and summoned an Armoured Vehicle Royal Engineers Churchill tank mounting the short-barrelled 12-inch demolition gun called a petard. He also urged Major Bob Forbes to "take chances and hurry the completion of his job, for obvious reasons."[21] The Churchill rolled up to a position practically on top of the strongpoint and fired several of its forty-pound square-shaped rounds, nicknamed "flying dustbins," against the concrete walls.

While the petard wreaked havoc on the central pillbox, a section of the North Shores's Bren carrier platoon accompanied by the antitank platoon advanced up a narrow alley bordering the southern edge of the strongpoint to cover the right flank of 'B' Company's attack. The carriers crept slowly forward, with the crews aboard bringing their Bren guns to bear on any Germans who dared betray their presence. Whenever a position proved too strong to be quickly overcome by machine-gun fire alone, carrier platoon commander Captain J.A. Currie called on Captain C.H. "Chuck" Murphy to deploy his antitank guns. The gun crews, who were pushing their six-pounders by hand up the street ahead of their own carriers, then proceeded to rip the German position apart with a few well-placed rounds.[22]

"We were right beside the rifle-company," antitank platoon

Sergeant Jack Springer later recalled. "Mostly we just fired ahead of us to clear the resistance. Somebody would say, 'There's someone over there. Fire at them!' And we did."[23]

Captain Currie was increasingly perplexed by the fact that half the time a building that had been swept clean by 'B' Company's platoon would suddenly blossom a new force of Germans who had to be shot out by the Bren guns and antitank guns. "We could not figure it out at the moment," he wrote, "but by persistent fire and rushes 'B' Company got them out and took a lot of prisoners."[24]

One prisoner passing Captain Murphy suddenly pulled a gun and started to draw a bead on him. Before the man could fire, however, Murphy managed to snatch a Sten gun from one of his men in time to kill the German with a long burst.[25]

Finally, the advancing unit reached the end of the alley to find the hulking edifice of a large building standing between it and the German strongpoint. Currie summoned Lieutenant B.S.A. McElwaine's pioneer platoon. The pioneers were regular infantrymen with specialized training in handling explosives, clearing mines, and carrying out other basic engineering tasks. Not given much to finesse, the pioneers infiltrated into the building and planted enough explosives inside to reduce the place to a pile of rubble. "This exposed the German gun position," Currie wrote, "and the anti-tanks gave it hell. Just five shots and the Jerries were pouring out with their hands up."[26]

The silencing of the right portion of the strongpoint coincided with the devastating shelling of its centre by the petard. The combined effect threw the surviving Germans into a panic. Out of the gun apertures, white flags appeared, and lieutenants Richardson and McCann moved forward to accept the German surrender. As they closed on the giant fortification, 'B' Company's second-in-command, Captain Bill Harvey, was stunned to see several of the approaching Canadians cut down by gunfire as the Germans opened fire. By this time, however, two Fort Garry Horse tanks had attained good covered positions from which they could fire on the German position. As the tankers pounded the fortification with shells, Richardson and McCann pressed the attack home, ignoring the sudden reappearance of the white flags. "The North Shore had had enough of that trickery,"

Harvey wrote, "and went in with bombs, cold steel and shooting. They inflicted many times the casualties we had suffered and cleaned the place out." The vicious battle ended abruptly at 1115 hours when the surviving forty-eight Germans in the strongpoint surrendered. At least that number again had been killed.[27]

WITH THIS POSITION finally silenced, St. Aubin-sur-Mer was firmly in Canadian hands, with just scattered snipers offering continued resistance. 'B' Company's badly thinned ranks, assigned the task of mopping up the snipers, warily probed any houses not yet cleared. Also moving through the town were Chaplain Miles Hickey, Medical Officer John Patterson, and a team of stretcher-bearers intent on collecting North Shore wounded. In many cellars they found instead cowering French civilians. Most were unhurt, but unfortunately some had been injured.

One man ran across the street to beg Hickey for help. The chaplain and Patterson ran to his house and found the man's young wife lying badly wounded on the floor with their three daughters huddled beside her. While Patterson quickly stanched the bleeding with a field dressing, the woman attempted to bless herself. Explaining he was a priest, Hickey offered her absolution and extreme unction. He then tried to calm the obviously frightened little girls by handing out three chocolate bars that were to have been part of his day's ration. "The terror vanished from six brown eyes and ... three little girls attempted a smile as I patted their curly heads," Hickey wrote.

"I think she'll live," Patterson reported. Hickey translated the prognosis for the husband.

"Thank God, thank God and you," the man replied. Hickey noted, "a new light was dancing in three sets of big brown eyes as Doc and I hurried away."

The two men stepped out into the street just as a stonk of mortar fire rained down and they dashed to take shelter with some other civilians in a cellar. After huddling there for a few minutes, Patterson said, "We're no good here, Father." Dashing through the explosions, they went back to bringing aid to other wounded civilians and soldiers.[28] The medical officer's dedication, repeatedly exposing himself to enemy fire in order to help the wounded, led to his being awarded a Military Medal.[29]

Throughout St. Aubin, surviving North Shores sought to learn the fate of friends and relatives serving in the regiment. Sergeant Jack Springer was told that his youngest brother Marven, a stretcher-bearer with 'A' Company, had been wounded but that his other brother Charles had got through okay. The sergeant's three other brothers were also all in the service but with different units than the North Shores. Springer walked along the beach until he found Marven lying on a stretcher. He had been badly injured by shrapnel in the left leg and also had a head wound. "I'll be back," Marven said. "You go back to England and stay there," Springer told him.[30]

Elsewhere on the beach, Lance Corporal Bud Daley asked a passing sergeant major about the fate of his brother Harold. "I'm afraid he got it," the sergeant said. Daley found his brother's body lying on the side of a road and gathered up his personal belongings to send home. Then he heard his company officers shouting for the men to get ready to move out again and rushed to fall in. When Corporal Alden Daley, the third brother in the family to have landed at St. Aubin that day, heard about Harold's fate, he was struck with a "terrible feeling of loss and a feeling of this is the real thing; there's no joke about this."[31]

Eliminating the strongpoint opened the way for No. 48 Royal Marine Commando to pass through the town's eastern edge and drive along the coast to secure Langrune-sur-Mer on the extreme left flank of Juno Beach. The commandos had met with disaster during their landing when a German machine gun caught them in a deadly rain of fire the moment the ramp of their Landing Craft Infantry, Small was dropped. Lieutenant Colonel Buell had watched in horror as the "poor devils just folded in the middle and fell overboard as though they were a row of wheat sheaves tumbling into the water. The craft then pulled out, leaving its ramp down and those men who had not been hit, jumped into the water." As the survivors of the Commando passed his position, Buell spoke to its commander, who reported grimly that he had lost 40 per cent of his four-hundred-man strength in those seconds of slaughter.[32]

Buell could only assure the officer that St. Aubin was clear, so he could count on being able to form his remaining men up on their start line without worry of enemy interference. What lay between St. Aubin and the commando objective was anyone's guess; something Buell was beginning to appreciate was true for his battalion as well. The North Shores' next objective was the village of Tailleville. 'C' Company was already forming up on the outskirts of St. Aubin preparatory to leading the advance forward. 'A' Company would trail 'C' Company. 'D' Company, meanwhile, was to establish a firm base of support at the junction of St. Aubin's main street and the road leading to Tailleville.

The North Shore company commanders gathered briefly at the church to work out the operation and took a few minutes to catch up with each other. The Support Company commander, Captain C.C. Gammon, was delighted to see Major Archie McNaughton. "Gosh, Archie, I'm glad you made it," Gammon said.[33] McNaughton smiled, not letting on that he had been shot in the hand during the fighting.

'D' Company's Major J. Ernest Anderson saw the bloody wound, but noticed that McNaughton seemed oblivious to the pain it must have caused. "His only concern," Anderson said later, "was for the boys he had lost. He mentioned them all by name and ended with Hughie McCormick." Then he marched towards the next battle.[34]

14

Go! Go! Go!

"**F**OLLOW ME!" Major Charles Dalton gallantly shouted at 0812 hours before dashing down the ramp of an LCA bearing on the beach directly fronting Bernières-sur-Mer and plunging over his head into water eight feet deep. Swimming until his feet found a purchase, Dalton started wading in, noticing with a kind of curious dread how the water to his immediate right was being whipped by bullets. The soldier closest to him on that side staggered under the impact of four slugs that punched ragged holes in his chest and stomach before he flopped lifelessly into the sea. Looking beyond the stricken man, Dalton realized that every man he could see in that direction was floating lifelessly in the water. Yet he remained untouched.[1]

Every soldier of the Queen's Own Rifles' 'B' Company to touch down in two LCAS on Dalton's right-hand side clambered off the ramps into a deadly maelstrom of fire coming from a concrete fortification standing immediately in front of their position. It was the major's miraculous good fortune that none of those machine guns could traverse the few extra inches to include him in their killing zone.

When Sergeant Fred Harris and Corporal John Gibson on No. 10 Platoon led the men out of their LCA into waist-deep water, a machine gun burst instantly killed Harris. The three men ahead of Rifleman Doug Hester fell in turn as each jumped off the ramp. Last to die was his friend, Rifleman Doug Reed. Hester plunged into water frothing with the blood of fallen comrades and wallowed frantically after Gibson, who seemed blessedly bulletproof.[2]

Lance Corporal Rolph Jackson, in the same section as Hester, was almost on the beach when a bullet hit his left hand and twirled him back into the water. Bouncing back to his feet, Jackson snatched up his rifle and raced for the protection of the seawall. Throwing himself behind it, Jackson shouldered his Lee Enfield, only to discover it was too clogged with sand to fire.[3]

Hester joined Gibson by the wall just as a machine-gun burst shredded the corporal's pack. Gibson grinned. "That was close, Dougie."

"Yes, Gibby, there goes your lunch," Hester joked. "We'll have to share." Suddenly Gibson pitched over as a second burst killed him. Hester attempted to remove the dead man's ID bracelet and the silver wristwatch that his wife had sent only the week before, but was forced to abandon the task when another burst of fire nearly hit him. He crawled to the scant cover offered by the wall of one of the pillboxes drenching the beach with fire. Looking over his shoulder, Hester saw Rifleman Ted Westerby from his shredded section staggering across the beach under the weight of a ladder the men were supposed to use to scale the seawall. Three slugs punched into the man and he fell dead in a spray of blood.

Hester decided to climb onto the pillbox and throw a grenade into an aperture above him, but before the rifleman could act a hand darted out of the same opening and dropped a grenade that landed about four inches from his left foot. There was time only to double up in an attempt to make himself a smaller target before the grenade exploded. When the smoke cleared, Hester was amazed to see that he was unharmed except for a small piece of steel that had nicked his Achilles tendon. Abandoning the idea of trying to single-handedly knock out the pillbox, Hester looked about and saw that the only men apparently still alive in this sector of beach were gathered alongside Major Charles Dalton about a hundred yards east of his position. He ran to join them. Dalton was standing with rifle shouldered, firing carefully aimed single shots towards the pillbox Hester had just left, when a bullet struck him in the head. Stretcher-bearer Alex Greer immediately jumped to Dalton's side and discovered the bullet had glanced off the major's skull. Although Dalton was momentarily stunned, the only damage was a deep furrow on the side of his head that Greer quickly bandaged.[4]

Off to the right of Dalton's position, Jackson was in a frenzy of anger that the Germans could so easily slaughter his comrades. The lance corporal was looking for someone to shoot with a Bren gun he had picked up from a dead rifleman, when suddenly a potato-masher grenade dropped from the top of the wall to land three feet from his head. Shrapnel riddled his tunic and a chunk pierced the heavy clothing to penetrate his right shoulder. A quick glance revealed a hole in his flesh the size of a pea, which was bleeding lightly. So far he had been shot in the hand and taken shrapnel in the shoulder, but he counted himself extraordinarily lucky compared to the other men in his section. Only Rifleman Bob Nicol and himself seemed to be still alive. Riflemen David Boynton, Fred Eaman, Ted Westerby, Albert Kennedy, Doug Reed, and Corporal Gibson were all dead, for sure. And Doug Hester had disappeared. Jackson and Nicol began crawling along the wall towards Major Dalton's position. It seemed impossible that less than five minutes had passed since 'B' Company had come up on the beach aboard five LCAS.[5]

The Germans in the pillboxes were still shredding 'B' Company. Sergeant G.W. Morrison was dead. More than half the company was either wounded or dead. Lieutenants John McLean and William Herbert, along with Company Sergeant Major W. Wallis, had been wounded. In the small Bible in his left breast pocket, McLean still had the letter he had accepted from one of his soldiers on the boat during the channel crossing. The man who had given it to him was floating lifeless at the tide line. McLean vowed to make sure he sent the letter, so full of apologies for a life of largely imagined wrongdoing to the young man's mother, but to add one of his own explaining how well the man had performed his duty this day. Assuming he lived to write it, of course.[6]

Although hit in the head and left leg by shrapnel, Lieutenant Herbert managed to round up two of his men, Corporal René Tessier and Rifleman William Chicoski, and carry out an attack on one of the pillboxes. Herbert led the way, alternating bursts from his Sten gun with hard-thrown grenades to close on the fortification. Then the three men lashed the Germans inside with gunfire through the apertures, followed up by several grenades. This action won Herbert a Military Cross and Tessier and Chicoski Military Medals, but the other pillbox still stood.[7] With Dalton down, nobody was exerting command control over the remaining soldiers. Taking the second fortification by direct frontal assault would be suicidal and 'B' Squadron of the Fort Garry Horse was still bringing its DD Tanks ashore from a launch point a thousand yards off the beach, so there were no tanks yet to provide fire support.

It was then that an apparent mishap turned the tide in the company's favour. During the run-in, the rudder of the LCA on the extreme left flank had jammed, causing it to veer far off course. Lieutenant Hank Elliot and his platoon landed on a beach devoid of German defences and immediately worked inland to attack the remaining fortification from the flank. It took Elliot a dozen minutes or so to reach and attack the position. The sudden assault from the flank surprised the Germans inside and convinced them to surrender.[8]

At the same time Elliot was making his attack, Rifleman Don Hester tackled another strongpoint constructed of logs with an antitank gun inside that was pointed to the sea. Hester crawled up on the position and chucked a grenade in one of the openings. After it exploded, three Germans abandoned the post and fled towards a nearby seaside hotel. Among them was an officer, who fired at Hester with a Luger pistol. Shouldering his Lee Enfield, Hester shot the man dead and then calmly retrieved the Luger for a souvenir.[9]

The simultaneous silencing of these strongpoints opened the way for the remnants of 'B' Company to enter Bernières-sur-Mer. Hester and Rifleman John Humenyk headed up a dory ramp to mount the seawall. Despite the fortifications having been knocked out, there was still a lot of machine-gun fire coming from smaller German positions. Mortar and artillery rounds were also exploding all over the beach and around the seawall. A nearby explosion sent Hester somersaulting down the ramp. When the smoke cleared, he saw that his left leg was bleeding from multiple shrapnel wounds. Finding his commando knife too dull to slit the trouser leg open, Hester was forced to apply a field dressing to the top of the fabric. The crude first-aid attempt seemed to work, as the flow of blood stopped. The explosion had left Humenyk untouched, although the breech of his rifle had been shattered by a piece of shrapnel.

ON 'B' COMPANY'S right flank, Major Elliott Dalton's 'A' Company had also been cut to pieces. The LCA carrying Dalton had zigzagged with amazing agility between the many beach obstacles to gain the sand, but in doing so had moved a little too far to the left for Dalton's liking. Leaning over to ask the coxswain to alter course, he saw blood coming from a bullet hole between the man's eyes. For some minutes, the LCA had been steering itself. With a grinding sound, the craft slammed up on the sand and Dalton ordered everyone out.[10]

"Move! Fast! Don't stop for anything! Go! Go! Go!" Company Sergeant Major Charlie Martin yelled over his shoulder as the ramp on his nearby LCA dropped. Most of the men here were from No. 9 Platoon, his old command before promotion, and they responded reflexively to his orders. Ahead stood a tall half-timbered house flanked by a pillbox on either side. Streams of machine-gun fire reached out of the apertures in the pillboxes towards the men. The platoon's commander, Lance Sergeant Jack Simpson, was cut down.[11] Then somebody stepped on a mine and riflemen Jamie McKechnie, Ernie Cunningham, and Sammy Hall died. The three soldiers had been carrying a ladder for scaling the wall. Rifleman Jack Culbertson was wounded in the blast.[12]

Martin ran towards a gap in the wall that appeared to have been left by the Germans as a vehicle access to the beach. On either side of him were 'A' Company's two snipers, riflemen Bill Bettridge and Bert Shepherd. A German MG42, manned by a single German, covered the gap. The enemy soldier was waving an arm wildly while looking over his shoulder, as if trying to summon a mate to feed the ammunition belt while he fired the gun. Firing their rifles from the hip, Martin and the snipers charged the gun. Fearing the gunner would bring them under fire before they overran him, Bettridge paused, took careful aim, and killed the gunner with a single shot. Martin led the way through the gap and across the backyard of the half-timbered house towards the railroad station, but found their route blocked at the tracks that parallelled the beach by heavy tangles of barbed wire.[13] They took cover in a shallow ditch next to the wire.

As they did so, Bettridge saw Rifleman Herman Stock, an Iroquois from the Gibson Reserve near Bala, Ontario, standing astride the track. Stock, a tall, powerful Bren gunner, had cut his hair Mohawk fashion for the invasion. Everyone else was crouched, lying prone, or running to avoid presenting a still target, but Stock was standing there glaring towards the houses of the town as if looking for a German to kill. The moment ended when a hidden sniper shot the man dead. Bettridge watched him fall and then got well down in the ditch. Bullets were chiming off the wire.[14]

Martin was on Bettridge's right and Shepherd on Bettridge's left, with a gap of about five feet between each man. The company sergeant major shouted to Bettridge, "Watch for these wire cutters. I'm going to throw them to you and you throw them to Shep and tell him to cut a hole through that wire." Once Shepherd finished the task, the whole platoon would go through the hole.

Bettridge didn't have time to pass on Martin's instructions before Shepherd bellowed: "You tell him to go fuck himself. He's making more money than we are."[15]

Knowing that Shepherd was the kind of man who would argue a detail to the end no matter what the circumstances, Martin set about doing the job himself and opened a hole just wide enough to crawl through. About fifteen men followed him through the little hole into a meadow of grass that had been allowed to grow up to almost three feet of height and so provided excellent cover. The Germans knew the Canadians were in the grass but, unable to see them crawling towards the buildings, could only search for them with random bursts of fire.

Martin was almost through to the buildings when the grassy meadow gave way to an open stretch of ground marked by minefield signs. Forming the men up on the minefield's edge, Martin signalled them forward. Advancing at a steady walking pace, scanning the ground as they did so, the men tried to ignore the German fire coming their way. Ten paces into the minefield, Martin heard a telltale click just as his foot met some resistance. The CSM realized he had depressed the detonating trigger of a Schützenmine. The moment his foot came free of the trigger, a canister loaded with 350 ball bearings would bounce three feet into the air ahead of him to rip his guts open. Knowing that as long as his foot remained on the trigger the mine would not be released, Martin froze in place while the rest of the platoon exited the minefield by clambering over a fence and entering the back gardens of the first row of houses.

Martin was calm, for he had been trained to escape this kind of mine's kill radius by simply dropping to the ground right beside it so that the ball bearings would spray out harmlessly overhead. But just as he made his move, a bullet struck his helmet, pierced right through the steel, and began spinning round and round inside the liner before exiting with such force that it tore the helmet clear off his head. Fortunately, the force of the bullet striking his head had also knocked him flat and the mine had exploded harmlessly overhead just as Martin had planned. Not bothering to retrieve his helmet, Martin fled the minefield and joined his small band in the gardens. Then he led them warily into the streets of Bernières-sur-Mer.

They met surprisingly little resistance. It seemed the Germans defending Bernières-sur-Mer had put all their defences in the shop window directly on the beach. So while Martin could hear a lot of gunfire and explosions still coming from the waterfront, an eerie calm hung over the streets of the town. 'A' Company's objective was to secure a road running through the southwest part of Bernières, so Martin headed that way while telling Bettridge and Shepherd to lead the advance by moving alternately up two streets on either side of a block of houses.[16] Reaching the end of the block, Bettridge carefully poked his head out to see into the cross street, only to have a bullet chip masonry off the wall right above his helmet. Peering around the opposite corner was Shepherd, rifle shouldered and smoking. "I never did think you were much of a bloody shot," Bettridge yelled at his fellow sniper.[17] Martin's team reached the objective at 0845 without encountering any resistance. There was nobody else around. The CSM had no idea whether the rest of 'A' Company had been wiped out on the beach or would soon be coming up through the town. He figured the best thing to do was to dig in on the objective and sit tight, for 'C' and 'D' companies should be landing about now and would surely get through.[18]

THE TWO RESERVE COMPANIES started landing at 0830 hours. More than half the LCAs were crippled just off the beach by mines. In 'C' Company, No. 15 Platoon's LCA had its ramp mangled and the craft started settling heavily to one side as water poured onto its deck. Sergeant Dave Kingston turned to the tallest man in the section at the rear of the boat and said, "Leap overboard and see how deep it is." Despite the fact that nobody could tell in the rough sea whether the water depth was four feet or twelve feet, the man went over the side without hesitation. He sank up to his chest and then found bottom. "Let's go," Kingston yelled and all but one of the men instantly clambered over the side. "I can't swim," the lingering soldier told Kingston. "I can't either," the twenty-two-year-old sergeant from Toronto said. The two men went over the side together.

Kingston waded onto a beach littered with the dead and dying of the initial assault wave. A long line of wounded were lying or sitting in front of the seawall. The beach was being heavily bombarded by mortar and artillery rounds and a few German machine guns still chattered. Most of the fire seemed concentrated to the left of where No. 15 Platoon had landed on the right edge of the town.[19]

No. 1 Troop of the Fort Garry Horse's 'B' Squadron touched down about the same time as 'C' and 'D' companies, formed a line at the water's edge, then growled up to the seawall to take up positions that enabled them to fire over it into Bernières. Lacking a way over the six-foot-high wall, the Shermans were stuck on the beach until the engineers could open up a vehicle exit. As more of the tanks waded ashore, the Shermans offered whatever fire support they could to the beleaguered Queen's Own 'A' Company. Sergeant Bill McLean's No. 5 Troop headed towards a house on the shoreline that concealed a machine-gun position, while No. 1 and No. 2 troops fired smoke rounds at the building to screen the attack. McLean rumbled his tank right up to the house and pumped several high-explosive rounds through a window, which put an end to the German resistance there.[20]

'D' Company of the Queen's Own, meanwhile, set down right in front of the town, using the half-timbered house as its guiding point. Rifleman Jim McCullough, one of the company's runners, saw all the shells exploding in the water around his little LCA and thought, "Holy Christ, I'm not even going to get to the beach!" There was a loud bang and the engine died. The soldiers in front started trying to force the ramp down, anxious to get off. "Stick with it, stick with it," the coxswain shouted as he used the rudder to keep the LCA directed towards the beach. They coasted in on the tide until the coxswain thought the water shallow enough to unload his passengers. McCullough waded through chest-deep water past the floating bodies of other Canadian soldiers and figured he would be lucky to live another thirty seconds. But he made the beach and sprinted for the protection of the wall.[21]

Rifleman Jack Martin was on an LCT carrying two Fort Garry Horse tanks and the two Bren carriers of his mortar section. The sergeant in command of the section said that the beach was still too hot for them to all go off aboard the carriers, so only two of the men on each mortar crew would stay with the vehicle. The other three men from each crew would go in on foot and temporarily attach themselves to 'C' Company. Martin had been so sick during the crossing from Britain that he had spent the night lying on the gunwale throwing up overboard, but now he felt fine despite the still pitching sea. He and the other two men from his section relegated to foot-sloggers got up right behind the ramp.

A second later, the LCT gently ground on the sand and the ramp dropped. The first thing Martin saw was Major Charles Dalton with blood running down his face from a head wound. "Oh, my God, what the hell have we got into now?" Martin wondered. Dalton shouted, "Get up to the wall." Jumping over bodies and equipment, the twenty-year-old soldier made a beeline to the wall, thinking as he did so that nobody had really needed to risk his life to encourage him to do the obvious.[22]

All of the Fort Garry Horse's 'B' Squadron was now ashore and being joined by some of the non–Duplex Drive Shermans of 'A' Squadron. There were also numerous armoured bulldozers, flail tanks, AVRES, and other engineering equipment coming off LCTS, as well as the Priests of the 14th Field Regiment, Royal Canadian Artillery. The beach was suddenly a very crowded place.

But the Queen's Own Rifles were moving quickly now, pushing inland and wiping out the last resistance facing the beach. A Royal Engineers' Churchill tank broke up a section of the wall with its massive petard and Lieutenant Jack Arber led No. 15 Platoon in a scramble up to the railroad track. The rest of 'C' Company followed hot on the platoon's heels and headed across a grassy knoll towards an orchard on the town's western flank.[23]

With the tanks and Priests ashore, the last resistance by the Germans defending the shoreline crumbled and the Queen's Own moved in strength into the town. They still lacked tank support, as the Shermans were left milling on the beach while the engineers began cutting the ramps necessary to get over the seawall. Major McGregor Young, the 14th Field Regiment's acting commander on the beach, managed to find a narrow route off the beach ahead of the engineers and led two Priests into the town. Coolly preceding the self-propelled guns on foot, the major pointed out potential German strongpoints that the gunners shot to pieces with their 105-millimetre guns by firing over open sights. Young cleared a route through Bernières to the southern outskirts that could be used by the rest of the motorized vehicles starting to finally escape the beach. His action earned the officer a Distinguished Service Order, the first such award to be won by a Canadian gunner during the invasion.[24]

By the time Young finished cutting a swath through the town, most of the Germans had quit Bernières. And the moment a street was freed from the heel of the German boot, the townspeople there started to emerge. One of the most amazing sights to greet the Canadians was a bar just off the beach that by 0900 had thrown open its doors and was selling wine and cognac to civilians and soldiers alike.[25] As the Queen's Own moved along streets, still warily hugging the walls because isolated snipers remained active, young children and beautiful laughing women thronged around them offering embraces, or trying to press wine, calvados brandy, and roses into their hands. They called on the men to join them in a victory party, but the soldiers pushed on through the throngs with their officers urging them to haste. Their job was to get inland, and already the clearing of Bernières had taken longer than planned. Ahead of them were more Germans and they would be better prepared to meet the Canadian advance if time was lost fraternizing with the townspeople. As well, the troops had been cautioned in pre-invasion briefings to accept no wine or food from French civilians. These were a people who had been living under the German occupation for four years, people who may have come to terms with that and might prove hostile to the Allies. It was the Canadians, after all, who had just landed in the wake of a naval bombardment that had demolished whole sections of the town and undoubtedly killed at least some residents. There was a fear of poisoned wine and cheese, of flowers and ribbons being fastened to officers' tunics to mark them for German snipers. So the rifle companies of the Queen's Own tromped through Bernières and out the other side, leaving it to the reserve and support units to determine whether the citizenry should be considered friend or foe.

Despite the orders and pre-invasion briefings, however, the men of the rifle companies were young and trusting in a typically Canadian way. So more than one ignored the proscriptions against fraternization and stuck the proffered bottle of calvados into his pack or munched a chunk of cheese. Accepting a kiss on one cheek and then another was even easier and did something to ease the hard lump of fear that had gathered in a stomach during the fierce battle for the beach.

'D' Company's Sergeant Dave Fletcher was passing a little school in the midst of the town when a small girl of about eight years old approached. Having been studiously studying a French-English dictionary for several months to hone his language skills, Fletcher said with careful enunciation and flagrant disobedience of the fraternization order, "Avez-vous les oeufs?" The girl looked at him for a thoughtful moment and then answered in perfect English, "Come back at 6:00 and we'll have some fresh eggs for you." As soon as he was out of sight of the girl, Fletcher threw away the French-English dictionary. "Christ," he muttered, "if everyone can speak English like that, I don't need it."[26]

Rifleman Jim McCullough's platoon from 'D' Company was moving slowly, cautiously up the main street running south through the town. Hearing what sounded like breaking glass in a courtyard, McCullough opened a gate, and with his gun at the ready, peered in. The courtyard was empty save for two old women sweeping up the glass of windows that had been broken by the concussion of the naval bombardment.[27] Much of the town was a shambles, having been pounded by heavy shelling and aerial bombardment.

Although the Germans had given up Bernières, they were still aggressively trying to prevent the Canadians breaking out into the country beyond. No. 15 Platoon no sooner entered the orchard than it was heavily shelled. An explosion tore Lieutenant Arber's right leg and part of his chin off. Lying on the ground with his leg beside him, the lieutenant looked up at Sergeant Dave Kingston and said, "Get a fighting patrol together and get out front to see who we're facing." Kingston was amazed at the man's calm demeanour and determination to continue commanding his platoon despite the terrible injury he had suffered.

Gathering the platoon's corporals together, Kingston explained how the patrol was to be conducted. He was just finishing up when a German half-track bore down on the group with two MG42s blazing. All six corporals were immediately killed or wounded, but not a round hit Kingston. The platoon responded with a torrent of rifle and Bren gun fire, wiping out the half-track crew. Up until then, No. 15 Platoon had seemed fortunate, for only one man had been lost on the beach. Now, except for Kingston, it was leaderless. The sergeant assigned a man from each section as its leader and then led the patrol out to try locating the German positions ahead of them.[28]

PART THREE

BREAKOUT

[15]

Nothing for Shame

EVEN AS THE GREAT barrage had lifted and the first glimmer of
light filtered through the thick cloud cover above the Normandy
beaches, 6th British Airborne Division's fight for control of its objectives between the River Orne and River Dives had continued unabated. Although small numbers of paratroops had managed to reach
their rendezvous points by dawn and begin their assigned tasks,
many more were still widely scattered across the countryside. Some
wandered lost, others were pinned down in firefights with German
reaction forces, and many were dead, wounded, or prisoners; but a
surprising number were still on the move and heading with clear
purpose towards assigned objectives or rendezvous points. Despite
having been scattered chaotically far beyond the designated drop
zones, the airborne troops took the disaster in stride.

This was as true for 1st Canadian Parachute Battalion as any of the
British battalions comprising the division. The men in Lieutenant
Philippe Rousseau's stick from 'C' Company had suffered as great
misfortune as those in Lieutenant John Madden's, which had ended
up practically in front of Sword Beach well west of the River Orne. In
Rousseau's case, the stick had been dumped out of its plane on the
eastern bank of the River Dives. By dawn, only eight men in this stick
had managed to stay together. Rousseau, the last man out of the

plane, had never been located. When Private Mel Oxtoby insisted on looking for the lieutenant, he simply disappeared into the darkness, never to re-emerge.*

Soon after first light, the small band encountered thirteen British paratroopers and the two groups joined forces. Then they picked up Corporal Boyd Anderson and Private Jim MacPherson, who had also been in Rousseau's stick. The party was working its way around a large hedge-bound field when a much larger German unit attacked it. Private Gordon Conneghan was killed and the rest of the men pinned down. Privates Morris Ellefson, James Broadfoot, Kenneth Pledger, and George Robertson had been out ahead on the western flank of the paratroops and now lay down covering fire to enable the larger group to extract itself from the enemy fire. As the main group made good its escape, the Germans turned their attention on these four Canadians. Robertson was just moving through a gap in the hedge when enemy fire ripped into the other three men. Pledger and Broadfoot fell mortally wounded, while Ellefson whirled around with his Bren gun and returned fire until he was shot dead. Robertson managed to dash away, suffering only a bullet crease on his right arm.

There ensued a hot pursuit that ended with five of the surviving Canadians, including Robertson, and most of the British paratroops being surrounded and forced to surrender. Only Corporal Boyd Anderson managed to elude the Germans, hiding behind cider barrels in a small shack. He would remain on the lam for several days before finally being captured.[1]

Also captured soon after dawn was Medical Officer Colin Brebner, who had been rendered helpless by a broken pelvis after free-falling out of a tree. Surprisingly, Brebner's left wrist, broken and badly deformed in the fall, had proven to be more painful than the injury to his pelvis during the night. By dawn, however, this situation was beginning to reverse itself. A keen birdwatcher since he was a child, Brebner attempted to distract himself from the increasing pain by

---

* Both men were subsequently discovered to have been killed, but the circumstances behind their deaths remain unknown.

identifying the various birds in nearby trees that were welcoming the day with song. When it became too agonizing to turn his head in search of the birds, the doctor tried instead memorizing the songs for future identification.

Eventually, Brebner was found by another paratrooper, who put him on an old garden trellis and then dragged the doctor to an aid post that some British medics from one of the other 6th Division units had established. The place was full of wounded and injured paratroops all being treated by one British medical officer. After being injected with morphine, Brebner fell asleep only to be wakened some time later by the sounds of falling bombs and the following explosions as Allied planes pounded a nearby target.

At 0730 hours, a German patrol swooped down on the aid station and took the mobile wounded off as prisoners, but left the more seriously injured paratroopers to die where they were. To save Brebner from this fate, two of the medics put him back on the old trellis again and dragged him along behind the party of walking wounded.[2] With some of the more badly wounded men, Brebner was transported to a civilian hospital in Caen and then transferred in July to a spa south of the city, where he was liberated in August.[3]

WHILE THE ARRIVAL of daylight greatly increased the likelihood that the scattered parties of paratroopers would be killed or captured by the many German units actively hunting them, it also made life more difficult for the small elements of Canadians who had successfully reached their objectives. At Robehomme, Captain Griffin's band of about fifty troops from 'B' Company had withdrawn from the destroyed bridge into the clutch of rough houses and barns that constituted the village and were frantically fortifying the position in expectation of counterattacks.[4]

Situated on a piece of high ground largely surrounded by land flooded by the German diversion of the River Dives and on one side by the river itself, the village was a good defensible position. Griffin set up a Vickers machine gun to cover the road and bridge and then distributed the rest of the force to ensure a 360-degree defensive ring around the small church whose tower served as an observation post.

From its heights, Griffin could see Varaville and Bavent, about a half-mile to the northwest and southwest respectively.

Bavent was a German base and within its streets Griffin could see troops mustering and then moving out towards Varaville, where the Canadian Parachute Battalion's 'C' Company was to have destroyed a gun position at the nearby Le Grand Château de Varaville and secured the village. Hearing the distant sound of gunfire from Varaville, Griffin knew that at least some paratroops had reached that objective and were involved in a battle there. But he had no way of warning them that a German reaction force was headed their way.[5]

Griffin's men had barely completed digging in around the church when three trucks loaded with German troops appeared on the east bank of the river. Quickly piling off the vehicles, the Germans swarmed two paratroopers—privates L.E. "Doc" O'Leary and L.D. Ross—who had been standing guard there and took them prisoner. After spreading out in the thick brush near the riverbank, the Germans attempted to deter the Canadians from firing on the trucks by putting the captured men up on the hood of one vehicle to serve as human shields. They then tried to cross the river, apparently expecting that the presence of the two prisoners on the truck would ensure no reaction from the paratroopers in Robehomme.

Instead, the paratroopers ripped into the Germans with deadly fire. In the ensuing gunfight, Ross was killed, but O'Leary managed to escape his captors and swim across the river to safety. When the Germans withdrew, they left behind numerous dead and, more importantly, weapons and ammunition that Griffin's men quickly rounded up to bolster their depleted stocks. Private W.J. Brady was particularly pleased to be given a "German sniper's rifle with lots of ammunition, telescope and cheek rest—the best!"[6] The two sides hunkered down to scowl across the river at each other and pick away at anyone who moved with small-arms fire. At best, the situation was a stalemate, but the Germans had the surety of being able to eventually summon reinforcements.

In the event, however, the scales tipped in favour of the Canadians, the sounds of gunfire serving as a beacon for lost paratroopers making their way out of the flooded terrain around the River Dives. Throughout the day, ever more men filtered in, ultimately adding another hundred men to the Canadian force's strength before dawn of June 7. For their part, the Germans confined themselves to trying to infiltrate the village throughout the course of June 6, but without success. Still it was dangerous, anxious work for the men in the most advanced fighting holes to determine whether it was friend or foe approaching the lines. This became particularly difficult once darkness fell.[7]

As the initial firefight had broken out at Robehomme, the paratroops holed up in Varaville and the gatehouse of Varaville Château overlooking the German strongpoint had also greeted the morning trading bullets with the enemy. In Varaville, Lieutenant Sam McGowan perched in the steeple of the village's church, where he had established a platoon headquarters and around which his troops were dug in. Soon a party of German troops, possibly those from Bavent, were observed closing on the village through a small wood. As a German section started crossing a large bomb crater towards the churchyard, the paratroopers opened fire. Three of the enemy fell dead, while the others ran back into the woods. After digging in among the trees and several outlying farm buildings, the German force added its weight to the mortar, machine-gun, sniper, and artillery fire all being directed at McGowan's men. Yet the Canadians suffered few casualties and noted that the Germans seemed content to merely harass them rather than trying to overwhelm the position with a direct attack.

For their part, the paratroopers had neither the strength in manpower nor abundance of ammunition to even contemplate going on the offensive. McGowan was satisfied to sit tight and keep his men sniping at any Germans foolish enough to expose themselves.[8] The small force of paratroopers was soon being significantly assisted by many of Varaville's villagers. Several women insisted on setting up an aid station in the church, where they bandaged the wounded as best they could with first-aid supplies the paratroopers had with them or with white sheets fetched from their homes. Some of the men volunteered to serve alongside the Canadians in the slit trenches and positions inside buildings. The paratroops gave one villager a maroon beret and rifle, after which he quickly demonstrated a deadly eye by killing three German snipers.[9]

The situation at the château's gatehouse, meanwhile, remained deadlocked. Captain John Hanson's thirty-man force from 'C' Company was keeping the Germans pinned down in the concrete emplacement and trench system with sniper fire, but it was unlikely this situation could be sustained indefinitely. As the Germans were heavily armed with machine guns and the 75-millimetre artillery piece, going on the offensive was not an option. Taking stock of his situation, the captain determined that he had a single Bren gun, four Sten guns, twenty rifles, a couple of pistols, and a small number of grenades and Type 82 grenades. Nicknamed "Gammon bombs" after British paratroop Lieutenant Jock Gammon, who invented the explosive to provide airborne troops with a lightweight but effective antitank weapon, these were basically a canvas bag filled with two pounds of plastic explosives fitted with a tumbler fuse. When a protective plastic cap was removed to expose the detonator atop the fuse, the explosive would explode at the slightest motion or impact.[10] Ideal for placing on roads to disable any passing tank, they were less functional as a thrown explosive and the German bunkers were out of range anyway.

Private Esko Makela was packing the Bren gun. Since his welcome appearance a couple of hours earlier, he had set up a firing position in the room on the second floor next to the one in which Major Murray MacLeod and the others had been killed by the 75-millimetre shell. Standing a few feet back from the window—to prevent the Bren's muzzle flash betraying his position—Makela had set the gun on single shot and was using it like a sniper rifle to shoot at the enemy. He had killed several men this way and was a major reason the Germans were keeping their heads well down.[11]

Before dawn, Hanson had sent two men to le Mesnil crossroads to advise Lieutenant Colonel G.F. Bradbrooke of the situation at Varaville. He had also asked them to find out if the battalion's 17-pound antitank gun had survived the landings and, if it had, to fetch it to the château. But it would be hours before he could expect any help from that quarter. The only advantage the Canadians enjoyed was that the Germans were as immobile as they were.

Hanson was still pondering his options and getting nowhere, when help materialized in the unexpected form of thirty-year-old Mademoiselle Laura Hiervieux, who arrived at the gatehouse from her home in Varaville. The daughter of a French father and English mother, Hiervieux and her brother Rene had both been educated in England before the war. After the occupation, Rene had emerged as a leading figure in the local Resistance and just two days before the invasion had been forced to flee into a large forest near Bavent to escape a Gestapo squad. Hiervieux told Hanson that he faced about eighty heavily armed Germans amply supplied with ammunition and commanded by an Austrian major. However, she also knew some of the soldiers. While the non-commissioned officers were all Germans, the troops were mostly Poles, Russians, and Romanians not particularly eager to die in the war.

Offering to act as an intermediary, Hiervieux proceeded to establish contact with the enemy soldiers in the trench close to the gatehouse and started urging them to surrender or the Allies would soon kill them. Calling to them from a window in the gatehouse, the Frenchwoman alternated between cajoling and haranguing the men, while the Canadians punctuated her remarks with gunfire aimed at the trench and apertures of the concrete bunker.[12]

SOON AFTER Mademoiselle Hiervieux's arrival, Corporal Dan Hartigan and Private Eddie Mallon, who had trekked through the night from Merville Battery to reach Varaville, also appeared. The two men had almost not made it. Dawn's half-light had found them lying in a field across from the château trying to perceive whether there were any friendly forces there or not. At last, they ventured out in the field and were about halfway across when a group of soldiers suddenly materialized out of the misty haze that blanketed the area. "Punch," Hartigan called fearfully and was relieved when someone answered, "Judy."

The troops proved to be British paratroopers from 3rd Parachute Brigade's Headquarters group, of which the Canadian battalion was part. As far as the British soldiers had been able to tell, Varaville appeared to be in Canadian hands and any battle over. Relieved at this news, Hartigan and Mallon slung their rifles and strode nonchalantly towards the village, looking forward to a rest. They had passed the château and started up the lane leading to the gatehouse when some men from No. 7 Platoon, hunkered in the adjacent antitank ditch, shouted for them to get down. Training kicking in immediately, the two men dived headfirst into the ditch just in time to avoid being killed by a savage burst of machine-gun fire that ripped down the lane from a German position.

Hartigan was shocked to learn that his company commander, Major Murray MacLeod, was dead and that a number of other men had been killed so far in the fight at the château. He was also disgusted by what he considered a wait-and-see attitude on Hanson's part. Hartigan confronted Sergeant Mosher MacPhee and demanded that an assault on the position be launched. MacPhee eventually was persuaded to let Hartigan reconnoitre the German lines to see if there was a way in. The sergeant told the corporal he was agreeing to this mostly because Hartigan had with him a two-inch mortar that might provide sufficient firepower to open a gap in the wire, through which an assault force could get into the enemy defences.

Hartigan stepped behind a big Lombardy poplar beside the ditch and peered around it to get a feel for the general layout of the German positions. Satisfied, he ducked back into the ditch a moment before the 75-millimetre gun banged loudly and an armour-piercing round "tore a slab like a railroad tie off the tree.... Jagged chunks and shards of wood splayed around the ditch. None of us," Hartigan later wrote, "were injured but some were badly bruised."

Undaunted, Hartigan crawled to the gatehouse and ascended to the second storey where Makela was sniping at the enemy. The Bren gunner had stacked some furniture in front of the window and was using it as an aiming rest for the machine gun. "Don't go in there," Makela warned as Hartigan opened the door to the room

Southampton's port, like many in southern England, was crammed to over-flowing by hundreds of landing craft. Taken on June 4, this photo shows many Landing Craft, Tanks loaded with trucks, tanks and other equipment bound for Juno Beach on D-Day. Frank L. Dubervill, NAC PA–132653.

top left · At Camp Shilo, Manitoba, 1st Canadian Parachute Battalion troops faced gruelling, highly realistic training to prepare for their forthcoming role in the vanguard of the Allied invasion of Normandy. Here, paratroops advance through mock defensive positions in a live-fire exercise. NAC PA–209720.

left · Personnel of the Royal Winnipeg Rifles on June 1, 1944, combat gear close at hand, in an embarkation camp awaiting loading onto the invasion ships. Donald I. Grant, NAC PA–132473.

above · Spirits ran high aboard the multitude of landing craft onto which the men of 3rd Canadian Infantry Division were loaded for the crossing of the English Channel. The men jammed onto this LCT likely had no idea how rough and uncomfortable their trip would prove in the cramped space. Dennis Sullivan, NAC PA–129053.

above · Telegraphist Stan Richardson (foreground with Sten gun) and Signaller L.D. "Duke" Fallon (rear with Bren gun) aboard HMCS *Bayfield*, using automatic fire to detonate German mines swept up during operations off the Normandy coast on D-Day. Photo courtesy of Stan Richardson.

top right · Aboard HMCS *Prince Henry*, the Reverend Robert Seaborn leads a group of Royal Canadian Engineers in a prayer prior to their boarding a Landing Craft, Assault for the run into Juno Beach. Dennis Sullivan, NAC PA–129054.

right · HMCS *Algonquin* fires a broadside with its 4.7-inch guns against targets on the Normandy coast. Herb Nott, NAC PA–170770.

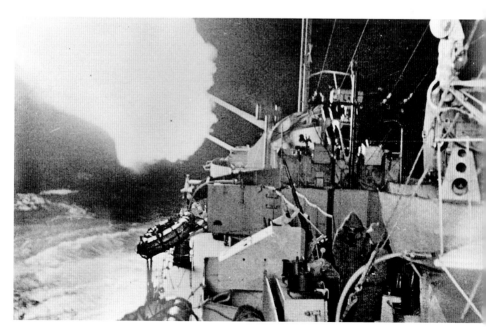

above · Soldiers of Le Régiment de la Chaudière descending scramble nets from HMCS *Prince David* into LCAS on June 6. Richard Graham Arless, NAC PA–169304.

top right · View from German gun position looking out at Juno Beach. Note the landing obstacles in the surf. Donald Grant, NAC PA–128792.

right · Major Lochie Fulton, commander of Royal Winnipeg Rifles 'D' Company, would win the Distinguished Service Order for his bravery during the D-Day fighting. Donald I. Grant, NAC PA–131271.

top left · Soldiers of the Highland Light Infantry wade through heavy surf towards the beach in front of Bernières-sur-Mer at 1140 hours on June 6. Gilbert Alexander Milne, NAC PA–137013.

left · Canadian troops at St. Aubin-sur-Mer. The tank on the right is a Churchill mounted with a 14-inch petard gun. Frank L. Dubervill, NAC PA–128789.

above · Highland Light Infantry troops eat a hasty meal aboard LCI(L) 299 while awaiting the order to land as part of the reserve 9th Canadian Infantry Brigade on D-Day morning. Gilbert Alexander Milne, NAC PA–136980.

above · Just before noon on D-Day, Major General Rod Keller and his staff landed at Bernières-sur-Mer. Pictured left to right are Captain Charles Turton, Captain W.H. Seamark, Major General Rod Keller (wearing beret), and Brigadier Bob Wyman. Frank L. Dubervill, NAC PA–115534.

top right · Canadian tank crews removing waterproofing from their tanks just off the beach. Ken Bell, NAC PA–132898.

right · An anti-aircraft gun guards the beach on June 6. In front of it is a knocked-out Duplex-Drive tank with its screen collapsed. Frank L. Dubervill, NAC PA–132897.

above · Canadian wounded lying behind the protection of a wall on Juno Beach in the afternoon of D-Day. Frank L. Dubervill, NAC PA–133971.

top left · After completing its minesweeping operation in the advance of the invasion fleet, HMCS *Bayfield* took up a position off the invasion beaches to await further orders. The beach in areas was completely obscured by fires burning ashore. Courtesy of Stan Richardson.

left · German troops under guard in front of the seawall at Bernières-sur-Mer. Frank L. Dubervill, NAC PA–133754.

above · German prisoners (one a stretcher-bearer) carry a wounded soldier back towards the beach. Frank L. Dubervill, NAC PA–132469.

top right · Within hours of the first landings, Royal Canadian Engineers began clearing the hundreds of German mines. Frank L. Dubervill, NAC PA–131441.

right · The main Canadian column during the advance inland with Le Régiment de la Chaudière in the lead. Frank L. Dubervill, NAC PA–131436.

On the night of June 6–7, the few German planes that dared venture over the great armada standing off the Normandy coast were greeted by hundreds of anti-aircraft guns whose tracers eerily illuminated the skies. Joseph J. Scott, NAC PA–138754.

where MacLeod and the others had died. "The room was a shambles, but more. A pair of legs hanging by the crotch of the trousers over a part of a wrecked bunk bed. A torso—no arms, head, legs or hips— lying on a pile of brick and covered in brick mortar dust; simply an insignificant little remnant clothed in a dirty [T-shirt]. It was something which had been a young man a few minutes earlier."

Despite the horror of the room, Hartigan took his time to examine the enemy position from its window. Then, leaving the gatehouse, he carefully circled the entire fortification, crawling through thick hedges and along ditches. Returning to the gatehouse, the corporal told MacPhee that there was no easy way through the wire and the only way to do any damage was to bombard the position by setting the mortar up in the ditch alongside the lane. MacPhee told him to save the mortar ammunition. The angle of fire from the ditch was too poor for effective fire.[13]

At 0830 hours, a white flag appeared aloft over the enemy fortification and a German sergeant approached the gatehouse. Hanson met him in the open ground between gatehouse and enemy position and soon determined that the Austrian major had been wounded. The sergeant said he sought a truce because he had a considerable number of casualties, no medical supplies, and the humane thing would be for the paratroops to share their supplies with the Germans.

Mademoiselle Hiervieux, who knew the German, firmly warned the man that the Canadians would soon overwhelm the position and kill them to a man. She urged him to impress on the others the urgent need to surrender. Tiring of the exchange, Hanson abruptly instructed the German that he could take a two-wheeled cart from the wagon house back to his lines, load the wounded on it, then return to this position and the Canadians would tend them.

While this parlay unfolded, Hartigan crept off on another reconnaissance and discovered a shallow, disused three-foot-deep trench completely concealed by cast-off rotting hay and overgrown weeds, which ran from the antitank ditch next to the lane over to the German gun position. Hartigan suspected the Germans were no more aware of its existence than had been the Canadians. From where the ditch ended near the German position, he would be able to fire the mortar at the 75-millimetre gun with good effect.

Hartigan excitedly explained his discovery to Sergeant MacPhee, who agreed with the plan. "I'm coming with you to make any judgement about calling it off if things become too hazardous," he cautioned Hartigan. The two men then set about gathering up all the two-inch mortar bombs they could lay hands on.[14]

As the two men firmed up their plans, a cluster of Germans emerged from the fortification. Two soldiers strained under the burden of the cart, in which they had propped up the three immobile casualties, while another three walking wounded hobbled along beside. Just short of the château, a German machine-gun crew suddenly fired a long burst from behind the casualty party that riddled the cart and wounded inside with bullets and also cut down the walking wounded. Having been protected by the cart, the two men who had been pulling it fled to the château to become prisoners.[15] The paratroopers could only surmise that some Nazi fanatic had objected to the mission of mercy and killed the wounded rather than see them surrender to the Allies.

After witnessing this tragedy, Hartigan and MacPhee crawled up the ditch with the mortar, moving cautiously to ensure that no swaying of weeds betrayed their presence to the Germans. Eventually, they reached the trench's end and wormed into a position behind a half-buried rock from which they could clearly see the 75-millimetre. MacPhee whispered to Hartigan that the trajectory to the target should be almost flat, a possible angle for the two-inch mortar because it had only a two-by-six-inch base plate and no bipod to regiment its deployment. The corporal loaded the mortar and then lowered the barrel with one hand until it was only a couple of degrees from flat on the ground, with the base plate braced against the rock. He sighted it by looking along the side of the barrel. "Handled this way," Hartigan wrote, "it acted much like a small infantry antitank gun and was surprisingly accurate. I fired two or three shrapnel shells at the enemy field gun, followed by a couple of smoke shells to help conceal our getaway.

"Our nerves were stretched to the limit because we expected the big gun to return fire. I went out of control as we scurried down the sloping ditch on our hands and knees. Without realizing it, I overtook MacPhee by clawing my way right over him and landed in our deep antitank ditch ahead of him."[16]

The mortaring, combined with Mademoiselle Hiervieux's continuing urging that the Germans surrender, had the desired effect. A few minutes after Hartigan and MacPhee's attack, the white flag again appeared over the fortification and at 1030 hours forty-two Germans emerged from the position with hands raised. Four Canadian paratroops captured earlier by the Germans were released.[17] Lying by the 75-millimetre gun was a dead German killed by Hartigan's mortar fire. Other corpses were strewn throughout the fortification.

Corporal John Ross, the radio signaller at Varaville, soon learned of the victory and transmitted "Blood," the coded message to confirm that 'C' Company had captured the German field piece. Hanson moved his men into the fortified position, intent on holding it against any counterattacks by turning the many captured machine guns and the field piece on the enemy. Instead of Germans, however, the next troops approaching Varaville proved to be two platoons of the British No. 6 Commando astride bicycles, who had landed that morning on Sword Beach and ridden through the day to relieve the Canadian paratroopers at Varaville. At 1500 hours, Hanson handed the position over to the commandos, gathered those German prisoners who were not wounded, and marched the Canadian paratroopers around Varaville towards le Mesnil crossroads to link up with the rest of the battalion.[18]

Hanson reported to Lieutenant Colonel Bradbrooke at 1730 hours. The battalion commander and his force had reached the crossroads at 1100 hours and since then more paratroops had been filtering into the position, bolstering the ranks. But they still remained terribly few. 'A' Company, whose D-Day task had been to cover the rear of 9th Battalion's attack on the Merville Battery, completed that mission with only twenty men and two officers. Lieutenant Jack Clancy, lacking any idea where the rest of his company or officers were, led the little force that had completed the task without serious incident and then marched towards le Mesnil, arriving thirty minutes after 'C' Company.[19] He was relieved to find that most of his company, scattered far away from their rendezvous point, had opted to make for le Mesnil crossroads and either had already arrived or were beginning to filter in.

With 'C' Company's success at Varaville, Bradbrooke was able to report to 3rd Parachute Brigade's commander, Brigadier James Hill, that 1st Canadian Parachute Battalion had completed all its assigned missions for D-Day. Bradbrooke, who had proven himself to be more than a competent peacetime officer this day, then set about establishing a defensive position around a brick factory that dominated the crossroads. As men trickled in, he was able to establish an all-round defence. The lieutenant colonel was greatly relieved seeing the ranks grow because, as late as noon, he had had no idea of the whereabouts or fate of about 250 Canadians. Now he could count 390 at le Mesnil and another 30 to 40 at Robehomme, but still there were many unaccounted for as night fell. As for the force at Robehomme, which, including British paratroopers, numbered about 100, it was perilously exposed to the threat of counterattack, but Captain Griffin had determined that a German force stood between it and le Mesnil crossroads. He decided to stay put until this enemy blocking force's strength could be determined in the morning.

AMONG THOSE STILL unaccounted for were Lieutenant John Madden and his little band, which had been dropped practically on Sword Beach. Once the naval bombardment had lifted, they had started off on a ten-mile journey towards the original drop zone with ears still ringing, walking through air thick with dust and smoke. A shell splinter he could not remove stuck out of the stock of Private G.H. Pidluberg's rifle. Madden spied a patrol of German infantry poking about in a way that told him it was a search party trying to find the paratroopers. They were fanning out from the parachutes abandoned near the German anti-aircraft gun position.

He pondered holing up until the British troops landed at Sword and overran the area, but always in the front of his mind was the mantra, "Get to the objective, get to the objective." That objective was Varaville and Madden hoped to shake the hunters on his track, cross the River Orne at the Ranville bridge, and get to the objective before day's end.[20]

Eventually, Madden could no longer see the pursuing Germans and realized they had either lost the trail or given up. This enabled the paratroopers to move more quickly, although they were still careful to not move in the open. Madden had no intelligence on where German positions might be located, because the paratroops had not been briefed on operating anywhere west of the River Orne.

As they crept past a group of farmhouses, the paratroopers heard a babble of voices from inside that seemed to be speaking Czech or Polish rather than German. Suddenly, a German soldier wearing a soft field hat and with a rifle slung on his shoulder pedalled past the Canadians with barely a glance, but then turned slowly around towards them. Madden fired a burst from his Sten gun and the man wobbled as if hit. Then he swung the bike around and started riding away. The lieutenant let go three more short bursts, emptying the magazine. "The bicycle wobbled. With a clatter, he fell and lay gurgling on the road. In the awful silence that followed the chatter of my Sten, we heard the rattle of equipment, the scuffle of feet running towards us. One moment of searing fright and we too were fleeing for our lives, even as the cyclist had tried to flee for his. There is nothing for pride in the way I killed that man; there is nothing for shame in the way we ran."[21]

The cross-country scurry turned eerily surreal when Madden's party stumbled half-lost into the village of Colleville-sur-Orne later in the morning, only to find it full of British troops from a Suffolk Regiment that had landed on the beach several hours earlier. "Khaki-clad soldiers sat at the tables of an outdoor café, sipping drinks, while a jeep-mounted 20-millimetre cannon fired round after round into a distant church steeple in an attempt to dislodge a sniper." Madden rounded up another seven men from 'C' Company and hitched a ride on a truck carrying supplies through to British paratroops, who had secured the vital crossing of the River Orne and Caen Canal near Ranville. Now designated Pegasus, the crossing would hopefully provide the paratroops with a way to get on the eastern side of the river and back into the lines of 6th Airborne Division.

Upon arriving at the bridges, Madden saw they were in British hands but still disputed by German snipers for anyone trying to cross over them. After glassing the situation for a while with his binoculars, Madden ordered the men to sprint over one at a time. Leading the way, Madden heard bullets chiming off the metal girders. After each perilous crossing, the men regrouped on the east bank of the river, but three men failed to dash through. Madden was angered to discover they appeared to have fled the scene in order to search out a safer crossing point. This was not the kind of behaviour he expected of paratroopers.*

From here, Madden and his remaining men walked as far as Amfreville, but a group of British commandos holding one side of the road warned that there was a strong German force between the village and his route to Varaville. As night was beginning to settle, Madden told his men to dig in on the other side of the road and secure the right flank of the commandos for the night. D-Day had proved little more than frustration broken with moments of fear and hazard for the young lieutenant, which had in no apparent way contributed to the successful outcome of the battalion's operations. Regardless of problems encountered tomorrow, Madden decided he would damn well reach his assigned objective.[22]

---

* After the war, Madden happened into one of the paratroopers who shirked and listened to a long explanation of how one of the men had suffered an injury which precluded the dangerous crossing. The lieutenant was unimpressed and chalked the failure up to personal cowardice.

16

In Good Fettle

HITLER WOKE AT NINE. It was the Führer's habit to convene two daily operational briefings attended by about twenty of the highest-ranking and most politically powerful officers in the German military. Normally, these briefings began respectively at noon and midnight, with the late-night session often not beginning until 0100 hours. Due to Hitler's increasing penchant to lecture the officers on military strategy and tactics in a manner that gave the impression he was speaking "out the window" rather than to anyone in particular, the briefings could drag on for hours.[1]

After the late-night session ended, the insomnia-plagued Führer required a sleeping draft or injection from his doctor, and to function effectively had to be allowed to waken naturally each morning from his drug-induced rest. Consequently, by the time Germany's supreme military commander rose from his bed on June 6, the Allied assault waves were ashore and a toehold on the beaches already won.

Oberkommando der Wehrmacht's chief of staff, Generalfeldmarschall Wilhelm Keitel, also slept late that morning, while its chief of operations, Generaloberst Alfred Jodl, who had risen at 0600 hours, did not warrant the reports emanating from Normandy sufficiently serious to merit wakening him early. Jodl was surprised to learn that Oberbefehlshaber (Commander-in-Chief) West, Generalfeldmarschall Gerd von Rundstedt's headquarters in St. Germain near Paris had on its own initiative put two armoured divisions on alert for an intended move towards the Normandy coast. He immediately directed Oberst Horst von Buttlar-Brandenfels of the operations department general staff to inform von Rundstedt that this order was to be rescinded.

It had been General der Infanterie Günther Blumentritt, von Rundstedt's Chief of Staff, who issued the alert order to the 12th ss Panzer (Hitlerjugend) Division and the Panzer Lehr Division. He had done so at 0400 hours following a frustrating conversation with Buttlar-Brandenfels, in which the officer had refused to authorize release of these divisions. By this time, Blumentritt and his intelligence staff were convinced that reports of parachute drops between the River Dives and the Cotentin Peninsula constituted the beginnings of the major invasion. Blumentritt hung up the phone and immediately "began to move one detachment . . . of each division in the general direction of Caen" in defiance of okw's instructions.[2]

But at 0630 hours, Buttlar-Brandenfels rang to say that these divisions "should forthwith be stopped, because the principal landing was expected at an entirely different place." Only the Führer, the okw staff officer snapped, could decide to deploy these divisions. Blumentritt had no choice but to comply. He also could not know "for certain whether this was the decisive main landing or only a preliminary diversion."[3]

Meanwhile, in accordance with orders issued days earlier, the 12th ss had started a planned move from its assembly point near Dreux, about forty miles west of Paris, towards Elbeuf on the south side of the River Seine across from Rouen. This was to better position the division to respond to the expected Pas de Calais invasion. While the invasion developed in Normandy, the tanks and mechanized vehicles of one of the most elite German divisions in France trundled in the wrong direction.[4]

As one hour followed another and the divisions defending the Normandy coast filed sporadic and confused reports of massive amphibious landings following the airborne drops, von Rundstedt directed Blumentritt to press okw harder for authorization to dispatch the Panzer divisions.[5] For his part, von Rundstedt was so disdainful of Hitler, whom he called "that Bohemian Corporal," and his toadies at OKW that he would not deign to talk directly to anyone at Hitler's headquarters.[6] Despite repeated calls in which Blumentritt argued the case with Buttlar-Brandenfels, Jodl, and other OKW staff, he was left with the impression that "OKW still had its doubts whether a landing would also be made in the Fifteenth Army area [between the Somme and Seine rivers]." He wondered also whether reports of wide-ranging landings by paratroop and glider forces not only between the Dives and Orne rivers, but also on Fifteenth Army's left flank to the east, might actually constitute the first stage of this feared larger attack. That the paratroops landing east of the Dives had been an error was not considered, nor did Blumentritt have accurate intelligence that would expose how few men actually constituted this unintentional and fully disorganized force.[7]

The inability of the Commander-in-Chief (West) to respond decisively to the invasion with an immediate counterattack by the armoured divisions in reserve meant that the coastal defence divisions were left to fight and die alone during the most critical hours. Responsibility for defending the beaches upon which British Second Army landed rested on the shoulders of Generalleutnant Wilhelm Richter, commander of the 716th Infantry Division. Having first donned an officer's uniform in 1914, Richter had seen extensive World War I service. Before assuming command of the 716th in March 1943, he had also served in Poland, Belgium, and Russia. Nothing in this experience had prepared the general for June 6. In the space of only a few hours, Richter's weak division, largely deployed in fixed coastal fortifications, was faced by four British and Canadian divisions attacking both from the sea and air. Lacking any significant reserves or inherent transport to quickly move inland units to reinforce his shore defences, Richter was rendered largely impotent to affect the battle's outcome. All he could do was plead unceasingly to both Seventh Army commander Oberstgeneral Friedrich Dollman and von Rundstedt to secure the release of the Panzers, but in the absence of orders from Hitler neither officer could offer any resources of substance. Instead, Richter was assured that help would be forthcoming and that in the meantime his division must hold regardless of casualties.

BY THE TIME HITLER had awakened to learn of the invasion, the Royal Winnipeg Rifles had tipped the battle on the beach in Mike Sector in their favour. Major Lochie Fulton was already pushing 'D' Company through the seemingly endless mine and wire fields in front of the hamlet of la Valette, with the intention of hooking into Graye-sur-Mer from the left. 'B' Company, meanwhile, had crossed the River Seulles into the neck of land east of Courseulles-sur-Mer and was methodically clearing a pillbox and trench system there. This still left a gap of ground facing the beach where several fortifications remained intact. It was in front of this position that the reserve companies and an advance party of battalion headquarters landed in the midst of heavy mortar and machine-gun fire at about 0900 hours.[8]

Dragging behind them a No. 22 wireless set mounted on a hand-pulled carriage, the headquarters section presented an easily identifiable target that immediately drew a swarm of mortar fire. The men dived for cover and ended up pinned on the beach for two hours until finally the German artillery observers were forced back to inland positions from which they could no longer see to accurately direct fire onto the beach.

While the Winnipeg Headquarters Company hunkered down, its reserve rifle battalions attempted to pursue their assigned tasks. 'A' Company, under Major Fred Hodge, was to advance on St. Croix-sur-Mer, while Major Jimmy Jones's 'C' Company would simultaneously break through to Banville-sur-Mer by way of Graye-sur-Mer.[9] Both companies had first, however, to get clear of the beach. The LCA carrying 'C' Company's No. 13 Platoon had dropped it three hundred feet out in deep water. With their Mae West life preservers inflated, the men started swimming awkwardly under the weight of their packs towards shore while trying to keep their weapons dry. About halfway in, Rifleman Jack McLean, who topped six feet, managed to touch bottom with his toes and started tiptoeing towards the sand. McLean staggered out of the water exhausted.

A major wire obstacle about thirty feet deep and an average height of two feet blocked the platoon's advance just short of the dunes. Having lost the platoon's bangalore torpedo in the water when the man carrying it had been shot and killed, the men had no option but to try carefully picking their way through the wire. McLean was halfway through when a blast knocked him down with stunning force, leaving him badly tangled in the sharp barbs and staring up at the ghastly sight of bits of bloody cloth and flesh hanging from the wire to his right. Dazed by concussion, the soldier was convinced he was looking at the remnants of his legs hanging there until a glance assured him that he was still intact. Lying nearby, however, he saw the corpse of another soldier from whom both legs had been torn. Several other men—either wounded or dead—were snarled in the wire close by. McLean realized that either one of the soldiers had tripped a mine or they had all been hit by an exploding mortar round.

From the dune side of the wire, Rifleman Wheeler Graham shouted at McLean to free himself from the barbs and join him in the shelter of a shellhole. Tearing flesh and clothing in the process, McLean managed to wrench himself free of the wire's grasp and ran to the hole. Throwing his rifle in ahead of him, McLean dived into the hole only to have the weapon's fixed bayonet strike his throat. "My God, I've killed myself," he thought, before realizing the blade had merely broken the skin. Graham, however, pulled apart a tear in the clothing on McLean's back and discovered a deep shrapnel wound, which he quickly slapped a field dressing on.

Bullets were spitting sand up all around the shellhole, so the men huddled in its shelter were pinned down. Unable to see any muzzle flashes to tell where the German fire originated, they started firing randomly up into the dunes, hoping to at least make the enemy duck. Finally, Lieutenant Lewis McQueen, the platoon's commander, arrived and reorganized the men for an advance through the sand dunes. Corporal James Kyle's section, which included McLean, took point with the men moving in single file. Kyle was nineteen and McLean's closest friend.

Passing through the dunes, they met only sporadic sniper fire and soon reached a canal that ran west from the River Seulles behind the dunes, constructed as a tank obstacle. Having been briefed on the existence of this canal, 'C' Company had retained its Mae Wests to help the men swim it. This No. 13 Platoon did without incident and then pressed past fenced-off areas marked with signs that read: "Achtung Minen."

Coming upon a road that cut across their front, the platoon drew enemy fire and dashed to take cover in a deep roadside ditch. Hoping to determine where the fire came from, McLean and several others crawled up to the edge of the road for a better vantage. As the man beside McLean raised his head, a bullet immediately smacked into his forehead, killing him. Three more men were hit before the platoon managed to drive off the sniper.[10]

They started closing on Graye-sur-Mer. With every step, however, McLean felt his right leg stiffening. It also felt like someone was jabbing the leg with a hot poker that was being left on red coals for longer periods before being pushed into his flesh. Glancing down, the soldier realized for the first time that his right pant leg was pocked with shrapnel holes through which blood was seeping at a quickening rate. Upon seeing the man's wound, Lieutenant McQueen ordered him to go back to the beach and get it dressed by medics. The rifleman said a quick goodbye to Kyle and his other buddies, reassuring everyone that he would see them again in a day or two. It seemed to take far longer to return to the beach than it had to advance inland. Reswimming the canal left McLean drenched through and shaking with cold. At the base of the sand dunes on the beach side, he found a long line of wounded, some wrapped in blankets. The wind off the water made him shiver all the harder and his teeth began chattering. A captain with a wounded arm offered to share his blanket. Gratefully, McLean crawled under it and the two men huddled together. "Inside pocket of my tunic has a flask in it," the officer said, "but can't reach it with this arm like it is." McLean fished the flask out and the two men proceeded to polish off the rum inside. After that, the rifleman felt a lot better.[11]

HIDING IN THE SMALL homes of Graye-sur-Mer were about five hundred French civilians who had endured the terrific shelling of the beaches. Among them was fourteen-year-old Georges Lecarpentier, who lived with his parents, aged grandmother, and twin sister Georgette in a small house that faced the beach. Before dawn, the two teenagers had gone outside and listened to the great roar of the navy shells flying overhead, while staring in awe at the gun's muzzle flashes. When it turned light, Georges and his sister had joined five other teenagers in climbing a tower that the Germans had constructed on top of one of the buildings in town as an observation post. Georges looked out to sea "and it was filled with boats. It was magnificent!" At first, the young boys and girls on the tower hoped to stay there through the landings, for they could see small boats filled with soldiers racing towards the shore and knew this must be the long-awaited invasion that BBC Radio had so long promised. But shells started exploding in and around the village, so they dashed to their homes. Looking over his shoulder as he ran, Georges saw the tower take a direct hit and disappear in a spray of splintered wood. As Georges was ducking into the front door of his home, a shell exploded nearby and a piece of shrapnel lodged painfully in his right heel. Unable to remove the little chunk of steel, his parents could only bandage the small wound.*

Occasionally, as the morning wore on, Georges risked furtive glances out a window to follow the progress of the various landing craft, but the sound of gunfire and exploding shells warned him it was dangerous to be exposed for long. He feared for the men who must land on the beach. During the last few months, the Germans had planted a deep minefield just back of the beach that extended right up to the road running in front of Graye-sur-Mer, and surrounded the field with vast wire entanglements. Signs had been posted warning the civilians to stay away from the beaches and mined areas. There had also been talk of their forcible evacuation to somewhere inland so that the village itself could be used as a fortification, but that had not developed. Now Georges hoped it was too late for the Germans to

---

* Lecarpentier still carries the piece of shrapnel in his heel, having been unable to have it surgically removed in the weeks following the invasion.

move them. He hoped the Allied landing would succeed and the Germans would soon be thrown out of all France.

It seemed to the young teenager that the battle for the beach passed very quickly and in no time at all Allied soldiers entered the village. Everyone poured out onto the street to greet them. Georges was surprised when some of the troops spoke to him in French. One soldier, who looked to be an officer, shouted that the people should go back into their homes where it would be safer, which was probably true, as German mortar and artillery rounds were still periodically exploding nearby. Georges saw strange-looking tanks with some kind of drum that rotated and lashed the ground with "huge chains" working through the minefields. The chains were detonating the explosives, but that appeared to be the tank's purpose.

As the civilians started returning to their houses, some of the soldiers pressed forward to hand the younger people chocolates and strange packets containing a hard little stick that smelled rather sweet. A man with a face blackened as if by gunsmoke grinned at Georges when he stared in puzzlement at the substance. The soldier unwrapped a stick identical to the one Georges held in his hand, popped it into his mouth, and then rather than swallowing it began methodically chewing like a cow might his cud. Georges mimicked his actions and the two stood happily munching away while the soldier kept saying, "Chewing gum, chewing gum." Although he had no idea what the stuff was made out of, Georges decided that it was pretty good and was pleased when the soldier gave him an entire pack to keep. Then he rushed to join his family inside the house even as the soldier hurried on his way inland.[12]

THE WINNIPEG RIFLES pushing towards St. Croix and Banville were still unaware that a German counterattack force that had gathered in these villages was advancing in their direction. Blocking their advance, however, was 'C' Company of the Canadian Scottish Regiment. At about 0900 hours, Major Desmond Crofton had first engaged this force by having destroyers standing off the coast hammer the villages with 4.2-inch guns. He then ordered Lieutenant

Roger Schjelderup to close on the Germans with No. 13 Platoon and keep them bottled up while his other two platoons provided covering fire.[13]

Moving into the waist-high wheat in an extended line, Schjelderup's men walked towards the gap between the two villages. Schjelderup was anxious, worried about the location of the Winnipeg Rifles, who were to have been closing on St. Croix and Banville on the left of 'C' Company's line of advance. When a light machine gun ripped off a burst from about 150 yards away in that direction, he thought it sounded like a Bren gun. "We hit the dirt," Schjelderup later wrote, "and I shouted: 'This must be the Winnipegs—when I say U P—all up together and shout Winnipegs.' We did, and to our surprise two enemy infantry sections stood up in their slit trenches just 125 [to] 150 yards ahead. They too were a picture of amazement and looked rather odd with their painted faces below helmets covered with grass. Their camouflage was perfect and it was no wonder we did not see them earlier. But the stunned silence did not last long.

"There was only one course of action and to a man the platoon rushed the enemy position. It was a bitter encounter with much hand-to-hand fighting. Enemy supporting machine gun fire from the area on the northern outskirts of St. Croix and mortar fire from St. Croix made our task more difficult."[14]

Unable to get a clear field of fire against the enemy while lying down with the Bren gun braced on its bipod stand, Private V.C. Paulson strode forward, firing the gun from his shoulder. Other soldiers were running and shooting Lee Enfield rifles from the hip.

From his position behind the attacking platoon, Crofton could see Germans "in the area of St. Croix darting between hedgerows and ducking down through the wheat and . . . working their way . . . towards us. But . . . the fine work of [the platoon] stopped this attack. In fact, all ranks fought like veterans while under heavy machinegun and mortar fire."

The Germans skulked back into the villages and No. 13 Platoon fell back on the rest of the company. Schjelderup had been shot in an arm, but refused to relinquish command. His heroism in this action would win him a Military Cross. With his platoons all heavily reduced by casualties, Crofton was worrying about 'C' Company's ability to withstand an attack should the Germans recover from the surprise of the engagement in the wheat field and renew the offensive. So it was with great relief that he saw 'A' Company coming up on his rear with Lieutenant Colonel Fred Cabeldu striding vigorously along in its midst. Adding to the impression of the cavalry arriving was the presence of several tanks from the 1st Hussars.[15]

NEITHER THE TANKERS nor the rest of the Canadian Scottish Regiment had met an easy time getting ashore. As the twenty-six LCAS carrying the reserve element of the battalion started the run shoreward, the persistently rough seas disrupted the orderly formation. In the battalion headquarters LCA, Lieutenant Colonel Cabeldu stood next to the Royal Canadian Navy commander in charge of the flotilla that had departed from *Queen Emma, Duke of Argyll,* and *Prince Henry,* listening as he used a loud-hailer to coax and bully the other LCA crews into their assigned positions. The navy officer was a veteran of landings in North Africa and at Salerno, Italy, so knew his business well. But suddenly the man became violently seasick and collapsed. With the naval officer rendered helpless, Cabeldu had to take over. The thirty-seven-year-old officer and former real estate agent from Victoria was not overly worried by this development, as the directions required to land the troops in the right place had been something on which he had been briefed many times. Looking shoreward, he saw the church steeple and water tower of Graye-sur-Mer standing well back of the beach. Taking up the loud-hailer, Cabeldu used these markers to direct the LCAS towards their assigned landing zone to the right of the village.

As the flotilla closed on the beach, Cabeldu realized that the rising tide and rough seas had prevented the engineers from clearing paths through the obstacles and he had to order the LCAS to each find its own way through.[16] Mines holed two LCAS as they did so.[17]

Seeing the listing wreck of an LCT with its bow almost on the sand, Cabeldu directed his craft to be pulled up alongside its stern. His party then scrambled onto the LCT, raced down its length, and piled almost feet dry onto the sand. Several LCAs from 'A' Company, including that carrying Major Arthur Plows, followed suit when they were unable to find a path through the beach obstacles.[18] Aboard the LCA carrying Private Jack Daubs, a twenty-year-old from London, Ontario, one of the Royal Navy crewmen calmly took off his shoes and socks, folded the socks and laid them on the precisely aligned shoes, and then rolled up his pants to just below his knees. Moments later, the ramp dropped and the man jumped into waist-deep water and ran to shore pulling a long rope behind him. Daubs and the others piled out, using the rope to help maintain their balance as they slogged under the burden of their heavy equipment to the sand. "Good luck, Canada," the sailor said to each passing man.

Daubs looked at him standing there with no helmet, no shoes, or protection of any kind and was struck by his calm courage, which stood in stark contrast to his own feelings. "I just wanted to get the hell off the beach," Daubs later recalled, "as there were dead guys around and smoke and people hollering." The private was sopping wet. Right ahead of him, Private Neil McPherson, a twenty-one-year-old from Vancouver, had a mortar round plow into the sand directly between his legs and the blast tore his legs off. As Daubs passed, he saw that the skin on the stumps was "all pink and black around the edges." McPherson was pleading, "Help me, help me." But there was nothing anyone could do, so the platoon left him lying there and ran hard for the sand dunes.[19]

The LCA carrying 'B' Company's Major R.M. Lendrum had been jockeying towards the LCT with an eye to following 'A' Company's method of getting ashore, when it was bracketed by heavy mortar and artillery fire. Realizing the Germans had cottoned on to the fact that the listing vessel was being used as an improvised wharf, the LCA crew commander swerved and made a run through the beach obstacles, with the rest of the company's craft following close behind. Private V.R.D. Garcia was killed when mortar fire hit the LCA carrying No. 10 Platoon. The platoon commander, Lieutenant J.H. Russell, and several other men were seriously wounded.[20] As the lieutenant was carried through the waist-deep water to shore, "he reviled the fates for [being so quickly wounded] after three years waiting."[21]

'B' Company's second-in-command, Captain P.F. Ramsay, was surprised to find the beach, supposed to have been secure by this point in the invasion, still a "no-man's land. Shells and mortar bombs ... landing in fairly regular succession on the sand, which was fortunately loose and absorbed most of the shrapnel. God knows it would have been a different story if it had been rock or solid shingle."[22]

The battalion paused to regroup in the sand dunes. The Canadian Scots had been assigned two immediate missions. 'D' Company under Major G.T. MacEwan was to seize two bridges over the River Seulles before they could be destroyed. One bridge was about three miles inland between Banville-sur-Mer and Reviers and the other stood a half-mile farther south at Colombiers-sur-Seulles. A platoon under Lieutenant Tom Butters was given the task of capturing the bridge near Reviers, and responsibility for the one south of Colombiers-sur-Seulles fell to Lieutenant A.C. Peck's platoon. To hasten each platoon's passage, the men were equipped with folding bicycles. Because the company had lost some of its bicycles during the landing, MacEwan was forced to give those of his HQ section to the leading platoons. This left his headquarters and the company's third platoon to follow on foot towards the bridge near Colombiers, which was the company's final rallying point. The second mission, to be carried out by the rest of the battalion, was to advance five miles to the high ground west of le Fresne-Camilly.

'D' Company quickly took off on its task and Cabeldu led the remaining two companies inland. Having received Major Crofton's urgent report that 'C' Company had successfully blocked the counterattack out of St. Croix-sur-Mer but was unsure if it could stave off another, Cabeldu decided to push through to Crofton with 'A' Company and the battalion headquarters. 'B' Company would meanwhile advance left of 'A' Company into the gap between St. Croix and Banville. 'C' Squadron of the 1st Hussars under Major D'Arcy Marks was to support the move forward, but it was having difficulty finding a route off the beach because of the canal behind the sand dunes. Cabeldu decided the infantry would have to proceed alone and hope the Hussars could soon catch up.

The advance inland by the Winnipeg Rifles had been so hasty that a lot of pockets of German infantry had been bypassed and were "now coming to life."[23] Captain Ramsay of 'B' Company, wanting to get off the beach quickly because it was proving "hazardous in the extreme as small-arms fire whistled around like angry bees," led the men to a point where an exit across the water obstacle reportedly existed. They arrived to find that an AVRE Churchill tank had tried crossing this supposedly shallow area and was now sunk right up to its turret top. Jumping on the tank, Ramsay scrambled through knee-deep water washing over the deck and managed to vault the rest of the distance onto a road parallelling the watercourse. Seeing some scrub brush about two hundred yards up the road, he dashed "hell for leather" to its shelter. Once under cover, Ramsay scanned the ground ahead and determined the enemy fire that had been chipping the road behind his feet was coming from the Graye-sur-Mer church tower.

Ramsay signalled Company Sergeant Major Frank Fisher to rally on his position by having the company come up the highway in extended order. With machine-gun fire whistling around them, the men clambered over the tank and then sprinted up the road to join the captain. Through his binoculars, Ramsay observed that "fighting was still strong in Graye-sur-Mer and figures could be seen on roof tops." Lieutenant Ian MacDonald's No. 12 Platoon had been specially trained for street fighting and was spoiling to join the fight, but Major Lendrum reminded the men that they had "other fish to fry" and would stick to the plan by moving inland alongside the River Seulles.[24]

On the right flank of the Scottish advance, 'A' Company commander Major Plows watched a Staghound armoured car flying the bright red and yellow pennon of the British Inns of Court Regiment race across the sand dunes towards la Valette. This British reconnaissance unit had landed on Juno with the mission of quickly dashing inland to seize several bridges and road intersections to deny them to the enemy. Plows was just thinking that the armoured car's speedy and very exposed advance showed that its crew commander had more pluck than brains, when there followed the heavy crump of an 88-millimetre gun and the Staghound "just disintegrated." Plows looked around in time to see a puff of smoke coming from a haystack off to his right.[25]

Cursing himself for not noticing the haystack earlier and having his men check it out, Plows ordered Lieutenant Bernard Clarke to knock out the gun. "Who, me?" Clarke replied, before quickly ordering his platoon forward. The lieutenant and his men crawled across seventy-five yards of open ground to gain a small knoll overlooking the haystack. Reaching the top just ahead of a group of Germans crawling up the other side, the Canadians quickly disarmed the enemy soldiers without firing a shot. Leaving half his men to guard the prisoners, Clarke and Sergeant W.A. Paterson led a charge towards the side of the haystack that faced away from the beach. As they closed in, Clarke realized the haystack was actually a concrete gun emplacement with hay piled on its roof for camouflage. One of his men yanked the back door open and tossed in a grenade that killed the gun crew. Turning from a job well done, Clarke and his small band were astonished to see that in charging the gun emplacement they had overrun a network of slit trenches without realizing it contained about fifty Germans—all now standing up with hands raised in surrender. Captain Bill Matthews, 'A' Company's second-in-command, ran up. "What the hell are you trying to do? Win the V.C.?" he shouted at the lieutenant.[26]

Having lost about twenty minutes waiting for 'A' Company to take out the gun position, Cabeldu hurried the men towards 'C' Company's position in front of St. Croix. He was also issuing urgent requests by radio for the 1st Hussars to marry up with him.

ON THE BEACH, congestion was nearing gridlock as infantry battalion support vehicles, self-propelled guns, engineering unit vehicles, ambulance teams, and a host of other men and motorized equipment piled off landing craft and started seeking a route inland. The 12th Field Regiment, Royal Canadian Artillery had unloaded its Priest 105-millimetre guns at 0900 hours and immediately started firing on enemy targets as directed through radio links with the regiment's forward observation officers serving alongside the infantry battalions. The FOO and reconnaissance teams landing to establish gun positions had taken disproportionately high casualties because the whip antennas of the radios served as beacons for German snipers. Major E. Pickering, the regiment's second-in-command, Major J.D. Ross, commander of 16th Battery, Captain G.M. Wright, Lieutenant E.C. Gothard, and Gunner A.A. Ellman had all been wounded, while Signalman E.G. Swan was killed. The 12th Field's SPGS started firing, sometimes over open sights, on targets either assigned by the FOOS operating inland or spotted by the gunners themselves. The regiment's commander, Lieutenant Colonel R.H. Webb, wrote later, "to the confusion of men and vehicles on the beach was added the roar of the guns, firing from the water's edge, with RHQ [Regimental Headquarters] behind them literally in the water." The 12th Field was the first artillery regiment to "bring down arty fire from land," he proudly noted.[27]

Frantically looking for a way over the water obstacle behind the sand dunes were the tankers of 'C' Squadron, 1st Hussars that were to support the Canadian Scottish. Battle Captain Brandon "Brandy" Conron led a group of Shermans through a gap in the dunes he had discovered about two hundred yards left of their original assigned exit. Topping the final dune, they had a short firefight with a group of Germans entrenched in a fortification. After wiping this position out, the tankers had to cross a thousand yards of heavily mined ground to reach a bridge spanning the water.

Conron jumped off his tank and started dragging a wire obstacle free while machine-gun fire "clipped the ground all about him."[28] When the wire was clear, he ran back to the line of tanks and jumped onto the back of No. 2 Troop commander Lieutenant Bill McCormick's Sherman. "You can't use that," the twenty-four-year-old troop commander told Conron, as he pointed at the rickety bridge. The battle captain agreed that it would never handle the weight of tanks and was just going to report as much over McCormick's radio when a mortar bomb landed alongside the tank and shrapnel struck him in both legs. While Conron climbed around to the front of the tank for protection, McCormick quickly wheeled the Sherman about and carried the wounded man to the Regimental Aid Post.[29] The lieutenant led the tanks back to the original beach exit, where 'C' Squadron waited impatiently until the engineers managed to clear the mines and obstacles to let it through the gap in the sand dunes. Once through the dunes, the engineers spanned the water obstacle by driving an Ark tank into it that mounted steel bridging ramps on its deck in place of a turret. After trundling over the bridge and gaining the road on the other side, they headed off. Shortly thereafter, the tanks linked up with the Canadian Scottish facing St. Croix.

In a hasty Orders Group, Cabeldu directed 'A' Company with 'C' Company following to pass between St. Croix and Banville to reach Colombiers-sur-Seulles and then make for the village of Pierrepont. Clearing St. Croix and Banville would be left to the Winnipeg Rifles and its supporting elements of 1st Hussars. As Cabeldu finished issuing his orders, 'D' Company reported its two bridges secure and that the reserve platoon and headquarters section were several hundred yards south of Banville where the Banville-Tierceville road intersected with one coming from St. Croix. Wanting to consolidate his company's hold on the bridge at Colombiers, Major MacEwan dispatched the reserve platoon on the remaining bicycles to reinforce Lieutenant A.C. Peck's platoon, leaving his small headquarters section to follow on foot.[30]

When Cabeldu's two-company force, with 'C' Squadron of the 1st Hussars, advanced into the gap between villages, it found the route "hazardous . . . as we were moving through thick grain fields and this appeared to be our only protection from many machine gun posts still held by the Jerry." In the middle of a field, a machine gun opened up on the section in which Private Jack Daubs served. The long burst of fire caught the man on point, missed the two behind him, struck down the next man in line, missed another, then hit the soldier directly ahead of him, missed the private, and killed the man following him. Everyone who had been missed dived for cover and stayed put until another section of the platoon wiped the gun position out.[31]

Few of the German gunners proved as good a shot as this one and even fewer chose to fight to the death. A pattern quickly emerged whereby the Germans opened up with sustained bursts but immediately surrendered when closed upon. Once they surrendered, the Germans proved so passive that fifty or more could be safely escorted back to the beach by one guard—a fact that Cabeldu, with his battalion's ranks badly thinned by casualties, greatly appreciated.[32]

Meeting no opposition from German tanks or self-propelled guns, 'C' Squadron had a "picnic steadily taking out machine-gun nests and entrenched positions whenever the infantry bogged down. The tanks scurried back and forth working madly behind and on the flanks of the infantry."[33]

Meanwhile, Major MacEwan's 'D' Company headquarters section on the Banville-Tierceville road heard the sharp sounds of gunfire from the direction of Cabeldu's advance and turned in time to see a small German car barrelling down the road from St. Croix towards them. Sergeant J.D. Blacklock killed the driver with a head shot and the vehicle "did a somersault off the road. A short while later," MacEwan later recounted, "a second car rushed along. A shot at this one wounded the driver who stopped and was placed in a ditch. By now we could see more people coming out of the village.... Captain J.T. Bryden, my 2 IC, with our two runners stood behind the parked car and as the Germans, in ones and twos on bicycles—and one on a motorcycle—rushed away from the village ... we stepped out and held them up." Eventually, after sending a bag of prisoners back to the beach, MacEwan and Bryden decided they could use the captured car to overtake their bicycling platoons. Bryden "drove and after grinding a gear or two got underway. To avoid being shot by our own troops," MacEwan wrote, "I stood up with my head out of the open top. This was fine until a sniper took a potshot at us and we left the car very quickly."[34]

MacEwan soon reached Colombiers and tied in with the 'D' Company platoons holding the bridge there. When Lieutenant Tom Butters radioed from the bridge near Reviers that the Regina Rifles were passing his position to the east, MacEwan ordered him to rejoin the rest of the company, as there was no longer any German threat to the bridge. Cabeldu's force was nearby, looking out from a knoll astride the Banville-Tierceville road towards the medieval fortress village of Creully to the south of Tierceville. "By this time it was about 1:30 in the afternoon," Cabeldu wrote, "and my clothes were starting to dry out ... but my cigarettes wouldn't puff, they were still too wet. We had now taken the crossings at Colombiers-sur-Seulles and also a battery of heavy German artillery guns intact.... Our fellows were in good fettle."[35] As well they should be, for, despite heavy casualties, the Canadian Scottish Regiment had secured the right flank of Juno Beach with its rapid advance inland.

TO THE LEFT of the Canadian Scots, the Winnipeg Rifles had made their way through "mortar and artillery fire of astonishing accuracy" to clear Banville and St. Croix. Whereas Banville proved to be largely abandoned, the Germans in St. Croix offered stubborn resistance to 'A' Company that was only quelled when 'A' Squadron of the 1st Hussars went to its assistance. The Winnipeg war diarist wrote admiringly that the tankers, "with cool disregard for mines and anti-tank guns, beat down the machine-gun positions and permitted 'A' Company to mop up and advance to the south." With these two villages clear, the Winnipeg Rifles hooked right across the line of advance being taken by the Canadian Scottish to follow the Banville-Tierceville Road to Tierceville and then south to secure Creully. Meeting only scant resistance, the advance proceeded quickly with few casualties.[36]

For the Regina Rifles, leaving Courseulles-sur-Mer after the seaside town was secured proved no easy task. Once the main German resistance was silenced, civilians emerged from cellars to clog the streets and press flowers, wine, and precious food upon the marching men. The company commanders hustled the men along and by 1215 'C' Company reported it was in Reviers and that 'D' Company's forty-nine-man force had arrived a little earlier. The rest of the battalion began consolidating on this village for the next stage of the advance, which would begin once 8th Canadian Infantry Brigade—having faced a tough time subduing the Germans in Bernières-sur-Mer and St. Aubin-sur-Mer—came up on the left flank.[37]

17

An Awful Shambles

THE ADVANCE FROM Bernières-sur-Mer had been badly delayed
by difficulties the engineers encountered constructing vehicle
exits through the seawall and an increasing state of general confusion as ever more units poured onto the beach with nowhere to go.
Contributing to 8th Canadian Infantry Brigade's problems renewing
the offensive was the fact that the reserve battalion, Le Régiment de
la Chaudière, had suffered grave misfortune during its landing—
beginning a trend of ill luck that was to dog the French-Canadian
unit the rest of the day. Not only were most of its LCAS damaged or
sunk by mines, but the soldiers were also lashed by mortar and
artillery fire. Every LCA carrying 'A' Company foundered so far off the
beach that the men were forced to discard much equipment and
weapons to enable them to swim to safety.[1] The other companies
fared little better. 'B' Company lost almost all of No. 11 Platoon either
killed or wounded to a mine that sank its LCA. Although suffering
, from wounds to his head and arms, Lieutenant D. Paré managed to
get the survivors ashore and then reorganize them as a functioning
unit. "Most LCAS have been sunk," wrote the Chaudière war diarist,
"and there are many dead and wounded."[2]

'A' Squadron of the Fort Garry Horse attempted to join the infantry's advance from the beach, but was caught in a massive traffic
jam that had built up despite efforts by the beach masters to limit

access to the primary vehicle road running south out of Bernières. Dozens of infantry Bren carriers, ambulance jeeps, 105-millimetre Priests from the 14th Field Regiment, and engineering vehicles clogged the route, snaring the tankers in a gridlock. Captain Eddy Goodman, 'A' Squadron's battle captain, "decided to cut across some open fields and circumnavigate the infantry vehicles. I came to one ploughed field and saw a sign reading *Achtung Minen*. Somewhere in the back of my mind I remembered an intelligence officer saying that often instead of mines the Germans put up signs to slow the enemy's advance. I decided that this was one of those times and went bowling across the field, only to blow up my tank, completely destroying the right track.... I grabbed together another tank and [led the squadron] to my support position with the Régiment de la Chaudière."[3]

According to the brigade plan, the Chaudière Regiment was to have passed through the Queen's Own and taken over the advance inland from Bernières through Bény-sur-Mer, Basly, and Colomby-sur-Thaon, on to the Anguerney heights. The QOR would be close behind in support.[4] At 0940 hours, the Chaudières, the Fort Garry Horse's 'A' Squadron, a battery of the 14th Field Regiment's 105-millimetre Priest self-propelled guns, and a heavy machine-gun section of Cameron Highlanders of Ottawa aboard Bren carriers congregated in an orchard on the town's west flank. This was the forming-up position for the advance on Bény-sur-Mer, a little over two miles away. As they passed through Bernières, the civilians were delighted to discover that among the liberating troops were men who spoke their own language. They greeted the French-Canadians enthusiastically, "some standing gamely among the ruins of their houses." Much of the town, the Chaudière war diarist noted, was "in ruins with numerous houses aflame."[5]

'C' and 'D' companies of the Queen's Own Rifles were also gathered in the orchard, so the area was quickly choked with people and machines. Rifleman Jack Martin was waiting impatiently for the Bren carrier with his three-inch mortar to arrive when a German machine gun suddenly opened up. He and a dozen or so other soldiers hit the dirt behind a nearby carrier's bogey wheels while they tried to figure out the enemy gun's location. The battalion's Lieutenant Colonel

Jock Spragge stumped over and glared down at the prone men. "For Christ's sake," he barked, "you don't duck for every one of them." Martin and the other men got sheepishly to their feet, as a section of riflemen went to work wiping out the German gun position.[6]

Because a dug-in 88-millimetre gun near the town cemetery blocked the line of advance, nobody was venturing up the road into the wheat fields beyond the orchard. So when Martin's Bren carrier arrived with the rest of his mortar team and its weapon, he quickly got it firing at the enemy gun. After loosing only a few rounds, Martin turned for another mortar bomb only to find that the rest of his crew had disappeared. He presumed they had gone for more ammunition, but it still meant laboriously firing the mortar single-handed.

Born in Toronto's East End, Martin had joined the 48th Highlanders of Canada in 1939 at age sixteen, but had been dismayed to discover that, at the slightest provocation, Highland regiments insisted on their pipers squalling away on the blessed pipes. He had jumped at the chance to transfer to the Queen's Own. Soon after joining the battalion for training at Camp Borden, Martin had been rendered deaf in his left ear by a Bren gunner who fired several continuous bursts from his weapon right next to his head. Martin's hearing worsened with every mortar shoot—a fact he was at pains to prevent the medical officer discovering, lest he be sent back to Canada on a disability discharge. He was a skilled mortarman and so the task of re-aiming after each round, dropping in a new charge, and then firing it at the hidden gun position was completed at a pace not much slower than if his mates were present. Whether the fire had any effect or not, however, was impossible to tell.

Off to his right, four Priests from the 14th Field Regiment were strung out in a field on the opposite side of the coastal road that ran westward from Bernières to Courseulles-sur-Mer. One of the Priests was only about a hundred feet from Martin's mortar.[7] Around the SPGS, the Chaudières were forming up by companies in preparation for an attack on the gun position.[8]

The four Priests were an ad hoc formation, drawn two each from 'A' Troop and 'C' Troop of the 66th Battery under command of 'C' Troop's Lieutenant Garth Webb. These four SPGS had managed to unload from the LCTS more quickly than the rest and so formed a temporary combat group. Webb had been directed to the position by the battery's command post officer, Lieutenant Al Lee, who had landed earlier aboard an LCA with the Queen's Own Rifles to scout out safe firing positions for the battery. At the time, Lee had been more worried about open fields being mined than the possibility of the Priests coming into range of enemy antitank guns, as there was no sign of such opposition about. "You don't need to worry about mines," the lieutenant said as he pointed out the field the guns were to occupy, "because here's this cow."

Observing that the animal was fastened to a six-foot tether, Webb replied, "It doesn't look like that cow would hit very many mines if that's all the distance he can move." Then he got busy deploying the guns according to directions given by Lee to bring them into a firing line towards likely inland targets that lay in the path of the advance.

Like all the Priests landing on Juno Beach, those of the 14th Field Regiment were heavily loaded with extra ammunition for the 105-millimetre guns, cases of bullets for the infantry, and mines and other explosives for the engineers. Webb and another man were out in front of the guns, lying on the grass in order to set up aiming markers, when the Priest on the far right of the line exploded.[9]

Rifleman Jack Martin was preparing to pop out another mortar round, when this first SPG took a direct 88-millimetre hit that not only exploded the machine but triggered secondary explosions of the Priest's entire ammunition and mine load. Martin buried his face in the ground just in time to miss being struck by a monstrous chunk of steel armour off the SPG that grazed the mortar as it whirled overhead to land about a hundred feet away. The force of the impact knocked the mortar over and left a knick in the tube that served as a lasting reminder to Martin of how close he had come to being "squashed like mashed potatoes." Propping the mortar back up, Martin got it back into action firing at the German position while trying to ignore the carnage suddenly developing around him.[10]

In quick succession, the 88-millimetre gun fired three more shots and two more Priests died as the German gun crew systematically worked along the line from right to left. Although the German fire was deadly accurate and the crew able to reload with stunning speed, the driver of the fourth Priest was able to back it into a lane that hid the gun from view in the nick of time to avoid being hit by the last round.[11] Six gunners aboard the other SPGS—two from 'A' Troop and one from 'C' Troop—were killed and five others wounded out of total crew complements of twenty-one.[12] This constituted almost half of 14th Field Regiment's total June 6 casualties.[13]

'B' Company of the Chaudières, still reeling from the loss of almost an entire platoon in the landings, was also caught in a series of gargantuan explosions as the three Priests were engulfed in flames and all the ordnance aboard ignited. Lieutenant R. Lapierre and a dozen men died instantly. Several more were wounded. The company had been reduced by two calamities from about 120 men to barely 40.

While the remainder of 66th Battery regrouped back towards Bernières in a church courtyard, the Chaudières hastily rallied for an attack on the gun that had wreaked such havoc. Major Hugues Lapointe's 'A' Company, supported by the Fort Garry's 'A' Squadron and the Vickers heavy machine guns of a platoon of Cameron Highlanders laying down covering fire, attacked the gun by the cemetery—overrunning the position and taking three prisoners.[14]

THE INFANTRY AND TANKS then started up a long, straight country lane that led towards Bény-sur-Mer, but after an advance of only about a thousand yards, the leading Chaudière element walked into the crossfire of several well-concealed machine guns that had the road covered. On either side of the road stretched grain fields that offered little cover, so the only way to prevent a World War 1–style slaughter was for the battalion to go to ground. Its commander, Lieutenant Colonel Paul Mathieu, sent scouting parties crawling into the fields to pinpoint the enemy positions hidden in the tall stands of wheat. Such work was dangerous and time-consuming, so a long delay was inevitable.[15] Yet initial radio messages from the Chaudières to 8th Canadian Infantry Brigade failed to impart the seriousness of the situation.

Further confusing the communication string running from the front lines back to division headquarters aboard HMS *Hilary* was the fact that 8 CIB's headquarters had only recently landed and established an advance base south of the church in Bernières. Consequently, its staff was just beginning to develop a picture of the location of its battalions. Brigadier K.G. "Ken" Blackader was well out to the front with Lieutenant Colonel Jock Spragge of the Queen's Own, trying to discover the cause of the delay on the Bény-sur-Mer road. But at 1054 hours, nobody at 8 CIB HQ was in contact with the brigadier when they reported to the division that the Chaudières were "making progress slowly."[16]

Aboard *Hilary*, 3rd Canadian Infantry Division commander Major General Rod Keller had been forced a few minutes earlier to make a difficult decision based on only a scant understanding of events on Juno Beach. At 1050 hours, Keller had issued orders instructing his reserve brigade—the 9th Canadian Infantry Brigade—to begin landing. As the morning had progressed, with a harder battle being fought to win the beachhead than expected, Keller became increasingly "jumpy and nervous."[17] The initial invasion plan had set out two alternatives for putting 9 CIB ashore, the preferred one being to distribute the brigade's battalions between Nan White in front of Bernières and Nan Red at St. Aubin-sur-Mer. Such a landing would well position 9 CIB to leapfrog 8 CIB and make for Carpiquet airport by the shortest possible route. Alternatively, the landing could be made at Courseulles-sur-Mer, but this lengthened the distance the brigade must travel to reach the airport.

Very little news was coming out of 7th Canadian Infantry Brigade headquarters at Graye-sur-Mer to the right of Courseulles, although it seemed the brigade's advance was progressing fairly well. Circumstances on the beach in the brigade's sector, however, were less than ideal for putting 9 CIB ashore quickly and with minimal casualties. The Royal Canadian Engineers tasked with clearing the beach obstacles here had been hampered by the lateness of the assault, the rising tide, and bad luck. The poor luck occurred when two sections of the 18th Field Company, RCE managed to create a fifty-foot gap by dragging or dynamiting beach obstacles clear, only to have the opening immediately plugged when two damaged LCTs drifted into its midst and lodged there. As far as a route for getting off the beach went, only one exit had been completed and the engineers constructing another in the sector of Mike Green were having trouble cutting a usable track through the sand dunes and spanning the flooded section behind.[18]

In 8 CIB's sector, Keller had at least two beach exits—one at St. Aubin and another at Bernières—with roads extending inland from both towns, providing good routes for breaking through to Carpiquet airport. Acting on the best information available, Keller ordered Brigadier D.G. "Ben" Cunningham to land his brigade at St. Aubin and Bernières. As Cunningham started acting on this order, however, the Royal Navy officer serving as 3 CID's beach master declared Nan Red at St. Aubin too hot for the brigade to use because the German strongpoint there had yet to be silenced. Anxious to get the landing moving, Keller told Cunningham to put his entire brigade ashore at Bernières.[19]

No sooner had this order been issued than Canadian Press correspondent Ross Munro found the major general standing on the ship deck gazing towards the beach. Keller showed Munro the text of a message he had just wired to First Canadian Army commander Lieutenant General Harry Crerar that read: "Beach-head gained. Well on our way to our intermediate objectives."

"It is hard fighting," Keller told Munro, "but our troops are doing great. I'm committing the reserve brigade now and it is landing at Bernières where the best beach exits have been made." Munro was elated by the news, for it seemed the invasion was going far better than anticipated.[20]

While Keller made his report to Crerar, Cunningham and Royal Navy Commodore G.N. Oliver decided to land one battalion of the "highland" brigade after the other. They would touch down in the order by which they were to advance inland: the North Nova Scotia Highlanders first, then the Stormont, Dundas and Glengarry Highlanders, and finally the Highland Light Infantry of Canada. The tanks of the Sherbrooke Fusiliers would also go ashore at Bernières to support the brigade's advance. Unlike the first two brigades, which had gone ashore in LCAS, 9 CIB's battalions were to land from more substantial Landing Craft Infantry, Large.

Lieutenant Peter Hinton, commanding LCI 262, received his orders to head for the beach with a contingent of about two hundred North Nova Scotia Highlanders at about 1130 hours—two hours behind schedule. As his vessel closed on the shore, Hinton thought the scene there "looked pretty chaotic. It was apparent that the planned clearance of beach obstacles had not been carried out."[21] A great number of listing, hung up, or sunken landing craft blocked most of the possible approaches to the beach. Hinton managed to narrowly steer between a row of steel tripods and almost got up on the sand. The ramps were then slung off the sides of the LCI and four of his sailors ran through the water, dragging the heavy lines for the infantry to use to steady their walk. Unloading the troops proved a slow process, for the men were hampered going down the ramps by the folding bicycles most of them carried.

As the last of the men departed, Hinton realized with some despair that he had forgotten to drop the stern anchor that would enable the LCI to winch itself off the sand. As the RCN lieutenant considered ways out of his beached predicament, the commander of LCI 276, Lieutenant Andy Webb, addressed him by loud-hailer. The diesel engine that powered the unloading ramps on Webb's LCI had failed and he suggested coming alongside LCI 262 so the North Novas aboard could cross onto Hinton's boat and disembark from its still lowered ramps. Hinton readily agreed, but the impact of Webb's LCI banging against the side of the boat shoved it against several beach obstacles and exploded two mines. One blast ripped a hole in the engine room's port side and the other blew out part of the tiller. Fortunately, the engineers were all on the other side of the engine room, where the ramps' diesel engine was located, at the moment of the explosion, so there were no casualties. But the room quickly filled with water and had to be abandoned. LCI 262 was immobilized.

With the North Novas unloaded, Webb called over to Hinton to cast off the lines they had used to lash the two vessels together, so he could head back out to sea. "No bloody way," Hinton shouted back. "You're going to tow me off here first."

Webb reluctantly agreed. Lines were hooked from the bow of lci 276 to the stern of lci 262 and "after much grinding and crunching he managed to get us off the beach. We assessed that the bulkheads forward of the engine room and between it and the tiller flats would hold." With most of the crew serving in a damage control party to work the lcis portable pumps as well as a couple more borrowed from lci 276, Hinton ordered his craft out to sea and started limping slowly towards Portsmouth.[22]

Hinton's lci was not alone in being damaged during the landing. Indeed, the rcn and Royal Navy vessels involved in landing troops on Juno Beach suffered the heaviest losses incurred in the British-Canadian sector of the invasion. In an after-action report, Force J Commander Oliver determined that ninety landing craft of various types were either sunk, badly damaged, damaged, or disabled on June 6. The lcas were hit hardest, with thirty-six lost or damaged (25 per cent of the total complement).[23] But Oliver's statistics were conservatively drawn. Although he reports just seven lcis either badly damaged, damaged, or disabled, 262nd Flotilla alone had eleven of twelve craft holed by mines—five seriously enough that emergency repairs had to be conducted before they could depart the beach.*

Of the eleven lcis in rcn 260th lci Flotilla, three were so badly holed by mines that they took twenty-two hours to limp back across the Channel, with lci 298 towing lci 249. Near the end of the voyage, the tow was taken over by a fortuitously passing tug that sped the badly listing craft into Portsmouth "in a sinking condition."[24]

Oliver also reports no lcas lost. However, lca 1021 from *Prince Henry*'s 528th Flotilla was holed by a mine departing the beach and sank. The five lcas of 529th Flotilla from *Prince David* involved in landing troops in the first assault wave were all lost. Mines holed lca 1059 and 1150 on the port side, lca 1137 was holed aft by an

---

* One would be floated off later that evening, but the others would require two more days to be rendered seaworthy.

explosion and suffered starboard bow damage in a collision with an obstacle, and LCA 1138 had its bottom completely ripped out by a mine. Royal Canadian Naval Reserve Lieutenant J. Beveridge aboard LCA 1138 suffered multiple shrapnel and blast injuries that included a fractured right leg and slight head injuries.

Only LCA 1151 was able to embark its load of troops and pull off the beach successfully. But it was then caught in the midst of a maze of beach obstacles draped in mines, with insufficient engine power to escape to sea in the face of the rising tide and pounding surf. The coxswain of this craft ended up locked in a hazardous dance that lasted for about ninety minutes as he added or cut power while working the rudder frantically to keep from being tossed on the mines. At 0950 hours, Lieutenant D. Graham, an RCN reserve officer, decided to risk the return trip, but when forced to swerve out of the way of an LCT bearing down on LCA 1151, the smaller craft struck an obstacle that ripped its hull open, sending 1151 to the bottom. Despite the loss of all five LCAS, Beveridge was the flotilla's only casualty.[25]

WHILE THE NAVY finished landing 9 CIB on Nan White at Bernières, 8th Canadian Infantry Brigade's advance inland continued to bog down in the face of opposition from well-concealed machine guns—leaving the newly arrived battalions packed on the beach. Crowding men and equipment ever more closely together was the fact that the tide was still rising, pushing towards its highest point. Streaming off several LCIS at 1140 hours with bicycles shouldered, the Highland Light Infantry discovered a beach shrunk to "about 25 yards ... in front of the promenade which was heavily wired so that there were only the exits put up by the beach group." The beach, reported the HLI war diarist, was "jammed [with] troops with bicycles, vehicles and tanks all trying to move towards the exits. Movement was frequently brought to a standstill when a vehicle up ahead became stuck. It was an awful shambles and not at all like the organized rehearsals we had had. More than one uttered a fervent prayer of thanksgiving that our air umbrella was so strong. One gun ranged on the beach would have done untold damage but the 9th CIB landed without a shot fired on them. Against this welling mass of movement the Beach Group was trying to set up and function in all its branches [including setting up first aid and casualty clearing stations], but the opposition was too great. They had to be content to 'nest' casualties until we had passed on."[26]

Bicycles still shouldered, the HLI finally managed to enter Bernières, where they found many side streets blocked with rubble from damaged or destroyed houses. Near the church, "we could go no farther as the roads were blocked by the transport of the assaulting battalions.... Everyone piled up behind, choking the roads, while the [enemy] positions up forward were cleared." The battalion's commander, Lieutenant Colonel F.M. Griffiths, finally abandoned pushing against the unyielding log-jam and ordered the HLI to gather in the grounds of an estate behind the church. "Here," the HLI war diarist wrote, "we had a chance to drink a can of self-heating soup or cocoa and eat some bully beef and hard tack. Here the sun broke through and the day became quite hot and sultry."[27]

Griffiths's decision to temporarily abandon the advance until the traffic congestion eased coincided with Keller's arrival on the beach with his divisional tactical headquarters section. Several key members of his staff, 2nd Canadian Armoured Brigade commander Brigadier Bob Wyman, and a number of news correspondents, including Ross Munro, accompanied him. While photographers captured images of the tall general looking very much the tough and determined commander in beret and battle dress, Keller glared about at the apparent chaos on the beach.

Brigadier Cunningham was frantically trying to sort out the situation, but the fact that 8 CIB's advance had stalled left him with few viable forming-up positions that were clear of the beach. Keller furiously demanded that immediate action be taken to get the battalions heading towards their objectives. He then stomped off to where his general staff officer, Lieutenant Colonel Don Mingay, had established a temporary divisional headquarters in an orchard next to the Bernières church. Mingay reported receiving a message at 1215 hours from 8 CIB's HQ that the Chaudières were making slow progress up the road and were now under fire not only from MGS but also a battery of between four and six artillery pieces.[28] The German guns were firing from a position to the right of Bény-sur-Mer near the hamlet of Moulineaux, but the 14th Field Regiment Forward Observation Officer with the Chaudières was unable to fix its location for accurate counter-battery fire.

He was also unable to direct the regiment's guns against the machine guns holding up the Chaudières, despite knowing fairly accurately where they were located. The FOO's problem was that, although the 14th Field now had eighteen guns scattered in a series of small fields about two hundred yards out from the beach, this position was behind a low hillcrest that hampered their ability to fire on targets at such close range.[29] He kept radioing map references for targets that were about 1,000 yards from the gun positions, but, because of the high trees topping the crest, the gun crews were unable to attain a firing angle against targets at ranges of less than 2,800 yards. After several fruitless attempts to respond to the FOO's fire requests, 'C' Troop's Lieutenant Peter Cox ordered the crews of his three surviving 66th Battery SPGs to cease firing. As the men started brewing up some tea, Cox reflected that the gunners would just have "to wait for the infantry to move up a little way from us or for someone to find a target further away."[30]

With the artillery unable to help, the Chaudières started crawling forward under covering fire from the Vickers of the Cameron Highlanders to take out the enemy machine-gun positions the hard way. Progress was slow, but shortly after 1300 hours enemy resistance was reported cleared and the French-Canadian battalion renewed its advance towards Bény-sur-Mer.[31]

No sooner had the Chaudières got back on the move, however, than another nearby 88-millimetre gun betrayed its position by firing on the beach exit. Without waiting for orders, Lieutenant Walter Moisan immediately led his No. 8 Platoon of 'A' Company in an attack on the gun. The platoon's leading section, under Corporal Bruno Vennes, was within two hundred yards of the German position when it was pinned down by heavy fire from infantry manning a trench in front of the 88-millimetre. Seeing the section's predicament, Moisan crawled forward and helped lead the men in a low crawl to a thicket of brush that provided some cover only thirty yards from the gun. Just as the section was preparing to wipe out the gun crew with rifle fire, a bullet or piece of shrapnel struck and detonated a phosphorous grenade attached to Moisan's web belt. The phosphorous set the lieutenant's clothing aflame and burned deeply into his flesh but, despite the agony of his injuries, the officer ordered Vennes to take out the gun before giving him any first aid.

Vennes dashed madly with his men into the trench system and, while the others became locked in a melee with the infantry, the corporal knocked out the 88-millimetre by killing its crew with several hand grenades. He then rejoined the section in clearing the trench before running back to where Moisan lay badly wounded to provide rudimentary first aid until stretcher-bearers could evacuate the lieutenant to the Regimental Aid Post. For their respective parts in this brief action, Moisan was awarded the Military Cross and Vennes the Military Medal.[32]

Silencing this gun broke the German resistance in the immediate area. The long snaking line of Canadians again started moving up the road towards Bény-sur-Mer, with the Shermans of the Fort Garry Horse's 'A' Squadron out front, closely followed by the Chaudières with 'B' Squadron and the Queen's Own Rifles in trail. Just short of the town, the tanks bounced some snipers and small groups of dug-in infantry that opened up with machine guns. Major George Sévigny's 'C' Company quickly moved out in a screen ahead of the tanks and was soon engaged in a hot fight that brought the slowly advancing column to another standstill. Well back in his regimental headquarters troop, the Fort Garry commander, Lieutenant Colonel Ronald Morton, was much vexed by the delay. If the tankers and infantry were to get to the 8 CIB objective of the Anguerny ridgeline so that 9 CIB and the Sherbrooke Fusiliers could pass through and dash on to Carpiquet airport before dark, the pace had to be quickened. Morton thought the Chaudières were being far too "slow clearing such opposition" as was being offered.

The tank commander noted that the Queen's Own Rifles, waiting impatiently in the rear for Bény-sur-Mer to be cleared so they could break off to the left of the Chaudières at Basly and drive through to Anguerny ridge on their own line of advance, were also "complaining of this."[33] Finally, at about 1430 hours, 'C' Company broke into the town and quickly swept out the last German resistance. This opened the way for Major J.F. Lespérance's badly depleted 'B' Company to set out on its primary task—capturing the German artillery battery near Moulineaux. The heavy 100-millimetre guns of this battery were persistently harassing the beach stretching from Bernières clear over to Graye-sur-Mer.

While 'B' company numbered barely forty men, it had available some heavy assistance in the form of HMCS *Algonquin*, already teed up to deliver a barrage on the battery as soon as Captain Michael Kroyer, a British Forward Officer Bombardment (FOB) was able to direct the destroyer's fire.[34] So while the rest of the French-Canadian battalion passed through Bény-sur-Mer on a line of advance up the road towards Basly, 'B' Company moved cross-country towards the gun battery, accompanied by Kroyer and his radio signaller. Soon the British captain had the battery in sight and established radio contact with Captain Desmond Piers, *Algonquin*'s skipper.[35]

"In order to make our shooting more accurate," Piers later wrote, "I moved the ship close inshore and anchored. This seemingly dangerous action was necessary because of the strong tide and the tremendous concentration of shipping in the vicinity. As we could not see our target, the firing had to be done from maps. The fall of shot was observed by the ... officer ashore, and he told us by wireless where the shells were landing."[36]

It was an exacting process reliant on relatively primitive technology. Kroyer's target information was given to another Royal Artillery officer on *Algonquin*'s bridge, Captain G. Blunt, the destroyer's Bombardment Liaison Officer (BLO). Blunt checked Kroyer's range and bearing calculations to the target on a standard grid map of the invasion area. He then passed this target information over to the Gunnery Officer, Lieutenant Corky Knight, who in turn punched the figures into a gunnery control clock. This primitive computer transmitted ranges to the fire-control system that set the pointers in each of the turrets housing the 4.2-inch guns. Once the gun crew drew a bead on the pointer, a ready-to-fire report was given and the gunnery officer released the guns to fire. Kroyer called the first salvo two hundred yards short and three hundred yards to the right. The second salvo was closer and with another minor adjustment he declared the third a hit and ordered a saturation.[37]

"We then fired for effect, four 4-gun salvoes, every one of which was reported as a hit. This was good shooting! A second and then a third group of four 4-gun salvoes were fired and again every single one found the target with direct hits. That was 13 salvoes out of 13. After that the ... officer told us to cease fire, as the battery had been demolished. He added in his brief code: 'Very accurate.' I only wish," Piers lamented, "we could have observed the results ourselves. The Germans must have been very shaken, not being able to see where the shells were coming from."[38] Kroyer was equally delighted, so much so that he later had HMCS *Algonquin* painted across the front of his jeep in honour of the moment.[39]

Things proved not quite as easy as Piers and Kroyer believed, for even though the German guns had been destroyed by *Algonquin*'s barrage, the infantry positioned to defend the battery shook off the effects of the shelling and fiercely resisted 'B' Company securing the position. Fighting from trenches surrounded by thick entanglements of barbed wire, the Germans were impervious to the weak rifle and Bren gun fire that forty scattered soldiers could mount. The battle seemed hopelessly deadlocked until Lieutenant J. Bureau found a gap in the wire and led his No. 12 Platoon in, with Lieutenant A.P. Ladas's platoon hot behind.[40] A fierce fight with bayonets and grenades ensued before the superior German force surrendered en masse. Seconds later, 'B' Company was disarming fifty-four prisoners. Lespérance's company suffered no casualties in this short action while demonstrating great courage under fire.[41]

[18]

A Fairly Rugged Day

<hr>

THE 3RD CANADIAN INFANTRY DIVISION's original invasion plan had assumed that once Bény-sur-Mer was secured 8th Canadian Infantry Brigade's three battalions would use this as a base for forming a solid foundation halfway between Juno Beach and the Caen-Bayeux Road based on Colomby-sur-Thaon and Anguerny. From this base, 9th Canadian Infantry Brigade would strike out to seize Carpiquet airport just to the south of the road objective. However, the slowness of 8 CIB's advance and the traffic snarl created by all of 9 CIB coming ashore at Bernières-sur-Mer had thrown the scheduled timing of the entire operation out the window. Further jeopardizing the plan's successful completion was the fact that the North Shore (New Brunswick) Regiment, held up initially by the St. Aubin strongpoint, had subsequently marched into another protracted firefight—this time for control of the village of Tailleville. According to the plan, the North Shores were to have established a blocking position in front of La Délivrande and Douvres-la-Délivrande to prevent any counterattacks from this direction threatening either Juno Beach or the left flank of 9 CIB's advance. At first light on June 7, the North Shores were then to overrun these villages, with a major objective being a heavily fortified Luftwaffe radio station just west of Douvres.[1]

Further complicating 8 CIB's situation was that ever since the initial landing by the North Shores at St. Aubin, all direct radio communication from this battalion to Brigadier Ken Blackader's headquarters had been lost.[2] The only word from Lieutenant Colonel Donald Buell was derived second-hand by way of reports on the fire missions the navy Forward Officer Bombardment (FOB) called in shortly after noon, which consisted of requests for two destroyers to fire their 4.2-inch guns on the château at Tailleville.[3] Whether Buell was instinctively softening up the next objective or was aware of strong resistance there remained unclear, leaving Blackader in the dark about the situation on his left flank except for the troubling fact that the North Shores had yet to push out of St. Aubin. The only course open to the brigadier was to chivvy the two battalions leading the main column to make haste in the face of resistance that was proving decidedly more determined than he had been led to expect by divisional intelligence and hope the New Brunswick regiment soon caught up.

As the North Shores formed up by the St. Aubin church on the town's southern edge, the men could clearly see the village that was their next objective by looking up the narrow road running through a wide expanse of grain fields interspersed by small orchards and cow paddies. In the typical Norman manner, hedgerows fenced in most of these fields. Surrounding the town itself was a twelve-foot-high, three-foot-thick stone wall that hid all but the rooftops and upper stories of the buildings inside. The hulking structure of the château, however, overlooked the wall and offered an excellent view of St. Aubin to any German observation officer in its upper levels, which Buell suspected explained why the beach was still subject to accurate shelling and mortaring. Until Tailleville was cleared, the engineers and other beach party teams on Nan Red would continue to have their work disrupted by the deadly fire that was still killing and wounding men on the beach. With 'C' Company only now moving towards Tailleville, all Buell could do to help ease the pressure on the beach was to tell his FOB to continue having the destroyers harass the village with heavy shelling.

At about 1230 hours, Buell instructed 'C' Company commander Major Ralph Daughney to begin the advance on Tailleville. Having

just returned from a brief reconnaissance up the road aboard a pur-
loined bicycle, the major had discovered no immediate enemy forces
and was hoping to get through to Tailleville without a fight. Just in
case, however, he had convinced Buell to secure a troop of Fort Garry
Horse tanks to support the infantry advance. Following behind 'C'
Company was Major Archie MacNaughton's 'A' Company, while the
Bren carrier platoon commanded by Captain J.A. Currie moved on its
tracked vehicles across an open field on the west side of the road to
cover the right flank. Lieutenant William Little's No. 5 Troop provided
the tank support.

'C' Company set off with one platoon to the right of the road, one
on the road itself, and one to the left. The two companies on either
side of the road spread out in a line across the fields. Little's tanks
started out in a file on the road behind the infantry platoon there.
Captain Hector LeBlanc, 'C' Company's second-in-command, was on
the road and bringing up the rear. With him was Sergeant Albanie
Drapeau's three-inch mortar team aboard a Bren carrier.

It quickly became evident that the Germans had opted to lie low
and not fire on Major Daughney during his earlier bicycle gambol up
the road, as the advancing force started being harassed by sniper fire
the moment it moved towards Tailleville. Then mortars and artillery
began to dog the advance, which probably would have ground to a
halt had it not been for the support provided by Little's tank troop.
The tankers hammered identified German positions with their 75-
millimetre gun and machine guns, often grinding out into the fields
ahead of the infantry to overwhelm the opposition. Daughney later
complimented Little, saying "that without his excellent and energetic
support [my] company would not have been able to advance at all."[4]

Radio signaller Private Joe Ryan was sticking to Daughney like
glue, even though the battery in his radio was dead and the spare battery he should have been carrying was somewhere out at sea aboard
the LSI from which they had disembarked, what seemed like ages before. His absentmindedness was embarrassing, but there was little
time to think on the mistake, as it took all his concentration to run,
dodge, and fall in rhythm to the screaming descent of the mortar and

artillery shells that ripped great gouges out of the earth when they exploded. Ryan thought the noise of the explosions was like a cry of agony raised by the earth itself "protesting being raped. The smell of cordite and earth spewed up made me almost sick to my stomach."[5]

Just before the village itself, dense hedgerows surrounded a few small orchards. As 'C' Company closed on these, several machine guns hidden in the hedges started raking the men. Caught in the open, the North Shores faltered and looked for cover. Daughney, up with the leading platoons as he had been throughout the advance, re- alized something had to happen quickly to keep the attack going for- ward. He sent a runner back to LeBlanc with instructions for Sergeant Drapeau's mortar team to immediately engage the German positions. The sergeant later wrote that LeBlanc "showed me the exact clump of trees he wanted fire brought down on. Luckily I made a quick correction in degrees and the first ranging rounds fell exactly where he wanted them. In a few minutes the mortars had quieted the German machine guns. Luck was with me that day for each time I was able to score direct hits."[6]

Captain Eloi Robichaud of the North Shore Headquarters Com- pany would have begged to disagree. While still a lieutenant, he had commanded the company of which Drapeau's mortar platoon was a part. What Drapeau called "luck," Robichaud countered "was skill. I knew [Sergeant] Drapeau well, and . . . he was an exceedingly capable mortar sergeant who had a complete knowledge of the weapon and it was not unusual for him to score direct hits even with ranging rounds."[7] It was the kind of skilled handling of weapons, honed by years of training, that was repeatedly proving itself in 3rd Canadian Infantry Division's first day of combat—as brutal a baptism of fire as any Canadian division in World War II may have seen.

Although Drapeau's precise fire had silenced most of the machine guns, one position remained active and was so sited that it was im- possible to knock out from any of the covered positions the company had managed to crawl into. Realizing the advance would remain stalled as long as this gun was able to fire directly across the fields 'C' Company had to cross, Private Herbert Butland stood up and charged the machine-gunners while firing his Bren gun from the hip. The MG42 machine gun shrieked a long burst of fire at the running Canadian that clipped the suspenders holding up his web belt right off his shoulders, but miraculously not a slug scratched the soldier's flesh. Butland closed on the gun and killed its crew with a lethal burst. The private's bravery was rewarded with a Military Medal.[8]

While 'C' Company rooted out the last German defenders in the fields and orchards north of Tailleville, Fort Garry Horse 'C' Squadron commander Major Roy Bray instructed his second-in-command, Captain Alexander Christian, to reinforce Little's tank troop with three more tanks. Having served a brief stint as an officer on loan to the British 17/21st Lancers during the African campaign in 1943, Christian was one of the few officers in 3 CID with any previous battle experience. He was also in some pain, having had the tip of a finger shot away by a sniper's bullet shortly after landing on the beach. Christian raced to Tailleville and found the North Shores laying siege to the village.

Daughney and Little were pressed up against the massive wall surrounding the village for cover while they discussed how to break into Tailleville. The infantry major was completely perplexed by the bizarre situation, which resembled something from the days when knights and archers might have attempted to pillage the medieval château, only to be confounded by an insurmountable wall. Daughney could find no way for his infantry to get through or over it. With his company all hunkered against the wall, the Germans were unable to fire directly at the Canadians. Since neither side could see the other, both had resorted to chucking occasional grenades over the wall whenever they heard voices or other sounds that might betray the position of an enemy. The fight had reached a standoff.[9]

Rumbling up in his tank at about 1400 hours, Christian jumped down from the turret and joined the other two officers. Christian and Little quickly conferred and agreed that all the tankers could do to help the situation was to hook around the town with their tanks and shoot over the wall with the hope of somehow dampening the German enthusiasm for the fight. Daughney told them to go to it. As the meeting was breaking up, a German grenade arced over the wall and landed directly between the two tankers. The blast knocked both men flat and left them dazed. Although Christian was unharmed, Little suffered multiple lacerations and had to be hastily spirited to St. Aubin by stretcher-bearers for treatment at the Regimental Aid Post.[10]

Quickly regaining the protection of his tank turret, Christian led his six-tank force around the village, "carrying out speculative shooting over the high wall." The Germans responded with small-arms fire that ricocheted deafeningly off the tanks. To better direct the fire, Christian had his turret hatch open and was hunkered down in the cupola peering out while trying to expose himself as little as possible. "Suddenly," he later wrote, "an impact like a sledge hammer hit the back of my head and I slumped on the floor, but regained consciousness and felt better after a drink of water. A bullet had pierced my helmet, grazed the back of my head and had gone out the other side of the helmet." After his wireless operator bandaged the wound, Christian went back to harassing the Germans.[11]

During their foray around the town, the tankers discovered a 75-millimetre gun, several other artillery pieces, and an ammunition dump dug into positions outside the village. They quickly destroyed these, but their fire into Tailleville appeared ineffective. Finally, Christian returned to Daughney, and the two men—whose exploits this day would result in each winning the Military Cross—decided the only solution was to find a viable entry into the village through which tanks and infantry might pass together. Casting about, Christian and Daughney discovered a "group of French inhabitants ... huddled below a large solid, wooden gate which was the entrance of the château's courtyard. I ordered my driver to advance and we battered open the gate and entered."[12]

Lieutenant Hector Robert MacQuarrie's platoon dashed through the breach and took up a fire position in the courtyard. Then Lieutenant George Malcolm Fawcett's platoon slipped through and leapfrogged under the protective cover of MacQuarrie's men from the château's grounds into the western part of the village. The tankers set up in the courtyard and blasted targets at close range, while the company's mortars fired over the wall at targets reported by the two lieutenants. It was quickly discovered that Tailleville was far more than a minor fortified position. In fact, it was the headquarters of the 2nd Battalion, 736th Grenadier Regiment. It had been cleverly constructed so that almost all of its facilities were in underground bunkers beneath the village itself. First aid posts, garages, stables, barracks, munitions dumps, and mess kitchens were all situated in a subterranean complex linked by tunnels. Other tunnels locked in with a series of defensive gun pits and firing trenches scattered throughout Tailleville. Virtually every approach from one street to another was covered by at least one gun pit, and snipers ranged freely through the village's buildings, using hidden accesses inside that led into the tunnel system.[13] The North Shores no sooner entered the village than they were caught in a vicious battle where each platoon's rear was always exposed to the appearance of Germans using the trenches and tunnels to reoccupy positions just taken.

WHILE 'C' COMPANY fought for control of Tailleville, Lieutenant Colonel Buell came up the road with his tactical headquarters to find out what was delaying the battalion's advance. He was still anxious to push on past the village and establish the blocking position in front of La Délivrande and Douvres-la-Délivrande, the North Shores's final objective, and already the fight for Tailleville was a couple of hours old.

With Buell was Lieutenant Colonel L.G. Clarke, the commander of the 19th Army Field Regiment, which was providing artillery support to the North Shores. The tactical HQ also consisted of Buell's intelligence officer, Lieutenant Blake Oulton, Buell's batman, and a radio signaller. As the small party approached Tailleville's outskirts, a soldier waved them off the road and warned that there was a German sniper still active outside the walls that nobody could locate. Crawling on their stomachs through a field of grain, Buell and his group managed to reach the entrance to the village.

The battalion commander soon found Daughney, who reported Tailleville all but cleared. Buell doubted that, as there was still very accurate German shellfire hitting the beach and he was certain a fire control post within the village directed those guns. He instructed the major to clear the village again until the shelling ceased. "Even if you have to do it four or five times," Buell insisted. Daughney was visibly unhappy about the order, but to Buell it seemed "obvious that our beachhead was of little value if the enemy could direct fire on all craft landing there."

Having dispatched 'C' Company to clear the buildings they had thought well swept, Buell told Major Archie MacNaughton to follow him through the village. The lieutenant colonel would personally allocate the section he wanted 'A' Company to hold and set out the boundary lines between the two companies. Buell's concern was not only to ensure the entire village was subjected to a house-to-house sweep, but that the two companies not end up in a firefight between friendly forces. "We had not moved more than a few steps on our way through the village," Buell later wrote, "when an automatic weapon was fired at us at close range. We all went flat on the ground instinctively. I was lying in the middle of the roadway, so I got up in a hurry and ran forward and squeezed into the projection of an archway that led into the château courtyard. While on the ground looking to see where the German was, I heard a movement in the bushes near by, so I fired my Sten into the bushes with no enemy reaction. Then I took a smoke bomb from a pouch and told Archie [McNaughton] that when the smoke emitted he was to move his party back ten yards and around the corner of the château wall, then for him to get a section of his company and we would close out this particular little pocket of resistance. I threw the grenade and it took a little time to emit smoke. Archie moved on the explosion of the grenade and simultaneously another burst of automatic fire occurred. Archie, his runner, and . . . his signaller fell dead. Another signaller lay wounded. I remained where I was and another burst of fire chipped the stone corner facing just alongside me. The wounded signaller pulled himself across the road to me on his hands, dragging his legs and body, and I started to dress his wounds when from somewhere a bomb was thrown which hit the roof of the archway above our heads."[14]

Buell threw himself over the badly wounded signaller to protect him from the falling slate broken off the roof by the explosion. Four more grenades followed the first, but each hung up on the roof and exploded harmlessly there, so the lieutenant colonel guessed that the German wasn't strong enough to cast them all the way over the roof. Each grenade seemed a bit closer, though, and Buell was anxious to find a way to get himself and the wounded signaller out of the deadly trap they were in. Fortunately, deliverance arrived in the form of a Fort Garry Horse tank that rumbled around the corner and took up a position between Buell and the German machine-gunner who had butchered MacNaughton's tactical headquarters section.

With the tank slowly backing up behind him so that its armoured hide deflected the German bullets, Buell carried the wounded signaller to safety. A section from one of 'C' Company's platoons immediately moved through the area and managed to kill the men in the machine-gun position and also the grenade thrower. They discovered that the machine-gunners had been firing from a position dug into the street that resembled a manhole access to a sewer system.[15]

Slowly the resistance in Tailleville was being eliminated, but the process was taking a painfully long time. Yet again the 716th Division, so disdained by Allied intelligence, were proving stout fighters. For every German who quickly surrendered, there were two more willing to fight to the death. Captain LeBlanc attempted to help some of them realize that ambition by having a private packing a flame thrower pour its deadly flame into a suspicious dugout, but was disappointed when all that emerged from the hole was a badly scorched German and an equally burned horse. A Bren gunner put the animal out of its misery and the German was marched to where a growing number of prisoners were being formed into a column for escort back to the beach.

Realizing the tide was turning, some Germans attempted to slip from the south side of the village and flee into a nearby wood, but Captain Currie raced around that flank with several Bren carriers and cut off their escape.[16] After the Bren carriers closed this avenue of retreat, the remaining Germans in Tailleville surrendered. The North Shores rounded up sixty prisoners and estimated about the same number had died in the drawn-out six-hour fight. It was 2000 hours and daylight was fast fading.[17] Buell ordered Daughney's exhausted 'C' Company to continue digging about in the subterranean complex to ensure that no Germans still hid there, while he started organizing 'A' Company, under Captain J.L. Belliveau since MacNaughton's death, to sweep the wood south of the village. The lieutenant colonel had every intention of still trying to fulfill his battalion's final mission for June 6 of establishing a blocking position in front of the German radar station at Douvres-la Délivrande.

Just as Belliveau's men were preparing to move out, however, Buell finally established radio contact with Brigadier Blackader, who told him to forget about the final objective and instead consolidate his grip on St. Aubin and Tailleville. With his entire left flank exposed from St. Aubin to Tailleville, Buell ordered 'B' Company to dig in to the east and south of St. Aubin to provide immediate cover for the beach. 'D' Company was ordered up to secure Tailleville's eastern flank while 'A' Company was positioned on the southern edge of the village and 'C' Company in its centre. Soon after each company re-ported itself in position, a final section of 'C' Company emerged from clearing another chamber of the underground warrens with more prisoners in tow. Buell thought it somewhat comical that the latest bag included two wounded German officers sporting monocles, so that they looked very much like Allied propaganda caricatures. The lieutenant colonel was, however, "disappointed at not running through all the objectives planned," but thought perhaps it was just as well, for the North Shores "had had a fairly rugged day."[18]

Just how rugged a day it had been became clear as the companies settled in their assigned positions for the night and started carrying out roll calls. That the battalion had lost a sizable number of men killed or wounded came as no surprise, but the extent of the losses surpassed Buell's expectations. Total casualties tallied 125 out of about 800 men. Of these, one officer and 33 other ranks were dead, while 2 officers and 89 other ranks had been wounded.[19] The only officer killed was Major MacNaughton, the forty-seven-year-old from New Brunswick's Black River Bridge. MacNaughton had served with the North Shores so long he was considered a tradition by the rest of the officers, who by comparison were mere youngsters. Immensely popular with the men, well respected by his colleagues, and always durable in the face of the physically demanding task of leading a rifle company, MacNaughton "could not be made to believe he was too old for the job." It had been a source of pride to him for his company, which was probably the least well turned out during inspections, to always emerge on top during any training exercise or sports activity. Captain Eloi Robichaud later wrote, "it was an irony of fate that [MacNaughton] had won still another first—the first senior officer to be killed in action."[20]

Hardly a man among the remaining North Shores was not somewhat astonished to still be alive and unhurt. Private Ian McFarlane felt particularly lucky. As McFarlane had come off the LCA that morning, Private Donald Young had been hit in the shoulder by a bullet and pitched back into the landing craft right beside him. Then he was running for the seawall when Corporal White had been shot down at his side. On the road to Tailleville, a shell landed on his platoon section and killed Private E.R. Palmer and Corporal Fraser. Next, his platoon sergeant, William Girvan, was wounded. In the melee in the village, Private C.W. McLaughlin was shot through the spine and left a paraplegic at the age of twenty-two. There had followed four terrifying forays into the underground warrens of the German headquarters system in search of the enemy, with wild firefights in narrow rooms and passageways that were night black. Through all of this, McFarlane had lived and emerged whole at day's end. But he could not stop thinking of the chums he had trained with for so long, who had one after the other fallen at his side. It seemed mere chance that determined who lived, who was maimed, who died.[21]

[19]

Beginning of the End

WHILE THE NORTH SHORE REGIMENT had advanced inland and then fought the long battle for control of Tailleville, the Germans had ponderously been trying to reinforce the beleaguered 716th Infantry Division. The nearest reinforcement immediately available was the 21st Panzer Division under command of Generalleutnant Edgar Feuchtinger, which was spread out across a twenty-five-square-mile area in the vicinity of Caen. Panzer Group West commander General der Panzertruppen Leo Freiherr Geyr von Schweppenburg, who ostensibly oversaw the operations of Panzer divisions in France, had opposed this scattered disposition as "a striking example of wretched Panzer tactics and the result of Rommel's orders." That order to create mobile reserves close to the coast by spreading some Panzer divisions out rather than keeping them together further inland had been vigorously opposed by Schweppenburg without effect. Now he believed the Germans were to pay the price of this folly because the division was too distributed to effectively regroup and lash out with the intended power of an armoured formation against the still weakly established Allied landings.

The 21st Panzer Division's 125th Panzer Grenadier Regiment was situated northeast of Caen on the east bank of the River Orne. A second group, consisting of the division headquarters, the 22nd Panzer Regiment (the division's tank unit), one artillery battalion, and weak elements of the Panzerjäger (antitank) battalion formed a reserve southeast of Caen. Committed to front-line positions along the coast and under command of 716th Infantry Division were a battalion of 192nd Panzer Grenadier Regiment and the rest of the Panzerjäger battalion. The placing of these units under direct control of General-leutnant Wilhelm Richter, who had no experience in tank warfare, contradicted standard German command doctrine for the control of Panzer forces. Finally, the 193rd Panzer Grenadier Regiment, less a battalion, was situated north of Caen.[1]

Elements of Major Hans von Luck's 2nd Battalion of the 125th Panzer Grenadier Regiment had been skirmishing through the night with paratroops of the 6th British Airborne Division, who had landed right in the midst of the battalion's night training exercise. Shortly after those landings started, von Luck had interrogated a captured British Medical Officer and the man's guarded responses left the major in no doubt that this was the invasion and no diversionary operation.

But when he contacted Feuchtinger's divisional headquarters, the major had been unable to secure permission to launch a concentrated night attack against the airborne division. The orderly officer on duty had only been able to tell him that Feuchtinger and his general staff officer were in Paris, Generalfeldmarschall Erwin Rommel was away from Army Group B headquarters on a visit to Germany, and there was therefore nobody available to authorize such an aggressive response. As the hours passed, von Luck could sense the opportunity to destroy the paratroopers slipping from his grasp. "We were becoming filled with anger," he later wrote. "The hours passed. We had set up a defensive front where we had been condemned to inactivity. The rest of the division . . . was equally immobilized, though in the highest state of alert."[2]

One phone call followed another, but von Luck was unable to get his orders changed. Finally, at dawn, the major sent his adjutant, Leutnant Helmut Liebeskind, to divisional command with express instructions to not return until he had secured "immediate clearance for a counterattack." If only Rommel was here, von Luck thought, "he would have disregarded all orders and taken action."

Liebeskind arrived at divisional headquarters just a few minutes after Feuchtinger's return from Paris and overheard the generalleutnant having a heated telephone discussion with someone at OKW. "I've just come back from Paris," Feuchtinger shouted, "and I've seen a gigantic armada off the west coast of Cabourg, warships, supply ships, and landing craft. I want to attack at once with the entire division east of the Orne in order to push through to the coast." After several seconds of listening to a voice on the other end, Feuchtinger banged the telephone into its cradle and told the room that permission had been denied.[3]

Feuchtinger had never seen combat and as an artilleryman had no training in tank warfare. His previous experience had been largely confined to organizing the participation of military units in Nazi Party rallies back in Berlin, which had resulted in his developing close ties to Hitler and other Nazi political figures. Recognizing his own military shortcomings, Feuchtinger had wisely developed a habit of delegating responsibility down the chain of command to those divisional officers, who, like von Luck, were veterans of the great tank battles of North Africa and Russia. But he could not delegate to these men the decision to act without orders and ended up vacillating for several hours while continuing to get direction from von Rundstedt, who in turn was hamstrung by OKW.[4]

In his command post at Bellengreville about four miles from the most southerly concentrations of the paratroopers, von Luck "paced up and down and clenched [his] fists at the indecision of the Supreme Command in the face of the obvious facts. . . . So the tragedy took its course. After only a few hours, the brave fighting units in the coastal fortifications could no longer withstand the enemy pressure . . . while a German Panzer division, ready to engage, lay motionless behind the front. . . . In the early hours of the morning, from the hills east of Caen, we saw the gigantic Allied armada, the fields littered with transport gliders and the numerous observation balloons over the landing fleet, with the help of which the heavy naval guns subjected us to precision fire."

Although refused authorization to go on the offensive, the 21st Panzer Division made every effort to regroup while being harassed by navy and air bombardment, in order to be so positioned that when a counterattack was ordered it could respond with lightning speed. Major von Luck broke his regiment into two strong combat units, with one standing on either side of the Orne, despite the fact that the officer believed "there was no longer much chance of throwing the Allies back into the sea.... A successful invasion ... was the beginning of the end."[5]

While von Luck despaired, his superiors hesitantly began to mobilize to meet the invasion with the reserve divisions. Having engaged in a number of fruitless discussions with Richter and then Richter's superior, General der Artillerie Erich Marcks, who commanded LXXXIV Corps, Feuchtinger decided to take the fight to the enemy on his own initiative. He ordered the division's regimental commanders to immediately go on the offensive with their sixteen thousand men by moving to the east of the River Orne to wipe out the airborne units.[6]

Feuchtinger and his staff believed it was "of paramount importance to capture this sector." Otherwise, the paratroops would pose "a standing menace to the division's east wing ... be in a position to reinforce this bridgehead [and] constantly tie down strong German forces." This was also where the Allies would logically gather their forces in from the beaches to effect a breakout from the beachhead onto the Falaise plains, which were ideal for tank operations. If 21st Panzer Division could regain this ground, however, the Germans would be able to form a bridgehead at Ranville from which to attack the Allied east flank and threaten the beaches themselves, particularly Sword and Juno.[7]

Just a few hours earlier, the division's tanks and vehicles could have moved from the holding areas south of Caen under the cover of darkness, but now they were exposed to constant harassment by the low-flying Allied Expeditionary Air Force's fighter-bombers. Still, by maintaining a space of one hundred yards between each tank, the German columns were able to warily creep from one position of cover to another and advance on the Orne without suffering any losses. As his regiment was already close, and in some places actually engaged in sporadic contact with 6th Airborne Division, von Luck was soon in position to begin the offensive upon arrival of the rest of the division. But at 1030 hours, a new set of orders altered Feuchtinger's attack.[8]

At his headquarters in St. Lô, Marcks had finally received word that Hitler, having at last awakened and been fully briefed, had ordered okw to clear 21st Panzer Division for offensive action under lxxxiv Corps command. He also learned that Seventh Army's Oberst-general Friedrich Dollman was working on getting 1st ss Panzer Corps released to him as well. This would bolster his forces significantly by freeing the Panzer Lehr Division and the 12th ss Panzer (Hitlerjugend) Division to support Marcks's right flank with counterattacks on the British and Canadian beachheads. But, although both these divisions had been ordered to begin moving towards Caen, they would be hours arriving. So for now Marcks would have to make do with the 21st Panzer Division.[9]

Marcks immediately informed Feuchtinger that "the bulk of the 21st Panzer Division will attack the enemy forces that have landed *west* of the Orne; only elements of von Luck's combat group will attack the bridgehead east of the Orne."[10] Orders issued, the one-legged Marcks jumped into an armoured scout car and raced to intercept the 22nd Panzer Regiment with the intention of personally sending it into battle. Marcks, who had just turned fifty-three in the early hours of June 6, had been instrumental—along with Heinz Guderian, presently serving as Inspector General of Armoured Troops—in developing fundamental aspects of the German blitzkrieg tactics and was no stranger to tank command. When he arrived at 22nd Panzer Regiment's forming-up area, Marcks grimly approached the regimental commander, Oberst von Oppeln-Bronikowski. "If you don't succeed in throwing the British back into the sea," he warned, "we shall have lost the war."[11]

TURNING THE BULK of the Panzer division around and moving in the ordered direction proved chaotic, and it was not until 1200 hours that Feuchtinger could report his force fully assembled and starting towards the beaches. The march itself was hellish. Whereas the tankers and mechanized troops had earlier managed to largely avoid detection by the Allied flyers while moving towards the east side of the Orne, their approach to Caen brought them directly into an area being heavily bombed and shelled. "There was only one usable bridge in Caen," Feuchtinger later wrote. "A further light bridge was available at Colombelles. The approaches of the various combat teams had to be fixed correspondingly."[12]

To von Luck, the move meant the majority of the division "had to squeeze through the eye of the needle at Caen, [which] was under virtually constant bombardment from the navy and the fighter-bombers." The major, however, was not concerned about trying to get his own regiment through Caen, for Feuchtinger had given him a more demanding immediate task. His job was to "crush the 6th Airborne's bridgehead, recapture the two Orne bridges at Bénouville [on the opposite side of the river from Ranville] and establish contact with the coastal units. Elements of artillery will support you. Start of the attack; as soon as all elements have reached you." In short, he was to carry out Feuchtinger's original plan with less than a quarter of the division's available strength. The major's 2nd Battalion was to be reinforced by the 21st Panzer Reconnaissance Battalion, 200th Assault-gun Battalion, and a platoon of 88-millimetre guns. For tanks, he would receive No. 4 Company of the 22nd Panzer Regiment, but had to send his own 1st Battalion to support the armoured regiment.[13]

Complicating von Luck's problem was that several elements of his 2nd Battalion were already locked in heavy fighting to hold back the attempts by the paratroops to extend their bridgehead. This meant that he could only free some of the battalion to participate in the attack. He was also greatly concerned that his only additional infantry reinforcement was in the form of the reconnaissance battalion, which was lightly armed and "not equipped for direct attacking operations."[14]

It took until 1700 hours for No. 4 Company to show with its tanks. Word came that the assault-gun battalion could not possibly arrive in the area until sometime in the early morning hours of June 7. As the main divisional attack had already started at 1600 hours, von Luck decided to wait no longer. He ordered the reconnaissance battalion to assume the point and start moving. His route would be via Escoville-Hérouvillette to Ranville and the two bridges there.

"The reconnaissance battalion went straight into the attack from its march," von Luck wrote, "and, supported by the Panzer company, penetrated to Escoville against their surprised opponents. Then all hell broke loose. The heaviest naval guns, up to 38-[centimetre], artillery, and fighter-bombers plastered us without pause. Radio contacts were lost, wounded came back, and the men of the reconnaissance battalion were forced to take cover."

From a position just behind the reconnaissance troops, von Luck "saw the disaster" and ran to the commander with fresh instructions. He told the officer to assume a defensive position on the southern edge of Escoville, with the tanks in support to block any advance by the paratroops. Then he radioed Leutnant Liebeskind and said to inform Feuchtinger that he was unable to break through on the eastern side of the Orne.

Feuchtinger had divided the main part of the division into two teams—one a mixed force of armour and mechanized infantry and the other mechanized infantry supported by artillery. The Armoured Combat Team's backbone was 22nd Panzer Regiment with the 1st Battalion of the 125th Panzer Grenadier Regiment, while the Combat Team consisted of 1st Battalion of the 192nd Panzer Grenadier Regiment with a company of the 220th Panzer Engineer Battalion in lightly armoured half-tracks. Although the armoured team at first glance appeared quite formidable, its one hundred tanks were mostly outdated Mark IVs mounting short-barrelled 75-millimetre guns with an effective range against armour of only two thousand feet. Still, Feuchtinger intended the armoured team to crash out from Caen along a road passing through Lébisy to Hermanville-sur-Mer and clear the coast from the mouth of the Orne to the eastern outskirts of Lion-sur-Mer. The 192nd Panzer Grenadier's team, meanwhile, would guard the armoured force's left flank and secure Lion-sur-Mer itself. With Sword Beach effectively destroyed, the 21st Panzer Division could be reinforced by the 12th SS Panzer and Panzer Lehr divisions in the morning. Then, together, this massive armoured juggernaut could roll up the invasion beaches from the most easterly to the most westerly, with Juno Beach the first marked for elimination.[15]

The counterattack enjoyed initial success as the tanks came up sharply on the 2nd King's Shropshire Light Infantry (KSLI), which was approaching Lébisy in a dash for Caen, and forced it to scramble back a mile to the protection of a ridge at Bieville. Breaking to the left, the German armour swung into a gap between Épron and Mathieu to gain Périers Ridge, less than two miles from the open left flank of 3rd Canadian Infantry Division's main line of advance. It was a move intended to enable the use of the ridge as a screen to protect the tanks from exposure to the antitank guns of the regiments guarding 3rd British Infantry Division's western flank. But the Germans were unaware that the British and Canadian armoured brigades possessed a new, deadly answer to the might of their Panzers.

Hidden on the opposing Hermanville Ridge, little more than a mile to the east, were three troops of Firefly Sherman tanks mounting 17-pounder guns. Their commander, Lieutenant Colonel J.A. Eadie of the Staffordshire Yeomanry, had anticipated that the Germans would launch a counterattack precisely into the gap between the Canadian and British divisions and use Périers Ridge to mask the move. As the Mark IVs came over the crest of the ridge, Eadie launched his ambush.[16] The big guns ripped into the German tanks at a range of just over 6,500 feet and the Germans were helpless to fight back. Sixteen tanks were knocked out in minutes and the rest scuttled back to the safety of the ridgeline.

An attempt by von Oppeln-Bronikowski to sideslip his combat group west to evade the British fire turned into a confused muddle because Allied radio-jamming efforts were so effective that he was unable to establish contact with individual tank crews. Progress by the tanks slowed to a crawl and then stopped entirely when the Germans saw hundreds of gliders descending to land in their rear.

This was the 6th Airlanding Brigade, arriving as scheduled at the end of the day to reinforce 6th British Airborne Division. When the tug planes crossed the coast almost over the heads of the Panzer troops, they released 228 Horsa and 30 Hamilcar gliders that began their descent. Unable to elevate the barrels of the tank and SPG main weapons to engage the British gliders, the Germans sprayed the air with machine-gun fire. Although Feuchtinger later claimed that this fire brought down 26 gliders, the fact was that the British troops were descending towards a drop zone just north of Ranville, well east of the German division's rear.[17] The main purpose of this landing was to strengthen the airborne bridgehead around the Ranville bridges crossing the Orne and Caen Canal to ensure that this vital position was not overrun by expected German counterattacks on June 7 and 8.

To the men of 21st Division's armoured team, however, it seemed eerily as if the Allies had somehow deliberately mounted a stunning *coup de main* with glider troops to cut off their lines of retreat. Badly pummelled by British tanks that stood far outside the range of their own guns, and now threatened from the rear, the Germans panicked and began a hasty retreat that was quickly endorsed by Feuchtinger.[18]

The 192nd Panzer Grenadier Regiment, meanwhile, was already too far forward to think they could escape the illusory trap of the British airborne forces. While the tankers had attempted to work around the deadly Staffordshire Yeomanry tanks, the 192nd Regiment's commander, Oberst Josef Rauch, had slipped his force along the west flank of Périers Ridge through to Plumetot. From here, it dashed northward along a local road to reach Lion-sur-Mer, and linked up with some elements of the 111th Battalion of the 736th Infantry Regiment dug in before the beach there. But on learning that there was no chance his smaller force would be reinforced by the tank team, Rauch decided he must turn around and withdraw. Poor communications plagued Rauch as badly as had been true for the armoured team and he lost contact with a number of self-propelled guns and the majority of his 1st Company of Panzer grenadiers during the withdrawal. They ended up straying into the lines of the Germans defending the radar station at Douvres-la Délivrande. When Rauch managed to establish radio contact with this lost element and reported their situation back to divisional headquarters, he was informed it would be too dangerous for it to attempt withdrawing and that the troops should strengthen that defensive position until relieved.[19]

The confusion that mired the 21st Panzer Division's counterattack had been greatly exacerbated by the actions of its commander. First,

Feuchtinger had shifted his headquarters from outside Caen to a new position at St. Pierre-sur-Dives near Troarn to be closer to the offensive he had ordered executed between the Dives and Orne rivers. This placed him a good twelve miles east of Caen and far from the action when Marcks ordered the offensive directed to the west of the Orne. Belatedly desiring to get closer to where the main strength of his division was engaged in battle, Feuchtinger had taken his entire staff— excepting the division's first general staff officer—off to Richter's headquarters on the Caen outskirts. In their haste, nobody had thought to take along a wireless set, leaving Feuchtinger dependent on the telephone for communicating through the staff officer to his fighting units. As the telephone exchanges and lines around Caen had been badly disrupted by massive Allied bombing and shelling, he was often unable to establish a link with his own headquarters.[20]

20

A Great Initiation

BY THE TIME 'B' COMPANY of La Régiment de la Chaudière had
finished mopping up the Moulineaux Gun Battery and shep-
herding the prisoners to Bény-sur-Mer for escort back to the beach,
Major George Sévigny's 'C' Company had pushed off towards Basly.
And, as had been the case since the company first assumed its position at the head of the column departing Bernières-sur-Mer, it immediately started tripping one sniper and machine-gun position after
another. Despite the complaints being registered by officers farther
back in the column, Sévigny and his men could do little more than
slowly, cautiously close on each cluster of German defenders and either force a surrender or eliminate them. Sévigny was, as he had
been throughout the advance, right at the front to ensure the platoon
section leaders were as aggressive as possible without recklessly risking lives. Beyond that, there was little he could do to hasten the
process of clearing the endless pockets of resistance.

The remaining Chaudière companies were too confined by the
road and its bordering hedgerows to offer any support. To deploy into
the neighbouring fields to come up on 'C' Company's flanks would
only have further delayed the advance. The 14th Field Regiment's
Forward Observation Officer, Lieutenant J.B. Leslie, was incapable of
providing artillery support because the German positions were only
revealed when 'C' Company was practically on top of them. Trying to
shell the enemy would likely cause friendly-fire casualties.[1]

Although the German 716th Infantry Division, whose 726th Infantry Regiment was defending this sector, had been declared by Allied intelligence to be of poor fighting quality, the division had proven capable of offering a determined fight from fixed positions. As had been true during the battle for the beach itself, the Germans encountered on the march from Bernières towards Anguerny and Colomby-sur-Thaon largely lacked armoured fighting vehicles and motorized transport. This meant they could seldom take the offensive or successfully withdraw from a defensive position. Consequently, the German infantry tended to fight stubbornly until the position was on the verge of being overrun, whereupon they generally surrendered rather than fight to the death—a pragmatic approach that still enabled the Germans to effectively hobble the Canadian advance.

The stiff resistance slowed 8th Canadian Infantry Brigade's advance to a crawl and left the three battalions of 9th Canadian Infantry Brigade and the Sherbrooke Fusiliers virtually shuffling along on the leading brigade's heels. It was not until 1645 hours that the North Nova Scotia Highlanders in the vanguard and the Sherbrookes reached their designated forming-up position outside Bény-sur-Mer, codenamed "Elder." From here, they were to close up on 8 CIB with the intention of overtaking the Chaudières at Colomby-sur-Thaon and passing through in a rapid mechanized dash to the Caen-Bayeux highway and Carpiquet airport.

In the North Novas ranks, as No. 12 Platoon of 'B' Company was forming up for the advance, several civilians came over and offered the men some wine from bottles. "Don't even think of it, because you never know," Private Jack Byrne warned the other soldiers. Even though Byrne was only a private, the other men immediately refused the wine. Just nineteen on D-Day, Byrne had been only fifteen when he volunteered in 1940. Being five-foot-eleven, 157 pounds, and an avid athlete, Byrne had succeeded in duping the recruiters into thinking he was of legal age. Posted in England to be an instructor at the Canadian Battle School, Byrne was quickly promoted to the rank of sergeant serving in the school's demonstration platoon. When Byrne realized the invasion was imminent, he requested a transfer to the

North Novas to get in on the show and gladly accepted a demotion to private in order to do so. Upon reporting for duty to No. 12 Platoon's lieutenant, Byrne recognized the officer as one of many who had gone through Battle School under his tutelage, where the officer had been required to defer to the then sergeant. "I'm here. I'm a private, and I'll remain that until I leave," Byrne assured his lieutenant. "I understand," the officer responded. But Byrne had a natural talent for leadership, and despite his lowly rank and young age the other men in the platoon often turned to him for guidance.[2]

While the North Novas were getting organized, the Sherbrookes were busy de-waterproofing their tanks. It had taken the crews two weeks of steady work to install the various waterproofing devices, but the removal required only ten minutes' effort. When the drivers plugged a strand of electrical wire into a live socket, a series of Cordex explosives were set off that blew the fabric covers that had covered the gun muzzle, mantle, and ventilation ducts. Meanwhile, the crew commander "pulled a trigger and the towering breathing tubes clattered to the ground," the regimental historian wrote. "The remainder of the crew with wrenches and crowbars tore off the breathing tube mounting fixtures, and opened the engine compartment door to see how much water had been shipped, but 'there was hardly enough briny there to make a decent gargle.'"[3]

The North Novas by now were anxious to get moving because hanging about the assembly area had attracted the attention of some German mortars, which were firing from a position near the little hamlet of Moulineaux. When the increasingly accurate mortaring seemed to single out Major L.M. Rhodenizer's 'A' Company for particular attention, the platoons started getting intermixed as men ducked for cover rather than marshalling around their assigned tanks. Corporal L.E. Bishop called on the men to stand fast, but was quickly killed by a round when he stepped out into the open road to set an example for the others.[4] One other soldier was killed and three wounded in the next few minutes.[5]

So when the order to saddle up came, the North Novas did precisely that. Three companies rushed to board the Shermans of the

Sherbrooke Fusiliers, while the other climbed onto its bicycles. When there proved to be too little space on the tanks for all the men assigned to them, tankers and infantry rigged up an ingenious sled that could be pulled on ropes attached to the backs of the tanks. For the landing, each tank had been supplied with extra ammunition loaded in a metal canister, which attached to the bottom of the Shermans for release on the beach.[6] Dubbed a porpoise, these canisters were about one foot deep, eight feet long, and five feet wide. The tankers now hooked the porpoises back up to the tanks and the North Novas, like Private Byrne, who were still looking for a means of transport jumped on. As the tanks ground up the road, Byrne thought the porpoises slid along behind "just like a sled on snow" despite their heavy loads of as many as twenty men per sled compared to the ten or so that managed to find space aboard each tank.[7]

Realizing the mortars were so positioned that they could dog 9 CIB's advance all the way to Colomby, the Sherbrookes' Lieutenant Colonel Mel Gordon instructed 'A' Squadron to dispatch a troop of tanks to wipe out the position. Major W.L. Arnold assigned the job to No. 1 Troop under command of Lieutenant John H. "Jack" Casey of London, Ontario. Sergeants R.R. Beardsley and T.B. Murray were in charge of the other two tanks in the troop.

Corporal Richard Bryant, Casey's driver, was struggling to forget the grim image of several Canadian corpses lying on the edge of the beach with their clothes blown right off by the force of an explosion that must have resulted from one of the men triggering an antitank mine. Bryant kept thinking: "If I don't forget this, I'm not going to get through."[8]

Soon the tanks closed up on a German trench system and Casey tried to flush any Germans that might be in it by throwing grenades from his position in the top of the turret. When that failed to have any noticeable effect, Casey told Bryant to drive closer so he could be sure to put the grenades right into the trench. "Sir, you're going to get your head blown off if you're not careful," the driver warned.

But Casey was insistent and also frustrated by the lack of effect the grenades were yielding. To increase the power of the explosions in the trench, the lieutenant started wrapping a grenade and antipersonnel mine together and throwing one of these charges after another into the trench. Suddenly, a burst of machine-gun fire ripped out of the German position and wounded Casey horribly in the head. Bryant spun the tank around and raced towards Bény-sur-Mer and the Regimental Aid Post there while other men in the crew tried to treat Casey's wound. Although the twenty-nine-year-old officer was soon evacuated off Juno Beach to a hospital in England, he succumbed to his wounds on June 18.[9]

When Casey was wounded, Sergeant Beardsley assumed command of the troop and continued the search for the enemy mortar position, but stumbled instead upon a well-hidden battery of four 122-millimetre howitzers protected by several machine guns and light antitank guns. Despite being decidedly outgunned, the sergeant succeeded in silencing the German position with a rapid succession of well-placed 75-millimetre gun rounds. Murray, meanwhile, had tracked the mortar to a position in a dugout in front of the Moulineaux church and destroyed it with several high-explosive shells. The two tanks then rejoined the rest of 'A' Squadron, which was advancing towards Colomby-sur-Thaon.[10]

The opposition the North Novas and Sherbrookes had encountered prompted 8 CIB Brigadier Ken Blackader to worry that the higher ground overlooking the road from the right might harbour German forces gathering for a counterattack against the long, dangerously extended column. With the column completely exposed by a gap that existed between the two brigades on the east and 7th Canadian Infantry Brigade, Blackader had no way of knowing what German forces might be lurking in that direction. He therefore ordered Lieutenant Colonel Ronald Morton to detach 'B' Squadron of the Fort Garry Horse from its position in front of the Queen's Own Rifles and have it sortie out through this country in an arc. Morton instructed Major Jack Meindl to take 'B' Squadron out on a wide loop from Bény-sur-Mer to Fontaine-Henry and then back to Colomby-sur-Thaon. Meindl was cautioned to not get involved in any major fight but to ensure that no German force in this area got past him to attack the main column.[11]

The major's headquarters section was trailing along in company with No. 5 Troop at the very tail of 'B' Squadron, the Shermans

grinding up the road just south of Bény-sur-Mer behind the marching ranks of the Queen's Own Rifles, when this order came. On
either side, thick hedgerows presented a barrier too thick for the
tanks to easily break through to embark on their new assignment, so
No. 1 Troop under Lieutenant J.P. Milner could only bump along
behind the infantry while looking for a suitable exit point. From a
position much farther back in the column, Morton saw 'B' Squadron
still rolling up the road despite the fact that Meindl had indicated
that he understood the urgency of the task given him. Exasperated,
Morton demanded to know what was causing the holdup. Stuck near
the rear of the tank column, Meindl was powerless to personally lead
the squadron off on its mission. Responsibility for finding an exit
from the road lay completely with the lead tank, so the major
demanded that Lieutenant Milner get his troop heading in the right
direction. With each passing minute and no thinning of the
hedgerow, Milner's headset was buzzing ever more loudly with
exhortations to get the job done. Finally, a desperate Milner got on
the radio to Sergeant John Shineton, whose tank was at the head of
No. 1 Troop. "For God's sake, do something," he snapped.

Looking about frantically, the sergeant decided there was nothing
for it but to just try bursting through the hedge and hoping his Sherman didn't get hung up or lose a track in the effort. With much crash-
ing and clawing of tracks, the thirty-five-ton monster lunged through
the heavy foliage and rumbled out into an open field, followed by the
rest of the squadron in single file. The sudden appearance of the
tanks caught several pockets of Germans dug in behind the
hedgerow preparing to ambush the advancing Canadians. Before the
Germans could react, Shineton and the other crew commanders in
the leading 'B' Squadron tanks ripped into them with machine-gun
fire, causing a general panic.[12]

When all the tanks were spread out in formation in the field, the
Fort Garry regimental historian later wrote, "Meindl pushed on joy-
ously, as so far he had only been able to shoot up some German infantry and antitank guns near Bernières."[13] It was the hard-charging
gallop so dreamed of by tankers but seldom called for and rarely
possible in the uneven European countryside. The primary tank role

was to chug along at the pace of the infantry they were supposed to support. Now, if only briefly, 'B' Squadron was foraying out as horse cavalry had done for centuries to protect the flank of the main body, perhaps even to crash into the enemy from behind, leaving havoc and destruction in its wake.

The squadron was bound for Hill 70, a position that overlooked many small crossroads and the villages of Colomby-sur-Thaon and Anguerny. From here, the tankers would be able to lob shells down from the right to cover the main column's advance. Resistance en route was scant, only a few snipers that the tankers took out if it was possible to do so without slowing down. Barrelling along at full speed, 'B' Squadron roared up onto the summit of Hill 70 to see the Canadian column only just making its way out of Basly.

As No. 5 Troop and Meindl's headquarters section came up to join the rest of the squadron on the hill, several German high-explosive artillery rounds slammed down on the hill. By mischance, one round dropped directly through a hatch on Lieutenant Norman Brown's tank. The ensuing explosion instantly killed the No. 5 Troop leader and his entire crew. Shrapnel from another shell seriously wounded Meindl in the head. When the smoke cleared, Meindl insisted on walking back to the Canadian lines rather than put stretcher-bearers at risk by having them make the cross-country trek to evacuate him. Bleeding badly, the major made his way back safely. The severity of his wound, the regimental historian wrote, meant that "early in our first battle we lost the services of a brave and outstanding commander."[14]

The squadron's second-in-command, Captain Jim Hall, took over and was just beginning to consider the next course of action when Captain Robert Grant's Sherman arrived. Grant was the squadron rear-link officer, whose main task was to maintain radio contact with regimental headquarters. Hall and Grant jumped out of their tanks to confer. "What the heck do we do now?" Hall asked as Grant walked up. Neither man had any idea, for no orders were coming from Lieutenant Colonel Morton's HQ.[15]

In the distance, the hangars and runway of Carpiquet airfield were clearly visible. No enemy forces were apparent between Hill 70 and the airport, and the tankers were tempted to renew the charge straight through to that final objective. Suddenly, to the south, a large cluster of German vehicles came roaring out of Villons les Buissons and made towards the main road running from there directly to Caen. The two officers jumped back into their tanks, as every Sherman in the squadron drew a bead on the fleeing column of half-tracks, trucks, and cars. Grant wrote later, "This was really our first experience firing at these things. It was just like a shooting gallery. They were going across in front of us. It was a great initiation."[16]

Shineton "had a field day setting them on fire," but eventually ammunition started running low and, having re-established radio contact with the regimental HQ, the squadron was ordered to "hold back on engaging any more targets unless it was absolutely necessary."[17] It was to hold in place to anchor 8 CIB's right flank. 'B' Squadron's exhilarating charge was done.

MEANWHILE, IN AN EFFORT to hasten the main advance upon Basly, Major Sévigny of 'C' Company had requested permission from Chaudière commander Lieutenant Colonel Paul Mathieu to form a rapid attack force to seize the hamlet of la Mare and an intersection just beyond. The road the column had been travelling split at this intersection, with one fork running to Colomby-sur-Thaon and the other to Anguerny. The Queen's Own Rifles were to break off for Anguerny at this intersection, while the Chaudières pushed on to capture Colomby. Sévigny hoped to accelerate the column's ponderous pace by striking out ahead with a fully motorized unit comprised of Lieutenant W. Foy's No. 14 Platoon mounted on a troop of Fort Garry Horse's 'A' Squadron and the Chaudières' Bren carrier platoon, commanded by Captain Michel Gauvin. Mathieu thought the idea had a good chance of success and radioed 8 CIB commander Brigadier Ken Blackader for permission to cobble together the small force. Desperate to attain his brigade's final objectives despite all the delays, Blackader quickly approved.

Sévigny and Foy's men mounted the tanks and the force set off with Gauvin's Bren carriers following close behind the Shermans. Instead of rooting out the few German snipers they encountered,

Sévigny ordered them bypassed and the force rushed straight through to La Mare. They found the village undefended except for an anti-aircraft gun detachment of twenty soldiers who immediately surrendered. Sévigny radioed back to Mathieu that he was in possession of the hamlet, had captured four vehicles along with the AA gunners, and was en route to the intersection. He soon reported this objective firmly in his hands and said he was ready to proceed to Colomby as soon as the rest of the battalion came up to provide a base of support. For this action and those that had preceded it through the long march, Sévigny was awarded the Distinguished Service Order, while Gauvin and Foy won Military Crosses.[18]

At the intersection, the Fort Garry's 'A' Squadron took the left fork, striking out ahead of the Queen's Own Rifles towards Anguerny, while Sévigny's 'C' Company led the Chaudières on to Colomby-sur-Thaon. The two villages were barely a half-mile apart and slightly less than that from the intersection. Sévigny closed quickly on Colomby with the hope of carrying off the same kind of fast attack that had led to La Mare falling so easily, but found the village surrounded by a thick stone wall that he could not breach in the face of determined German resistance. Once again, his men were so close to the wall that it was impossible to call for artillery without risking friendly fire casualties. The major put out an urgent request for tanks, only to learn that 'A' Squadron had pushed off ahead of the Queen's Own and was heading independently for Anguerny. No other tanks were available.

A protracted firefight ensued, with several failed attacks during which Lieutenant L.E. Dupont was wounded, before the company managed to rout the German defenders and the Chaudières moved into the town. With his men establishing a perimeter defence around Colomby, Lieutenant Colonel Paul Mathieu was able to report to Brigadier Blackader that the way was now open for 9 CIB to pass through and head for its objectives.[19]

Meanwhile, the Fort Garry's 'A' Squadron had arrived at Anguerny and its commander reported his tanks "were prowling about mopping up enemy resistance [but] wished infantry as soon as possible." The prowling took some of the squadron as far as the outer edges of Anisy, but lacking infantry support the tankers were hesitant to attempt to hold any ground and instead kept roaming between the two villages.[20]

'C' Company was leading the advance of the Queen's Own and faced the same problems that Chaudières had encountered during the earlier phase and the march on Colomby—constant sniper harassment and stubborn machine-gun blocking positions that proved tough to eliminate. The company was also subjected to almost constant mortar and artillery fire. Throughout the advance, Rifleman Orville Cook had noticed that each village had at least one tall religious statue in a square and every time "you got close to one of these you were going to get shelled or mortared."[21] The Germans had pre-registered their guns to range in on the statues.

Farther back in the advance, 'A' Company's Company Sergeant Major Charlie Martin had come to the conclusion that the advance inland was "worse than the beach itself." Because the ground rose gradually the farther inland they went, the Germans enjoyed the advantage of having a clear view of the advance at all times. When a German machine gun opened up, the nearest platoon took to "the fields, picking out draws, sloughs and low ground when we could. We needed to locate the enemy's machine-gun fire in order to pinpoint our own fire and this was done in erratic bursts of running and flopping, stops and starts." It was exhausting and exceedingly dangerous work. All the companies were taking casualties during the march to Anguerny and it pained Martin to see 'A' Company, so hard hit on the beach, lose even more men as the long afternoon dragged on.[22]

Finally, at 1730 hours, the Queen's Own entered Anguerny, a small village of about 240 people living in 90 houses. Shortly thereafter, a jeep carrying two Queen's Own soldiers drove into Roger Chevalier's small farmyard and stopped outside his house. The family went out to greet them and one of the Canadians offered Chevalier's two-year-old daughter an orange, which she began happily tossing around in the mistaken belief that it was some kind of ball. Since the occupation, nobody had seen any kind of fruit other than those that grew locally. One of the Canadians spoke a little French and began questioning Chevalier about what defences the Germans might have on top of a hill that overlooked the farm. He told them that the hill had a water reservoir on it and the Germans had some kind of gun dug in on the summit.

The farmer was having a hard time concentrating on the Canadian soldier's French because of a grisly sight on the road running in front of his farm. In the approach to Anguerny, a German sniper had killed a Canadian soldier and the body still lay in the middle of the road. He watched in growing horror as a line of Fort Garry tanks leaving Anguerny ground one after another over the corpse, the tracks scattering the man's "guts all over the road." It was the cruellest thing he had ever seen, but when Chevalier pointed out to the soldiers what was happening they shrugged as if such matters were routine.[23]

While most of the Queen's Own Rifles began taking up defensive positions in Anguerny, Lieutenant Colonel Jock Spragge sent Major Neil Gordon's 'D' Company on to secure Anisy. After a "sharp brush" with a small force of Germans that attempted a stand in the little village, Gordon reported it cleared. He had seen no sign of the Fort Garry Horse tanks that were supposed to have been in the vicinity.[24] Spragge set 'A' Company up in the eastern part of Anguerny with 'B' Company holding the westerly side, which was further protected by the presence of the Chaudières in Colomby-sur-Thaon. 'C' Company was given the task of conducting roving patrols between Anguerny and Anisy to tie 'D' Company into the battalion's defensive layout.[25]

Most of the Queen's Own had no sense that the tankers had beaten them to Anguerny or Anisy. This was possibly because, within minutes of the infantry's arrival, the Fort Garry Horse had received orders from 2nd Canadian Armoured Brigade to return to Bény-sur-Mer in order to regroup and replenish fuel and ammunition stocks so that it would be immediately operational come the morning. As a result, by 2000 hours 'A' and 'B' squadrons along with the regimental headquarters were rumbling back along the road towards the rear. Only 'C' Squadron, after much pressure by North Shore (New Brunswick) Regiment's Lieutenant Colonel Donald Buell, was instructed to overnight with the infantry at Tailleville because of the strong likelihood of a counterattack from the German strongpoint at Douvres-la Délivrande.[26]

With the tankers already departing from the area, Spragge faced a difficult time summoning tank support for the one remaining piece of real estate he was determined to acquire before night fell. This was Hill 80, a small height of ground to the east of Anguerny near Roger Chevalier's farm, believed to be a key German observation point that enjoyed an excellent view of Juno Beach. Spragge ordered Captain Stanley Biggs, commander of the Bren carrier platoon, to gather a small force and take the hill after it was heavily shelled by two Fort Garry Horse tanks. Once atop the summit, Biggs was to transform it into a Canadian observation post by keeping an eagle eye open for the presence of German artillery batteries or the approach of counterattacking forces.[27] That no serious counterattack had yet materialized was a source of increasing puzzlement to Spragge and every other commander of 3rd Canadian Infantry Division, which had by now expected to be fending off elements of the heavily mechanized 21st Panzer Division and even the 12th ss Panzer (Hitlerjugend) Divison.

Biggs took just nine men with him to carry out the attack. As the Queen's Own had closed on Anguerny, they had come under fire from the hill, so the captain knew he was going to have to fight for its possession. But he was counting on the tank fire to force the Germans to cower in their trenches long enough for his men to get on top of the hill in a flat-out charge that would be better executed by a small group than a full platoon. His men also had the advantage of being heavily armed, with one soldier carrying a PIAT, another a two-inch mortar, and the rest Bren guns. For his part, Biggs had a Sten gun and two grenades. His batman, Rifleman "Red" McBride, was lugging a wireless that would be used to alert Spragge to any artillery targets or approaching German forces that Biggs spotted after the hill was taken. Rifleman Orville Cook was among the men dragooned by Biggs for the task.

The ground was good for an attack, Biggs noted. "There was cover in an orchard at the base of the hill, an assortment of trees, mounds and ditches. In the infantry one reads ground and cover in a very quick and special way." His reading was that the approach up the hill was perfect for his purposes.[28]

Biggs spread his men out in the orchard and everyone settled down to await the supporting tanks. It seemed an inordinate amount of time before Biggs heard the clanking of tank tracks and saw a single Sherman lumber into view behind him. Expecting to lead his men in a full-tilt rush up the hill, Biggs brought his whistle up in readiness to signal the men to begin the attack immediately after the tank blasted the hilltop with a few rounds. A sharp crack of the tank gun firing was followed immediately by the explosion of the shell in the middle of the orchard rather than on the hilltop. Biggs hurled himself into a nearby ditch as one high-explosive round after another tore the orchard to pieces. Leaves, branches, and splinters of trunks flew everywhere. Biggs "didn't know what the hell to do. In a desperate moment, I raised my Canadian helmet—without my head in it of course—above the ditch and prayed."[29]

The tank suddenly ceased firing and, after a moment of chuffing back and forth, turned its gun on the correct target with a fury that matched its earlier assault on the men in the orchard, which incredibly had failed to hurt anyone. Biggs watched happily as what seemed to the infantry officer to be hundreds of rounds were punched out of the 75-millimetre main gun in rapid succession. Finally, the tanker stopped shooting and Biggs "blew my whistle and got back to trying to be brave and successful. Our group was on its way, spread out and charging up the hill. At the top, we found ten slit trenches each about five feet deep." Heading down the hill on the other side was a German half-track with a bunch of men crowded in its open troop compartment. Biggs and his men opened up with long bursts of automatic fire that may have killed some of the men but failed to stop the vehicle's escape.[30]

Even over the slow thudding bark of his Bren gun, Cook could hear the Germans in the "half-track hollering as they were hit."[31] With the hill taken, Biggs split his force up so that there were two men in the five trenches closest to the summit and then set to work trying "to detect any forming-up of enemy troops and tanks." Biggs was also watching for German artillery—either visible batteries or the flash of guns firing—with the intent of knocking them out with counter-battery fire.

As dusk fell, Biggs could see smoke from fires burning in Caen only about four to five miles away. Out to sea, the flash of naval guns was visible, the shells being lobbed far inland on predetermined targets such as road intersections and bridges. Biggs radioed Spragge to report that the hill was secure and was told to dig in for the night. The captain didn't tell Spragge that such labour was mercifully unnecessary as the Germans had left them with perfectly good trenches.[32] After a long day of being constantly on the move with the likelihood of being killed or wounded, Cook was "dead tired, just beat."[33] Biggs was equally fatigued but also "inspired" by the day's events. He ordered the men to follow a routine whereby one of the men in each trench would sleep for four hours while the other remained on watch.[34]

ABOUT THE TIME Biggs's small band had seized Hill 80, the North Nova Scotia Highlanders and Sherbrooke Fusiliers finally started pushing through Colomby-sur-Thaon, with the hope that they could still achieve the division's key objectives of cutting the Caen-Bayeux highway and capturing Carpiquet airport. Night was less than two hours off, but the force was entirely mechanized and, so long as German resistance proved weak, it might still cover the five miles lying between 8 CIB's forward position and the objectives.

Forming a protective screen ahead of the main body were the Honey tanks of the Sherbrooke Fusiliers Reconnaissance Troop under Lieutenant G.A. Kraus.[35] These outdated American-made Stuart tanks were lightly armoured and mounted only a 37-millimetre main gun, but were faster and more agile than Sherman tanks in cross-country travel. Closely following the Honeys was the North Novas' Bren carrier platoon with the battalion's 'C' Company mounted on eighteen vehicles by platoon sections. Immediately behind the carriers was No. 11 Platoon of the Cameron Highlanders of Ottawa, 3 CID's brigade support group, with its Vickers heavy machine guns loaded on carriers. They were trailed by a troop of M10 tank destroyers, two assault sections of the North Novas' pioneer platoon, one section of its mortar platoon, and four of the battalion's antitank guns. Captain E.S. Gray commanded the carrier platoon, while 'C' Company was temporarily under the orders of its second-in-command, Captain Hank Fraser, in order to leave Major Don Learment free to exercise overall command of this vanguard element.[36]

With the leading element forming the tip of an arrowhead formation, 'A' Company aboard the Sherbrookes' 'A' Squadron tanks moved out on the right flank, while on the left 'B' Squadron carried 'B' Company. 'D' Company, riding on 'C' Squadron, brought up the rear and was responsible for mopping up any points of light resistance the vanguard bypassed. North Novas' commander, Lieutenant Colonel Charlie Petch, and his battalion headquarters were positioned in the middle of the diamond-shaped formation directly behind Learment's vanguard. "Everyone was feeling keen," the North Novas' regimental historian wrote, as the powerful battle group broke out into the open past Colomby. It was "as if they were on a new sort of scheme that played for keeps, but was exciting and not too dangerous. They knew the main objective was Carpiquet Airport and did not think there would be much trouble getting there."[37]

The carriers carrying 'C' Company were strung out in a line by platoons with Lieutenant Herby Langley's platoon in front, followed by that of Lieutenant Jack Veness, and then Lieutenant Bob Graves's platoon. For the first mile and a half, it was a happy romp, with only a few wildly inaccurate snipers that were left to 'D' Company to clean up. Soon they reached the crossroad that extended from Anisy across the main road they were travelling to Villons-les-Buissons. This was a pivotal intersection and the briefing officers had repeatedly cautioned that the force must turn right rather than carrying on straight. Going straight would put the battle group on a main road leading to Caen, but much more critically it also crossed into the British 3rd Division's operational area. Going right steered the Canadians onto a southerly running secondary road that led via Buron, Authie, and Franqueville to the highway objective and the Carpiquet airport directly to the south of it.

Given the insistence of the briefing officers about the need to make the right turn, it was with some consternation that Captain Gray of the carrier platoon saw Lieutenant Kraus's Honeys barrel right past it and on towards Caen. By the time he careened up the road at full speed in his carrier to head Kraus off, Lieutenant Langley's platoon had also overshot the turn. While Kraus and Langley started turning around, Gray signalled Lieutenant Veness to assume the lead.[38] Veness had gone less than a quarter-mile and was closing on Villons-les-Buissons when three machine guns in the village starting firing up the road at his platoon.[39] The lieutenant pulled up his No. 14 Platoon until Langley caught up with his men and then the two officers attacked. The fight was over in five minutes, with the greater number of a German platoon killed and three others taken prisoner, while the North Novas suffered no casualties.[40]

Night was falling fast now and the battle group was still four miles from Carpiquet airport, with no chance of reaching it or the highway objective before complete darkness set in. Increasingly anxious about the threat of a counterattack, Major General Rod Keller had no desire to see a large part of his leading brigade groping its way forward half-blind. Instead, he instructed 9 CIB to consolidate where each battalion could establish a fortified position to meet the expected German retaliation.[41] The battle group of North Novas and Sherbrookes accordingly "formed a fortress based on the high ground around the crossroads ... between Anisy and Villons-les-Buissons."[42]

For their part, the Stormont, Dundas and Glengarry Highlanders and the Highland Light Infantry were to hunker down around Bény-sur-Mer. Both battalions had endured sporadic bouts of mortaring in this vicinity as they waited for the order to advance on their final objectives. The SDG suffered one man killed and five wounded as it moved up to a position near the village's church.[43] More fortunate, the HLI reported no casualties during the day. In fact, the day had proved almost pleasant for the battalion as it languished in Bény-sur-Mer waiting for an advance order that never came. The war diarist noted that many of the troops "could be seen with a book in one hand reading off French phrases much to the amusement of the inhabitants." The village had been a German barracks and the citizenry wasted no time in beginning "to loot the place. Men struggled by with bags of flour, a wheelbarrow full of army boots, a hind leg of beef, chairs, clothes, boxes of black rye bread, butcher's saws and countless other articles. Women came by with chickens, butter, curtains, sheets, pillows, dishes, cutlery, bowls. Even the parish priest was seen to carry off a set of dishes. People were all excited and friendly, offering us their best luck, glasses of milk and wine."[44]

Although the troops in 9 CIB's advance force had the sensation as darkness descended that they were dangling in the air well ahead of the rest of the division, the Queen's Own Rifles were actually close by in the form of 'D' Company at Anisy. This company's presence served as a guard for the North Novas' and Sherbrookes' left flank. To the right, however, a serious gap did exist, for, although 7 CIB had also been vying to reach the Caen-Bayeux highway, its progress had been less than hoped with the result that its leading battalions were four miles away in the town of le Fresne-Camilly. The brigade's failure to reach its final objectives had certainly not been for want of trying.

21

At All Costs

THE BATTLE THAT THE Canadian Scottish Regiment and Royal Winnipeg Rifles of 7th Canadian Infantry Brigade had been embroiled in for control of St. Croix-sur-Mer and Banville-sur-Mer had thrown the advance on the right flank seriously behind schedule. Scattered pockets of resistance were still being mopped up when the Bren carrier platoon, itself delayed in the landing process at Courseulles-sur-Mer, arrived in the area at 1400 hours under command of Lieutenant Joseph James Andrews. The thirty-year-old Victoria native had been questing about for some time trying to find the main body of his battalion, which he understood to be somewhere on the road to Tierceville. When the carriers rolled through Banville-sur-Mer, a German hiding in the tower of a church opened fire with a Schmeisser submachine gun. As the carriers were all open-topped, Andrews realized that trying to make a run past the German would certainly result in casualties. "Oh no," he thought, "this is getting to be a bit hazardous."

Pulling the carriers back around the corner of a building out of sight of the German, he started organizing his men to attack the church but was interrupted by the arrival of a 13th Field Regiment, RCA's 105-millimetre Priest. Andrews hastened to wave the SPG down so that its crew would not be exposed to the German's fire. When Andrews told him he was going to take a section of men to clear out the sniper, the commander of the Priest said, "Don't bother, I'll do it. I'll do it." Carefully Andrews led the man to the corner of the building and then peeked around it to show him where the church was situated. The Priest then moved around the corner "and chopped the church down in three pieces," Andrews said later. "The inside was just a mass of dirt and debris and stuff."

After going only a short distance, the lieutenant was able to see Germans and Canadians still locked together in a melee around St. Croix and so decided to halt in the protective cover of a section of sunken road. He then ordered his men off the carriers and into positions that would enable them to provide an all-round defence while he tried to figure out who was embroiled in the "scrap down there." Andrews "had no desire to get mixed up in that" because he knew better than to "go rushing up if you don't know what you're doing."

As he was staring at the village through binoculars, one of his men facing back towards the sea yelled, "Somebody's coming." Andrews whirled around in time to see a scattering of soldiers creeping along a hedge towards the platoon. Everyone tightened their fingers on gun triggers and waited. Andrews grinned as he saw that the man leading the section of troops was not only wearing a Canadian uniform but "had his pants rolled up logger style, which only a west coaster would do." The lieutenant declared, "He's got to be Canadian Scottish."[1]

It proved in fact to be the leading section of 'A' Company. A few minutes later, Lieutenant Colonel Fred Cabeldu also emerged and instructed Andrews to spread his carriers out among the four companies, so that each had support of the mounted Bren guns. Cabeldu informed Andrews that the Canadians fighting in St. Croix were from the Royal Winnipeg Rifles, who were finishing mopping up the village with the help of 'A' Squadron of the 1st Hussars. The Canadian Scots, meanwhile, would push on to Colombiers-sur-Seulles, cross the bridge seized there earlier by a platoon from 'D' Company that had dashed inland on bicycles, and make for Pierrepont astride the Creully-Caen road as their next objective.[2]

German opposition to this phase of the advance was meager, little more than a bit of faint-hearted sniping by soldiers who fled after firing a few shots, so the battalion made good time to the bridge. Here they linked up with 'D' Company under Major G.T. MacEwan, which happily abandoned its bicycles and "joined the forward advance." Trailing along in the rear, his men had need to only keep pace and MacEwan soon noticed "the rapidity with which the men picked up souvenirs. Within a very short time ... most men seemed to have a memento." For one it was a German belt, for another "a German rifle ... he seemed willing to carry along with his own." Schmeissers were particularly popular. The major "even saw one man carrying a belt of German MG ammo. As the day wore on it was noticeable that the heavier items were discarded." MacEwan confined his own pickings to a bottle of champagne that he stowed aboard the company's headquarters Bren carrier. He noted ruefully that this was "not the best place for champagne storage."[3]

The battalion's line of advance had now swung to the southeast, with the main body following a side road running from Colombiers to Pierrepont. Major R.M. Lendrum's 'B' Company was moving through fields and along rough tracks on the left flank towards the hamlet of Amblie with instructions to root out any Germans dug in there. At this point, Lendrum's left shoulder was pointed almost due north back towards the beach and he was somewhat concerned to see no evidence of the Regina Rifles coming up from that direction out of the village of Reviers, which had fallen to this battalion some hours previously.

What he did see shortly thereafter were several Sherman tanks crawling towards a height of ground south of Reviers unaccompanied by supporting infantry. They managed only a short advance before being "one by one knocked out" by antitank fire from a position the major was unable to situate.[4]

HAVING HAD TWO COMPANIES mauled during the fight for the beach in front of Courseulles-sur-Mer, the Regina Rifles had been badly delayed in clearing the town and then bringing the majority of its surviving strength up to Reviers. The supporting 1st Hussars tanks of 'B' Squadron had fared little better, with only ten tanks, or half its total strength, making it past Courseulles—the others having been lost or damaged during the landing or knocked out in the ensuing fighting.[5] En route to Reviers, Lieutenant R.F. Seaman's tank ran over a mine. The ensuing explosion damaged the Sherman, badly injured the driver, and inflicted minor wounds on the rest of the crew. That reduced the squadron to nine tanks which acting commander, Captain H.L. Smuck, organized into three troops.[6]

It was 1800 hours before the Reginas were reorganized in Reviers and ordered by 7 CIB's Brigadier Harry Foster to renew the attack by advancing on Fontaine-Henry and le Fresne-Camilly. With 'A' Company numbering less than platoon strength at only twenty-eight men, and 'D' Company barely mustering forty-nine, Lieutenant Colonel F.M. Matheson really had only two effective companies at his disposal. He ordered 'B' Company to proceed to Fontaine-Henry, which would bring 7 CIB's left flank up adjacent to where 8 CIB was in control of the village of Basly. 'C' Company, meanwhile, would bypass Fontaine-Henry and strike out directly for le Fresne-Camilly astride the Creully-Caen road. Smuck's nine tanks were to provide support.[7]

As the infantry began its advance, Captain Smuck suggested to Matheson that two troops of 'B' Squadron should conduct a brief reconnaissance ahead of the main force to ensure that a forested ridge on a valley west of the road was not concealing any German positions. Matheson readily agreed. Smuck dispatched No. 1 Troop under Lieutenant E.L. Pease and Lieutenant C.M. McLeod's No. 2 Troop to carry out the scouting mission while he kept three tanks, including his own, back to provide covering fire from hull-down positions on a height of ground. Sergeant Léo Gariépy in McLeod's troop was surprised to get the order to move out, since nobody had bothered to brief the sergeants or corporals as to where they were going or the nature of the task. He suspected that even the two lieutenants might not have had a real briefing. As McLeod's radio was broken, Gariépy was unable to seek any further instructions from his troop commander.

The tanks followed the Reviers–Fontaine-Henry road for a short distance before breaking to the east into a small valley, with No. 1 Troop on the left and No. 2 Troop right. Bordering the valley's eastern flank was a small forested ridge. As the tanks clanked across the valley floor, the gunners pounded the edge of the wood with high-explosive rounds. No. 2 Troop was starting up the slope and about 150 yards short of the woods when a heavy mortar began ranging on it. Knowing his troop commander was incapable of radioing Smuck to find out if he wanted the tanks to keep going despite the risk posed by the mortar, Gariépy got on the radio himself. Smuck told him to get the tanks out of there. Having no way of communicating with McLeod, the sergeant told his gunner to fire smoke out ahead of the troop, which would help cover the withdrawal and also hopefully serve to alert his lieutenant to the change of plan.

McLeod responded instantly, swinging his tank around and starting back down the hill. No. 2 Troop headed towards home in a two-up formation, with McLeod and Corporal R. Pike's tanks up front and Gariépy about ten yards behind in trail. The sergeant kept popping smoke the entire way to keep the tanks screened from where he believed the German mortar was positioned on the forested ridge. As the two tanks started coming up on the Reviers–Fontaine-Henry road, Gariépy saw McLeod's tank suddenly burst into flames. "I halted," he later wrote, "[and] told my driver to reverse full speed and my gunner to traverse 106 degrees right. When this was almost completed I saw my corporal's tank blown up in turn."[8]

Scanning the ground around him for the German gun, Gariépy saw a deadly 88-millimetre dug into a hole next to the road between two burning tanks from No. 1 Troop so that it was all but invisible until the muzzle blast kicked up a plume of dust. The range was just sixty yards. Gariépy frantically directed his gunner's aim onto the enemy gun before it reduced their Sherman to another burning hulk and won the race. His gunner fired two rounds and the second was a direct hit.

The sergeant radioed Smuck and reported that the other five tanks had been knocked out. He was ordered back to Reviers, but Gariépy said that first he wanted to check for survivors. He wanted also to make damned certain the garrison of that German gun were dead. Despite being warned by Smuck not to take the risk, Gariépy rolled his tank right up onto the gun emplacement "and mercilessly shot all the gun crew of fourteen men who were cowering in the trench."[9]

Despite the fact that all five tanks burst into flames the moment they were hit, most of the crews managed to escape. Although Lieutenant McLeod was wounded, his crew was unhurt. Lieutenant Pease and three of his crew, however, were killed, with only the co-driver escaping. In all, seven 1st Hussars perished in those brief seconds.[10]

As Gariépy concluded his grim accounting of the dead, the Reginas came abreast of the scene. A passing officer mentioned that he thought there had been a sniper firing at the tank commanders from a nearby house, where some of the infantry were forming up. Spending most of their time with heads poked above the rim of the cupola of the turret hatch, tank commanders were favoured targets for enemy snipers. Sticking his headphones inside his beret, Gariépy approached the house while poking the phony head out of the turret hatch. Sure enough, a shot came from the attic of the house. The sergeant would have liked to blow the house apart with his main gun, but the infantry were still milling about and seemed not to have heard the sniper shot. Not wanting to risk the sniper escaping while he pointed the German position out to the infantry, Gariépy and his loader/operator jumped out of the tank, ran to the house, and kicked the door in. An old man and woman crouched inside began imploring the two men in German, which neither Canadian could understand. They brushed past the pair, dashed up the stairs, and broke into the attic to find a young woman of about nineteen. In her hands was a German Mauser rifle held low but pointed in their direction. Gariépy gunned her down with his Sten gun.

"Angry, irritated, probably scared, I could not hesitate," he later said. "We learned from the old people that this girl's 'fiancé' had been shot by a Canadian tank that morning and she had sworn she would liquidate all crew commanders."[11]

When Gariépy caught up to the other three surviving tanks, he not surprisingly "found the morale of the squadron was extremely low but everyone [was] wishing revenge."[12]

While the tankers were recovering from the debacle with the 88-millimetre gun, the Reginas' advance continued. Having lost radio contact with both 'B' and 'C' companies, however, Lieutenant Colonel Matheson was at a loss to know where they were or whether they had run into any difficulty. Hoping to re-establish some link with them, he dispatched the Bren carrier platoon commander with a section of carriers to determine the situation and report back. New communication links were soon established and 'B' Company reported that it had entered Fontaine-Henry at 1900 hours. 'C' Company checked in thirty minutes later, with a report that it had finished clearing le Fresne-Camilly.

Leaving the battered 'A' Company at Reviers to guard the bridge crossings of the River Seulles and await reinforcements, Matheson set off with 'D' Company for le Fresne-Camilly. Soon after this force arrived, the battalion received orders at 2100 hours from Brigadier Foster to consolidate for the night. Fifteen minutes later, 'B' Company reported that German artillery fire had hammered its headquarters in Fontaine-Henry and that both commander Major F.L. Peters and his second-in-command, Lieutenant G.D. Dickin, had been killed. So too had been Rifleman A.J. Kennedy. These were the Reginas' last casualties in what had been an extremely costly day for the regiment. Despite the many terrible setbacks the Reginas had endured, however, they could be, as the regimental historian noted, proud of having reached the intermediate objective. "Get your intermediate objectives on D-Day at all costs," the officers had been told, and they had done that.[13]

THE SAME COULD NOT be said for the 21st Panzer Division or 716th Infantry Division. While the latter had been virtually eliminated in the day's fighting, the former had put in a disappointing performance, in part due to Generalleutnant Edgar Feuchtinger's questionable leadership. By 2200 hours, his divisional staff, relying on motorcycle couriers in the absence of a radio link with the fighting units, had managed to reorganize the troops to hold a defensive line extending from north of Buron to the west through Épron and Lébisy to Major Hans von Luck's position at Blainville. This enabled the division to safeguard the approaches to Caen against an advance by 3rd British Infantry Division while also being placed so as to renew the counterattack if that was ordered.[14] Responsibility for issuing such an order, however, no longer rested with LXXXIV Corps' General der

Artillierie Erich Marcks. In the late afternoon, Hitler had issued instructions through OKW placing the entire Orne front under the command of Generaloberst Josef (Sepp) Dietrich of 1st SS Panzer Corps.

Hitler's late rising that morning had crippled OKW's ability to react to the invasion in any effective manner. As General der Infanterie Günter Blumentritt later said, "The system of command under Hitler made it impossible for, say, Jodl to make a decision on his own, since Hitler reserved to himself the disposal of every single division. This system had been enforced since 1943; before then the German method of command prevailed and one could act very independently on one's own responsibility without asking permission."[15]

Having only received a full briefing by OKW staff at the midday meeting, it was not until 1500 hours that Hitler issued orders placing the 12th SS Panzer (Hitlerjugend) and Panzer Lehr divisions under Seventh Army control. Another clarifying order issued at 1540 hours put 1st SS Panzer Corps also under Seventh Army Commander Oberstgeneral Friedrich Dollman's authority. Finally, OKW was taking the invasion of Normandy seriously.

Dollman ordered 1st SS Panzer Corps and the two divisions to proceed with haste to the Caen area for the purpose of launching a counterattack against the British and Canadian beachheads, an order immediately confirmed by Commander-in-Chief West von Rundstedt.[16]

Dietrich's staff had received early warning that such an order was likely and the corps commander had himself hastened back from leave in Belgium upon learning of the invasion. Consequently, at 1600 hours, his staff and corps troops struck out for Caen after ensuring that both divisional commanders had received their new orders. By late afternoon, the heavy haze that had hung over Normandy during the morning and hampered operations by Allied fighter-bombers had dissipated. Much of France was now warmed by spring sunshine.

The corps staff and column of supporting troops were forced by the constantly hovering presence of Typhoons and Spitfires to stay off the main highway from Trun to Falaise to avoid easy detection. Instead, they snaked along narrow secondary lanes that were often covered by overhanging branches of the bordering ranks of trees. "Already there were burning vehicles of all kinds everywhere on the road," Dietrich's chief-of-staff Generalmajor Fritz Krämer later wrote. With no anti-aircraft guns positioned to fire upon the Allied planes and nary a Luftwaffe fighter to be seen, Krämer lamented that the fighters "were able to attack as though carrying out exercises. Air attacks had a paralyzing effect on some of our drivers. German soldiers were not accustomed to this type of attack, and it was several days before they became accustomed to it, placed observers in vehicles, and took necessary countermeasures. Whenever enemy fighters approached, the vehicles were raced, if possible, to a house, tree, slope of the road, or other cover, and the crew alighted."[17]

The decision to move a Panzer corps headquarters and two Panzer divisions in broad daylight infuriated Panzer Group West commander General der Panzertruppen Leo Freiherr Geyr von Schweppenburg. While accepting the need to turn 12th SS Panzer Division around and heading in the right direction despite the risks this entailed, he pleaded with von Rundstedt to rescind the order putting Panzer Lehr on the march. There would be no significant delay, he said, if the division waited until night to move. The old officer stiffly refused to countermand his orders.

On receiving the movement order, the Panzer Lehr's divisional commander, Generalleutnant Fritz Bayerlein, also pleaded for permission to delay until after nightfall. But von Rundstedt was unshakable, so the tanks and vehicles soon rolled out of their assembly point at Nogent le Rotrou, ninety-five miles southwest of Paris, en route to Caen. No sooner had it started on the march than the fighter-bombers pounced on one of the Panzer Grenadier regiments, destroying 123 personnel carriers and five trucks. Hearing this news, Schweppenburg bitterly reflected that he and Bayerlein "had experienced for years a considerable amount of stubborn Panzer fighting. Rundstedt, Jodl, and Blumentritt had not. The resulting two schools of thought represented the difference between the tactics of horse-drawn divisions of the Napoleonic Age and the 19th Century and that of mechanized divisions of the 20th Century. The tactical methods of one were hardly understandable to the other."

He was even more disturbed by the implication of the movement order itself and the fact that his precious divisions were being placed under Dollman's command. They were, he lamented, to now be "committed in the same manner as a reserve battalion of 1918 might have been thrown in to take back a segment of a trench captured by the enemy. Since Hitler had the last say, one would have hoped that experts were consulted. This was not the case. Neither Panzer Group West [Schweppenburg himself] nor Oberstgeneral [Heinz] Guderian was asked to express an opinion."[18]

When 12th ss Panzer Division's Brigadeführer (ss equivalent to Generalmajor) Fritz Witt had received the order at about 1600 hours to swing his command around, he could not believe the stupidity. Sending dispatch riders racing up and down the columns with the new instructions, the general steamed and worried while vehicles were laboriously shunted back and forth on the narrow roads to turn them in the right direction. Fortunately, the division had already been heading northwest towards Elbeuf and when a new route was mapped out to get the division to the area of Lisieux near Caen, Witt discovered it was only forty-four miles to the new assembly point. But he also knew that as the division neared Caen and the invasion beaches it would attract the Allied fighters like so many flies.[19]

One of Witt's favourite commanders, Standartenführer (ss equivalent to Oberst) Kurt Meyer, upon learning that the division was to march towards the sound of the guns rather than merely a possible invasion sight, felt a moment's anxiety. In Poland, Holland, Belgium, France, the Balkans, and Russia, the ss officer had led troops through the carnage of battle. Now he would do so again in France, but this time his men were young teenagers who had never before seen the face of war. They were, he believed, "superbly trained" and highly motivated. While his veteran officers and non-commissioned officers all met the 25th ss Panzer Grenadier Regiment commander's eyes with gazes filled with the same anxiety he felt, Meyer noted that, in comparison, "the magnificent young grenadiers look at us with laughter in their eyes. They have no fear. They are confident, they have faith in their strength and the will to fight. How will these boys prove themselves?"[20]

As the twenty thousand troops of the division moved towards Caen, the fighter-bombers and strafing fighter planes found the ss columns. Tanks dashed across open road junctions in single bounds to avoid the rockets and bombs of the Typhoons and Spitfires. Other fighters hurtled down the roads, raking the strung-out vehicles with machine guns. Meyer watched aghast as the "flourishing life" of his teenage troops was shredded by bullets or torn to pieces by explosions.

Before them, Caen was wrapped in a dark cloud of smoke. The ss troopers pushed down the Falaise-Caen road against a tide of refugees fleeing the burning ruin. Many of the civilian vehicles were caught in the Allied strafing attacks. Meyer drove past a burning bus. Mangled bodies hung out of the windows and blocked the door, barring the escape of others trapped inside and screaming in anguished pain as they were incinerated.

On the division went, under almost constant attack. But the orders were clear—they were to stop for nothing; they were to get to Caen and the battleground. Meyer wished he had some information about what lay ahead, anything about the Allied formations and strength that they would fight. He knew nothing, only that many of his soldiers were being killed or wounded long before they reached the field of battle.[21]

Elsewhere on the road, 1st ss Panzer Corps' Dietrich and Krämer met up with Witt. The ss divisional commander "gave some valuable hints about camouflage during marches." He also provided the corps officers with the whereabouts of 21st Panzer Division's new headquarters at St. Pierre-sur-Dives. As the corps journeyed deeper into Normandy, Krämer noted that many civilians were aware of the landings. They also gathered "before the doors of their houses in towns and villages. Their attitude was not hostile; rather, they showed a strong resentment towards the Allied air attacks, which oftentimes did not discriminate between German motor- and horse-drawn vehicles and French civilian vehicles. Likewise, the civilians were aware that enemy air attacks had almost demolished Falaise.

"When Corps arrived at Falaise, it was impossible to pass through the burning town, and we had to detour along a road that the local military police had cleared. This roundabout way was passable for tanks and heavy motor vehicles, so that delay was the only obstacle the air attack created."[22]

At about 2000 hours, Dietrich and Krämer burst into the command post at St. Pierre and were astonished to find nobody of importance there other than the division's first general staff officer. When the officer nervously related what he knew of the division's counterattack efforts on both the east and west sides of the River Orne, the two ss men were unimpressed that Feuchtinger would divide his forces in a way that denied them a concentrated impact.

Then they were told that the division commander was at Richter's headquarters, but had no radio with him. For a Panzer commander "to leave his headquarters without a radio set was ... tantamount to travelling without his head," Krämer fumed. Equally dismaying was the fact that, because of its move, the divisional headquarters had not yet established a telephone link to Seventh Army in le Mans. Dietrich demanded that such a connection be established forthwith while he consulted with Feuchtinger by telephone to get a better assessment of the Panzer division's situation.[23]

In a conversation frequently interrupted by failed connections and during which Feuchtinger's voice was often inaudible, Dietrich learned that the hapless commander "had no contact with his combat groups, except through messengers and special-mission staff officers." This, of course, was because he had no radio. The situation, Feuchtinger admitted, "was vague." He assured Dietrich, however, that he had sixty tanks ready for action that were sufficiently equipped with ammunition and fuel to return to the counterattack on the corps commander's order.[24]

By the time this call was concluded, a tenuous link to Seventh Army had been established that ran through an exchange in the midst of burning Falaise. The extent of damage to the town was causing severe problems for the communications people there, and broken connections and complete loss of volume constantly plagued Dietrich's conversation with Oberstgeneral Dollman. Finally, the two reverted to a ponderous conversation by Teletype in which the army commander urged Dietrich to carry out a "compact attack by Corps as soon as possible."

Dietrich responded that it would be impossible for Panzer Lehr Division to reach the area until the evening of June 7 and that a coordinated attack should not be expected before June 8. It would take at least until then to organize the three Panzer divisions with their various support elements for a counterattack on June 8 that would "throw the landed enemy back into the sea."[25]

While Dietrich and Dollman sparred over the details and timing of the counterattack, 12th ss Panzer Division's Kurt Meyer was tracked down by an ordnance officer from 21st Panzer Division. The ss officer was wanted immediately at the headquarters of 716th Infantry Division for consultations with Feuchtinger. Leaving his regiment of Panzer Grenadiers to make its own way to the assigned assembly point near Carpiquet airport, Meyer hastened towards Caen. The city was ablaze, dazed civilians wandering aimlessly or shifting listlessly through piles of rubble, streets jammed with debris, the air thick with a black and choking smoke.

Richter's headquarters was in a bunker dug deep into a sandspit near the river. The corridors were packed solid with wounded soldiers from both the 716th and 21st Panzer divisions. Working feverishly, doctors and orderlies carried out cursory treatments and then readied the men for evacuation in ambulances to hospitals in the rear.

Just before midnight on June 6, Meyer was ushered into the presence of Richter and Feuchtinger. The Panzer commander immediately launched into a long justification of his actions while simultaneously blaming the confused command structure under which he had served throughout the day as the reason for his initial inaction and then the scattered nature of the eventual counterattack. As Feuchtinger droned on, Meyer thought a pivotal opportunity to seriously disrupt the invasion had been frittered away. "Instead of driving like lightning into the massed concentration of landed enemy forces, the division was condemned to be burnt out in dribs and drabs." Ruefully he remembered the old-tank philosopher Guderian's admonishment: "Rather all at once than bit by bit."[26]

After hearing Feuchtinger out, Meyer was called to the telephone. It was Brigadeführer Witt calling from 21st Panzer Division's headquarters at St. Pierre and demanding a situation report. Meyer told him what he had learned. The immediate challenge, Witt said, was to deny the Allies Carpiquet airport and entry to Caen. Therefore, the 12th ss Panzer Division would form up alongside the 21st Panzer Division to launch an attack on those areas where the Allies were closest to either of these strategically vital targets. Much of that attack would fall directly on 3rd Canadian Infantry Division's 9th Canadian Infantry Brigade. Witt stated that Meyer should plan on the attack going in sometime in the early afternoon of June 7.[27]

When Meyer hung up, he informed Richter and Feuchtinger of Witt's instructions. The ss officer was anxious to get going. He found the pessimistic mood that hung over the bunker oppressive. Not that he failed to appreciate the scope of the disaster that had befallen Richter's 716th Division or the setback Feuchtinger's Panzer troops had suffered. For all practical purposes, the 716th Division had ceased to exist, having been wiped out in small clustered groups within their fortified strongpoints on the beach or cut down while trying to delay the advance inland. From six battalions, Richter estimated he had less than the strength of one remaining. The general told Meyer that he was also no longer in contact with any of the division's regimental headquarters.

Just as Richter made this pronouncement, however, the phone rang. On the other end was one of his regimental commanders calling from his bunker for orders. "The enemy is standing on the top of the bunker," the desperate officer shouted. "I have no means to fight him, nor any contact with my units. What shall I do?"

The room went silent as every man there looked to Richter. "I cannot give you any further orders, you may act on your own initiative," the divisional commander said icily. "Goodbye!"[28] With that, Richter cradled the phone. Meyer gratefully fled the bunker and stepped into a night eerily illuminated by the burning pyre of Caen.

22

A Degree of Gallantry

WHILE THE OVERALL German response to the invasion had been hesitant and fumbling, it was also true that 716th Infantry Division had succeeded in denying the British and Canadian divisions their assigned final objectives for the day. But there was an exception to this result, which had come on the extreme right flank of 3rd Canadian Infantry Division's advance from Juno Beach and developed in the form of a daring sortie behind enemy lines carried out by just three Sherman tanks of the 1st Hussars.

By mid-afternoon, the Royal Winnipeg Rifles were well on the way to their intermediate objective. This was the capture of the medieval fortress of Creully, followed by an advance south of the Creully-Caen road to a large chalk-pit quarry near Lantheuil. Major Lochie Fulton's 'D' Company had led the way from Banville-sur-Mer to Creully, with No. 2 Troop from 'C' Squadron of the 1st Hussars in support. During the two-hour march, only minimal resistance was encountered that proved easily brushed aside. Each short engagement, however, led to Lieutenant Bill McCormick and his tankers idling impatiently while the infantry rooted the Germans out of holes. Bordering the Banville-Tierceville road the Winnipegs followed were numerous thickets of woods that made it a poor line of advance for tanks to hang about on or travel through slowly. McCormick was worried that the woods might hide a German antitank gun or even an infantryman armed with a deadly Panzerfaust antitank rocket launcher. By the time he came onto a ridge and saw Creully across the way, with its castle hulking on the side of a steep cliff overlooking the River Seulles, he was seriously considering abandoning the infantry for a high-speed run to the Caen-Bayeux Highway objective.[1]

At the base of the cliff, a bridge crossed the river and then the road snaked up a narrow wooded draw into the village itself, which was impossible to see behind the soaring towers and turrets of the castle. Fulton ordered Lieutenant Jack Mitchell to secure the bridge. To the right of the road stood a grand estate fronted by a large pasture that ran unbroken to the river and bridge. On the left, just before the bridge, stood Creullet, a huddle of ancient stone buildings surrounded by a wall, which looked as if it might have provided farm quarters for serfs serving the castle lord hundreds of years before. The bridge itself was set amid a thicket of poplar and elm trees that grew densely along the riverbank.

Mitchell was up with the forward section as his platoon started across the bridge. The officer was well ahead of his men, looking the bridge over for signs of demolition explosives, when a machine gun on the south side opened up with a shrieking long burst. A bullet clipped one of Mitchell's hands and two men on the bridge were cut down. The rest of the platoon was just coming up onto the bridge and everyone dived for cover.[2] Mitchell neither fled nor hunkered. Instead, the lieutenant began madly dashing about on the bridge, tearing up land mines that had been sown on its surface and throwing them into the river—all the time with the machine gun trying to score a deadly hit.[3] This done, he raced to the north side of the river and signalled frantically for Lieutenant McCormick to bring his tanks forward to wipe out the German position now that it would be relatively safe for armour to cross the bridge. Mitchell's incredible calmness under fire earned him a Military Cross.[4]

Machine-gun bullets raking the armoured skin of his Sherman, McCormick barrelled onto the bridge. So much lead was chipping away at the tank that the lieutenant was hunched inside the turret with the hatch closed, using the commander's periscope to search for the enemy machine-gun position, when a burst of fire shot away the protruding end of the device. His tank was square in the middle of the bridge, so McCormick ordered the driver to reverse to the end and then rolled forward with the co-axial and bow machine guns spraying the other side. After repeating this process a couple of times, McCormick drove off the other end and spotted the German machine gun and its now dead crew lying at the corner of the bridge.

With Major Fulton's infantry following behind, McCormick's troop of tanks trundled up the road leading to the castle and village on top of the ridge. As they turned the sharp corner and faced the square, McCormick was presented with the imposing sight of the towering steeple of Creully's large cathedral. Each angled section of its octagon-shaped belfry contained a narrow five-foot-high opening. A hell of a place for a sniper, McCormick thought, as he ordered his gunner to knock the steeple down with a few rounds from the 75-millimetre gun. Seconds later, the steeple was just so much broken masonry lying around the church, and McCormick's tank led the way into the village. The twin barrels of a 20-millimetre gun poked around the corner of a building and spat its light high-velocity shells harmlessly at the Sherman until being reduced to smoking wreckage by McCormick's gunner.

That was it for the German opposition in Creully. The village consisted of several short streets lined by large two- and three-storey buildings, all of the same dull chalk colour as the castle, and the cathedral that dominated the large central square. A few minutes after the Canadians secured the village, a company of troops from the British 50th Division that had advanced from Gold Beach on the Canadian right flank arrived to "liberate" Creully. The Winnipeg Rifles left them to it, marching east along the road towards the quarry. McCormick's anxiety over travelling at the pace of infantry when there were so many places to hide antitank weapons was increasing. Keep moving at this speed and "you're a dead duck," he thought. Finally McCormick told Major Fulton that he was going to move ahead independently and signalled the two other crew commanders of No. 2 Troop, Corporal Jackie Simmons and Corporal Bill Talbot, to follow his lead.[5]

After the tanks took off, Fulton's company marched on about a mile to the large chalk-pit quarry, arriving at 1700 hours. When Fulton reported being on the intermediate objective to Royal Winnipeg commander Lieutenant Colonel John Meldram, he was told that the battalion would pause there for the night. This would allow time to regroup and bring up reinforcements to replenish the badly depleted ranks, particularly of 'B' Company. By the time Meldram arrived to set up his battalion headquarters in the quarry, the battalion's companies were starting to get well dug in for the night and a first draft of reinforcements had come up from the beach. This amounted to five officers and seventy-eight other ranks, all of which were posted to 'B' Company.

"A very special note ... should be made about the general tone of the [battalion] during this day," the Royal Winnipeg war diarist wrote in his last notation for June 6. "Not one man flinched from his task, no matter how tough it was—not one officer failed to display courage and energy and a degree of gallantry. It is thought that the Little Black Devils, by this day's success, has managed to maintain the tradition set by former members."[6]

Showing at least "a degree of gallantry" during the late afternoon of D-Day was McCormick's No. 2 Troop. Well before 'D' Company of the Royal Winnipeg had reached the chalk-pit, this tiny force of fifteen men and three 1st Hussars tanks was concluding a remarkable run that had taken it almost to Carpiquet airport via the Caen-Bayeux highway. After leaving the infantry at Creully, the tankers had run into nothing but scattered groups of German infantry "who either came out and surrendered or tried to crawl away through the wheat. As a tank troop we could not handle prisoners, so we disarmed them and sent them back down the road [towards Creully]. The rest we pursued with machine-gun fire and shell fire and continued on our way," McCormick later wrote.[7]

Instead of the main Creully-Caen road, No. 2 Troop travelled on a side road that passed through the hamlets of Cainet and le Fresne-Camilly, which the Reginas had not yet reached by the time McCormick led his tanks through it. At Camilly, another road turned due south to Bretteville-l'Orgueilleuse on the Caen-Bayeux highway. McCormick was by now so convinced that nothing stood between his tanks and Carpiquet airport that he had the driver barely ease the pressure off the throttle going through the hamlets. Barrelling out of Camilly on a narrow road, the lieutenant was suddenly presented with a small German scout car speeding along in the opposite direction. When the car's driver swerved to try to squeeze past the tank, Trooper O.K. Hunter raked it with a burst of machine-gun fire a second before Trooper Gord Perkins slewed the Sherman head-on into the vehicle and crushed it against a stone wall. The car exploded into a ball of flames as the car's driver pitched forward to lie draped over the windshield and the German beside him was flung burning onto the road.

Also thrown from the car was a German officer, who had been riding in the back seat. Although the man had been wounded in the legs by the machine-gun burst Hunter had fired and his feet were burning, he rolled onto his stomach and seemed to be reaching for a gun. McCormick quickly pulled his own pistol and levelled it at the officer, but couldn't bring himself to shoot him in the back.

Instead, followed by Perkins, he jumped down from the tank. While Perkins ran over and grabbed the officer, McCormick directed Corporal Simmons to move his Sherman out to guard the front and Corporal Talbot to cover an intersecting lane. Then he turned to the two German soldiers, who had been thrown out of the front seat of the scout car. Both had been charred to black by the fire that had engulfed the vehicle and would likely have consumed the tank as well had not the Sherman's driver and co-driver quickly used fire extinguishers to douse the flames that had spread to the camouflage net. The German driver was already dead and it was obvious that the soldier lying on the road was beyond help. Every muscle and nerve in the man's body was twitching violently and McCormick wondered whether to put him out of his misery with a bullet.

Still pondering the matter, McCormick, pistol dangling from his right hand, walked over to where the officer lay. By now, his driver and co-driver had liberated the man's pistol, watch, wallet, and other valuables before propping him up against the wall. As McCormick approached, the German took a deep breath and looked resignedly at the gun in the lieutenant's hand. Realizing the man thought McCormick was going to shoot him, he stuffed the weapon back in its holster and then walked back to the Sherman while ordering the crew to mount up.[8]

Advance renewed, the tanks went about a mile south on the road before coming to a section of it that went through a cut. McCormick knew that his crews had been going nonstop since the launch of their Duplex-Drive tanks that morning and the drivers were exhausted, so he called a short breather. As the tankers sat around on the Shermans relaxing in the waning afternoon sun, McCormick spotted a German marching purposefully up the road towards them. The crews jumped back into their tanks and six Browning machine guns were soon tracking his advance while McCormick covered him with a pistol. The German strode right up to the tank, clicked his heels together, and offered a formal salute. Suddenly, the enemy soldier's eyes widened as he took in the shape of the tanks and their markings. Diving off the side of the road, the German ran like a panicked hare into the fields with such speed that McCormick got off only one shot at him and the men on the Brownings had no chance to fire at all before he disappeared.

This German's obvious expectation that no Allied forces could be this far inland only confirmed McCormick's belief that the Canadians had a great opportunity to take Carpiquet airport before the enemy could respond and establish a proper defensive line. But his attempts to raise 'C' Squadron commander Major D'Arcy Marks on the radio to report the opportunity and get the entire squadron or even regiment racing up went unanswered. "Come up, come up," McCormick repeatedly pleaded into the radio, only to be met by static. It was obvious the troop was no longer netted into the regiment's radio grid. Finally, after turning onto the Caen-Bayeux highway (part of the Canadian final objective for June 6) and pushing east almost a mile from the undefended outskirts of Bretteville-l'Orgueilleuse to la Villeneuve, McCormick acknowledged that the joyride had to come to an end. Although he suspected it would be possible to go right through to Carpiquet airport, there was no way that his little troop of tanks, low on fuel and ammunition as they were, could establish a viable position there and hold it against an attack. Somewhat dejectedly, he ordered the troop to turn around and retrace its route.[9]

WHILE MCCORMICK TURNED his back on Carpiquet airport, the main force of the Canadian Scottish Regiment was coming astride the Creully-Caen road, duly reported at 1630 hours by Lieutenant Colonel Cabeldu to Brigadier Foster. 'B' Company, meanwhile, had scooped up a number of prisoners as it closed on Amblie and its second-in-command, Captain P.F. Ramsay, had observed a number of Germans fleeing out the other side of the village. When Sergeant Gerry Burton suggested that he and a few of the men from No. 12 Platoon could jump on some nearby horses and take off bareback after the Germans, Ramsay reminded him that "maintenance of the objective" had priority. As the platoon had been specially trained for the role of street fighting but had yet to put such skills to use, he directed Lieutenant Ian MacDonald and Burton to lead the way into Amblie and quash any resistance there. Looking for a fight, the "Merry Men," as Company Sergeant Major Frank Fisher had dubbed the platoon, "searched thoroughly and painstakingly for enemy, however, other than frightened women huddled in one house there was [nobody] encountered."[10]

The moment Amblie was declared clear, the company renewed its advance, pushing on "across the open fields up the slope towards the high ground overlooking the valley of the Mue River." The Mue River valley ran south to north and its wide base was filled with open farm fields and little villages. Two rivers ran through it—the Mue and its tributary Chiromme—with the latter following the valley's westerly flank near Camilly and then running past Thaon before joining the Mue. The larger river originated well south of the Caen-Bayeux Highway, crossing it at la Villeneuve, and then flowing through Rots and Cairon. This last community was astride the Creully-Caen road about two miles from le Fresne-Camilly. The high ground that 'B' Company had ascended was a little south of le Fresne-Camilly, so the Canadian Scottish were protecting the right flank of the Regina Rifles holding this village.

Upon learning of 'B' Company's position, Cabeldu decided to bring the rest of the battalion up on the company's left. He ordered Major Crofton's 'C' Company to push on to a crossroads about a thousand yards south of the little hamlet of Cainet and more than a mile south of the Creully-Caen road. 'A' Company, meanwhile, would move cross-country towards Camilly to the immediate south of le Fresne-Camilly, while 'D' Company settled around Cainet, and Cabeldu's battalion headquarters set up near Pierrepont. The various positions would be protected by some of the 1st Hussars tanks of 'C' Squadron under Major D'Arcy Marks.

Major G.T. MacEwan's 'D' Company encountered no enemy resistance at all and was quickly in position at Cainet. The headquarters section took over a tidy little farmhouse and decided to celebrate by dining "well on our first evening in France. Local chickens provided us with boiled eggs and our bottle of champagne, although warm and fizzy from its bouncing about, made a grand feast."[11]

The entire operation for the Canadian Scottish went off smoothly, with the only serious opposition posed by an enemy mortar and machine-gun position that tried to block 'C' Company, but was quickly overrun. As 'A' Company drove towards its objective, Captain Bill Matthews followed behind with a party of soldiers that swept through farm buildings, flushing numerous German stragglers who generally surrendered without a fight. Just outside Camilly, a German artillery piece opened fire but was quickly silenced as the troops skillfully used the lay of the land to approach the position and eliminate the gun crew. At 1715, 'A' Company commander Major Arthur Plows radioed that his company had "captured battery position of 109 Artillery Regiment together with large amount of signal equipment."[12]

Plows was closing on Camilly, when out of the blue and coming from the wrong direction for Allied tanks appeared Lieutenant Bill McCormick and his troop of 1st Hussars. The tanker told Plows there was no opposition in the village, but the infantry officer insisted on putting in a proper attack anyway, as he was already formed up for it. McCormick arrayed his tanks to provide support and they started moving across a field towards the village. An old lady sitting on a stool in the middle of the field milking a cow "never even looked up as this battalion of infantry and tanks went by," McCormick remembered. "We just walked into the village. There was nothing there."[13]

As Plows ordered the infantry to start digging in, a Bren carrier roared up carrying Lieutenant Colonel Matheson of the Regina Rifles, who was conducting a personal reconnaissance forward of his battalion's position. "What the hell are you Scottish doing here?" he demanded, while extending his hand to shake Plows's.[14] With that, 7 CIB's advance inland came to a halt.

After helping the Canadian Scottish secure their position for the night, McCormick received word to withdraw his tanks to Pierrepont, where the 1st Hussars were regrouping. He headed back with the tantalizing vision of the airport still in his mind and the worrisome thought that by morning the Germans might well have pulled themselves together after the beating they had taken this day and be ready to put up a fight to stop the Canadian advance. Mostly, however, he wanted just to sleep. Like everyone else in the Allied invasion force, the lieutenant was dead tired from an incredibly long day of almost constant battle.[15]

[23]

Such a Sad Day

MCCORMICK'S BOLD DASH with No. 2 Troop of the 1st Hussars 'C' Company was the deepest penetration into Normandy achieved by any Allied forces coming off the invasion beaches on D-Day—nine miles as the crow flies or about twelve miles via the actual route taken. More importantly, by the end of the day, the Canadians had advanced farther from the shore than any of the British or American divisions. Having landed later than the rest, they had pushed up to six miles inland despite fierce opposition from the Germans on the beach and doggedly persistent resistance during the advance. It was a stunning feat of arms of which the soldiers of 3rd Canadian Infantry Division and 2nd Canadian Armoured Brigade could be proud.

The cost in blood for this achievement was certainly high but the impact was somewhat softened by its being less than half what the invasion planners had feared. At day's end, 340 of the Canadians who landed on Juno Beach were dead and another 574 wounded. Twenty-six of the wounded subsequently succumbed to their injuries between June 7 and June 28, bringing the total number of dead to 366.

Considering that by the end of D-Day, 14,500 Canadians had been landed on Juno Beach, 914 casualties seems high enough at roughly one out of every fifteen. Since time immemorial, the "poor bloody infantry" paid the bitterest price in battle and so it was for the battalions that led the assault onto the beaches. The six battalions of 7th and 8th

Canadian Infantry Brigades suffered 696 of the total D-Day casualties. Hardest hit was the Queen's Own Rifles with 143 men killed or wounded, 61 of whom died. The Royal Winnipeg Rifles had 57 dead and 66 wounded for a total of 123, while the North Shore (New Brunswick) Regiment had 125 casualties, of which 33 were fatal. The men of 'A' Company paid the highest price in casualties of the Regina Rifles. Mustering only 28 men after the debacle on the beach at Courseulles-sur-Mer out of about 120, they accounted for most of the battalion's total losses of 108 men, of whom 45 died. The Canadian Scottish Regiment was the only first-wave assault unit with fewer than 100 casualties—22 dead and 65 wounded for a total of 87—no doubt because only 'C' Company participated in the initial landing. Le Régiment de la Chaudière had 48 men wounded and 18 killed during its landing and advance at the head of the column moving from Bernières-sur-Mer to Colomby-sur-Thaon.

Although few infantrymen fancied switching places with their tanker colleagues out of a fear of dying in the cramped confines of a burning Sherman, the armoured regiments fared better than the leg units on D-Day—the usual case in World War II combat. But while the odds of becoming a casualty was less for tankers, the likelihood of being killed versus wounded ran about equal. The 1st Hussars had 22 men killed and 21 wounded, while the Fort Garry Horse had 14 dead compared to 11 wounded.

Oddly, 3rd Canadian Infantry Division compiled casualty statistics more thoroughly than the British or American divisions, making it difficult to compare relative casualty rates between one beach and another. Hardest hit, however, was the 1st U.S. Infantry Division, with a regiment of 29th U.S. Infantry Division attached to it, that landed on Omaha Beach. U.S. official historians estimated casualties here at about 2,000, but conceded they might have been higher. Meanwhile, at Utah, the 4th U.S. Infantry Division had the easiest time of all, suffering just 197 casualties. The British kept casualty figures only of those killed or wounded in the beach assault itself and made no effort to track casualties that occurred during the push inland. Their calculations for Sword Beach show 630 casualties and 413 for Gold.

In addition to the Canadian casualties suffered in the Juno Beach sector of the invasion, a further 243 British soldiers who landed with the Canadians were reported as killed or wounded. For the beach assault phase, British Second Army officials identified 805 soldiers as having been killed or wounded on Juno Beach. However the figures are examined, it is indisputable that the battle for Juno Beach was won at a loss in men killed or wounded that was only exceeded by that of the Americans at Omaha.

For 1st Canadian Parachute Battalion, the grim toll of casualties was felt less in soldiers killed or wounded than in those lost as prisoners due to their being badly scattered in the night drop. Of the battalion's 113 reported casualties on D-Day, 84 were taken prisoner. Only 19 paratroopers died and 10 suffered wounds that day. But the total loss of 113 in just twenty-four hours out of the 543 men who jumped into Normandy represented a casualty rate of just over 20 per cent.

All airborne forces suffered heavily on D-Day. The two American divisions reported 2,499 casualties at day's end, while the estimated toll for 6th British Airborne Division was 1,500 men killed, wounded, or missing (with most ending up in captivity).

The U.S. has estimated total Canadian, British, and American army and marine casualties at the most conservative figure of 8,443. Canada's World War II Army historian pegged the total at 9,000, while British military authorities decided on 10,865. All agreed that about one-third of the casualties were fatal.[1]

Of the approximately 9,400 Canadian naval personnel involved in Operation Neptune on June 6, no casualty estimate is possible—the navy seeming to concern itself more with damage to ships than men in its overall accounting. The majority of Royal Canadian Navy casualties would have been suffered by the sailors crewing the landing craft that took damage from mines, collisions with beach obstacles, and hits by German shell and mortar fire. The 262nd LCI Flotilla, for example, reports 6 crew being wounded during its landing operations on June 6 out of about 253 personnel serving on eleven craft.[2] Although most of the Canadian LCAS from *Prince Henry* and *Prince David* suffered damage, only three sailors were reported as casualties, none of which proved fatal.[3]

No determination of the number of Royal Canadian Air Force personnel engaged in operations supporting the invasion was prepared. Given the fact that 3,258 RCAF and Royal Air Force aircraft of all types were directly engaged in the invasion as part of the Allied Expeditionary Air Force commitment, the majority of the 22,727 Canadians serving as aircrew in either RCAF or RAF units must have had some involvement.[4] Although the Luftwaffe hardly ventured from the ground on June 6, anti-aircraft guns remained active and took their toll on aircraft.

Flight Officer Frederick Wilson of 'A' Flight of RCAF 441 Squadron was "pranged by flak" when he strayed over Caen. The twenty-five-year-old had been tasked with patrolling the beachhead in his Spitfire Mark IX, but had become disoriented in the low, thick morning cloud cover. Suddenly he was over the city, ducking and turning through a sky smudged with black explosions. After four or five shells slammed into the plane, the oil pressure gauge plunged from 120 to 20, warning him that an engine seizure was imminent. Somehow he managed to keep it sputtering along until he was back over England. Unable to lower his wheels and now with no oil pressure at all, Wilson belly-flopped in the open just off the runway in order not to damage the landing surface and walked away from the wrecked aircraft without a scratch.[5]

Also patrolling over the beach was Flight Officer Gordon Ockenden of 443 Squadron, which along with 441 and 442 squadrons comprised 144 Wing, RCAF under command of Wing Commander Johnnie Johnson. The young pilot from Alberta flew an afternoon patrol that circled over Gold, Juno, and Sword beaches, watching closely for any sign of German fighters. Although none appeared, the patrol lost one of its pilots when Flight Leader MacLennan's Spitfire sprang a glycol leak and he was forced to land behind German lines. One of the other pilots on the patrol last saw MacLennan jumping from the aircraft and dashing towards a nearby farmhouse. It was soon learned that he had been taken prisoner.[6]

J. Danforth "Danny" Brown, an American who had enlisted in the RCAF before the U.S. joined the war because his mother hailed from

Nova Scotia, was 144 Wing's Deputy Wing Commander on D-Day. He led planes from 441 Squadron on four separate missions over Normandy on June 6, with the first one starting at 0625 hours. He and the other pilots were pumped up and ready to rip into any Luftwaffe flyers that dared to test the covering flights of fighters swarming over the great armada below. But the ceiling was down to less than two thousand feet most of the day and not a single German fighter was to be seen, so the flights became an exercise in tedium.

Once night fell, a couple of German fighters did duck in to try strafing the ships and were greeted by every gun aboard the more than four thousand ships still standing offshore blasting flak into the sky. "No one ever turned on fireworks like they [the ship gunners] turned on," Brown later wrote. Allied fliers quickly learned to stay well clear of the trigger-happy gunners, who tended to fire at anything that flew near rather then making any attempt at friend-or-foe recognition, giving the invasion fleet a very wide berth.[7]

BY NIGHTTIME ON JUNE 6, Major General Rod Keller began to take stock of his division's situation with a mind to preparing for operations on June 7 that would secure the original D-Day final objectives. On the three British Second Army beaches, 75,215 soldiers had been put ashore, while another 7,900 British and Canadian paratroopers had landed from the sky. Farther to the west, the Americans had some 57,500 troops on the ground. Also crossing the British and Canadian beaches had been more than 6,000 vehicles, including about 900 tanks and armoured vehicles, 240 field guns, 80 light anti-aircraft guns, 280 antitank guns, and over 4,000 tons of supplies. From a tenuous toehold in the early morning hours, Juno Beach had been transformed into a sprawling military encampment swarming with Royal Canadian Army Service Corps personnel whose job it was to ensure the supplies got from the beach to the fighting troops inland.[8]

Despite the great buildup in men and equipment on the beaches, Keller still had fewer than 20,000 Canadian and British troops on Juno Beach and only about 10,000 of these gave the division its fighting teeth. The rest were part of the vital tail that enabled the division to fight, but the numbers on the ground gave a deceptive appearance of strength.

As the day had passed, Keller's anxious demeanour and hesitancy in decision-making increasingly concerned his staff officers and brigadiers. Brigadier Ben Cunningham ended the day feeling over-whelmed by the two distinct duties of trying to keep Keller "steadied down" while also maintaining control over his 9th Canadian Infantry Brigade's landing on the beach and movement inland.[9] Also proving invaluable in bolstering Keller's confidence was 2nd Canadian Armoured Brigade's Brigadier Bob Wyman. Deputy Adjutant and Quarter Master General (DAQMG) Lieutenant Colonel Ernest Côté noted Wyman's frequent visits to Keller's headquarters after the divisional staff came ashore. The brigadier, he later said, "gave Keller much guidance which Keller appreciated."[10]

Côté was no more concerned about Keller's jumpiness than he had been about the divisional commander's heavy drinking, which did not seem to be a factor influencing his behaviour on the beach. The quartermaster general considered that Keller had won the confidence of his staff, who would serve him "as best we could" de-spite any personal failings. What mattered more than Keller's person-ality and leadership in an extensively pre-planned operation such as the invasion was the ability of the infantry, tank, and artillery brigadiers to handle the troops under their command on an ever changing battlefield. Côté, who considered the "division's brigadiers rock solid competent individuals," believed "the performance of their brigades during and right after the landing was marvellous."[11] He expected the division to continue operating smoothly as it pushed inland in the morning.

On the Canadian right flank, the Royal Winnipeg Rifles had tied in with the 7th Green Howards of the 50th British Division at Creully in the afternoon so that the two divisions presented a solid front. To the left, however, the large gap into which the 21st Panzer Division had launched its abortive counterattack remained. The stretch of beach from Langrune-sur-Mer to Lion-sur-Mer was still in

German hands, but the units fixed inside the fortifications here were isolated. This was also the case for the Luftwaffe and part of a company of the 21st Panzer Division that was dug in around the radar station at Douvres-la Délivrande.

According to the invasion plan, the Langrune to Lion section of beach was to have fallen to the Royal Marine's No. 48 Commando and No. 41 Commando—the former landing on the left flank of Juno and the latter the right flank of Sword and then advancing towards each other. Setting down at 0843 hours directly in front of the strongpoint at St. Aubin-sur-Mer, No. 48 Commando had been shredded, losing about 40 per cent of its strength. The survivors attempted to complete the mission, but were soon brought to a standstill by the strength of the fortifications in Longrune. At Lion, No. 41 Commando had been similarly stalled.[12]

Closing the gap between the Canadians and their British counterpart on the left was to have been the responsibility of the 3rd British Division's 9th Brigade, which was to drive southwestward to Cambes and then St. Contest. This would not only tie the two divisional fronts together at the end of D-Day, but enable 9th Brigade to attack Caen from the west on D-Day + 1 if it were not taken on June 6 itself. Setbacks suffered during the early fighting at Sword Beach, however, led to 9th Brigade being diverted to other tasks. One battalion was rushed to support No. 41 Commando's stalled attack on Lion-sur-Mer, while the other two were swung completely over to the division's left flank to assist the embattled paratroopers of 6th Airborne Division. These moves scuttled any hope of linking the two divisions together and created the dangerous gap that threatened the Canadian left and British right flanks at the end of June 6.[13]

BACK ON THE SAND of Juno Beach, Canadian Press correspondent Ross Munro had spent the late afternoon inspecting the German beach defences and considering the great battle that had been fought in an attempt to understand all he had witnessed. Having barely slept in the past two days, something he realized was equally true for most of the soldiers who had fought so hard through this long day, Munro "was dopey with weariness." To clear his mind enough so that he could write, the reporter "munched a Benzedrine tablet every four hours."[14]

Munro was drawn with macabre fascination to the system of pill-boxes that had met the Queen's Own Rifles at Bernières-sur-Mer and exacted such a terrible toll. Picking through the tunnels and concrete chambers, he had seen the smashed German machine guns and artillery pieces that had eventually been overrun. Munro confessed to feeling, as he gazed about at the sheer enormity of the defensive work, an "intense pride" in the Canadians who had taken it. But the "sight of wounded friends who talked to you with pain in their faltering words" served as reminder of the cost paid in blood for the achievement.[15]

On the beach in front of Bernières, the divisional medical units had established a central facility to handle the wounded. In one area fronting the wall, more than 150 wounded Canadians and Germans had been collected. "They lay on stretchers and on the ground wrapped in blankets, their faces ashen grey. Doctors and medical orderlies were with them."[16]

Three Canadian Field Ambulance units—Nos. 14, 22, and 23—had been attached respectively to the 7th, 8th, and 9th Infantry Brigades for the initial landings. As the assault battalions had pushed inland, the ambulance sections had followed along behind, gathering in the wounded and evacuating them to dressing stations established behind the advancing lines. By 1100 hours, No. 14 Canadian Field Ambulance had a dressing station up and running at Banville-sur-Mer, while No. 22 established a matching facility at Bény-sur-Mer shortly after 1800 hours. Closer to the beach, the medical units of No. 102 British Beach Sub-Area—responsible for administering and maintaining Juno Beach—landed two field dressing stations, two field surgical units, one field transfusion unit, one surgical team, a field sanitation detachment, Pioneer Company stretcher-bearers, and a casualty evacuation unit. In from the beach, the British medical units set up two advanced surgical centres—one at Bernières-sur-Mer and the other at Graye-sur-Mer. Both of these were fully operational by 1100 hours.[17]

Queen's Own Rifles Lance Corporal Rolph Jackson, who had been shot in the hand on the beach, had stayed with his No. 10 Platoon of 'B' Company throughout the advance inland because it was so short of men. The platoon ended the day with just seven men standing. Jackson was ordered to report to the Medical Officer to get his wound treated, so with a feeling of great sadness he left the remaining six soldiers huddled in their slit trenches at Anguerny. After seeing the Medical Officer, who despite also being wounded was still treating injured men, Jackson started on a trek back towards the rear. He was picked up at a crossroads by an ambulance team operating a Bren carrier and driven to the dressing station at Bény-sur-Mer, which turned the wounded on the carrier away because it was full. The next station at Bernières-sur-Mer was set up under the cover of a large tent with the sides removed. Lacking a power generator, the inside was lit by coal-oil lamps. Each of the wounded men was quickly assessed and given a number. Then the walking wounded, like Jackson, were sent to wait in a courtyard until called for treatment.

While Jackson waited for his number to come up, he saw a man, stripped down to a singlet and wearing an apron, step outside the tent to smoke a cigarette. As the man's match flared, Jackson saw that he was covered in blood from the tips of his fingers to his elbows. "The surgeon," one of the other wounded said. It soon became evident that Jackson's wounded hand was very low in priority for treatment, so he settled down in the courtyard and catnapped as best he could while the night dragged by. Jackson's thoughts often strayed to all the friends who had died or been maimed around him so few hours before.[18]

As the sun had set on Juno Beach, war correspondent Ralph Allen had found a soldier of the Queen's Own Rifles still hanging in the barbed wire that had been strung along the railroad tracks behind the seawall. "I knelt beside him," Allen said, "and discovered he had bled to death. Beside him was a pack of Canadian cigarettes—open, with one cigarette out and beside it a lighter. I tried the lighter. It was clogged. This poor man had been trying to have one last smoke and the lighter hadn't worked. Nothing had worked for him that day."[19]

OUT ON THE FRONT LINES, emotions numbed by the horror of the day's combat began to make themselves felt. At Tailleville, Sergeant Jack Springer had learned that the North Shores had lost twenty men killed or wounded from his hometown of Chatham—a terrific loss for a town of barely three thousand souls. He walked out to the edge of the lines and saw his antitank platoon commander, Captain "Chuck" Murphy, sitting beside a gun and softly "crying like a baby." When Springer asked him what was wrong, the officer said he could not get the memory of the German prisoner who had tried to pull a hidden weapon on him out of his mind. He kept seeing the man's expression as he died from the Sten gun burst that Murphy had fired into his body. "Chuck, he'd have got you if he could have," Springer said softly. "Don't worry about it."[20]

To the southeast of Tailleville at the Queen's Own Rifles position in Anguerny, Company Sergeant Major Charlie Martin had completed his evening tally of men still on 'A' Company's strength and been dismayed to find that it mustered only about half of those who had climbed down the scramble nets into the LCAS that morning. He walked behind a wall for privacy and let the tears come. "So many had been lost. I found myself questioning—idiotically—why war was conducted this way. Four years of training and living together, a common purpose, friends who became brothers—then more than half of us gone. Why didn't they just round up any collection of men in uniform and throw them into this killing machine? Why these, when anyone— somebody else, but not these—could have paid this price in human life? In grief there is not always good sense. It was one of those times. Gradually though, in asking helplessly what we could do, we would find an answer—we could carry on and do our best, that's what."[21]

Returning to his slit trench, Martin stared out at the eerie blackness of no man's land, beyond which it was easy to imagine that a branch moved by the breeze or a crackle of brush caused by a mouse was evidence of a German counterattack creeping slowly up on the Canadians. A little before midnight, the lines off to one side erupted in wild firing. Men shouted and machine guns chattered to be answered by hoarse bellows in German and the higher-pitched screech of Schmeisser submachine guns. Martin realized that a patrol of

Germans had infiltrated the position. "Dealing with them was difficult. This was our first experience with night fighting, and while the enemy knew who and where we were, we didn't know where or what about them. We had to be careful about our targets. A shadow in the dark could be an enemy or it could be one of our own."[22]

As quickly as it had begun, the firefight abruptly ended with four Germans from the 12th ss Panzer (Hitlerjugend) Division taken prisoner and three Queen's Own wounded. The ss patrol's officer had attacked Rifleman Frank Mumberson in his trench, but the soldier had managed to bayonet the German in the stomach. Mumberson and the German were now swearing loudly at each other because in the confines of the three-foot-wide trench the rifleman was unable to pull the bayonet from the ss man's guts. Finally some other Queen's Own were able to extract the two from the trench and free the bayonet. They sent the wounded ss officer back to the aid post and tried to settle down for the rest of the night.

Out to the front, a match flared as somebody tried to light a cigarette. Martin shouted at the man to douse the cigarette, that he was lucky such foolishness had not ended in his being killed by a sniper. Then the CSM realized by the shape of the man's body that he was dressing down Lieutenant Colonel Jock Spragge. He stomped over to the battalion commander and "gave him plain hell. As far as NCOS and senior officers and all that business might go, combat is far different from the Parade Square. I told him he should be back at Battalion HQ, not up at the front with us—the last line between our forces and the enemy. He was too good and too necessary to be killed or wounded. He gave me one of those looks that anyone who ever knew Jock Spragge would recognize and said, 'Charlie, it's such a sad day. We've lost so many good men.' He said goodnight and turned away, but not before I saw the tears in his eyes."

Martin "walked back to 'A' Company with some heavy thoughts about the Colonel's burden and about the Queen's Own Rifles of Canada, 8th Brigade, 3rd Division, and our landing in Normandy that day. That any of us had survived seemed like a miracle."[23]

Juno Beach in Memory

I STAND ON JUNO BEACH, back to Courseulles-sur-Mer, and look upon a sea whipped into frenzy by a stiff westerly. Chill drizzle falls from a leaden sky. Grey light, grey sea, grey sand. Similar weather to that which greeted more than 14,000 Canadians that morning of June 6, 1944. Then, the Baie de la Seine brimmed with ships. Today, only a couple of small fishing boats have ventured out of the port directly west of me to dip nets and lines into the stormy waters. Then, the air was rent with a cacophony of gunfire, exploding shells, the cries of young men dying. Today, there is only the plaintiff call of a single gull drifting on the wind. Hard today to imagine that morning sixty years past, and yet how can any Canadian visiting this long stretch of sand not? For it is here on this grey beach that Canada fought and won one of the nation's most important battles. Five Allied divisions landed that day—two American, two British, one Canadian. A David hit the beach alongside two Goliaths and did as well or better than the giants.

A David that was largely forgotten in the collective Allied memory of the event. In most American histories of the invasion, Canada's presence figures as little more than a footnote. Because they fought on loan to the British Second Army, British histories are generally more inclusive, while still curiously remaining more focussed on not only what their own divisions experienced but also the American divisions. So while Canada is less a footnote, it is not a chapter either. It falls then to Canadians to tell their own story, which is probably as well.

How have we done with that? Until recently, books on the invasion of Normandy have tended to take in the entire campaign from the landing on Juno to August 28 when the Falaise Gap was finally closed—a lengthy span of time usually compressed into a slight number of pages. During that time, of course, First Canadian Army landed in its entirety and 3rd Canadian Infantry Division reverted back to its control to join in the large and bitter summer battles. That the Canadian experience on June 6 merited singular attention was not seriously considered by most writers or publishers turning their hand to World War II subjects.

Perhaps this is because the official history, *The Victory Campaign*, published by the Canadian Army in 1960 and written by Colonel C.P. Stacey, compressed the day's events into twenty-two pages. While arguably a necessary economy of words in a book spanning the entire northwest Europe campaign, the effect was to create a false impression of June 6's unfolding, particularly as more pages are devoted to describing the invasion plan and German defences than to the fighting itself. The afternoon's drive inland from Juno and build-up of reserves and supplies on the beach passes in just five pages. The reader is left with the sense that once the Canadians exited the beach, the march inland was not seriously contested, which was clearly not the case at Tailleville or St. Croix-sur-Mer or anywhere along the main column's embattled advance from Bernières-sur-Mer through Bény-sur-Mer to Anisy and Villons-les-Buissons.

There has also been a sense in many writings that the Canadian performance on D-Day was disappointing because the final June 6 objectives were not attained. Coupled with an oft-drawn conclusion that the opposing 716th Infantry Division had neither the heart nor ability to offer serious resistance, the inference is drawn that the Canadians, those landing on Juno and paratroopers alike, could and *should* have done better. Seldom do Canadian writers addressing the subject credit the fact that 3rd Canadian Infantry Division ended the day ahead of either the U.S. or British divisions despite the facts that they landed last and that only the Americans at Omaha faced more difficulty winning a toehold on the sand.

While it is true that the Germans and Eastern Europeans of the 716th Infantry Division were not elite troops, neither were they incapable, and they enjoyed the advantage of fighting from fixed and well-armed fortifications. Most did so until the fall of their position was clearly imminent, whereupon they surrendered or fled if possible. More than a few fought to the bitter end.

Could the Canadians have reached the final objectives on D-Day? Beyond mere speculation, it is difficult to say. While the three 1st Hussars tanks of Lieutenant Bill McCormick's troop did gain the Caen-Bayeux highway, it seems improbable the foot-slogging infantry could have pressed through in the face of the defense offered by the remnants of the 716th and the assembling strength of the 21st Panzer Division. By nightfall, this latter division had established several strongpoints ahead of the Canadian position, and the 12th SS Panzer (Hitlerjugend) Division was already probing the front lines with intent to counterattack on June 7 and drive right through to the beach.

What is evident is that the failure of the Allied naval and air bombardment of the German defences both on Juno Beach and inland of it left the Canadians facing an enemy little disrupted or reduced by the great storm of steel that had been flung its way. This resulted in a far more prolonged and bloody fight for the beach than the planners had anticipated or the soldiers had been led to expect. By the time the last strongpoints on the beach were cleared, the invasion timetable was in tatters and the assaulting battalions staggering from the heavy casualties suffered. The fact that these casualties were less than half of what had been predicted does not diminish their effect. The Queen's Own Rifles and Regina Rifles, for example, had companies reduced to fractions of their starting strength, only a couple of hours earlier. That the survivors gathered their weapons and kept on fighting for the rest of the day is telling testimony to the endurance, resilience, and innate courage of these soldiers.

It also speaks of the effectiveness of the training the Canadians had in preparing for this day. The Canadian army in Britain from

1940 to 1944 engaged in steadily improving its combat prowess. When 3rd Canadian Infantry Division and 2nd Canadian Armoured Brigade were tipped to form one of the five invasion forces, the training for these soldiers quickened and intensively focussed on the principle task that would make or break the invasion's ability to succeed—getting ashore. Despite the many problems that beset the assault forces on June 6 as they took to the water and started heading in, the soldiers did not falter. When they found the fortifications virtually unscathed by the bombardment, the assault battalions attacked and eliminated them according to their training.

An essential characteristic of the Canadian soldier was his ability to stay in the fight no matter how casualties reduced the command structure of the battalion in which he served. Perhaps because of Britain's class structure and the fact that its army was one of conscription, there was a tendency for the common soldier to hesitate and take to defensive positions if his officers were killed or wounded. The same has been said of American troops, who also served in an army reliant as much on conscription as volunteerism. In June 1944, Canada's army was still entirely a volunteer one, for the government would not implement conscription until late November of that year. The fact that the soldiers were volunteers greatly increased their esprit de corps. Another key contributing factor to the spirit of Canadian troops was that the battalions were regionally raised, so soldiers marched into battle alongside men they had known in civilian life or who shared similar backgrounds. This was true for the officers of these battalions, too, so there was a lessened gulf between those of rank and the men they commanded. Many veterans relate that they were on a first-name basis with their officers and sergeants. And that, if those leaders fell, the platoon or company would carry on even if it meant being led by a corporal or private. In this, the Canadians excelled to a degree unseen in any of the other forces that fought in Normandy, whether Allied or Axis. This combination of independent spirit strengthened by a sense of community is uniquely Canadian and contributed enormously to the extent of the victory gained at Juno Beach.

TODAY, FEW OF the Canadians involved in the Normandy invasion remain and their numbers shrink with each passing year. Until recently, it was reasonable to fear that as the last veterans passed away the national awareness of this seminal event in our history would be lost. Yet there are signs that this will not be the case. Although it is late in the eyes of many veterans, there is a trend towards Canadians taking active interest in our military heritage. Remembrance Day ceremonies draw larger crowds than was true two or three decades ago. The number of books dealing with Canada's experience of war is growing and these are being more strongly received by readers than was the case in the 1980s or 1990s. In Canadian universities, the study of military history, once a backwater of history departments, is enjoying a renaissance of popularity with students.

I believe that one of the strongest influencing factors in this upsurge in interest stems from a desire on the part of younger generations to understand how World War II affected their forebears—whether great-grandparents, grandparents, or parents. Raised in times when the quest for self-understanding and comprehension of personal motivations is germane to life, we cannot believe that a cataclysm as profound as war did not indelibly influence the lives of those who endured it. And we are right to believe that it did, even when so many of the old warriors try to downplay its effect on their lives after peace came. Theirs was a generation not given to displays of emotion or the exposing of inner feelings. There was also a natural modesty that is Canadian to the bone.

It is at the Bény-sur-Mer Canadian War Cemetery, a few miles inland from Juno Beach, that I see one veteran lower his emotional guard. It is here that the majority of those Canadians who died on D-Day lie alongside more than two thousand others who fell during the subsequent fighting in Normandy. The cemetery is atop a rise from which it is possible to see Juno Beach in the distance. Interspersed among the row upon row of white marble headstones, roses and other flowers grow and the grassy lanes between the ranks of graves are meticulously maintained.

As has been my wont for these years spent researching books on Canada's World War II experience, I slowly pass down each lane, noting the names, ages, ranks, hometowns, units, and inscriptions on each headstone. In this cemetery, like all the others, the Canada of 1940 to 1945 is poignantly depicted. Here a significant portion of that small nation's youth of the time remains ever young.

In a lane near the one I am walking, an elderly man in a brown jacket, upon which a row of medals is pinned, stands with his gaze fixed on the headstone in front of him. Although tears glisten on his cheeks, the old soldier makes no move to wipe them aside. I turn away quietly, not wanting to affront or embarrass. The palpable nature of his grief is deeply moving. I wonder who it is that he weeps for, but when I look again he is striding off as if to rejoin a marching column and I had failed to fix the headstone's location. Just as well. He has come to this cemetery as an act of remembrance and whether his tears related to one fallen soldier or all those lying here matters not.

From the cemetery I drive to St. Aubin-sur-Mer and then follow the coast back to Courseulles-sur-Mer via Bernières-sur-Mer, pausing often to walk out onto the sand and to examine the various German casemates that can still be found along Juno Beach's length. In each town, plaques have been erected to commemorate the battalions that landed in front of them. The three towns are now pleasant seaside resorts that cater to French sun-seekers from the big interior cities. And to those engaged in pilgrimages of remembrance. Most of this latter group are veterans with their families, but others come, too—largely from Britain, the United States, Germany, and Canada.

They journey from Utah Beach up to Pegasus Bridge, where a new museum honours the 6th British Airborne Division and has a special section set aside to relate the story of 1st Canadian Parachute Battalion. Until 2003, this museum, the plaques, a few armoured vehicles transformed into monuments, and the cemetery at Bény-sur-Mer were about all there was to signify the Canadian participation in the invasion.

Today, however, there is the Juno Beach Centre. Costing more than $8 million, the Juno Beach Centre stands immediately west of the River Seulles opposite Courseulles-sur-Mer and was opened on June 6, 2003. From the beach, its low grey structure gives the impression of an oversized German fortification the Canadians might have had to take in bloody battle. It is, however, the most significant Canadian World War 11 interpretative history museum to be found anywhere outside this country. The federal government and several provinces contributed most of the money required to build the centre. France put in $1 million. And Canadian veterans of D-Day and the Normandy campaign raised more than $1 million. Inside the museum, displays include one that provides a simulation of the approach to the D-Day beaches by landing craft. Others give extensive explanations of relevant military hardware and tactics employed to make the invasion successful. There is also a "children's circuit" aimed at children aged eight to thirteen.

The centre was brought to fruition largely through the efforts of veterans who lobbied the federal government for almost seven years to build a significant museum of Canada's experience on D-Day at Juno Beach. It is a significant achievement, of which they can be proud, and is arguably now the most compelling museum regarding the invasion to be found anywhere along the Normandy coast, which has many such facilities.

But museums can only do so much to preserve the knowledge of Canada's contribution to winning the war for future generations or particularly the contribution of those soldiers, airmen, and sailors who took part on June 6, 1944 in the Normandy invasion. Ultimately, it falls to all of us to keep that memory alive. It lies with us to do hon-our by all those young men who faced the grey sky, sea, and sand of Juno Beach that morning so long ago, which is still only yesterday for those veterans alive today.

3RD CANADIAN INFANTRY DIVISION
7th Reconnaissance Regiment
(17th Duke of York's Royal Canadian Hussars)
—observer elements only

The Royal Canadian Artillery:
12th Field Regiment
13th Field Regiment
14th Field Regiment
19th Army Field Regiment (attached)
3rd Anti-tank Regiment
4th Light Anti-Aircraft Regiment

Corps of Royal Canadian Engineers:
6th Field Company
16th Field Company
18th Field Company
3rd Field Park Company
5th Field Company (attached)

Brigade Support Group:
The Cameron Highlanders of Ottawa (MG Battalion)

7th Canadian Infantry Brigade:
The Royal Winnipeg Rifles
The Regina Rifle Regiment
1st Battalion, Canadian Scottish Regiment

8th Canadian Infantry Brigade:
  The Queen's Own Rifles of Canada
  Le Régiment de la Chaudière
  The North Shore (New Brunswick) Regiment

9th Canadian Infantry Brigade:
  The Highland Light Infantry of Canada
  The Stormont, Dundas and Glengarry Highlanders
  The North Nova Scotia Highlanders

2ND CANADIAN ARMOURED BRIGADE
  6th Armoured Regiment (1st Hussars)
  10th Armoured Regiment (The Fort Garry Horse)
  27th Armoured Regiment (The Sherbrooke Fusiliers Regiment)

1ST CANADIAN PARACHUTE BATTALION
  (Landed Drop Zone V near River Dives)

APPENDIX B:
ROYAL CANADIAN NAVY SHIPS
IN THE INVASION
(EACH SHIP CLASS LISTED BY SENIORITY
OF COMMANDING OFFICER)

A. FLEET DESTROYERS ('V' CLASS)
HMCS *Algonquin*
    Sioux

B. FLEET MINESWEEPERS (BANGOR CLASS)

HMCS *Caraquet*	HMCS *Bayfield*
Blairmore	*Mulgrave*
Cowichan	*Guysborough*
Fort William	*Kenora*
Malpeque	*Vegreville*
Milltown	*Georgian*
Minas	*Thunder*
Wasaga	*Canso*

C. ASSAULT FORCES
Landing Ships, Infantry (Medium)

HMCS *Prince Henry*	HMCS *Prince David*
(528th LCA Flotilla)	(529th LCA Flotilla)
LCA 856	LCA 1150
LCA 1372	LCA 1375
LCA 736	LCA 1059
LCA 1033	LCA 1151
LCA 850	LCA 1138
LCA 1021	LCA 1137
LCA 925	
LCA 1371	

Landing Craft Infantry, Large

(260th LCI Flotilla)	(262nd LCI Flotilla)
LCI 117	LCI 115
LCI 121	LCI 118
LCI 166	LCI 125
LCI 177	LCI 135
LCI 249	LCI 250
LCI 266	LCI 252
LCI 271	LCI 262
LCI 277	LCI 263
LCI 285	LCI 270
LCI 298	LCI 276
LCI 301	LCI 299
	LCI 306

(264th LCI Flotilla)

LCI 255
LCI 288
LCI 295
LCI 302
LCI 305
LCI 310
LCI 311

D. ASSAULT AREA DEFENCE FORCES: COVERING AND SUPPORT FORCES

Motor Torpedo Boats

(29th MTB Flotilla)	(65th MTB Flotilla)
MTB 459	MTB 726
MTB 460	MTB 727
MTB 461	MTB 735
MTB 462	MTB 743
MTB 463	MTB 746
MTB 464	MTB 745
MTB 465	MTB 748
MTB 466	

Tribal Class Destroyers
HMCS *Haida*
    Iroquois
    Huron
    Athabaskan

Destroyers

Escort Group 11	Escort Group 12
HMCS *Ottawa*	HMCS *Qu'Appelle*
Kootenay	*Saskatchewan*
Chaudière	*Skeena*
St. Laurent	*Restigouche*
Gatineau	*Assiniboine*

Frigates

Escort Group 6	Escort Group 9
HMCS *New Waterford*	HMCS *Matane*
Waskesiu	*Swamsea*
Outremont	*Stormont*
Cape Breton	*Port Colborne*
Grou	*St. John*
Teme	*Meon*

Corvettes

HMCS *Prescott*	HMCS *Mayflower*
Calgary	*Louisburg*
Mimico	*Rimouski*
Alberni	*Trentonian*
Woodstock	*Moose Jaw*
Regina	*Port Arthur*
Baddeck	*Lindsay*
Camrose	*Kitchener*
Lunenburg	*Summerside*
Drumheller	

LCA   Landing Craft, Assault
LCI(S) Landing Craft Infantry, Small
LCI(L) Landing Craft Infantry, Large
LCT   Landing Craft, Tank
LSI(H) Landing Ship, Infantry (Hand Hoisting)
LSI(M) Landing Ship, Infantry (Medium)
LSI(L) Landing Ship, Infantry (Large)
LST   Landing Ship, Tank

APPENDIX D:
CANADIAN INFANTRY BATTALION
(TYPICAL ORGANIZATION)

HQ COMPANY:

No. 1: Signals Platoon

No. 2: Administrative Platoon

SUPPORT COMPANY:

No. 3: Mortar Platoon (3-inch)

No. 4: Bren Carrier Platoon

No. 5: Assault Pioneer Platoon

No. 6: Antitank Platoon (6-pounder)

A COMPANY:

No. 7 Platoon

No. 8 Platoon

No. 9 Platoon

B COMPANY:

No. 10 Platoon

No. 11 Platoon

No. 12 Platoon

C COMPANY:

No. 13 Platoon

No. 14 Platoon

No. 15 Platoon

D COMPANY:

No. 16 Platoon

No. 17 Platoon

No. 18 Platoon

APPENDIX E:
CANADIAN ARMY ORDER OF RANK
(LOWEST TO HIGHEST)

Private
Rifleman (rifle regiment equivalent of private)
Gunner (artillery equivalent of private)
Trooper (armoured equivalent of private)
Lance Corporal
Corporal
Lance Sergeant
Sergeant
Company Sergeant Major (CSM)
Regimental Sergeant Major (RSM)
Lieutenant
Captain
Major
Lieutenant Colonel
Colonel
Brigadier
Major General
Lieutenant General
General

Because the German Army had a ranking system where rank also usually indicated the specific type of unit in which one served, only basic ranks are given here. The translations are roughly based on the Canadian ranking system, although there is no Canadian equivalent for many German ranks.

Schütze	Private, infantry
Grenadier	Private, infantry
Kanonier	Gunner
Panzerschütze	Tank crew member
Pionier	Sapper
Funker	Signaller
Gefreiter	Lance Corporal
Obergefreiter	Corporal
Unteroffizier	Lance Sergeant
Unterfeldwebel	Sergeant
Feldwebel	Company Sergeant Major
Oberfeldwebel	Battalion Sergeant Major
Leutnant	Second Lieutenant
Oberleutnant	Lieutenant
Hauptmann	Captain
Major	Major
Oberstleutnant	Lieutenant Colonel
Oberst	Colonel
Generalleutnant	Lieutenant General
Generalmajor	Major General
General der Artillerie	General of Artillery

General der Infanterie	General of Infantry
General der Kavallerie	General of Cavalry
General der Pioniere	General of Engineers
General der Panzertruppen	General of Armoured Troops
Generaloberst	Colonel General
Generalfeldmarschall	General Field Marshal

Canadian military personnel won many military decorations on
June 6, 1944. The decoration system that Canada used in World
War II, like most other aspects of its military organization and
tradition, derived from Britain. A class-based system, most military
decorations can be awarded either to officers or to "other ranks," but
not both. The Canadian army, navy, and air force also have distinct
decorations. Only the Victoria Cross—the nation's highest award—
can be won by personnel from any arm of the service or rank.

The decorations and qualifying ranks are:

VICTORIA CROSS (VC): Awarded for gallantry in the presence of the
enemy. Instituted in 1856. Open to all ranks. The only award that
can be granted for action in which the recipient was killed, other
than Mentioned in Despatches—a less formal honour whereby an
act of bravery was given specific credit in a formal report. No Victoria
Crosses were awarded to Canadian military personnel on D-Day.

DISTINGUISHED SERVICE ORDER (DSO): Army officers of all ranks,
but more commonly awarded to officers with ranks of major or
higher.

DISTINGUISHED SERVICE CROSS (DSC): Navy officers ranging in
rank from commander down to lieutenant.

MILITARY CROSS (MC): Army officers with a rank normally below
major and, rarely, warrant officers.

DISTINGUISHED FLYING CROSS (DFC): Air force officers and warrant officers for acts of valour while flying in active operations against the enemy.

AIR FORCE CROSS (AFC): Air force officers and warrant officers for valour while flying, but not while in active operations against the enemy.

DISTINGUISHED CONDUCT MEDAL (DCM): Army warrant officers and all lower ranks.

CONSPICUOUS GALLANTRY MEDAL (CGM): Navy chief petty officers, petty officers, and men.

DISTINGUISHED SERVICE MEDAL (DSM): Navy chief petty officers, petty officers, and men.

MILITARY MEDAL (MM): Army warrant officers and all lower ranks.

DISTINGUISHED FLYING MEDAL (DFM): Air force non-commissioned officers and men for valour while flying in active operations against the enemy.

AIR FORCE MEDAL (AFM): Air Force non-commissioned officers and men for valour while flying, but not in active operations against the enemy.

NOTES

INTRODUCTION: GREEN ON

1 Lochie Fulton, interview by Ken MacLeod, Victoria, BC, 9 February 1998.
2 Col. C.P. Stacey, *The Victory Campaign: The Operations in North-West Europe, 1944–1945*, vol. 3 (Ottawa: Queen's Printer, 1960), 38.
3 Fulton interview.
4 John R. Madden, recorded recollections, 1987, University of Victoria Special Collections.
5 Brian Nolan, *Airborne: The Heroic Story of the 1st Canadian Parachute Battalion in the Second World War* (Toronto: Lester Publishing, 1995), 79.
6 Madden reminiscences.

I: MAXIMUM FORCE NEEDED

1 Col. C.P. Stacey, *The Victory Campaign: The Operations in North-West Europe, 1944–1945*, vol. 3 (Ottawa: Queen's Printer, 1960), 4.
2 Ibid.
3 Ibid.
4 Ibid.
5 Ibid., 5–6.
6 Ibid., 7.
7 Ibid.
8 Ibid.
9 Ibid., 14.
10 Ibid., 13–15.
11 Ibid., 29.
12 Ibid., 34.
13 Ibid.
14 F.E. Morgan, "War Document, F.E. Morgan to British Chiefs of Staff," *Encyclopedia Britannica*, 15 July 1943, 1998–1999., n.p.
15 Stacey, 19–21.
16 Carlo D'Este, *Decision in Normandy: The Unwritten Story of Montgomery and the Allied Campaign* (London: Penguin Books, 2001), 50–51.
17 Stacey, 21.

18 Maj. J.R. Martin, "Report No. 147 Historical Section Canadian Military Headquarters: Part One: The Assault and Subsequent Operations of 3 Cdn Inf Div and 2 Cdn Armd Bde, 6–30 June 44—N.W. Europe," Directorate of History, Department of National Defence, 3 December 1945, para. 12.

19 Stacey, 21.

2: THE WEB-FOOTED DIVISION

1 Crerar Papers, "Appointments and Promotions—Officers, Period Feb. 1942 to January 1943," MG 30 E157, vol. 5, National Archives of Canada.

2 Ibid.

3 Granatstein Papers, newspaper story, n.p, n.d., York University Archives and Special Collections, Scott Library.

4 Granatstein Papers, "Royal Military College of Canada Report of Gentleman Cadet R.F.L. Keller of the 3rd Class for the Term ending 20 July, 1918," York University Archives and Special Collections, Scott Library.

5 Granatstein Papers, "Royal Military College of Canada Report of Gentleman Cadet R.F.L. Keller of the 1st Class for the Term Xmas, 1919."

6 J.L. Granatstein, *The Generals: The Canadian Army's Senior Commanders in the Second World War* (Toronto: Stoddart, 1993), 16–17.

7 Ernest Côté, interview by Michael Boire, Ottawa, 14 November 2003.

8 Harold Bertrand Gonder, interview by Mark C. Hill, 23 July and 7, 8, 9 August 1985, University of Victoria Special Collections.

9 Granatstein, *The Generals*, 166.

10 Gonder interview.

11 Canadian Operations in North–West Europe, June 1944: Extracts from Memoranda (Series 1), R.F.L. Keller, "The Techniques of the Assault: Comments on Operation 'Overlord'," 21 June 1944, Directorate of Heritage and History, Department of National Defence, 1.

12 Will R. Bird, *The Two Jacks: The Amazing Adventures of Major Jack M. Veness and Major Jack L. Fairweather.* (Toronto: Ryerson Press, 1954), 2.

13 Bird, 3.

14 Lochie Fulton, interview by Ken MacLeod, Victoria, BC, 9 February 1998.

15 Dave Kingston, interview by John Gregory Thompson, Mississauga, ON, 10 September 2003.

16 Rolph Jackson, interview by John Gregory Thompson,Toronto, 2 September 2003.

17 James Douglas Baird, interview by William S. Thackray, 17, 27 June and 18 July 1980, University of Victoria Special Collections.

18 Maj. H.S. Patterson, "Artillery Communications in Operation Overlord, Account by Maj. H.S. Patterson, OC 2 Coy, 3 CDN INF DIV SIGS," 018(D2), Directorate of History, Department of National Defence, 6.

19 Baird interview.

20 Patterson, 7–8.

21 Col. C.P. Stacey, *The Victory Campaign: The Operations in North-West Europe, 1944–1945*, vol. 3 (Ottawa: Queen's Printer, 1960), 35–36.

22 N.a., "Second Canadian Armoured Brigade: Operation Overlord—The Assault on the Beaches of Normandy, 6–11 June 1944—Sequence of Events and Lessons Arising Therefrom," vol. 104S5, RG24, National Archives of Canada, n.p.

23 Ibid.

24 Phil Cockburn, interview by John Gregory Thompson, Ravenswood, ON, 11 August 2003.

25 Jim Simpson, interview by John Gregory Thompson, Windsor, ON, 13 September 2003.

26 Keller, "The Technique of the Assault: Comments on Operation 'Overlord,'" 21 June 1944, 1.

27 Don Mingay speech, 2002, copy in possession of the author.

3: LEARNING NEW SKILLS

1 Peter Hinton, interview by Mark Hill, 22 July 1985, University of Victoria Special Collections.

2 "The Royal Canadian Navy's Part in the Invasion," Directorate of History, Department of National Defence, 27.

3 Ibid.

4 Ibid.

5 Hinton interview.

6 Ibid.

7 Ibid.

8 "The Royal Canadian Navy's Part in the Invasion," 5–6.

9 Ibid., 20.

10 Ibid., 20–21.

11 Stan Richardson diary, copy in possession of the author.

12 Ibid.

13 "The Royal Canadian Navy's Part in the Invasion," 21.

14 Richardson diary.

15 "The Royal Canadian Navy's Part in the Invasion," 21.

16 Richardson diary.

17 "The Royal Canadian Navy's Part in the Invasion," 21–23.

18 Ibid., 25.

19 Ibid., 25–26.

20 Col. C.P. Stacey, *The Victory Campaign: The Operations in North-West Europe, 1944–1945*, vol. 3 (Ottawa: Queen's Printer, 1960), 37.

21 "The Royal Canadian Navy's Part in the Invasion," 28.

22 Ibid.

23 Hinton interview.

24 "The Royal Canadian Navy's Part in the Invasion," 29.

25 Hinton interview.

26 Lochie Fulton, interview by Ken MacLeod, Victoria, BC, 9 February 1998.

27 Will R. Bird, *North Shore (New Brunswick) Regiment* (Fredericton, NB: Brunswick Press, 1963), 192.

4: DEATH OR GLORY

1 Trafford Leigh-Mallory, "Air Operations by the Allied Expeditionary Air Force in N.W. Europe from November 15th, 1943 to September 30th, 1944," Fourth Supplement, *The London Gazette*, 31 December 1946, 37.

2 Ibid.

3 Ibid., 38.

4 Ibid., 43.

5 Brereton Greenhous, Stephen Harris, et al., *The Crucible of War, 1939–1945: The Official History of The Royal Canadian Air Force*, vol. 3 (Toronto: University of Toronto Press, 1995), 288–89.

6 Ibid., 279.

7 Ibid.

8 David Bashow, *All the Fine Young Eagles: In the Cockpit with Canada's Second World War Fighter Pilots* (Toronto: Stoddart, 1996), 256.

9 Jean E. Portugal, *We Were There: The Navy, the Army and the RCAF—A Record for Canada*, vol. 7 (Shelburne, ON: The Battered Silicon Dispatch Box, 1998), 3283.

10 Greenhous et al., 278.

11 Bashow, 263.

12 Greenhous et al., 279.

13 Ibid.

14 Ibid., 289.

15 Ibid., 284.

16 Ibid., 289–90.

17 Bashow, 263.

18 Greenhous et al., 281.

19 Bashow, 264–65.

20 Leigh-Mallory, 42.

21 Ibid., 50.

22 Ibid., 51.

23 Greenhous et al., 805.

24 Don Cheney, interview by Glen Cook, 16 November 2000, Ottawa, Canadian War Museum Oral History Project Collection.

25 Ibid.

5: THE INTELLIGENCE FOG

1 Ralph Bennett, *Ultra in the West: The Normandy Campaign, 1944–45* (London: Hutchinson & Co., 1979), 49–50.

2 Col. C.P. Stacey, *The Victory Campaign: The Operations in North-West Europe, 1944–1945*, vol. 3 (Ottawa: Queen's Printer, 1960), 46.

3 Bennett, 64–67.

4 Ibid., 42.

5 Hans Speidel, "Ideas and Views of Genfldm Rommell, Commander of Army Group B, on Defense and Operations in the West in 1944," in *Fighting the Invasion: The German Army at D-Day*, David C. Isby, ed. (London: Greenhill Books, 2000), 41.

6 Ibid., 42.

7 Ibid., 41.

8 Ibid., 42.

9 Stacey, 55.

10 Walter Warlimont, "The Invasion," in *Fighting the Invasion: The German Army at D-Day*, David C. Isby, ed. (London: Greenhill Books, 2000), 92.

11 Stacey, 57.

12 Ibid., 59.

13 Ibid., 55.

14 Ibid., 69.

15 Ibid., 56.

16 Roger Chevalier, interview by author, Courseulles-sur-Mer, 23 May 2003.

17 Warlimont, 88.

18 Max Pemsel, "Seventh Army, June 1942–6 June 1944: Report of the Chief of Staff," in *Fighting the Invasion: The German Army at D-Day*, David C. Isby, ed. (London: Greenhill Books, 2000), 55.

19 Warlimont, 88.

20 Ibid., 89.

21 Bennett, 50.

22 Speidel, 39.

23 Stacey, 60.

24 Bennett, 50.

25 Ibid., 51.

26 Stacey, 66–67.

27 Speidel, 38.

28 Trafford Leigh-Mallory, "Air Operations by the Allied Expeditionary Air Force in N.W. Europe from November 15th, 1943 to September 30th, 1944," Fourth Supplement, *The London Gazette*, 31 December 1946, 51.

29 Ibid.

30 Ibid.

31 Brereton Greenhous, Stephen Harris, et al., *The Crucible of War, 1939–1945: The Official History of The Royal Canadian Air Force*, vol. 3 (Toronto: University of Toronto Press, 1995), 284.

32 Ibid.

33 Canadian Operations in North-West Europe, June 1944: Extracts from Memoranda (Series 1), R.F.L. Keller, "The Techniques of the Assault: Comments on Operation 'Overlord'," 21 June 1944, Directorate of History, Department of National Defence, 2.

34 N.a, "Second Canadian Armoured Brigade: Operation Overlord, The Assault on the Beaches of Normandy—6–11 June 1944—Sequence of Events and Lessons Arising Therefrom," vol. 104S5, RG 24, National Archives of Canada, 1.

35 Jean E. Portugal, *We Were There: The Navy, the Army and the RCAF—A Record for Canada*, vol. 6 (Shelburne, ON: The Battered Silicon Dispatch Box, 1998), 2784.

36 Ernest Côté, interview by Michael Boire, Ottawa, 14 November 2003.

37 Ibid.

38 Portugal, vol. 6, 2784.

39 Mingay, Don (Lt. Col.), documents. Canadian War Museum Archives.

40 Russell Frederick Choat, interview by James Murphy, 27 June and 5, 11 July 1977, University of Victoria Special Collections.

41 Maj. J.R. Martin, "Report No. 147 Historical Section Canadian Military Headquarters: Part One: The Assault and Subsequent Operations of 3 Cdn Inf Div and 2 Cdn Armd Bde, 6–30 June 44—N.W. Europe," 3 December 1945, Directorate of History, Department of National Defence, para. 155.

42 Ibid.

43 Cyril Merrott Wightman, interview by Cameron Falconer, 8 February 1983, University of Victoria Special Collections.

6: SPOILING FOR A FIGHT

1 Maj. G.W.L. Nicholson, "Report No. 138 Historical Section Canadian Military Headquarters: 1st Canadian Parachute Battalion: Organization and Training, July 1942–June 1944," Directorate of History, Department of National Defence, n.d., para. 8.

2 Ibid., para. 3.

3 Brian Nolan, *Airborne: The Heroic Story of the 1st Canadian Parachute Battalion in the Second World War* (Toronto: Lester Publishing, 1995), 34.

4 Nicholson, para. 9.

5 Nolan, 14.

6 Dan Hartigan, *A Rising of Courage: Canada's Paratroops in the Liberation of Normandy* (Calgary: Drop Zone Publishers, 2000), 2–5.

7 Nolan, 18.

8 Nolan, 25–31.

9 John R. Madden, recorded recollections, 1987, University of Victoria Special Collections.

10 Nolan, 38.

11 Madden recollections.

12 Nolan, 41–48.

13 Madden recollections.

14 Nicholson, paras. 22–23.

15 Ibid.

16 Ibid., paras. 24–25.

17 Nolan, 49.

18 Ibid., 48–49.

19 Nicholson, para. 26.

20 Ibid., para. 28.

21 Ibid.

22 Ibid., para. 29.

23 Ibid., para. 37.

24 Hartigan, 19.

25 Ibid., 20–21.

26 Ibid., 21.

27 Col. C.P. Stacey, *The Victory Campaign: The Operations in North-West Europe, 1944–1945,* vol. 3 (Ottawa: Queen's Printer, 1960), 71–72.

28 Hartigan, 21.

29 John A. Willes, *Out of the Clouds: The History of the 1st Canadian Parachute Battalion* (Port Perry, ON: Port Perry Printing, 1995), 51–52.

30 Hartigan, 21.

7: TO DIE GLORIOUSLY

1 Maj. J.R. Martin, "Report No. 147 Historical Section Canadian Military Headquarters: Part One: The Assault and Subsequent Operations of 3 Cdn Inf Div and 2 Cdn Armd Bde, 6–30 June 44—N.W. Europe," 3 December 1945, Directorate of History, Department of National Defence, para. 154.

2 John Clifford Cave, interview by Chris D. Main, 14, 24 August 1978, University of Victoria Special Collections.

3 Martin, paras. 77–78.

4 Col. C.P. Stacey, *The Victory Campaign: The Operations in North-West Europe, 1944–1945,* vol. 3 (Ottawa: Queen's Printer, 1960), 76.

5 Ibid., 76–81.

6 Martin, paras. 99–103.

7 Stacey, 77.

8 Martin, para. 83.

9 Ibid., paras. 83–91.

10 Stacey, 120.

11 Don Mingay speech, 2002, copy in possession of the author.

12 Peter Simonds, *Maple Leaf Up, Maple Leaf Down: The Story of the Canadians in the Second World War* (New York: Island Press, 1946), 129.

13 Ibid., 129–30.

14 Jean E. Portugal, *We Were There: The Navy, the Army and the RCAF—A Record for Canada*, vol. 1 (Shelburne, ON: The Battered Silicon Dispatch Box, 1998), 23–27.

15 Ibid., 35.

16 Hugh Lamb, interview by John Gregory Thompson, Mississauga, ON, 8 September 2003.

17 Desmond W. Piers, "HMCS *Algonquin*—Operation Neptune," University of Victoria Special Collections, 1.

18 "The Royal Canadian Navy's Part in the Invasion," Directorate of History, Department of National Defence, 17.

19 Piers, 1.

20 Ibid.

21 Ibid.

22 R.M. Hickey, *The Scarlet Dawn* (Campbellton, NB: Tribune Publishers, 1949), 184.

23 William Boss, *Up the Glens: Stormont, Dundas and Glengarry Highlanders, 1783–1994*, 2nd ed. (Cornwall, ON: Old Book Store, 1995), 183.

24 Ronald Shawcross, interview by Mark C. Hill, 14, 19 June 1985, University of Victoria Special Collections.

25 N.a., "Second Canadian Armoured Brigade: Operation Overlord—The Assault on the Beaches of Normandy, 6–11 June 1944—Sequence of Events and Lessons Arising Therefrom," vol. 10455, RG 24, National Archives of Canada, n.p.

26 Bill McCormick, interview by John Gregory Thompson, Gault, ON, 3 October 2003.

27 "Second Canadian Armoured Brigade: Operation Overlord," n.p.

28 "Second Canadian Armoured Brigade: Operation Overlord—The Assault on the Beaches of Normandy, 6–11 June 1944—Appendix B Narrative, 10 CDN ARMD REGT," 1.

29 Martin, para. 158.

30 Fort Garry Horse War Diary, June 1944, RG 24, National Archives of Canada, n.p.

31 Ibid.

32 Ralph Burley, interview by John Gregory Thompson, Toronto, 12 August 2003.

33 John Marteinson and Michael R. McNorgan, *The Royal Canadian Armoured Corps: An Illustrated History* (Toronto: Robin Brass Studio, 2000), 243.

34 1st Hussars War Diary, June 1944, RG 24, National Archives of Canada, 1.

35 Royal Winnipeg Rifles War Diary, June 1944, RG 24, National Archives of Canada, n.p.

36 Russell Choat, interview by James Murphy, 27 June and 5, 11 July 1977, University of Victoria Special Collections.

37 Peter Hinton, interview by Mark Hill, 22 July 1985, University of Victoria Special Collections.

38 Ibid.

39 B.B. Schofield, *Operation Neptune* (London: Ian Allan, 1974), 59.

40 Ibid., 66–67.

41 Stacey, 89.

42 Schofield, 67–68.

43 Carlo D'Este, *Decision in Normandy: The Unwritten Story of Montgomery and the Allied Campaign* (London: Penguin Books, 2001), 110.

8: NO BANDS OR CHEERING CROWDS

1 Maj. J.R. Martin, "Report No. 147 Historical Section Canadian Military Headquarters: Part One: The Assault and Subsequent Operations of 3 Cdn Inf Div and 2 Cdn Armd Bde, 6–30 June 44—N.W. Europe." 3 December 1945, Directorate of History, Department of National Defence, para. 164.

2 R.M. Hickey, *The Scarlet Dawn* (Campbelltown, NB: Tribune Publishers, 1949), 192.

3 19th Field Regiment, RCA War Diary, June 1944, RG 24, National Archives of Canada, n.p.

4 "Letters from Capt. Seaborn to wife Mary Elizabeth (Betty) Seaborn," 5 June 1944, Robert Lowder Seaborn and Family Papers, National Archives of Canada.

5 Ibid.

6 Jean E. Portugal, *We Were There: The Navy, the Army and the RCAF—A Record for Canada*, vol. 2 (Shelburne, ON: The Battered Silicon Dispatch Box, 1998), 612.

7 Highland Light Infantry of Canada War Diary, June 1944, RG 24, National Archives of Canada, 3.

8 Ibid.

9 Bill McCormick, interview by John Gregory Thompson, Gault, ON, 3 October 2003.

10 Jack Martin, interview by John Gregory Thompson, Scarborough, ON, 1 October 2003.

11 Peter Hinton, interview by Mark Hill, 22 July 1985, University of Victoria Special Collections.

12 B.B. Schofield, *Operation Neptune* (London: Ian Allan, 1974), 43–44.

13 "The Royal Canadian Navy's Part in the Invasion," Directorate of History, Department of National Defence, 73.

14 Anthony H.G. Storrs, interview by Chris Bell, 9, 16 September 1982, 13 June, 8 July, and 30 August 1983, University of Victoria Special Collections.

15 "The Royal Canadian Navy's Part in the Invasion," 73.

16 Stan Richardson Diary, copy in possession of the author.

17 Schofield, 51–54.

18 I.J. Gillen Diary, RG518-0-2-E, National Archives of Canada, 2.

19 John A. Willes, *Out of the Clouds: The History of the 1st Canadian Parachute Battalion* (Port Perry, ON: Port Perry Printing, 1995), 52.

20 Dan Hartigan, *A Rising of Courage: Canada's Paratroops in the Liberation of Normandy* (Calgary: Drop Zone Publishers, 2000), 65.

21 Brian Nolan, *Airborne: The Heroic Story of the 1st Canadian Parachute Battalion in the Second World War* (Toronto: Lester Publishing, 1995), 77.

22 Hartigan, 65–69.

23 John R. Madden, recorded recollections, 1987, University of Victoria Special Collections.

24 Nolan, 78.

25 G.W.L. Nicholson, "Report No. 139 Historical Section Canadian Military Headquarters: The 1st Canadian Parachute Battalion in France, 6 June–6 September 1944," Directorate of History, Department of National Defence, n.d, para. 8.

26 "Information re: dispersion on D-Day, 6 June 1944 1 CDN Para Bn," Directorate of History, Department of National Defence, n.p.

27 Brereton Greenhous, Stephen Harris, et al., *The Crucible of War, 1939–1945: The Official History of The Royal Canadian Air Force*, vol. 3 (Toronto: University of Toronto Press, 1995), 806.

28 Don Cheney, interview by Glen Cook, 16 November 2000, Ottawa, Canadian War Museum Oral History Project Collection.

29 Portugal, *We Were There*, vol. 1, 3252.

30 Col. C.P. Stacey, *The Victory Campaign: The Operations in Northwest Europe, 1944–1945*, vol. 3 (Ottawa: Queen's Printer, 1960), 121–22.

31 Max Pemsel, "Seventh Army, June 1942–6 June 1944: Report of the Chief of Staff," in *Fighting the Invasion: The German Army at D-Day*, David C. Isby, ed. (London: Greenhill Books, 2000), 70.

32 Max Hastings, *Overlord: D-Day and the Battle of Normandy* (New York: Simon & Schuster, 1984), 67–68.

33 B.H. Liddell Hart, *History of the Second World War* (New York: G.P. Putnam's Sons, 1970), 575.

34 Hans von Luck, *Panzer Grenadier: The Memoirs of Colonel Hans von Luck* (Westport, CT: Praeger Publishers, 1989), 136–37.

35 Ibid.

36 Ibid.

9: STICK TO THE OBJECTIVE

1 Dan Hartigan, *A Rising of Courage: Canada's Paratroops in the Liberation of Normandy* (Calgary: Drop Zone Publishers, 2000), 71.

2 Ibid., 72.

3 Ibid., 118–20.

4 Ibid., 117–18.

5 John P. Hanson, "Letter 12 November 1949 in Correspondence re Ops 1st Cdn Para Bn from various officers," Directorate of History, Department of National Defence, 2.

6 Ibid.

7 Hartigan, 113.

8 John R. Madden, recorded recollections, 1987, University of Victoria Special Collections.

9 Brian Nolan, *Airborne: The Heroic Story of the 1st Canadian Parachute Battalion in the Second World War* (Toronto: Lester Publishing, 1995), 79–80.

10 Madden reminiscences.

11 John A. Willes, *Out of the Clouds: The History of the 1st Canadian Parachute Battalion* (Port Perry, ON: Port Perry Printing, 1981), 78–79.

12 Hartigan, 110–13.

13 Willes, 79.

14 Ibid., 78–80.

15 T. Robert Fowler, *Valour on Juno Beach: The Canadian Awards for Gallantry, D-Day, June 6, 1944* (Burnstown, ON: General Store Publishing, 1994), 15–16.

16 Hartigan, 116.

17 N.a., "Information re: dispersion on D-Day, 6 June 1944 1 CDN Para Bn," 145.4013(D1), Directorate of History, Department of National Defence, n.p.

18 Ibid.

19 Nolan, 92–93.

20 Hartigan, 107.

21 Ibid., 90.

22 Ibid., 83–84.

23 Ibid., 96–97.

24 Willes, 75.

25 Hartigan, 86.

26 Willes, 75.
27 Hartigan, 120–25.
28 Willes, 76.
29 Hartigan, 149.
30 Ibid., 116–17.
31 Willes, 78.
32 Ibid., 82.

IO: ALL AFLAME

1 Anthony H.G. Storrs, interview by Chris Bell, 9, 16 September 1982, 13 June, 8 July, and 30 August 1983, University of Victoria Special Collections.
2 "The Royal Canadian Navy's Part in the Invasion," Directorate of History, Department of National Defence, 75–76.
3 Stan Richardson Diary, copy in possession of the author.
4 "The Royal Canadian Navy's Part in the Invasion," 75–76.
5 Ibid., 87.
6 Trafford Leigh-Mallory, "Air Operations by the Allied Expeditionary Air Force in N.W. Europe from November 15th, 1943 to September 30th, 1944," Fourth Supplement, *The London Gazette*, 31 December 1946, 56.
7 Brereton Greenhous, Stephen Harris, et al., *The Crucible of War, 1939–1945: The Official History of The Royal Canadian Air Force*, vol. 3 (Toronto: University of Toronto Press, 1995), 808.
8 Desmond W. Piers, "HMCS *Algonquin*—Operation Neptune," University of Victoria Special Collections, 4.
9 "The Royal Canadian Navy's Part in the Invasion," 89.
10 Piers, 4.
11 G.W.L. Nicholson, *The Gunners of Canada*, vol. 2 (Toronto: McClelland & Stewart, 1972), 275.
12 H.S. Patterson, "Artillery Communications in Operation Overlord, Account by Maj. H.S. Patterson, OC 2 Coy, 3 CDN INF DIV SIGS," 018(D2), Directorate of History, Department of National Defence, 6.
13 Piers, 4.
14 B.B. Schofield, *Operation Nepture* (London: Ian Allan, 1974), 94–95.
15 Ibid., 44–45.
16 Ibid., 94.
17 Nicholson, 276.
18 Patterson, 6.
19 Fred Rogers, videotaped recollections in possession of the author, n.d.
20 James Douglas Baird, interview by William S. Thackray, 17, 27 June and 18 July 1980, University of Victoria Special Collections.

21 Patterson, 6.

22 Baird interview.

23 Nicholson, 277.

24 G.E.M. Ruffee and J.B. Dickie, *The History of the 14 Field Regiment, Royal Canadian Artillery: 1940–1945* (Amsterdam: Wereldbibliotheek NV, 1945), 26.

25 Okill Stuart, "D-Day—The Longest Day," *Quadrant*, December 2000, 17.

26 Jean E. Portugal, *We Were There: The Navy, the Army and the RCAF—A Record for Canada*, vol. 4 (Shelburne, ON: The Battered Silicon Dispatch Box, 1998), 1881–82.

27 Col. C.P. Stacey, *The Victory Campaign: The Operations in North-West Europe, 1944–1945*, vol. 3 (Ottawa: Queen's Printer, 1960), 102.

28 "The Royal Canadian Navy's Part in the Invasion," 90–91.

29 Fort Garry Horse War Diary, June 1944, Appendix 1, National Archives of Canada, 2.

30 A. Brandon Conron, *A History of the First Hussars Regiment, 1856–1980* (n.p., 1981), 50.

31 Ralph Burley, interview by John Gregory Thompson, Toronto, 12 August 2003.

32 Conron, 50.

33 Stuart, 17.

II: ROLL ME OVER, LAY ME DOWN

1 Royal Winnipeg Rifles War Diary, June 1944, RG24, National Archives of Canada, 3.

2 Roy Whitsed, *Canadians: A Battalion at War* (Mississauga, ON: Burlington Books, 1996), 3.

3 Queen's Own Rifles War Diary, June 1944, RG24, National Archives of Canada, n.p.

4 Canadian Scottish Regiment 1st Battalion, Regiment War Diary, June 1944, Appendix C COY, 1 C. Scot R. 31 May to 6 June 44, National Archives of Canada, 1.

5 Canadian Scottish Regiment 1st Battalion, War Diary, June 1944, RG24, National Archives of Canada, n.p.

6 C.M. Wightman Personal Diary, University of Victoria Special Collections, Reginald Roy Papers.

7 "The Royal Canadian Navy's Part in the Invasion," Directorate of History, Department of National Defence, 90.

8 Wightman diary.

9 Robert Lowder Seaborn, interview by Cameron Falconer, 23 February 1983, University of Victoria Special Collections.

10 Reginald Roy, *Ready for the Fray: The History of the Canadian Scottish Regiment (Princess Mary's), 1920 to 1955* (Vancouver: Evergreen Press, 1958), 211.

11 N.a., *The Canadians at War, 1939/45,* vol. 2 (Montreal: The Reader's Digest Assoc. [Canada], 1969), 442.

12 Russell Choat, interview by James Murphy, 27 June and 5, 11 July 1977. University of Victoria Special Collections.

13 J.H. Hamilton, "Normandy: 1944, Juno Beach," *Perspectives,* Alex Kuppers, ed. (Royal Winnipeg Rifles Assoc. British Columbia Branch, 2003), 27.

14 Charles Martin, *Battle Diary: From D-Day and Normandy to the Zuider Zee* (Toronto: Dundurn Press, 1994), 3–4.

15 Bill Bettridge, interview by John Gregory Thompson, Brampton, ON, 14 October 2003.

16 Gerry Cleveland interview by John Gregory Thompson, Port Colbourne, ON, 4 November 2003.

17 Fort Garry Horse War Diary, June 1944, Appendix 1, National Archives of Canada, 2.

18 A. Brandon Conron, *A History of the First Hussars Regiment, 1856–1980* (n.p., 1981), 51.

19 Jean E. Portugal, *We Were There: The Navy, the Army and the RCAF—A Record for Canada,* vol. 3 (Shelburne, ON: The Battered Silicon Dispatch Box, 1998), 1008–9.

20 Stan Seneco, interview by John Gregory Thompson, East York, ON, 3 November 2003.

21 Ibid.

22 1st Hussars War Diary, June 1944, Appendix 8: Account written by Sgt. Gariépy, National Archives of Canada, 1.

23 Lochie Fulton, interview by Ken MacLeod, Victoria, BC, 9 February 1998.

24 Martin, 4–5.

25 Cleveland interview.

26 Anthony Hopkins, *Songs from the Front and Rear: Canadian Servicemen's Songs of the Second World War* (Edmonton, Hurtig Publishers, 1979), 135.

27 Charles Richardson, interview by John Gregory Thompson, London, ON, 30 October 2003.

28 Gerry Purchase and Owen Cooke, "A Rideau Canal Tragedy," *Canadian Military History,* Winter 2002, 49–53.

29 Richardson interview.

30 Cleveland interview.

31 Whitsed, 3.

32 Col. C.P. Stacey, *The Victory Campaign: The Operations in North-West Europe, 1944–1945,* vol. 3 (Ottawa: Queen's Printer, 1960), 99–100.

33 Choat interview.

34 Bill Bury, interview by John Gregory Thompson, Hamilton, ON, 20 August 2003.

35 Larry Allen, "WWII Diary of L. Allen—The Story of a D-Day Soldier," 1st Hussars Regimental Museum.

36 Seneco interview.

37 Conron, 51–52.

38 Seneco interview.

39 Conron, 52.

40 Seneco interview.

41 Ralph Burley, interview by John Gregory Thompson, Toronto, 12 August 2003.

12: MERRY HELL

1 Lochie Fulton, interview by Ken MacLeod, Victoria, BC, 9 February 1998.

2 J.H. Hamilton, "Normandy: 1944, Juno Beach," *Perspectives*, Alex Kuppers, ed. (Royal Winnipeg Rifles Assoc. British Columbia Branch, 2003), 27.

3 Regina Rifles Regiment War Diary, June 1944, Intelligence Log Appendix, RG24, National Archives of Canada, Sheet 1.

4 Royal Winnipeg Rifles War Diary, June 1944, RG24, National Archives of Canada, 3.

5 Reginald Roy, *Ready for the Fray: The History of the Canadian Scottish Regiment (Princess Mary's), 1920 to 1955* (Vancouver: Evergreen Press, 1958), 212.

6 Ibid., 212–13.

7 Canadian Scottish Regiment 1st Battalion, Regiment War Diary, June 1944, Appendix C COY, 1 C. Scot R. 31 May to 6 June 44, RG24, National Archives of Canada, 1–2.

8 Roy, 213.

9 Maj. D.G. Crofton, "'C' Company—Landing on D-Day," Directorate of History, Department of National Defence, 1–2.

10 Ibid.

11 Fulton interview.

12 T. Robert Fowler, *Valour on Juno Beach: The Canadian Awards for Gallantry, D-Day, June 6, 1944* (Burnstown, ON: General Store Publishing, 1994), 51.

13 A. Brandon Conron, *A History of the First Hussars Regiment, 1856–1980* (n.p., 1981), 52–53.

14 Peter Simonds, *Maple Leaf Up, Maple Leaf Down: The Story of the Canadians in the Second World War* (New York: Island Press, 1946), 147.

15 Jake Miller, "D-Day—June 6, 1944," *Perspectives*, 51.

16 Bruce Tascona and Eric Wells, *Little Black Devils: A History of the Royal Winnipeg Rifles* (Winnipeg: Frye Publishing, 1983), 146.

17 Jim Parks, "Recollections—Excerpts," *Perspectives*, 132–33.

18 Jim Parks, interview by Ken MacLeod, Vancouver, November 1997.
19 Fowler, 48.
20 Stewart A.G. Mein, *Up the Johns! The Story of the Royal Regina Rifles* (North Battleford, SK: Turner-Warwick Publishers, 1992), 111.
21 "The Recollections of the Regina Rifles: N.W. Europe World War 2, June 6, 1944–May 8, 1945," (n.p., n.d.), n.p.
22 Ronald Gendall Shawcross, interview by Mark C. Hill, 14, 19 June 1985, University of Victoria Special Collections.
23 Mein, 110–11.
24 Shawcross interview.
25 1st Hussars War Diary, June 1944, Appendix 8: Account written by Sgt. Gariépy, RG24, National Archives of Canada, 1.
26 Col. C.P. Stacey, *The Victory Campaign: The Operations in North-West Europe, 1944–1945*, vol. 3 (Ottawa: The Queen's Printer, 1960), 105.
27 Bill Bury, interview by John Gregory Thompson, Hamilton, ON, 20 August 2003.
28 Larry Allen, "WWII Diary of L. Allen—The Story of a D-Day Soldier," 1st Hussars Regimental Museum.
29 Bury interview.
30 "Recollections of the Regina Rifles," n.p.
31 Stacey, 105.
32 Mein, 111.
33 "Recollections of the Regina Rifles," n.p.
34 Fowler, 45.

13: THE REAL THING
1   Gerry Cleveland, interview by John Gregory Thompson, Port Colbourne, ON, 4 November 2003.
2   Will R. Bird, *North Shore (New Brunswick) Regiment* (Fredericton, NB: Brunswick Press, 1963), 206.
3   Cleveland interview.
4   Ibid.
5   Bird, 200–201.
6   Col. C.P. Stacey, *The Victory Campaign: The Operations in North-West Europe, 1944–1945*, vol. 3 (Ottawa: Queen's Printer, 1960), 70.
7   Reginald Roy, *1944: The Canadians in Normandy* (Toronto: Macmillan of Canada, 1984), 17.
8   Stacey, 70.
9   Charles Richardson, interview by John Gregory Thompson, London, ON, 30 October 2003.
10 Bird, 203.
11 Ibid., 204.

12 R.M. Hickey, *The Scarlet Dawn* (Campbellton, NB: Tribune Publishers, 1949), 194.

13 Ibid., 194–95.

14 T. Robert Fowler, *Valour on Juno Beach: The Canadian Awards for Gallantry, D-Day, June 6, 1944* (Burnstown, ON: General Store Publishing, 1994), 32.

15 Joe Ryan, interview by John Gregory Thompson, Cobourg, ON, 6 November 2003.

16 Ibid.

17 Fowler, 26–27.

18 N.a., *Vanguard: The Fort Garry Horse in the Second World War* (Doetincham, Holland: Uitgevers–Maatschappij, C. Misset NV, n.d.), 132.

19 Fort Garry Horse War Diary, June 1944, Appendix No. 1, RG 24, National Archives of Canada, 2.

20 G.W.L. Nicholson, *The Gunners of Canada*, vol. 2 (Toronto: McClelland & Stewart, 1972), 279–80.

21 Bird, 214.

22 Ibid., 218.

23 Jack Springer, interview by John Gregory Thompson, London, ON, 1 November 2003.

24 Bird, 218.

25 Ibid.

26 Ibid., 218–19.

27 North Shore (New Brunswick) Regiment War Diary, June 1944, RG 24, National Archives of Canada, 2.

28 Hickey, 196–97.

29 Fowler, 29–30.

30 Springer interview.

31 N.a., *The Canadians at War, 1939/45*, vol. 2 (Montreal: The Reader's Digest Assoc. [Canada], 1969), 441–42.

32 Jean E. Portugal, *We Were There: The Navy, the Army and the RCAF—A Record for Canada*, vol. 4 (Shelburne, ON: The Battered Silicon Dispatch Box, 1998), 1636.

33 Bird, 217.

34 Bird, 211.

14: GO! GO! GO!

1 N.a., *The Canadians at War, 1939/45*, vol. 2 (Montreal: The Reader's Digest Assoc. (Canada), 1969), 442.

2 Roy Whitsed, *Canadians: A Battalion at War* (Mississauga, ON: Burlington Books, 1996), 4.

3 Rolph Jackson, interview by John Gregory Thompson, Toronto, 2 September 2003.

4 Whitsed, 4–5.

5 Jackson interview.

6 Jean E. Portugal, *We Were There: The Navy, the Army and the RCAF—A Record for Canada,* vol. 2 (Shelburne, ON: The Battered Silicon Dispatch Box, 1998), 612.

7 T. Robert Fowler, *Valour on Juno Beach: The Canadian Awards for Gallantry, D-Day, June 6, 1944* (Burnstown, ON: General Store Publishing, 1994), 38–39.

8 W.T. Barnard, *The Queen's Own Rifles of Canada, 1860–1960: One Hundred Years of Canada* (Don Mills: Ontario Publishing Co., 1960), 195.

9 Whitsed, 5.

10 *Canadians at War, 1939/45,* 442.

11 Charles Martin, *Battle Diary: From D-Day and Normandy to the Zuider Zee* (Toronto: Dundurn Press, 1994), 6–7.

12 Bill Bettridge, interview by John Gregory Thompson, Brampton, ON, 14 October 2003.

13 Martin, 8.

14 Bettridge interview.

15 Ibid.

16 Martin, 9–11.

17 Bettridge interview.

18 Martin, 11.

19 Dave Kingston, interview by John Gregory Thompson, Mississauga, ON, 10 September 2003.

20 Portugal, *We Were There,* vol. 3, 1430–31.

21 Jim McCullough, interview by John Gregory Thompson, Loretto, ON, 9 September 2003.

22 Jack Martin, interview by John Gregory Thompson, Scarborough, ON, 1 October 2003.

23 Kingston interview.

24 G.W.L. Nicholson, *The Gunners of Canada,* vol. 2 (Toronto: McClelland & Stewart, 1972), 279.

25 Queen's Own Rifles of Canada War Diary, June 1944, RG24, National Archives of Canada, n.p.

26 Dave Fletcher, interview by John Gregory Thompson, Streetsville, ON, 2 September 2003.

27 McCullough interview.

28 Kingston interview.

15: NOTHING FOR SHAME

1 John A. Willes, *Out of the Clouds: The History of the 1st Canadian Parachute Battalion* (Port Perry, ON: Port Perry Printing, 1995), 83–84.

2 Brian Nolan, *Airborne: The Heroic Story of the 1st Canadian Parachute Battalion in the Second World War* (Toronto: Lester Publishing Limited, 1995), 100–101.
3 Dan Hartigan, *A Rising of Courage: Canada's Paratroops in the Liberation of Normandy* (Calgary: Drop Zone Publishers, 2000), 251.
4 Nolan, 100.
5 Willes, 77.
6 Hartigan, 154–155.
7 N.a., "Canadian Parachute Battalion in Normandy: Historical Sketch," 25 September 1952, 145.4013(D4), Directorate of History, Department of National Defence, 7.
8 Willes, 78.
9 1st Canadian Parachute Battalion War Diary, June 1944, RG24, National Archives of Canada, 4–5.
10 Napier Crookenden, *Dropzone Normandy: The Story of the American and British Airborne Assault on D-Day 1944* (New York: Charles Scribner's Sons, 1976), 31.
11 Hartigan, 126.
12 Ibid., 117–18.
13 Ibid., 127–28.
14 Ibid., 129–30.
15 Willes, 80–81.
16 Hartigan, 130–31.
17 1st Canadian Parachute Battalion War Diary, 5.
18 Willes, 81.
19 1st Canadian Parachute Battalion War Diary, 2.
20 John R. Madden, recorded recollections, 1987, University of Victoria Special Collections.
21 Nolan, 98.
22 Madden recollections.

16: IN GOOD FETTLE

1 Walter Warlimont, "The Invasion," *Fighting the Invasion: The German Army at D-Day*, David C. Isby, ed. (London: Greenhill Books, 2000), 92.
2 "Campaign in France, 1944: Answers by Gen. Blumentritt to questions submitted by Chester Wilmot," University of Victoria Special Collections, 2.
3 Ibid.
4 Fritz Krämer, "1st SS Panzer Corps Moves Up to Counterattack," *Fighting the Invasion*, David C. Isby, ed., 242.
5 "Campaign in France, 1944: Answers by Gen. Blumentritt," 2.
6 Tony Foster, *Meeting of Generals* (Agincourt, ON: Methuen, 1986), 306.

7 Ibid., 2–3.
8 Royal Winnipeg Rifles War Diary, June 1944, RG24, National Archives of Canada, 3.
9 Ibid.
10 John (Jack) McLean, "Remembering D-Day," *Perspectives*, Alex Kuppers, ed. (Royal Winnipeg Rifles Assoc. British Columbia Branch, 2003), 56–59.
11 Jack McLean, interview by Ken MacLeod, Vancouver, September 1997.
12 Georges Lecarpentier, interview by author, Courseulles-sur-Mer, 23 May 2003.
13 Maj. D.G. Crofton, "'C' Company—Landing on D-Day," 145.2C4013(D4), Directorate of History, Department of National Defence, 1–2.
14 Reginald Roy, *Ready for the Fray: The History of the Canadian Scottish Regiment (Princess Mary's), 1920 to 1955* (Vancouver: Evergreen Press, 1958), 221.
15 Crofton, 2.
16 Lt. Col. F.N. Cabeldu, "Battle Narrative of the Normandy Assault and First Counter-Attack," 145.2C4013(D2), Directorate of History, Department of National Defence, 2.
17 Roy, 215.
18 Ibid.
19 Jack Daubs, interview by John Gregory Thompson, London, ON, 9 October 2003.
20 Roy, 215.
21 Capt. P.F. Ramsay, "Battle Narrative: 'B' Coy, 1 C Scot R," 145.2C4(D6), Directorate of History, Department of National Defence, 1.
22 Ibid.
23 Cabeldu, 2.
24 Ramsay, 2.
25 Arthur Howard Plows, interview by Chris D. Main, 18, 31 August 1978, University of Victoria Special Collections.
26 Roy, 219–20.
27 Lt. Col. R.H. Webb, "12 Cdn Fd Regt. 23 June 44, Fd Arty in the Assault," 23 June 1944, Reginald Roy Collection, University of Victoria Special Collections, 1.
28 A. Brandon Conron, *A History of the First Hussars Regiment, 1856–1980* (n.p., 1981), 59.
29 Bill McCormick, interview by John Gregory Thompson, Gault, ON, 3 October 2003.
30 G.T. MacEwan, "D Day and the Counter-Attack on Putot-en-Bessin," 145.C4013(D3), Directorate of History, Department of National Defence, 4.
31 Daubs interview.

32 Cabeldu, 2.
33 Conron, 60.
34 MacEwan, 4.
35 Cabeldu, 2.
36 Royal Winnipeg Rifles War Diary, 4.
37 Regina Rifles Regiment, 1st Battalion War Diary, June 1944, RG 24, vol. 15198, National Archives of Canada, n.p.

17: AN AWFUL SHAMBLES

1 Col. C.P. Stacey, *The Victory Campaign: The Operations in North-West Europe, 1944–1945*, vol. 3 (Ottawa: Queen's Printer, 1960), 109.
2 Le Régiment de la Chaudière War Diary, June 1944 (trans. Tony Poulin from RG 24, National Archives of Canada), in possession of the author, n.p.
3 John Marteinson and Michael R. McNorgan, *The Royal Canadian Armoured Corps: An Illustrated History* (Toronto: Robin Brass Studio, 2000), 239.
4 W.T. Barnard, *The Queen's Own Rifles of Canada, 1860–1960: One Hundred Years of Canada* (Don Mills: Ontario Publishing Co., 1960), 195.
5 Le Régiment de la Chaudière War Diary, n.p.
6 Jack Martin, interview by John Gregory Thompson, Scarborough, ON, 1 October 2003.
7 Ibid.
8 Le Régiment de la Chaudière War Diary, n.p.
9 Jean E. Portugal, *We Were There: The Navy, the Army and the RCAF—A Record for Canada*, vol. 4 (Shelburne, ON: The Battered Silicon Dispatch Box, 1998), 1898.
10 Martin interview.
11 Portugal, 1898.
12 G.W.L. Nicholson, *The Gunners of Canada*, vol. 2 (Toronto: McClelland & Stewart, 1972), 279.
13 14th Field Regiment Royal Canadian Artillery War Diary, June 1944, RG 24, National Archives of Canada, 4.
14 Le Régiment de la Chaudière War Diary, n.p.
15 Canadian Operations in North-West Europe, June 1944: Extracts from Memoranda (Series 1), "Comments by Brig. K.G. Blackader, Commander 8 CDN INF BDE, as Given to Hist Offr, 24 June 44," Directorate of History, Department of National Defence, 5.
16 Terry Copp and Robert Vogel, *Maple Leaf Route: Caen* (Alma, ON: Maple Leaf Route, 1983), 56.
17 Ernest Côté, interview by Michael Boire, Ottawa, 14 November 2003.
18 A.J. Kerry and W.A. McDill, *History of the Corps of Royal Canadian Engineers*, vol. 2 (Ottawa: The Military Engineers Assoc. of Canada, 1966), 266–68.

19 Copp and Vogel, 56.

20 Ross Munro, *Gauntlet to Overlord: The Story of the Canadian Army* (Toronto: Macmillan Co. of Canada, 1946), 64.

21 Peter Hinton, interview by Mark Hill, 22 July 1985, University of Victoria Special Collections.

22 Ibid.

23 Stacey, 101.

24 "The Royal Canadian Navy's Part in the Invasion," Directorate of History, Department of National Defence, 100–101.

25 Ibid., 94–95.

26 Highland Light Infantry of Canada War Diary, June 1944, RG24, National Archives of Canada, 6.

27 Ibid., 7.

28 Copp and Vogel, 56–58.

29 14th Field Regiment, Royal Canadian Artillery War Diary, June 1944, RG24, National Archives of Canada, 3.

30 Portugal, 1883.

31 Canadian Operations in North-West Europe, June 1944, "Comments by Brig. K.G. Blackader," 5.

32 T. Robert Fowler, *Valour on Juno Beach: The Canadian Awards for Gallantry, D-Day, June 6, 1944* (Burnstown, ON: General Store Publishing, 1994), 59–60.

33 Fort Garry Horse War Diary, June 1944, Appendix 1, RG24, National Archives of Canada, 3.

34 14th Field Regiment, RCA War Diary, 4.

35 Bill McAndrew, Donald E. Graves, and Michael Whitby, *Normandy 1944: The Canadian Summer* (Montreal: Éditions Art Global, 1994), 43.

36 Desmond W. Piers, "HMCS *Algonquin*—Operation Neptune," University of Victoria Special Collections, 5.

37 McAndrew et al., 43.

38 Piers, 5.

39 McAndrew et al., 46.

40 Le Régiment de la Chaudière War Diary, n.p.

41 Jacques Castonguay and Armand Ross, *Le Régiment de la Chaudière* (Lévis, PQ: n.p., 1983), 245.

18: A FAIRLY RUGGED DAY

1 Col. C.P. Stacey, *The Victory Campaign: The Operations in North-West Europe, 1944–1945*, vol. 3 (Ottawa: Queen's Printer, 1960), 111.

2 Will R. Bird, *North Shore (New Brunswick) Regiment* (Fredericton, NB: Brunswick Press, 1963), 223.

3 Ibid., 213.

4 N.a., *Vanguard: The Fort Garry Horse in the Second World War* (Doetincham, Holland: Uitgevers–Maatschappij, C. Misset NV, n.d.), 133.

5 Jean E. Portugal, *We Were There: The Navy, the Army and the RCAF—A Record for Canada*, vol. 4 (Shelburne, ON: The Battered Silicon Dispatch Box, 1998), 1672–73.

6 Bird, 220.

7 Ibid., 221.

8 T. Robert Fowler, *Valour on Juno Beach: The Canadian Awards for Gallantry, D-Day, June 6, 1944* (Burnstown, ON: General Store Publishing, 1994), 62.

9 Portugal, *We Were There*, vol. 3 (Shelburne, ON: The Battered Silicon Dispatch Box, 1998), 1444–45.

10 *Vanguard*, 133.

11 Portugal, vol. 3, 1443–44.

12 Ibid., 1444.

13 Reginald Roy, *1944: The Canadians in Normandy* (Toronto: Macmillan of Canada, 1984), 22.

14 Bird, 222.

15 Ibid., 222–23.

16 Ibid., 224–25.

17 Roy, 22.

18 Bird, 223.

19 Stacey, 650.

20 Bird, 232–33.

21 Ibid., 226–27.

19: BEGINNING OF THE END

1 Freiherr Geyr von Schweppenburg, "The 21st Panzer Division's Situation (6 June 1944)," *Fighting the Invasion: The German Army at D-Day*, David C. Isby, ed. (London: Greenhill Books, 2000), 236.

2 Hans von Luck, *Panzer Grenadier: The Memoirs of Colonel Hans von Luck* (Westport, CT: Praeger Publishers, 1989), 137–38.

3 Ibid., 138.

4 Ibid., 132–33.

5 Ibid., 139.

6 Edgar Feuchtinger, "The 21st Panzer Division on 6 June 1944," *Fighting the Invasion: The German Army at D-Day*, David C. Isby, ed. (London: Greenhill Books, 2000), 222.

7 Edgar Feuchtinger, "Counterattack of the 21st Panzer Division," *Fighting the Invasion*, David C. Isby, ed., 241.

8 von Luck, 141–42.

9 Col. C.P. Stacey, *The Victory Campaign: The Operations in North-West Europe, 1944–1945*, vol. 3 (Ottawa: Queen's Printer, 1960), 122.

10 von Luck, 142.

11 Tony Foster, *Meeting of Generals* (Agincourt, ON: Methuen, 1986), 307.

12 Feuchtinger, "Counterattack of the 21st Panzer Division," 239.

13 von Luck, 142.

14 Ibid.

15 Feuchtinger, "Counterattack of the 21st Panzer Division," 239–40.

16 Carlo D'Este, *Decision in Normandy: The Unwritten Story of Montgomery and the Allied Campaign* (London: Penguin Books, 2001), 138–40.

17 Feuchtinger, "Counterattack of the 21st Panzer Division," 240.

18 Foster, 309.

19 Feuchtinger, "Counterattack of the 21st Panzer Division," 240.

20 Fritz Krämer, "1st SS Panzer Corps Moves Up to Counterattack," *Fighting the Invasion*, David C. Isby, ed., 244.

20: A GREAT INITIATION

1 14th Field Regiment, Royal Canadian Artillery War Diary, June 1944, RG24, National Archives of Canada, 4.

2 Jack Byrne, interview by John Gregory Thompson, St. Joseph, ON, 10 October 2003.

3 H.M. Jackson, *The Sherbrooke Regiment (12th Armoured Regiment)* (n.p., 1958), 122–23.

4 Will Bird, *No Retreating Footsteps: The Story of the North Nova Scotia Highlanders* (Hantsport, NS: Lancelot Press, 1983), 67–68.

5 North Nova Scotia Highlanders War Diary, June 1944, RG24, National Archives of Canada, 4.

6 Sherbrooke Fusiliers Regiment War Diary, June 1944, RG24, National Archives of Canada, 2.

7 Byrne interview.

8 Jean E. Portugal, *We Were There: The Navy, the Army and the RCAF—A Record for Canada*, vol. 5 (Shelburne, ON: The Battered Silicon Dispatch Box, 1998), 2535.

9 Ibid.

10 Ibid., 2428–29.

11 N.a., *Vanguard: The Fort Garry Horse in the Second World War* (Doetincham, Holland: Uitgevers–Maatschappij, C. Misset NV, n.d.), 17.

12 Portugal, *We Were There*, vol. 3, 1431–32.

13 *Vanguard*, 18.

14 Ibid.

15 Portugal, *We Were There*, vol. 4, 1457.

16 Ibid., 1458.

17 Ibid., 1433.

18 Jacques Castonguay and Armand Ross, *Le Régiment de la Chaudière* (Lévis, PQ: n.p., 1983), 247–48.

19 Le Régiment de la Chaudière War Diary, June 1944 (trans. Tony Poulin from RG24, National Archives of Canada), in possession of the author, n.p.

20 *Vanguard,* 18.

21 Orville Cook, interview by John Gregory Thompson, Holland Centre, ON, 7 October 2003.

22 Charles Martin, *Battle Diary: From D-Day and Normandy to the Zuider Zee* (Toronto: Dundurn Press, 1994), 14.

23 Roger Chevalier, interview by author, Courseulles-sur-Mer, 23 May 2003.

24 W.T. Barnard, *The Queen's Own Rifles of Canada, 1860–1960: One Hundred Years of Canada* (Don Mills: Ontario Publishing Co., 1960), 196.

25 Martin, 14.

26 *Vanguard,* 19.

27 Roy Whitsed, *Canadians: A Battalion at War* (Mississauga, ON: Burlington Books, 1996), 19.

28 Ibid.

29 Ibid., 20.

30 Ibid.

31 Cook interview.

32 Whitsed, 20.

33 Cook interview.

34 Whitsed, 21.

35 Sherbrooke Fusiliers War Diary, 3.

36 Bird, 66.

37 Ibid.

38 Ibid., 67.

39 North Nova Scotia Highlanders War Diary, 5.

40 Will Bird, *The Two Jacks: The Amazing Adventures of Major Jack M. Veness and Major Jack L. Fairweather* (Toronto: Ryerson Press, 1954), 5–6.

41 Reginald Roy, *1944: The Canadians in Normandy* (Toronto: Macmillan of Canada, 1984), 21.

42 Sherbrooke Fusiliers War Diary, 3.

43 Stormont, Dundas and Glengarry Highlanders War Diary, June 1944, RG24, National Archives of Canada, n.p.

44 Highland Light Infantry of Canada War Diary, June 1944, RG24, National Archives of Canada, 7.

21: AT ALL COSTS

1 Joseph James Andrews, interview by Cameron Falconer, 8 March 1983, University of Victoria Special Collections.

2 Reginald Roy, *Ready for the Fray: The History of the Canadian Scottish Regiment (Princess Mary's), 1920 to 1955* (Vancouver: Evergreen Press, 1958), 224–25.

3 G.T. MacEwan, "D Day and the Counter-Attack on Putot-en-Bessin," 145.C4013(D3), Directorate of History, Department of National Defence, 4–5.

4 Roy, 225.

5 A. Brandon Conron, *A History of the First Hussars Regiment, 1856–1980* (n.p., 1981), 56.

6 1st Hussars War Diary, June 1944, Appendix 8: Account written by Sgt. Gariépy, RG24, National Archives of Canada, 2.

7 Regina Rifle Regiment War Diary, June 1944, National Archives of Canada, n.p.

8 1st Hussars War Diary, Appendix 8, 2.

9 Alexander McKee, *Caen: Anvil of Victory* (London: Souvenir Press, 1964), 57–58.

10 Conron, 58.

11 McKee, 57–58.

12 1st Hussars War Diary, Appendix 8, 2.

13 Eric Luxton, ed., *1st Battalion, The Regina Rifle Regiment, 1939–1946* (Regina: The Regiment, 1946), 38.

14 Edgar Feuchtinger, "Counterattack of the 21st Panzer Division," *Fighting the Invasion: The German Army at D-Day,* David C. Isby, ed. (London: Greenhill Books, 2000), 240.

15 "Campaign in France, 1944: Answers by Gen. Blumentritt to questions submitted by Chester Wilmot," University of Victoria Special Collections, 3.

16 Ibid., 4.

17 Fritz Krämer, "1st SS Panzer Corps Moves Up to Counterattack," *Fighting the Invasion,* David C. Isby, ed. (London: Greenhill Books, 2000), 243.

18 Freiherr Geyr von Schweppenburg, "Invasion," *Fighting the Invasion,* David C. Isby, ed., 226.

19 Tony Foster, *Meeting of Generals* (Agincourt, ON: Methuen, 1986), 307–8.

20 Kurt Meyer, *Grenadier* (Winnipeg: J.J. Fedorowicz, 1994), 117.

21 Ibid., 117–19.

22 Krämer, 243.

23 Ibid., 244.

24 Ibid.

25 Ibid., 245–46.

26 Meyer, 118–19.

27 Ibid., 120.

28 Ibid., 118.

22: A DEGREE OF GALLANTRY

1 Bill McCormick interview, by John Gregory Thompson, Gault, ON, 3 October 2003.

2 T. Robert Fowler, *Valour on Juno Beach: The Canadian Awards for Gallantry, D-Day, June 6, 1944* (Burnstown, ON: General Store Publishing, 1994), 16.

3 Stan Creaser, "War Experiences: January 16, 1999," *Perspectives,* Alex Kuppers, ed. (Royal Winnipeg Rifles Assoc. British Columbia Branch, 2003), 29.

4 Fowler, 16.

5 McCormick interview.

6 Royal Winnipeg Rifles War Diary, June 1944, RG24, National Archives of Canada, 5.

7 Bill McCormick, "Armistice Day Address," n.d., in possession of the author.

8 Bill McCormick telephone interview by John Gregory Thompson, 14 February 2004.

9 McCormick interview, 3 October 2003.

10 Capt. P.F. Ramsay, "Battle Narrative: 'B' Coy, 1 C Scot R," 145.2C4(D6), Directorate of History, Department of National Defence, 2.

11 G.T. MacEwan, "D Day and the Counter-Attack on Putot-en-Bessin," 145.C4013(D3), Directorate of History, Department of National Defence, 5.

12 Reginald Roy, *Ready for the Fray: The History of the Canadian Scottish Regiment (Princess Mary's), 1920 to 1955* (Vancouver: Evergreen Press, 1958), 225–26.

13 McCormick interview, 3 October 2003.

14 Roy, 225–26.

15 McCormick interview, 3 October 2003.

23: SUCH A SAD DAY

1 Col. C.P. Stacey, *The Victory Campaign: The Operations in North-West Europe, 1944–1945,* vol. 3 (Ottawa: Queen's Printer, 1960), 650–52.

2 "The Royal Canadian Navy's Part in the Invasion," Directorate of History, Department of National Defence, 103–4.

3 Ibid., 94–96.

4 Trafford Leigh-Mallory, "Air Operations by the Allied Expeditionary Air Force in N.W. Europe from November 15th, 1943 to September 30th, 1944," Fourth Supplement, *The London Gazette,* 31 December 1946, 55.

5 Jean E. Portugal, *We Were There: The Navy, the Army and the RCAF—A Record for Canada,* vol. 7 (Shelburne, ON: The Battered Silicon Dispatch Box, 1998), 3277.

6 Ibid., 3284.

7 Ibid., 3312.

8 Reginald Roy, *1944: The Canadians in Normandy* (Toronto: Macmillan of Canada, 1984), 23.

9 Granatstein Papers, 17 April 1991 letter from B.D. Hunt, Royal Military College to Granatstein, York University Archives and Special Collections, Scott Library.

10 Ernest Côté, interview by Michael Boire, Ottawa, 14 November 2003.

11 Ibid.

12 Stacey, 114.

13 Ibid., 116.

14 Ross Munro, *Gauntlet to Overlord: The Story of the Canadian Army* (Toronto: Macmillan of Canada, 1946), 79.

15 Ibid., 72.

16 Ibid., 71.

17 W.R. Freadsby, ed., *Official History of the Canadian Medical Services, 1939–1945, Vol. 1: Organization and Campaigns* (Ottawa: Queen's Printer, 1956), 221–23.

18 Rolph Jackson, interview by John Gregory Thompson, Toronto, 2 September 2003.

19 N.a., *The Canadians at War, 1939/45,* vol 2. (Montreal: Reader's Digest Assoc. [Canada], 1969), 445.

20 Jack Springer, interview by John Gregory Thompson, London, ON, 1 November 2003.

21 Charles Martin, *Battle Diary: From D-Day and Normandy to the Zuider Zee* (Toronto: Dundurn Press, 1994), 14–15.

22 Ibid., 15.

23 Ibid., 15–16.

BOOKS

Barnard, W.T. *The Queen's Own Rifles of Canada, 1860–1960: One Hundred Years of Canada.* Don Mills: Ontario Publishing Co., 1960.

Bashow, David. *All the Fine Young Eagles: In the Cockpit with Canada's Second World War Fighter Pilots.* Toronto: Stoddart, 1996.

Battledress Ballads: 3 Canadian Infantry Division, n.p., n.d.

Bennett, Ralph. *Ultra in the West: The Normandy Campaign, 1944–45.* London: Hutchinson & Co., 1979.

Bird, Will R. *North Shore (New Brunswick) Regiment.* Fredericton, NB: Brunswick Press, 1963.

———. *No Retreating Footsteps: The Story of the North Nova Scotia Highlanders.* Hantsport, NS: Lancelot Press, 1983.

———. *The Two Jacks: The Amazing Adventures of Major Jack M. Veness and Major Jack L. Fairweather.* Toronto: Ryerson Press, 1954.

Boss, William. *Up the Glens: Stormont, Dundas and Glengarry Highlanders, 1783–1994,* 2nd ed. Cornwall, ON: Old Book Store, 1995.

The Canadians at War, 1939/45, vol. 2. Montreal: Reader's Digest Assoc. (Canada), 1969.

Castonguay, Jacques and Armand Ross. *Le Régiment de la Chaudière.* Lévis, PQ: n.p., 1983.

Conron, A. Brandon. *A History of the First Hussars Regiment, 1856–1980.* n.p., 1981.

Copp, Terry and William McAndrew. *Battle Exhaustion.* Montreal: McGill-Queen's University Press, 1990.

——— and Robert Vogel. *Maple Leaf Route: Caen.* Alma, ON: Maple Leaf Route, 1983.

Crookenden, Napier. *Dropzone Normandy: The Story of the American and British Airborne Assault on D-Day 1944.* New York: Charles Scribner's Sons, 1976.

D'Este, Carlo. *Decision in Normandy: The Unwritten Story of Montgomery and the Allied Campaign.* London: Penguin Books, 2001.

1st Battalion, The Highland Light Infantry of Canada: 1940–1945. Gault, ON: Highland Light Infantry of Canada Assoc., 1951.

Flatt, S.A. *History of the 6th Field Company Royal Canadian Engineers: 1939–1945.* Vancouver: Wrigley Printing Co., n.d.

Foster, Tony. *Meeting of Generals*. Agincourt, ON: Methuen, 1986.

Fowler, T. Robert. *Valour on Juno Beach: The Canadian Awards for Gallantry, D-Day, June 6, 1944*. Burnstown, ON: General Store Publishing, 1994.

Freasby, W.R., ed., *Official History of the Canadian Medical Services, 1939–1945, Vol. 1: Organization and Campaigns*. Ottawa: Queen's Printer, 1956.

———. *Official History of the Canadian Medical Services, 1939–1945, Vol. 2: Clinical Subjects*. Ottawa: Queen's Printer, 1953.

Granatstein, J.L. *The Generals: The Canadian Army's Senior Commanders in the Second World War*. Toronto: Stoddart, 1993.

——— and Desmond Morton. *Bloody Victory: Canadians and the D-Day Campaign*. Toronto: Lester & Orpen Dennys, 1984.

Greenhous, Brereton and Stephen Harris, et. al. *The Crucible of War, 1939–1945: The Official History of the Royal Canadian Air Force*, vol. 3. Toronto: University of Toronto Press, 1995.

Hanson, John P. "Letter 12 November 1949 in Correspondence re Ops 1st Cdn. Para Bn from various officers." Directorate of History, Department of National Defence.

Hartigan, Dan. *A Rising of Courage: Canada's Paratroops in the Liberation of Normandy*. Calgary: Drop Zone Publishers, 2000.

Hastings, Max. *Overlord: D-Day and the Battle of Normandy*. New York: Simon & Schuster, 1984.

Hickey, R.M. *The Scarlet Dawn*. Campbellton, NB: Tribune Publishers, 1949.

Holman, Gordon. *Stand by to Beach*. London: Hodder & Stoughton, 1944.

Hopkins, Anthony. *Songs from the Front and Rear: Canadian Servicemen's Songs of the Second World War*. Edmonton: Hurtig Publishers, 1979.

Isby, David C., ed. *Fighting the Invasion: The German Army at D-Day*. London: Greenhill Books, 2000.

Jackson, H.M. *The Sherbrooke Regiment (12th Armoured Regiment)*. N.p., 1958.

Kerry, A.J. and W.A. McDill. *History of the Corps of Royal Canadian Engineers*, vol. 2. Ottawa: The Military Engineers Assoc. of Canada, 1966.

Kuppers, Alex, ed. *Perspectives*. Royal Winnipeg Rifles Assoc. British Columbia Branch, 2003.

Liddell Hart, B.H. *History of the Second World War*. New York: G.P. Putnam's Sons, 1970.

Luxton, Eric, ed. *1st Battalion, The Regina Rifles Regiment, 1939–1946*. Regina: The Regiment, 1946.

McAndrew, Bill; Donald Graves, and Michael Whitby. *Normandy 1944: The Canadian Summer*. Montreal: Éditions Art Global, 1994.

McKee, Alex. *Caen: Anvil of Victory*. London: Souvenir Press, 1964.

Marteinson, John and Michael R. McNorgan. *The Royal Canadian Armoured Corps: An Illustrated History*. Toronto: Robin Brass Studio, 2000.

Martin, Charles Cromwell. *Battle Diary: From D-Day and Normandy to the Zuider Zee*. Toronto: Dundurn Press, 1994.

Mein, Stewart A.G. *Up the Johns! The Story of the Royal Regina Rifles*. North Battleford, SK: Turner-Warwick Publications, 1992.

Meyer, Kurt. *Grenadier*. Winnipeg: J.J. Fedorowicz, 1994.

Moir, John S., ed. *History of the Royal Canadian Corps of Signals, 1903–1961*. Ottawa: Corps Committee Royal Canadian Corps of Signals, 1962.

Munro, Ross. *Gauntlet to Overlord: The Story of the Canadian Army*. Toronto: Macmillan Co. of Canada, 1946.

Nicholson, G.W.L. *The Gunners of Canada*, vol. 2. Toronto: McClelland & Stewart, 1972.

Nolan, Brian. *Airborne: The Heroic Story of the 1st Canadian Parachute Battalion in the Second World War*. Toronto: Lester Publishing, 1995.

Portugal, Jean E. *We Were There: The Navy, the Army and the RCAF—A Record for Canada*, vol. 1–7. Shelburne, ON: The Battered Silicon Dispatch Box, 1998.

Ross, Richard M. *The History of the 1st Battalion Cameron Highlanders of Ottawa (MG)*. N.p, n.d.

Roy, Reginald H. *1944: The Canadians in Normandy*. Toronto: MacMillan of Canada, 1984.

———. *Ready for the Fray: The History of the Canadian Scottish Regiment (Princess Mary's), 1920 to 1955*. Vancouver: Evergreen Press, 1958.

Ruffee, G.E.M. and J.B. Dickie. *The History of the 14 Field Regiment Royal Canadian Artillery, 1940–1945*. Amsterdam: Wereldbibliotheek, NV, 1945.

Schofield, B.B. *Operation Neptune*. London: Ian Allan, 1974.

Service, G.T. *The Gate: A History of the Fort Garry Horse*. Calgary: n.p., 1971.

Simonds, Peter. *Maple Leaf Up, Maple Leaf Down: The Story of the Canadians in the Second World War*. New York: Island Press, 1946.

Stacey, Col. C.P. *The Victory Campaign: The Operations in North-West Europe, 1944–1945*, vol. 3. Ottawa: Queen's Printer, 1960.

Tascona, Bruce and Eric Wells. *Little Black Devils: A History of the Royal Winnipeg Rifles*. Winnipeg: Frye Publishing, 1983.

Vanguard: The Fort Garry Horse in the Second World War. Doetincham, Holland: Uitgevers-Maatschappij, C. Misset, NV, n.d.

von Luck, Hans. *Panzer Grenadier: The Memoirs of Colonel Hans von Luck*. Westport, CT: Praeger Publishers, 1989.

Warren, Arnold. *Wait for the Waggon: The Story of the Royal Canadian Army Service Corps*. Toronto: McClelland & Stewart, 1961.

Whitsed, Roy. *Canadians: A Battalion at War*. Mississauga, ON: Burlington Books, 1996.

Willes, John A. *Out of the Clouds: The History of the 1st Canadian Parachute Battalion*. Port Perry, ON: Port Perry Printing, 1995.

394 / JUNO BEACH

MAGAZINES, NEWSPAPERS, AND ARTICLES

Leigh-Mallory, Trafford. "Air Operations by the Allied Expeditionary Air Force in N.W. Europe from November 15th, 1943 to September 30th, 1944," Fourth Supplement, 1946. *The London Gazette*, 31 December: 37–62.

Morgan, F.E. "War Document, F.E. Morgan to British Chiefs of Staff," 15 July 1943, *Encyclopedia Britannica*, 1998–1999.

Purchase, Gerry and Owen Cooke. "A Rideau Canal Tragedy." *Canadian Military History*. Winter 2002: 49–53.

Stuart, Okill. "D-Day—The Longest Day," 2000. *Quadrant*, December: 17–19.

UNPUBLISHED MATERIALS

Allen, L. "WWII Diary of L. Allen—The Story of a D-Day Soldier." 1st Hussars Regimental Museum.

Andrews, J.J. (Maj.). "Battle Narrative—D Day and the Counter Attack at Putot-en-Bessin," 145.2C4(D5). Directorate of History, Department of National Defence.

"Attacks on Coastal Defence Batteries by Bomber Command," 181.003(D1957). Directorate of History, Department of National Defence.

Cabeldu, F.N. (Lt. Col.). "Battle Narrative of the Normandy Assault and First Counter-Attack," 145.2C4013(D2). Directorate of History, Department of National Defence.

———. "Narrative of Normandy Assault," 145.2C4013(D1). Directorate of History, Department of National Defence.

Cameron Highlanders of Ottawa (MG) War Diary, June 1944. RG24. National Archives of Canada.

"Campaign in France, 1944: Answers by Gen. Blumentritt to questions submitted by Chester Wilmot," University of Victoria Special Collections.

Canadian Operations in North-West Europe, June 1944: Extracts from Memoranda (Series 1), 018(D13). Directorate of History, Department of National Defence.

Canadian Operations in North-West Europe, August 1944: Extracts from Memoranda (Series 7). University of Victoria Special Collections, Reginald Roy Collection.

Canadian Parachute Battalion Correspondence re: Ops 1st Cdn. Para. Bn. from various officers (Cunningham, Hanson, Bradbrooke), 145.4013(D5). Directorate of History, Department of National Defence.

Canadian Scottish Regiment, 1st Battalion War Diary, June 1944. RG24. National Archives of Canada.

Crerar Papers. "Appointments and Promotions—Officers, Period Feb. 1942 to January 1943," MG30 E157, vol. 5. National Archives of Canada.

Crofton, D.G. (Maj.). "'C' Company—Landing on 'D' Day," 145.2C4013(D4). Directorate of History, Department of National Defence.

Dodds, R.V. "War Museum Query re: RCAF Activity on D-day," 16 July 1968, 181AH.003(D1). Directorate of History, Department of National Defence.

8th Canadian Infantry Brigade War Diary, June 1944. RG24. National Archives of Canada.

5th Canadian Field Company, Royal Canadian Engineers War Diary, June 1944. RG24. National Archives of Canada.

1st Canadian Parachute Battalion War Diary, June 1944. RG24. National Archives of Canada.

1st Hussars (6th Canadian Armoured Regiment) War Diary, June 1944. RG24. National Archives of Canada.

Fort Garry Horse (10th Canadian Armoured Regiment) War Diary, June 1944. RG24. National Archives of Canada.

14th Field Regiment, Royal Canadian Artillery War Diary, June 1944. RG24. National Archives of Canada.

Gillen, I.J. I.J. Gillen Diary, RG518-0-2-E. National Archives of Canada.

Granatstein Papers. York University Archives and Special Collections, Scott Library.

Highland Light Infantry of Canada War Diary, June 1944. RG24. National Archives of Canada.

"Historical Notes 1942–1945: First Canadian Parachute Battalion," 145.4013(D1). Directorate of History, Department of National Defence.

"Information re: dispersion on D-Day, 6 June 1944 1 CDN Para Bn," 145.4013(D2). Directorate of History, Department of National Defence.

"Interview with Maj. J.H. Gordon, Queen's Own Rifles 8bde 3 Canadian Division." Directorate of History, Department of National Defence.

Locke, J.E. (Capt.). "Narrative by Capt. J.E. Locke on D-Day Normandy, The History of the Jeep Platoon in Action on 6 June 44," 112.3H1.001(D21). Directorate of History, Department of National Defence.

McCormick, Bill. "Armistice Day Address." N.d. In possession of the author.

MacEwan, G.T. "D Day and the Counter-Attack on Putot-en-Bessin." 145.C4013(D3). Directorate of History, Department of National Defence.

Martin, J.R. (Maj.). "Report No. 147 Historical Section Canadian Military Headquarters: Part One: The Assault and Subsequent Operations of 3 Cdn Inf Div and 2 Cdn Armd Bde, 6–30 June 44—N.W. Europe." 3 December 1945. Directorate of History, Department of National Defence.

"Memo of Interview with Maj. J.A. Clancy, MC at Acton 14 June 45," 145.4011(D2). Directorate of History, Department of National Defence.

"Memo of Interview with Capt. D.W.W. Mascall at Army Headquarters, Ottawa, 16 November 49," 145.4011(D3). Directorate of History, Department of National Defence.

"Memo of Interview with Maj. D.W. Wilkins, 1st Canadian Parachute Bn., at CMHQ, 18 and 28 July 44," 145.4011(D1). Directorate of History,

Department of National Defence.

"Memorandum of Interview with Lt. Col. F.M. Matheson, OC, Regina Rifles by Historical Officer, 24 June 44," 145.2R11011(4). Directorate of History, Department of National Defence.

Mingay, Don (Lt. Col.). "Documents," Canadian War Museum Archives.

———. Speech, 2002. Copy in possession of the author.

Morton, Ronald. "Preparation for Invasion," MG31, vol. 1, National Archives of Canada.

Nicholson, G.W.L. (Maj.). "Report No. 138 Historical Section Canadian Military Headquarters: 1st Canadian Parachute Battalion: Organization and Training, July 1942–June 1944," 7 July 1945. Directorate of History, Department of National Defence.

———. "Report No. 139 Historical Section Canadian Military Headquarters: The 1st Canadian Parachute Battalion in France, 6 June–6 September 1944," 7 July 1945. Directorate of History, Department of National Defence.

19th Field Regiment, Royal Canadian Artillery War Diary, June 1944. RG24. National Archives of Canada.

9th Canadian Infantry Brigade War Diary, June 1944. RG24. National Archives of Canada.

"The Normandy Invasion—June, 1944: A Study prepared by the German Air Historical Branch (8th Abteilung), dated 6th August 1944." University of Victoria Special Collections, Reginald Roy Collection.

North Nova Scotia Highlanders War Diary, June 1944. RG24. National Archives of Canada.

North Shore (New Brunswick) Regiment War Diary, June 1944. RG24. National Archives of Canada.

Oliver, G.N. (Commodore). "Operation Neptune: Force 'J' Naval Operation Orders," Canadian War Museum Archives.

"Operation Overlord 7th Canadian Infantry Brigade Briefing Notes," Canadian War Museum Archives.

Patterson, H.S. (Maj.). "Artillery Communications in Operation Overlord, Account by Maj. H.S. Patterson, OC 2 Coy, 3 CDN INF DIV SIGS," 018(D2). Directorate of History, Department of National Defence.

Piers, Desmond W. "HMCS Algonquin—Operation Neptune." University of Victoria Special Collections.

Queen's Own Rifles of Canada War Diary, June 1944. RG24. National Archives of Canada.

Ramsay, P.F. (Capt.). "Battle Narrative, 'B' Coy, 1 C Scot R.," 145.2C4(D6). Directorate of History, Department of National Defence.

The Recollections of the Regina Rifles: N.W. Europe World War 2, June 6, 1944–May 8, 1945, n.p., n.d., looseleaf folder in possession of the author.

Le Régiment de la Chaudière War Diary, June 1944. RG24. National Archives of Canada.

Regina Rifles Regiment, 1st Battalion War Diary, June 1944. RG24, vol. 15198. National Archives of Canada.

Richardson, Stan. Diary. Copy in possession of the author.

Roy, Reginald (Lt.). "1 Canadian Parachute Battalion in Normandy: Historical Sketch," 25 September 1952, 145.4013(D4). Directorate of History, Department of National Defence.

"The Royal Canadian Navy's Part in the Invasion." Directorate of History, Department of National Defence.

"The Royal Canadian Navy's Part in the Invasion of Northern France— Operation 'Overlord' (a first narrative prepared by the RCN Historical Section—London)," Draft "A," Narrative "B," vol. 1, D779G7W3 V.5. Directorate of History, Department of National Defence.

Royal Winnipeg Rifles War Diary, June 1944. RG24. National Archives of Canada.

Seaborn, Robert Lowder. Robert Lowder Seaborn and Family Papers, MG31 F 18, vols. 2–6. National Archives of Canada.

"Second Canadian Armoured Brigade: Operation Overlord—The Assault on the Beaches of Normandy, 6–11 June 1944—Sequence of Events and Lessons Arising Therefrom," vol. 10455, RG24. National Archives of Canada.

2nd Canadian Armoured Brigade War Diary, June 1944. RG24. National Archives of Canada.

7th Canadian Infantry Brigade War Diary, June 1944. RG24. National Archives of Canada.

The Sherbrooke Fusiliers Regiment (27th Canadian Armoured Regiment) War Diary, June 1944. RG24. National Archives of Canada.

"Special Interrogation Report, Brigadefuhrer Kurt Meyer, Comd 12 SS PZ DIV 'Hitler Jugend' (6 June 1944–25 August 1944)." University of Victoria Special Collections, Reginald Roy Collection.

Stormont, Dundas and Glengarry Highlanders War Diary, June 1944. RG24. National Archives of Canada.

3rd Canadian Anti-Tank Regiment War Diary, June 1944. RG24. National Archives of Canada.

13th Field Regiment, Royal Canadian Artillery War Diary, June 1944. RG24. National Archives of Canada.

12th Field Regiment, Royal Canadian Artillery War Diary, June 1944. RG24. National Archives of Canada.

"War Diary Extracts, Vol. 19: HQ RCE 3 Cdn Inf Div, War Diary–June 44," University of Victoria Special Collections, Reginald Roy Collection.

Webb, R.H. (Lt. Col.). "12 Cdn Fd Regt, 23 June 44, Fd Arty in the Assault."

University of Victoria Special Collections, Reginald Roy Collection.

Whitby, Michael. "RCAF Strength and Casualties During Normandy Campaign," 8 April 1994. Directorate of History, Department of National Defence.

Wightman, Maj. C.M. Personal Diary. University of Victoria Special Collections, Reginald Roy Collection.

INTERVIEWS AND CORRESPONDENCE

Andrews, Joseph James. Interview by Cameron Falconer. Victoria, BC. 8 March 1983. University of Victoria Special Collections.

Baird, James Douglas. Interview by William S. Thackray. Victoria, BC. 17, 27 June and 18 July 1980. University of Victoria Special Collections.

Bateman, Merritt Hayes. Interview by Tom Torrie. Sidney, BC. 28 May 1987. University of Victoria Special Collections.

Beer, John Pope. Interview by David Gantzer. Victoria, BC. 26, 28 November 1979. University of Victoria Special Collections.

Bettridge, Bill. Interview by John Gregory Thompson. Brampton, ON. 14 October 2003.

Boyle, Art. Interview by John Gregory Thompson. London, ON. 30 September 2003.

Burley, Ralph. Interview by John Gregory Thompson. Toronto. 12 August 2003.

Bury, Bill. Interview by John Gregory Thompson. Hamilton, ON. 20 August 2003.

Butters, Thomas William Lowell. Interview by Tom Torrie. Victoria, BC. 19 August 1987. University of Victoria Special Collections.

Byrne, Jack. Interview by John Gregory Thompson. St. Joseph, ON. 10 October 2003.

Cave, John Clifford. Interview by Chris D. Main. Victoria, BC. 14, 24 August 1978. University of Victoria Special Collections.

Cheney, Don. Interview by Glen Cook. Ottawa. 16 November 2000. Canadian War Museum Oral History Project Collection.

Chevalier, Roger. Interview by author. Courseulles-sur-Mer. 23 May 2003.

Choat, Russell Frederick. Interview by James Murphy. Victoria, BC. 27 June and 5, 11 July 1977. University of Victoria Special Collections.

Clarke, Bernard. Interview by Tom Torrie. Victoria, BC. 18 August 1987. University of Victoria Special Collections.

Cleveland, Gerry. Interview by John Gregory Thompson. Port Colbourne, ON. 4 November 2003.

Cockburn, Phil. Interview by John Gregory Thompson. Ravenswood, ON. 11 August 2003.

Cook, Orville. Interview by John Gregory Thompson. Holland Centre, ON. 7 October 2003.

Corry, Geoffrey D. Interview by Tom Torrie. Victoria, BC. 12 August 1987.
University of Victoria Special Collections.

Côté, Ernest. Interview by Michael Boire. Ottawa. 14 November 2003.

Crabtree, Kenneth S. Interview by Chris Bell. Victoria, BC. 24 August 1982.
University of Victoria Special Collections.

Daubs, Jack. Interview by John Gregory Thompson. London, ON. 9 October
2003.

Eckenfelder, George V. Interview by Tom Torrie. Victoria, BC. 7 August 1987.
University of Victoria Special Collections.

Fletcher, Dave. Interview by John Gregory Thompson. Streetsville, ON.
2 September 2003.

Fulton, Lochie. Interview by Ken MacLeod. Victoria, BC. 9 February 1998.

Gonder, Harold Bertrand. Interview by Mark C. Hill. Victoria, BC. 23 July and
7, 8, 9 August 1985. University of Victoria Special Collections.

Gray, Raymond Skelton. Interview by Tom Torrie. Victoria, BC. 27 August
1987. University of Victoria Special Collections.

Hall, A.C. Vassar. Interview by Chris D. Main. Victoria, BC. 7, 11, 15 May 1979.
University of Victoria Special Collections.

Hinton, Peter. Interview by Mark Hill. Victoria, BC. 22 July 1985. University
of Victoria Special Collections.

Jackson, Rolph. Interview by John Gregory Thompson. Toronto. 2 September
2003.

Kingston, Dave. Interview by John Gregory Thompson. Mississauga, ON.
10 September 2003.

Lamb, Hugh. Interview by John Gregory Thompson. Mississauga, ON.
8 September 2003.

Learment, Don. Interview by John Gregory Thompson. Guelph, ON.
21 November 2003.

Lecarpentier, Georges. Interview by author. Courseulles-sur-Mer. 23 May 2003.

McCormick, Bill. Interview by John Gregory Thompson. Gault, ON. 3 October
2003.

———. Telephone interview by John Gregory Thompson. 14 February 2004.

McCullough, Jim. Interview by John Gregory Thompson. Loretto, ON.
9 September 2003.

McLean, Jack. Interview by Ken MacLeod. Vancouver. September 1997.

Madden, John R. Recorded Recollections. 1987. University of Victoria Special
Collections.

Martin, Jack. Interview by John Gregory Thompson. Scarborough, ON.
1 October 2003.

Mingay, Donald. Interview by Michael Boire. Collingwood, ON. November
2003.

Parks, Jim. Interview by Ken MacLeod. Vancouver, BC. November 1997.

Plows, Arthur Howard. Interview by Chris D. Main. Victoria, BC.
    18, 31 August 1978. University of Victoria Special Collections.
Richardson, Charles. Interview by John Gregory Thompson. London, ON.
    30 October 2003.
Richardson, Stan. Correspondence with author. 10 March 2003.
Rogers, Fred. Videotaped recollections in possession of the author. N.d.
Ruffee, George E.M. Interview by Tom Torrie. Victoria, BC. 28 July 1987.
    University of Victoria Special Collections.
Ryan, Joe. Interview by John Gregory Thompson. Cobourg, ON. 6 November
    2003.
Seaborn, Robert Lowder. Interview by Cameron Falconer. Victoria, BC.
    23 February 1983. University of Victoria Special Collections.
Seneco, Stan. Interview by John Gregory Thompson. East York, ON.
    3 November 2003.
Shawcross, Ronald Glendall. Interview by Mark C. Hill. Victoria, BC.
    14, 19 June 1985. University of Victoria Special Collections.
Simpson, Jim. Interview by John Gregory Thompson. Windsor, ON.
    13 September 2003.
Springer, Jack. Interview by John Gregory Thompson. London, ON.
    1 November 2003.
Storrs, Anthony H.G. Interview by Chris Bell. Victoria, BC. 9, 16 September
    1982 and 13 June, 8 July, 30 August 1983. University of Victoria Special
    Collections.
Stuart, Okill. Correspondence with author. 6 January 2003.
Wightman, Cyrill Merrott. Interview by Cameron Falconer. Victoria, BC.
    8 February 1983. University of Victoria Special Collections.

GENERAL INDEX

Ranks given for individuals are highest attained as of June 6, 1944

Adams, Pte. Bill, 147–48
Aldershot, 106
Alexander, Capt. H.L., 165
Alexander, Gen. Sir Harold, 28
Algonquin, HMCS, 107–8, 155–56, 270–71
Allan, Tpr. Larry, 177, 194–95
Allen, Ralph, 341
Allied Expeditionary Air Force (AEAF), 57, 59, 66, 81, 286
Amblie, 330
American Priest 105-mm SPG, replaces 25-pounder, 39–40
Anderson, Pte. Boyd, 89, 226
Anderson, Maj. J. Ernest, 209
Anderson, F/L Thomas G., 132–33
Andover, 94
Andrews, Lt. Joseph James, 310–11
Anguerny, 76, 101, 258, 269, 272, 294 300, 301–4, 342
Anisy, 101, 302, 303, 309, 345
Arber, Lt. Jack, 219, 221
Ardenne, 101
Argentan, 80
Arkansas, USS, 153
Arnold, Maj. W.L., 296
Arromanches, 97
Asnelles-sur-Mer, 80
Authie, 101, 307, 308

Baie de la Seine, 344
Bailey, Sgt. James Malcolm "Ace," 177–78, 194–95
Baird, Maj. James Douglas, 38–40, 160
Bangor Class Minesweeper, described, 49–50
Banville-sur-Mer, 185, 242, 246–47, 250, 254–56, 310, 324, 340
Banville–Tierceville road, 254, 256, 324

le Bas de Bréville, 148
Basly, 101, 258, 269, 299, 301, 313
Bavent, 228, 229, 231
Bayerlein, Generalleutnant Fritz, 318
Bayeux, 27, 82, 99
Bayfield, HMCS, 50–52, 124–25, 153
Beardsley, Sgt. R.R., 296–97
Beattie, Lt. Rod, 187–88
Bellengreville, 134, 135, 285
Belliveau, Capt. J.L. 281
Benouville, 140, 288
Bény-sur-Mer, 258, 261, 262, 268–70, 272, 293, 294, 297–98, 308, 340–41, 345, 349
Bény-sur-Mer Canadian War Cemetery, 348
Berlin, 61, 65, 68, 285
Bernières-sur-Mer, 100–2, 158, 167–68, 173, 175, 197, 256–59, 261–63, 270, 272, 293, 294, 298, 303, 334, 340, 341, 345, 349
battle for, 210–21
Bettridge, Rfn. Bill, 169–70, 214–16
Beveridge, Lt. J., 266
Bieville, 290
Biggs, Capt. Stanley, 304–6
Bishop, Cpl. L.E., 295
Bismutka, Pte. Peter, 138, 142, 144, 151
Black, Doug, 174
Black, Marvin, 174
Blackader, Brig. K.G. "Ken," 262, 273, 297, 300, 301
Blacklock, Sgt. J.D., 255
Blainville, 316
Blairmore, HMCS, 124
Blakely, Pte. Harry, 203
Blanchard, Pte. Alfred, 199
Blumentritt, General der Infanterie Günter, 240–41, 317

INDEX OF FORMATIONS,
UNITS, AND CORPS

ABOUT THE AUTHOR

MARK ZUEHLKE's critically acclaimed trilogy about Canada's experiences in World War II's Italian campaign—*Ortona: Canada's Epic World War II Battle, The Liri Valley: Canada's World War II Breakthrough to Rome,* and *The Gothic Line: Canada's Month of Hell in World War II Italy*—established him as the nation's leading writer of popular military history. He is also the author of *The Canadian Military Atlas: The Nation's Battlefields from the French and Indian Wars to Kosovo; The Gallant Cause: Canadians in the Spanish Civil War, 1936–1939;* and *Scoundrels, Dreamers, and Second Sons: British Remittance Men in the Canadian West. Juno Beach* is the first of a planned series that will trace the Canadian role in the Normandy campaign.

Also a novelist, he is the author of the popular Elias McCann series, which follows the misadventures and investigations of a community coroner in Tofino, British Columbia. The first in this series, *Hands Like Clouds,* won the 2000 Crime Writers of Canada Arthur Ellis Award for Best First Novel. It was followed by *Carry Tiger to Mountain* and, most recently, he has completed *Sweep Lotus,* with publication expected soon.

Zuehlke lives in Victoria, British Columbia, where, when not writing, he enjoys backpacking, cycling, kayaking, cooking Italian food, and gardening.